# SHAKESPEARE SURVEY

# ADVISORY BOARD

# SHAKESPEARE SURVEY

## AN ANNUAL SURVEY OF
## SHAKESPEARIAN STUDY AND PRODUCTION

34

EDITED BY
## STANLEY WELLS

CAMBRIDGE UNIVERSITY PRESS

CAMBRIDGE
LONDON   NEW YORK   NEW ROCHELLE
MELBOURNE   SYDNEY

Published by the Press Syndicate of the University of Cambridge
The Pitt Building, Trumpington Street, Cambridge CB2 1RP
32 East 57th Street, New York, NY 10022, USA
296 Beaconsfield Parade, Middle Park, Melbourne 3206, Australia

First published 1981

*Shakespeare Survey* was first published in 1948. For the first
eighteen volumes it was edited by Allardyce Nicoll.
Kenneth Muir edited volumes 19–33

Printed in Great Britain
at the University Press, Cambridge

Library of Congress catalogue
card number: 49–1639

*British Library Cataloguing in Publication Data*
Shakespeare Survey.
34
1. Shakespeare, William – Criticism
and interpretation
I. Wells, Stanley
822.3'3 PR2976 49–1639
ISBN 0 521 23240 6

# EDITOR'S NOTE

The first eight papers in this volume were delivered to the International Shakespeare Conference in Stratford-upon-Avon in 1980, except for Professor Weil's, delivered to the 1978 Conference. The next volume will have as its theme 'Shakespeare in the Nineteenth Century'. The theme of the subsequent volume will be 'Shakespeare in the Twentieth Century'. We hope to include a number of papers delivered to the International Shakespeare Conference in 1982. Other contributions are invited, and should reach the Editor at 40 Walton Crescent, Oxford OX1 2JQ by 1 September 1982 at the latest. Please send a non-returnable xerox, or include return postage. A style sheet is available on request. All articles submitted are read by one or more members of the Advisory Board, whose indispensable assistance the Editor gratefully acknowledges.

In attempting to survey the ever-increasing bulk of Shakespeare publications our reviewers have inevitably to exercise some selection. Review copies of books should be addressed to the Editor, as above; we are also very pleased to receive offprints of articles, which help to draw our reviewers' attention to relevant material.

I am honoured to succeed Kenneth Muir as Editor of *Shakespeare Survey*, and happy that this creates a further link with my mentor and friend, Allardyce Nicoll, founder of both this journal and the Shakespeare Institute of the University of Birmingham. Professor Muir has been characteristically generous with help in effecting the transition.

S.W.W.

# CONTRIBUTORS

---

RALPH BERRY, *Professor of English, University of Ottawa*

T. J. CRIBB, *Fellow of Churchill College, Cambridge*

MICHAEL GOLDMAN, *Professor of English, Princeton University*

KAREN GREIF, *Harvard University*

HARRIETT HAWKINS, *Linacre College, Oxford*

RICHARD LEVIN, *Professor of English, State University of New York, Stony Brook*

RUSS MCDONALD, *Assistant Professor of English, University of Rochester*

J. MCLAVERTY, *Lecturer in English, University of Keele*

GIORGIO MELCHIORI, *Professor of English, University of Rome*

KENNETH MUIR, *Emeritus Professor of English Literature, University of Liverpool*

A. D. NUTTALL, *Professor of English, University of Sussex*

GĀMINI SALGĀDO, *Professor of English, University of Exeter*

LEO SALINGAR, *Fellow of Trinity College and Lecturer in English, University of Cambridge*

BRIAN VICKERS, *Professor of English Literature, Swiss Federal Institute of Technology, Zürich*

ROGER WARREN, *Lecturer in English, University of Leicester*

HERBERT S. WEIL, JR, *Professor of English, University of Manitoba*

ROBERT WEIMANN, *Akademie der Künste der Deutschen Demokratischen Republik*

GEORGE WALTON WILLIAMS, *Professor of English, Duke University*

# CONTENTS

# PLATES

---

# SHAKESPEARE'S OPEN SECRET

## KENNETH MUIR

One of the embarrassments of writing about Shakespeare is to discover when one appears in print that, as Hector remarked about Troilus and Paris, one has glozed but superficially on the question at issue. I grew up in the age of Bradley; and, like most Shakespearians of my generation, I was later influenced by the criticisms made of his method by Edgar Elmer Stoll, Lily Bess Campbell, Levin Schücking, and L. C. Knights. I came to assume that Bradley read subtleties into the plays which would have astonished an Elizabethan audience or, indeed, the poet himself; that he was too little aware of theatrical considerations; and that (as Knights put it) he did not know that *Macbeth* was more like *The Waste Land* than *A Doll's House*. In fact, as we now know, Bradley was a keen playgoer and he always believed and asserted that Shakespeare's plays were essentially dramatic poems. Some of the most memorable passages in his *Shakespearean Tragedy* are on a subject he professedly omitted – the poetry of the plays; while, on the other hand, the most memorable passages of his critics are not those where the plays are considered specifically as dramatic poems, but rather those which concentrate on the moral issues raised in them. Leavis's quarrel with Bradley on Othello, and Knights's quarrel with him on Hamlet and Macbeth were largely due to their conviction that these tragic heroes were bad men who had been whitewashed by Bradley. He had been seduced by the poetry Shakespeare puts into their mouths, much as

we are seduced by advertisements which persuade us to buy nicotine and alcohol by associating these slow poisons with attractive and apparently accessible girls.

Some of the criticisms made of Bradley are unjustified. He was fully aware that there was a vital difference between characters in a play and living persons. He pointed out:

> To consider separately the action or the characters of a play . . . is legitimate and valuable, so long as we remember what we are doing. But the true critic in speaking of these apart does not really think of them apart; the while, the poetic experience of which they are but aspects, is always in his mind; and he is always aiming at a richer, truer, more intense repetition of that experience.[1]

Although he sometimes made the mistake of considering what happened off stage, or before the beginning of the action, he could never have made the kind of mistake into which Helen Faucit fell in her letters about Shakespeare's heroines. When she played Imogen she was convinced that that character would not long survive after the end of the play:

> Happiness hides for a time injuries which are past healing. The blow which was inflicted by the first sentence in that cruel letter went to the heart with a too fatal force. Then followed, on this crushing blow, the wandering hopeless days and nights, without shelter, without food even up to the point of famine. Was this delicately nurtured creature one to

---

1 *Oxford Lectures on Poetry* (1909), pp. 16–17.

go through her terrible ordeal unscathed? We see that when food and shelter came, they came too late. The heart-sickness is upon her: 'I am sick still – heart-sick'. Upon this follows the fearful sight of, as she supposes, her husband's body. Well may she say that she is 'nothing; or if not, nothing to be were better'. When happiness, even such as she had never known before, comes to her, it comes, like the food and shelter, too late. Tremblingly, gradually, and oh, how reluctantly, the hearts to whom that life is so precious will see the sweet smile which greets them grow fainter, will hear the loved voice grow feebler! The wise physician Cornelius will tax his utmost skill, but he will find the hurt is too deep for mortal leech-craft.[2]

Bradley did not read *Hamlet* as though it were *Middlemarch*. Nor was his aim to give separate character sketches of the dramatis personae, but rather to encourage people to 'read a play more or less as if they were actors who had to study all the parts . . . This, carried through a drama, is the right way to read the dramatist Shakespeare; and the prime requisite here is therefore a vivid and intent imagination.'[3]

Bradley's weakness, oddly enough, was not that he was a bardolater – though he once remarked that the appreciation of Shakespeare was the whole duty of man – but that he often seems to be apologizing for faults which would not be visible to an audience. He did not fully appreciate that things invisible to an audience should not be regarded as flaws. The performances he witnessed in the later years of the nineteenth century were adaptations, and he never understood that the plays were perfectly designed for the Elizabethan theatre. It may be added that Bradley sometimes invented psychological reasons for actions dictated by the plot; that he ignored the differences between Elizabethan and nineteenth-century psychological theories, and that his own theories did not make enough allowance for irrationality.

The situation has, of course, changed during the last seventy-five years. Everyone now agrees that Shakespeare's plays belong pri-marily to the theatre, and most of us believe that in all his mature plays Shakespeare was professionally as competent as modern directors, and wiser than most of his critics. We have had the opportunity, which Bradley's generation had not, of seeing productions which obeyed, or at least acknowledged, Elizabethan stage conventions. Everyone now knows about unlocalized scenes, the fluid construction of the plays, Shakespeare's scenic art, the use of rhetorical patterns, multiple consciousness, direct self-explanation, the use of imagery, and so on. One result of this critical revolution is that we have had to modify our views on Shakespeare's method of characterization. This does not mean that Bradley's method was absolutely wrong, or that Shakespeare was so careless an artist that he cheerfully allowed absurd inconsistencies in characterization – that he created a Macbeth who could not have murdered Duncan, an Othello who could not have developed into a jealous maniac, an Angelo who could never have lusted after a novice.

Bradley provides a useful introduction to the subject of my paper: how far ought we to modify Bradley's method of approach to Shakespeare's characters? To put it in another way, what are the means by which Shakespeare creates characters who seem to be more life-like than those of other dramatists?

In many ways, of course, Shakespeare's method is not very different from that of Racine, Molière, Chekhov or Ibsen. He, like them, creates credible characters by the actions they are made to perform, by what they say about themselves and others, by what other characters, friends and enemies, say about them, by the speech patterns they use, even by their silences. We may choose Hamlet as a convenient example because he is the best known of all Shakespeare's characters. Hamlet

---

2 *On Some of Shakespeare's Female Characters* (Edinburgh and London, 1885), pp. 278–9.
3 *Shakespearean Tragedy* (1904), p. 2.

feigns madness, spares Claudius, kills Polonius, sends Rosencrantz and Guildenstern to their deaths, grapples with Laertes at Ophelia's grave-side. He laments Gertrude's remarriage, vows to avenge his father's murder, admires an old play about Dido, inveighs against Ophelia, castigates his own delay, praises Horatio's imperturbability, meditates suicide, preaches to Gertrude. He is said by Ophelia to have had a noble mind, and to have been the observed of all observers; by Claudius he is said to be a fever in his blood, but also most generous and free of all contriving. To Horatio he is 'sweet Prince' and to Fortinbras one who would have made an excellent king. Any interpretation of Hamlet's character would have to take note of these and many other words and actions; but (as he tells us) he is not so easily played upon as a pipe. This is a *reductio ad absurdum* of the old method of character analysis, and no one would now regard it as adequate. If we consider some of its limitations we shall obtain an insight into Shakespeare's own method of creating character.

The main limitation is that such an attempt to pigeon-hole a Shakespeare character evades the ambiguities and ambivalencies which are an essential part of his method – what Maurice Morgann meant by the term 'secret impressions'. Our 'impressions and understanding of a scene may be at variance', and Morgann argued that this was an effect deliberately contrived by the poet and that 'the Principles of this Disagreement are really in human Nature'. He was arguing that we have conflicting impressions about our friends and acquaintances and Shakespeare's realization of this made his characters truer to life – more real – than the characters of other dramatists. Morgann was concerned with the conflicting impressions which are caused by what the characters do and say, and by what others say about them. I want to enlarge the question, so as to embrace five or six points that Morgann could ignore in writing on Falstaff.

First, we may consider the expectations of

the audience from their previous knowledge of the story, and the extent to which Shakespeare fulfilled or disappointed those expectations. This is a matter which is assumed by anyone who writes on Greek tragedy. The plays written by Euripides and Sophocles about Electra derive much of their interest and significance from their deviations from the Aeschylean version; just as, in our own day, Sartre and O'Neill assumed our knowledge of the Oresteia, and Cocteau and Anouilh played on our knowledge of the Oedipus story.

Most of Shakespeare's original audience would have been acquainted with the story of Lear, and they would all expect him to be restored to the throne. When Edmund sends his sword to countermand the death-sentence, most members of the audience must have believed – or at least hoped – that Cordelia would be saved.

*Hamlet* (to take another example) had been popular for a decade when Shakespeare transformed it. He relied on the fact that the audience would make comparisons. He tantalized the expectations of the audience and teased them into thought. Waldock and other critics have argued that Shakespeare was foolishly pouring new wine into old bottles, and that traces of the old motivations, of the old primitive avenger, blatantly conflict with the character of the introspective hero of the new version. The original Hamlet would doubtless have made obscene remarks to Ophelia, spared the King at his prayers so as not to send him to heaven, referred callously to the corpse of Polonius as 'the guts', and murdered his old friends Rosencrantz and Guildenstern without a qualm. But, we are told, the Prince who speaks the great soliloquies or meditates on the special providence in the fall of a sparrow, would never have done such brutal things. *But he did*: Shakespeare deliberately retained some of the characteristics of the old avenger. The conflict between the old avenger and the new – one might almost say between the Old and New Testaments – was one of the ways by which the character of the Prince was made stereoscopically real. It is not surprising that there have been several hundred interpretations of Hamlet's character, many of them based on the text, or a fraction of it, and therefore plausible.

There may well have been more than one play about Julius Caesar before Shakespeare wrote his. In any case – and this was the reason why Ernest Schanzer called *Julius Caesar* a problem play – Shakespeare could dally with conflicting views on the assassination: whether Brutus and Cassius were martyrs in the cause of freedom, or criminals who deserved to be relegated to the lowest circle of hell, alongside Judas.

The story of Coriolanus was also well known, but not previously dramatized. It was frequently used by political theorists to illustrate the evils of democracy: only Machiavelli condemned Coriolanus for his treachery. But Shakespeare could nevertheless set up conflicting impressions about his hero. He does this, more overtly than usual, in a curious speech by Aufidius, who advances a number of different explanations of Coriolanus's banishment:

I think he'll be to Rome
As is the osprey to the fish, who takes it
By sovereignty of nature. First he was
A noble servant to them, but he could not
Carry his honours even. Whether 'twas pride,
Which out of daily fortune ever taints
The happy man; whether defect of judgement,
To fail in the disposing of those chances
Which he was lord of; or whether nature,
Not to be other than one thing, not moving
From th'casque to th'cushion, but commanding
    peace
Even with the same austerity and garb
As he controll'd the war; but one of these –
As he hath spices of them all – not all,
For I dare so far free him – made him fear'd,
So hated, and so banish'd. But he has a merit
To choke it in the utt'rance. So our virtues
Lie in th'interpretation of the time,
And power, unto itself most commendable,

Hath not a tomb so evident as a chair
T'extol what it hath done.

(*Coriolanus*, 4.7.33–53)

Aufidius offers several explanations: pride, defect of judgement, trying to apply military discipline to peace-time government. There is some truth in all of them; but as Aufidius has good reason to hate Coriolanus, what he says is not the whole truth. We have to balance it with what his friends and relations say; what the choric figures who prepare the senate house for a meeting conclude about his virtues and defects; and above all we have to consider the subtext of his own speeches, his love for his wife, his fatal devotion to his dreadful mother, his feeling that compromise was the enemy of integrity – this is underlined by his repeated theatrical imagery – and his hatred of the common people which may be traced to his inadequate upbringing. It has often been pointed out that Valeria's description of the boy Marcius was intended to reflect on the immaturity of his father:

O' my word, the father's son! I'll swear 'tis a very pretty boy. O' my troth, I look'd upon him a Wednesday half an hour together; has such a confirmed countenance! I saw him run after a gilded butterfly; and when he caught it he let it go again, and after it again, and over and over he comes, and up again, catch'd it again; or whether his fall enrag'd him, or how 'twas, he did so set his teeth and tear it. O, I warrant, how he mammock'd it!

(*Coriolanus*, 1.3.57–65)

If one analyses any of Shakespeare's major characters one soon unveils similar complexities; and Morgann was surely right when he argued that the impression of overwhelming reality given by Shakespeare's characters was due to this. A similar impression of human reality is obtained by Paul Scott in the Raj Quartet, in which we get a variety of conflicting impressions of the different characters, according to the viewpoint of the person through whose eyes we see the events. This is rather different from the technique used by

Browning in *The Ring and the Book*; for although Browning uses as his spokesmen nine or ten different characters, there is no over-all ambiguity: we never doubt that Pompilia is an innocent and saintly victim and that her husband is a villain.

I turn now to another cause of conflicting impressions: the use of stage types as the basis of a character, though never as simply as the *commedia dell'arte* types in *Love's Labour's Lost*. Sometimes, indeed, there is an ingenious fusion of several different types. Falstaff, for example, is based on the *miles gloriosus*; but he is also a Vice or Riot, derived from moralities and interludes – and as such he represents the World, the Flesh and the Devil; and imposed on these is the allegedly hypocritical heretic, Oldcastle, whose characteristics survive in the occasional sanctimoniousness displayed by the fat rogue. (It may be added that several critics believe that the character reflects the feelings of the poet in his relationship with Mr W. H.) It was appropriate for Morgann to choose Falstaff as his chief exhibit in his essay on Shakespeare's method of characterization; and it is a pity that most commentators on Morgann have concentrated on his paradoxical defence of Falstaff's courage.

The influence of morality plays is more apparent in the tragedies; and it has often been shown that Shakespeare blends the influence of the metaphysical struggle between vice and virtue with a more modern, secular, psychological characterization. Iago is a demi-devil, anxious to bring Othello's soul to damnation; but he is also a character animated by jealousy, colour prejudice, and other very human motives. In addition to this blending of the psychological and the metaphysical, we have to remember (as Muriel Bradbrook reminds us) that Shakespeare was breaking the stereotypes of honest soldier and barbarous Moor. This, which so disgusted Rymer, was yet another way by which Shakespeare played with his audience. Rymer thought that a dishonest soldier was an incredible character: he did not

realize that Shakespeare made use of this assumption by making everyone refer to Iago's honesty. An audience, with its inevitably stock responses, would expect a white professional soldier to be a plain blunt man; so that Iago's deviousness, apparent in the opening dialogue with Roderigo, would upset their expectations. In the same way, they would believe that blackness was the devil's colour, and that a blackamoor would be cruel, evil, and passionate. Shakespeare in the first two acts depicts a Moor who falsifies these expectations.

It would be easy to show that both *Macbeth* and *King Lear* combine the metaphysical with the psychological. I am not, of course, arguing that they are morality plays, but merely that the background of the psychomachia adds a metaphysical dimension to the characters. In *Macbeth* the good and evil supernatural are continually presented, and in *King Lear* the good and evil children are as plainly differentiated as the sheep and goats in the parable. With *King Lear* there is an additional complicating factor. The story was not merely well-known and legendary, but archetypal and mythical, so that the audience has the feeling, as it watches the love test in the first scene, or the scene in act 4 where the proud King and the proud daughter kneel to each other, that they are witnessing, one might almost say *re-enacting*, something that happened 'A great while since, a long long time ago'. Such a feeling is bound to affect, if only subliminally, an audience's reactions to the characters of the play. Lear and Gloucester, Goneril and Regan, are vividly realized characters, with different speech patterns, characters so delusively real that they have attracted the attention of psychoanalysts. On the other hand, they are mythological figures as fated as Oedipus to fulfil their destinies.

Another branch of Shakespeare's art which affects his method of characterization is his use of verse. It is more difficult to differentiate characters in verse than in prose. Shakespeare's triumphs in the plays written at the end of the sixteenth century – Shylock, Beatrice, Falstaff, Rosalind – must have tempted him to abandon verse, as Ibsen did in mid-career, because, as he said, verse had done immense injury to the art of the theatre. Stendhal, earlier in the century, had reached the same conclusion. His reason for preferring Shakespeare to Racine was that blank verse is closer than rhymed alexandrines to natural speech. English verse, he declared enthusiastically, was able to say everything. The alexandrine was no more than a *cache-sottise*. He allowed that verse plays gave a great deal of pleasure, but it was not a dramatic pleasure. Audiences enjoyed listening to noble sentiments expressed in beautiful verse, poetry recitals rather than drama. The most precious moments in the theatre were the short moments of perfect illusion; and beautiful verse was the enemy of illusion. What was needed, Stendhal wrote in 1822, was prose tragedy. He quoted Macbeth's words on seeing the ghost of Banquo and asked: 'What verse, what rhythm could add to the beauty of such a sentence?'[4] The irony of this question is that the words he quoted were part of a regular line of verse. But he was right to feel that Shakespeare was able to express directly and simply things that were impossible for Racine. If Shakespeare had been born a hundred years later, he could not have used the words to which Dr Johnson objected in Lady Macbeth's invocation of the murdering ministers: 'peep', 'blanket' and 'knife'. To Shakespeare, born in the sixteenth century, nothing was common or unclean.

Yet Stendhal was wrong on several counts. His knowledge of English versification was apparently not enough for him to recognize a line of blank verse; his suspicion of anything poetic and his desire for prose tragedy showed that he appreciated only one part of Shakespeare's quality; and his belief in the supreme importance of illusion ignores the way an audience can believe in the reality of the scene at the same time as it enjoys the poetry. The illusion is never complete except for very naive spectators (such as Partridge in *Tom Jones*) but it is not destroyed or even minimized by the poetry. No one listening to one of Macbeth's or Hamlet's soliloquies thinks primarily of the poetry unless the actor destroys the rhythm or the sense: it is the failure to do justice to the poetry which distracts our attention from the meaning.

In some dramatists, verse does indeed have a levelling effect, so that the style of an old man is no different from that of a young woman. But Shakespeare was careful, after his earliest plays, to alter his style to suit the character speaking. Romeo's initial speeches reveal the artificiality of his love for Rosaline, whereas the equally artificial sonnet he shares with Juliet on their first meeting is a means of revealing a marriage of true minds. In *Hamlet* the rhetorical excess of the Dido speeches throws into relief the colloquial agony of Hamlet's ensuing soliloquy, and the rhymed couplets of *The Mousetrap* (being a stage further away from colloquial speech than the blank verse of most of the play) make us believe that Hamlet is speaking naturally, however poetical his speeches are. Hamlet, indeed, has the most varied styles of any character in the whole of Shakespeare's dramas; and in the theatre we are hardly aware when he moves from prose to verse, or from verse to prose.

Since Caroline Spurgeon, Mikhail Morozov and Wolfgang Clemen wrote on the way imagery can be used to differentiate character, it has been generally recognized that even when characters draw their images from the same field, the particular images are appropriate to the characters who speak them. Othello uses sea imagery in a romantic and imaginative way; Iago's use of the same imagery is technical and pedestrian. Othello uses jewel imagery; Iago, like the enterprising monetarist he is, has straightforward references to cash. Troilus and

---

4 Stendhal, *Oeuvres Complètes*, ed. V. del Litto and E. Abravanel, 50 vols (Geneva, [1968–74]), vol. 37, pp. 8, 19, 86, 146.

Pandarus both use cooking imagery, but in ways appropriate to their characters.

Imagery therefore provides another of the secret impressions which complicate our conceptions of the characters. The acting imagery used by Coriolanus reveals his revulsion against playing the part assigned to him by the patricians, the imagery used by Leontes when he falls a prey to the green-eyed monster conveys in the most economical way possible the turmoil in his soul, and Viola's image about her imaginary sister reveals something of her own secret passion – though she is far too sensible to pine away.

In the introduction to his translation of *Macbeth*, Maurice Maeterlinck suggested that Shakespeare used imagery to reveal the unconscious mind of his hero; and everyone recognizes that the prudential reasons he advances in the crucial soliloquy in act 1, scene 7 against murdering Duncan – universal condemnation, punishment in this life, compelled to drink the poisoned chalice – are all undermined and overturned by the sense of moral horror which the imagery discloses.

One other cause of conflicting impressions is the relationship of a particular play to those which immediately preceded it and, indeed, to the totality of the poet's work, and to the themes which occur in play after play. The seed of one play can sometimes be found in one he had written not long before (with which perhaps he was dissatisfied).

Now although Shakespeare was able to identify with a wide range of characters, wider than those of any other dramatist, he is more likely to identify with major characters, whether villains or heroes, than with a second sentry or a third citizen; with Angelo, Isabella and Claudio than with the Provost. To put it in another way, the reality of Macbeth, or Othello, or Hamlet, is so convincing to us because the poet imagined himself under the skins of those characters. Instinctively he was wondering how he would have felt, and what he would have done, if he had discovered that his mother

had committed adultery with the murderer of his father, what he would have done at Inverness or in Cyprus. I suggest that the presence of the poet as a secret and unacknowledged *dramatis persona* adds another and very potent secret impression to complicate our reactions to the characters. I am reminded by Inga-Stina Ewbank of a letter written by Strindberg about his *Son of a Servant*. He said he had not wished to write a biography or a volume of confessions, but that he had 'used his life, which he knew best of all lives, to try to formulate the history of the growth and development of a mind and to explore the concept of character on which the whole of literature rests'.

In the preface to the second edition of the book, Strindberg referred again to the same question: 'Whether the author has really, as he has at times believed, experimented with viewpoints, or incarnated himself in different personalities, polymerized himself, or whether a gracious providence has experimented with the author, must, for the enlightened reader, emerge from the texts.'

It was natural that Strindberg, simply because he was a dramatist, should speak, even about an avowedly autobiographical work, in such terms; and it can be said of Shakespeare too that he experimented with viewpoints, that he incarnated himself in different personalities, and that (to paraphrase *polymerize*) he passed through successive variations in his various characters. He would learn from his incarnation in different personalities, just as Edgar learnt from the various roles he assumed during the course of the play: Poor Tom, Demoniac, Peasant, Guide, Champion and Future King.

I turn now to a matter which applies not merely to Shakespeare but to all dramatists whose plays are regularly performed. Every new production of a play, whether good or bad, provides a different perspective on it; and, of course, no two performances of the same production can be identical. Let me give some examples from productions of *Troilus and Cressida*

7

in the present century. When Edith Evans played Cressida in 1913 she went all out for comedy. As she took leave of Troilus, she was pinning on her hat, visibly intent on her change of fortunes, and bored with his demands that she should be faithful. When the play was staged in 1922 by the Marlowe Society to an audience which included war veterans, it seemed bitterly relevant to those who had been additionally disillusioned by the treaty of Versailles. When the play was performed in modern dress at the Westminster Theatre at the time of Munich, the war scenes became more interesting than the love scenes. As Desmond McCarthy wrote: 'The interesting result of modernising the play and presenting the characters in contemporary dress – Thersites as a dingy war correspondent (wearing a red tie); Helen and Cressida as cocktail party lovelies &c – is to bring us straight into contact with the mood in which the play was conceived and written.'[5]

In the days of the Phoney War – the lull before the invasion of France – the play was revived by the Marlowe Society and the debates in the Greek camp and on war aims were 'followed with a fascinated recognition of the immediate relevance at every point'. There was a revival in Edwardian costume directed by Tyrone Guthrie at the Old Vic, in which the love plot became 'thoughtless undergraduate seduced by bitch'. There have been six revivals at the Memorial Theatre since the first International Shakespeare Conference. In the 1960 revival directed by Peter Hall and John Barton the part of Cressida was taken by Dorothy Tutin, who (we are told) was 'a wisp of rippling carnality that [was] almost unbearably alluring', 'sweltering with concupiscence', 'almost unbearably erotic'. An actress who could so arouse the sexual fantasies of the critics went far to explaining why Troilus found her so enchanting. But this was not the most important thing about the production. The directors showed that the play was 'a planned, architected, coherent and powerful drama,

with Hector and Achilles the symbols of a conflict between chivalry and brutal opportunism, to which the ruin of Troilus by the faithless Cressida is secondary'. After more than 350 years the play had come into its own. In later Stratford revivals, the play was made more negative and more cynical, so that one critic in 1968 headed her review 'THERSITES WAS RIGHT'. I am not concerned here with determining which production was closest to Shakespeare's conceptions (supposing these could be ascertained) but merely with the effect of the over-all idea of the directors on the way the characters were presented.

We are bound to have our views of characters modified by brilliant performances, even when they run counter to our preconceptions, as (I confess) both Edith Evans's and Dorothy Tutin's Cressidas ran counter to mine. But when Sybil Thorndike played Volumnia at the Old Vic and could not conceal her dislike of that creature's opinions; or when Edith Evans delivered Katherine's sermon to the other wives as an ironical attack on male chauvinism; or when Judi Dench as Lady Macbeth seemed literally possessed by the spirits of darkness, we may disagree with these interpretations, but we cannot forget them.

Actors collaborate with dramatists, as the player Shakespeare appreciated. Stanislavsky declared that when an actor speaks Hamlet's soliloquy, 'To be or not to be', he puts into the lines much of his own conception of life:

Such an artist is not speaking in the person of an imaginary Hamlet. He speaks in his own right as one placed in the circumstances created by the play. The thoughts, feelings, conceptions, reasoning of the author are transformed into his own . . . For him it is necessary that the spectators *feel* his inner rela-

---

5 The quotations from reviews of productions will be found in the newspaper cuttings in the library of the Shakespeare Centre, Stratford-upon-Avon. There is an admirable account of the stage history of the play by Jeanne T. Newlin in *Harvard Library Bulletin*, 17 (1969), 353–73.

tionship to what he is saying. They must follow his own creative *will* and desires.[6]

We may add that most directors and actors will have studied not merely the theatrical traditions of their roles, even when they strike out a new line, but they, and many members of the audience will know something, usually too much, indeed, of what the critics have said. Marvin Rosenberg's experiments with ignorant audiences showed that they often expected things to happen differently. More sophisticated audiences may not be fully conscious of what Coleridge, Bradley, Wilson Knight, L. C. Knights and Eleanor Prosser said about Hamlet, of what Bradley, Eliot, and Leavis said about Othello; but these ghosts will haunt us as persistently as the elder Hamlet haunted his son.

What I am arguing is that the conflicting impressions of a character which we get from all the factors I have been discussing – the disparity between source and play, the disparity between what different characters say about each other, the contrast between metaphysical and psychological motives, the shattering of stereotypes, the complicating effect of the poetry, the poet's presumed identification with some of his characters more than with others, the difference between one production and another, between one actor and another – these conflicting impressions are the means by which we are convinced that the characters are *real*, not real people, but startlingly natural.

Most of these effects were calculated and some were peculiar to Shakespeare. He must have known that in many of his dramas he was playing variations on old themes, that different opinions expressed by various characters would help to convert the subject of them from a flat to a round character, that he was modifying or fusing traditional types, and that some of the plays had a metaphysical dimension. When he was at the height of his powers he had as much delight in depicting an Iago as an Imogen or, one may add, a Cloten as a

Cordelia, a Desdemona as a Thersites. Sometimes, no doubt, as with the character of Iago, he could write from his inner knowledge of a dramatist's and an actor's psychology.

Shakespeare is the most popular world dramatist because of his unrivalled powers of characterization; and this power depends on the methods I have been describing. These methods run counter to all orthodox prescriptions of dramaturgy. William Archer, who thought that Elizabethan and Jacobean dramatists were inferior to Robertson, Pinero, Galsworthy, and Henry Arthur Jones, and wrote a treatise on play-writing, would have condemned Shakespeare too if he had had the courage of his convictions. Make certain, the pundits tell the aspiring playwright, that there is no discrepancy between your characters and the actions the plot requires them to perform. When you have worked out your plot, put down character sketches as a guide to your scenes. Generally speaking, avoid any inconsistencies of characterization, but if you cannot avoid them, prepare for them and explain them. Give all your characters an easily recognized and consistent manner of speech. Never let them speak out of character etc. This is all very unlike Shakespeare's method. But he knew, as Stendhal said, that *la vraisemblance* was the enemy of *la vérité*: or, as one may put it, that naturalism is the enemy of realism.[7]

---

6 *An Actor Prepares*, trans. Elizabeth Reynolds Hapgood (1937; Harmondsworth, 1967), p. 228.

7 I am not advocating a retreat to Bradley, but an advance from Bradley; but it would be disingenuous to pretend that Shakespeare's inconsistencies always have the effect of convincing us of the truth of his characters. The character of Ajax is a case in point. In some scenes (act 2, scene 1; act 3, scene 3) he is brainless, illiterate, foolish and vain. In the scene of his combat with Hector (act 4, scene 5), he is sensible, sympathetic and courteous. But the first we hear of him – the Jonsonian character sketch spoken by Alexander in the second scene of the play – has no relation to the boorish butt of Thersites's sarcasm, nor to the gentle knight who fights with Hector. This is one of the reasons why critics suspect that *Troilus and Cressida* underwent some re-writing.

# THE EMERGENCE OF CHARACTER CRITICISM, 1774–1800

## BRIAN VICKERS

An interest in Shakespeare's characters is as old as an interest in Shakespeare himself. Among the earliest allusions to his plays in the early seventeenth century we find tributes to the drawing-power of Falstaff, or Hamlet, or Malvolio,[1] and among the earliest pieces of formal literary criticism are praises for his skill in creating characters: in general terms by Margaret Cavendish, Duchess of Newcastle in 1662 (vol. 1, pp. 42 ff.), and more specifically by Dryden in his accounts of Falstaff (vol. 1, pp. 139 ff., 257 ff.) and Caliban (p. 260). Commentary on the characters continued as part of the discussion of a play under the traditional neoclassical categories of action, plot, characters, manners, instruction, diction and so on: we find discussions of varying lengths and subtlety by Rymer, Dennis, Rowe, Gildon, Steele, John Hughes, Lewis Theobald, Warburton, George Stubbes, Joseph Warton, Upton, Kames, and of course Dr Johnson. Such criticism is to be found in the footnotes to editions, in periodical and other essays, all of which give a complete account of the plays.

What is new in the last quarter of the eighteenth century is that essays and whole books are devoted to individual characters, and those alone. The critics abandon discussion of plot or language and write simply about the people of Shakespeare's creation. This was a decisive change of emphasis, as some of them were well aware. Thomas Whately, at the beginning of his excellent *Remarks on Some of the Characters of Shakespeare* (written *c.* 1768–9; pub-

lished 1785) declared that 'The writers upon dramatic compositions have, for the most part, confined their observations to the fable; and the maxims received amongst them for the conduct of it are emphatically called *The Rules of the Drama.*'[2] But, Whately argued, such rules are subordinate to another topic in criticism, 'I mean the distinction and preservation of *character*, without which the piece is at best a tale, not an action . . .' Since in other literary forms, 'the actors . . . are not produced upon the scene', then the presence of characters before us means that character – and not plot! – should be the main focus of critical interest. Occasionally a critic will even oppose the two in a rather cavalier manner. A writer in the *English Review* for 1784 said that 'in Shakespeare we forget the poet, and think only of the character' (vol. 4, p. 20), while George Colman, having stated that 'the nice discrimination of the various shades of the human mind, the pourtraying of character, was Shakespeare's excellence', went on to argue that 'his fable is often comparatively defective.

---

1 For early references to Shakespeare's characters see J. Munro (ed.), *The Shakspere Allusion-Book*, with preface by E. K. Chambers (Oxford, 1932), and Brian Vickers (ed.), *Shakespeare: the Critical Heritage, Volume 1: 1623–1692* (1974), pp. 27 ff. Future references to this latter collection will be incorporated into the text.

2 Brian Vickers (ed.), *Shakespeare: the Critical Heritage, Volume 6: 1774–1801* (London and Boston, 1981), p. 408.

What is the conduct of the story of *Hamlet* viewed with the person of Hamlet and the Ghost?' (*ibid.*).

Not all critics are as aggressive, or as one-sided, in justifying their interest in character. But whatever their reasons they produced extensive analyses: William Richardson wrote three whole books of *Essays on Shakespeare's Dramatic Characters* (1774, 1783–4, 1788–9; collected 1798, and with additions, 1812); Maurice Morgann published his *Essay on the Dramatic Character of Sir John Falstaff* in 1777, and was ably answered by Richard Stack in 1788; Whately's essay on Richard III and Macbeth led to a defence of Macbeth by J. P. Kemble in 1786, which he enlarged in 1817; in addition there are important essays on Hamlet by Frederick Pilon, Henry Mackenzie, and Thomas Robertson, as well as several anonymous writers; Richard Cumberland wrote on Macbeth and Richard III, as did George Steevens; Henry Mackenzie analysed Falstaff in two numbers of *The Lounger*, one W.N. wrote on Othello in *The Bee*, Wolstenholme Parr wrote on Othello and Coriolanus, while Richard Hole produced an ironic – at least, one hopes that it is ironic! – apology for Iago and Shylock.[3] That cursory listing will show the amount of criticism produced, and much of it is good, indeed the best critical work of the period was produced in responding to Shakespeare's characters. It was a topic which stimulated readers to become critics: the essays by Morgann, Richardson, Mackenzie, Robertson, Whately, Kemble, and Stack were all first publications.

The newness of the genre and of the writers might suggest that their critical approach was also innovatory. In some ways it was – as in the new interest in character psychology – but in others it was traditional. There seem to be two main theoretical expectations common to nearly all of these critics:

1. The concern that characters should be consistent – they should be 'preserved', 'sustained', or maintained as a coherent whole.

2. They should fulfil some moral purpose: they should seek virtue, avoid or condemn vice, and be rewarded or punished accordingly.

Both criteria are evidently part of traditional neoclassical theory, which indeed continued to provide the assumptions and methods for many readers, and writers, in this period. Many of them still expected poetic justice to be enforced, still believed that the three unities were essential.

New ideas, and new approaches, did emerge, however, but the first point I wish to make is that they emerged not as deliberate or conscious innovations in aesthetic theory – there was no 'group' of critics, no 'programme' or 'manifesto'. Rather, they appeared as a result of a specific critical method, which led to a sort of chain reaction within neoclassical theory. The development was internal, the result of a disagreement where both parties appeal to the same criteria, yet where the final position breaks the system that produced those criteria.

The first cause of change, as I see it, was the critical method, which was a very simple one of attack and defence. Where generations of orthodox neoclassical critics had attacked Shakespeare's characters for being inconsistent, and not morally improving – or at least not consistently so – this generation of critics, who shared the same belief in the need for consistency and morality, set out to defend

---

3 All these authors are represented in the above collection. Of the secondary literature, two older studies are still useful: T. M. Raysor, 'The Study of Shakespeare's Characters in the Eighteenth Century', *Modern Language Notes*, 42 (1927), 495–500, and David Lovett, 'Shakespeare as a Poet of Realism in the Eighteenth Century', *ELH*, 2 (1935), 267–89. R. W. Babcock, *The Genesis of Shakespeare Idolatry, 1766–1799* (Chapel Hill, 1931; New York, 1978) attempts to cover too much detail, resulting in a plethora of bibliography but a paucity of analysis. Much more illuminating is J. W. Donohue, Jr, *Dramatic Character in the English Romantic Age* (Princeton, 1979), on Macbeth and Richard III in the critical tradition and in the acting versions of Cibber, Garrick, and Kemble.

these characters. In the process a shift of emphasis occurred.

Strict neoclassical critics, from Rymer to Mrs Lennox to George Steevens, throughout a hundred-year period, applied the concept of consistency of character formulated in the *Ars Poetica*:

> Si quid inexpertum scaenae committis et audes
> personam formare novam, servetur ad imum,
> qualis ab incepto processerit, et sibi constet.
>
> (ll. 125–7)

('If it is an untried theme you entrust to the stage, and if you boldly fashion a fresh character, have it kept to the end even as it came forth at the first, and have it self-consistent.'[4])

This demand, reiterated in countless modern treatises, was applied to Shakespeare with vigour, and at times ferocity. Hamlet, as a character, was notorious as an example of the union of the most incompatible qualities: 'impetuous, tho' philosophical; sensible of injury, yet timid of resentment; shrewd, yet void of policy; full of filial piety, yet tame under oppression; boastful in expression, undetermined in action. . .'. Francis Gentleman, from whom I have been quoting,[5] laments that the hero 'should be such an apparent heap of inconsistency' (1770); George Steevens, attacking the hero for delaying his revenge, and the play for not getting anywhere after act 2, enlarged on 'the glaring inconsistencies in the character of the hero' in several essays and notes.[6] The critics who defended Hamlet might have simply retorted that the criterion of character-consistency ought not to be applied in such a severe way. Instead, they accepted the diagnosis of inconsistency, but then sought for an explanation of it within Hamlet's character. Thomas Sheridan, recorded in conversation by Boswell (in 1763: the account was not published until the 1950s),[7] described Hamlet as a 'young man who had led a studious contemplative life and so become delicate and irresolute', lacking the 'strength of mind' to revenge himself on Claudius. 'His timidity being once

admitted, all the strange fluctuations which we perceive in him may be easily traced to that source' (vol. 4, p. 8). Here the negative criticism is accepted but deflected into a search for a ruling principle that will integrate the character, turn contradiction into unity.

The unity discovered by these critics was the unity of a divided mind. Henry Mackenzie, writing in 1780[8] and trying to find the 'leading idea' which would reduce Hamlet's character to a 'fixed or settled principle', admitted all the 'variable and uncertain' facets of his personality, yet where earlier critics had cited these as evidence of Shakespeare's clumsy dramaturgy, in which they are involuntary blemishes, Mackenzie retorted that 'this is the very character which Shakespeare meant to allot him' (vol. 6, pp. 273 f.). Finding in real life such a person, 'endowed with feelings so delicate as to border on weakness, with sensibility too exquisite to allow of determined action', he made this divided mind the centre of the play. To Mackenzie Hamlet is 'a sort of double person', and William Richardson[9] followed him in diagnosing a continuous 'state of internal contest'. Thomas Robertson, lecturing to the Royal Society of

---

4 Horace, *Satires, Epistles and Ars Poetica*, trans. H. R. Fairclough (London and Cambridge, Mass., 1970).

5 Gentleman, *The Dramatic Censor; or, Critical Companion*, 2 vols. (London, 1770). Excerpts in Brian Vickers (ed.), *Shakespeare: the Critical Heritage, Volume 5: 1765–1774* (London and Boston, 1979), pp. 373–409.

6 For Steevens's attacks on Hamlet see vol. 5, pp. 447–59, 470–8, 479–83, 487–90, 539–43; and vol. 6, p. 199. He was answered by Joseph Ritson (vol. 6, pp. 342–8) and Malone (vol. 6, pp. 547 f.).

7 Sheridan is recorded in *Boswell's London Journal 1762–3*, ed. F. A. Pottle (London, 1950), pp. 234–5; excerpts in *Shakespeare: the Critical Heritage, Volume 4: 1753–1765* (London and Boston, 1976), pp. 4 f.

8 Mackenzie's essays appeared in his journal *The Mirror* (Edinburgh), nos. 99 (17 April 1780) and 100 (22 April 1780); reprinted in vol. 6, pp. 272–80.

9 Richardson, *Essays on Shakespeare's Dramatic Characters of Richard the Third, King Lear, and Timon of Athens. To which are added, an Essay on the Faults of Shakespeare: and Additional Observations on the Character of Hamlet* (1783); excerpts in vol. 6, pp. 351–70.

Edinburgh in 1788,[10] generalized the insights of Mackenzie and Richardson on to a higher plane with the suggestion that Shakespeare had balanced the discordant qualities in Hamlet deliberately, and 'in such an opposite manner, that one class of them should counteract, and render inefficient the other. It is this that suffered nothing to be done; it is this that constantly impeded the action, and kept the catastrophe back' (vol. 6, p. 483). There, it seems to me, whatever our opinion of the final estimate, Robertson has converted defects into assets, and linked character with the design of the whole play. He sees Hamlet paralysed by 'the fluctuation of his mind between contriving and executing', between his gentleness and his sensibility. There we find two of the key elements in the Goethe–Schlegel–Coleridge concept of Hamlet, the discord between the hero's character and his circumstances, and the pressure of events on a sensitive soul resulting in paralysis. It is surprising, perhaps, but none the less true, that the Romantic *Hamlet* derived directly from its apparent polar opposite, the flawed jumble condemned by the neoclassical critics, thanks to the mediation of this generation of critics – whom we would insult by calling transitional. Here is an instance of the internal dialectic of a critical tradition having a fruitful outgrowth. There were also less happy results. In this debate on Hamlet's inconsistency the aesthetic or formalist attack by orthodox neoclassical critics pushed the new critics of the 1780s into a defence by the appeal to Hamlet's psychology. A similar resort to psychology, and to hypotheses about hidden motives, resulted from attacks based on the other neoclassical principle, that of morality. But the defence here seems to me of dubious value. I review briefly two instances, the prayer scene, and the hero's madness.

First, Hamlet's stated reasons for not killing Claudius while he is praying, lest his soul should go to heaven: a few tough-minded critics could accept these reasons at face value – Joseph Ritson, for instance.[11] But most of them agreed with George Stubbes in 1736[12] that

there is something so very Bloody in it, so inhuman, so unworthy of a Hero that I wish our Poet had omitted it. To desire to destroy a Man's Soul, to make him eternally miserable by cutting him off from all hopes of Repentance; this surely, in a Christian Prince, is such a Piece of Revenge as no Tenderness for any Parent can justify. (vol. 3, p. 59)

Other critics, including Dr Johnson, Francis Gentleman, Reed, Thomas Davies, and Malone, agreed in condemning this 'horrid soliloquy'.[13] One remedy was to leave it out on stage, but as Frederick Pilon[14] pointed out, 'This principal link being omitted in the representation, and no other cause substituted for Hamlet's continuing to procrastinate, he appears weak and inconsistent during the last two acts' (vol. 6, p. 183). If you solve one problem by such drastic means you create others: plays are organisms or ecosystems whose balance can be easily upset, with unexpected consequences. Indeed, the common tactic of the defenders of Shakespeare on this head

10 Robertson, 'An Essay on the Character of Hamlet, in Shakespeare's Tragedy of *Hamlet*', *Transactions of the Royal Society of Edinburgh*, 2 (1788), pp. 251–67; excerpts in vol. 6, pp. 480–90.

11 Ritson, *Remarks, Critical and Illustrative, on the Text and Notes of the last Edition of Shakespeare* (1783); excerpts in vol. 6, pp. 334–48; the *Hamlet* discussion is given complete (pp. 342–8).

12 Stubbes, *Some Remarks on the Tragedy of Hamlet* (1736); excerpts in *Shakespeare: the Critical Heritage, Volume 3: 1733–1752* (London and Boston, 1975), pp. 40–69.

13 Dr Johnson judged it a speech 'too horrible to be read or to be uttered' (vol. 5, p. 159); Gentleman: 'sentiments more suitable to an assassin of the basest kind than a virtuous prince and a feeling man' (vol. 5, p. 379; repeated in his notes to Bell's edition: vol. 6, p. 90); Reed: see his revision of the Johnson–Steevens edition, 1785, vol. 10, p. 418; Davies: the soliloquy 'is more reprehensible, perhaps, than any part of Shakespeare's works' (vol. 6, p. 381); Malone: vol. 6, p. 24.

14 Pilon, *An Essay on the Character of Hamlet As Performed by Mr. Henderson* (1777); excerpts in vol. 6, pp. 180–3.

led to damaging side effects. William Dodd, in 1752,[15] was the first to argue that Hamlet 'is afraid to do what he so ardently longs for' (vol. 4, p. 474): in other words, all the business about hell is a mere rationalization of his own cowardice. Thomas Sheridan thought that the speech was just another excuse for his delay (vol. 4, p. 8). Richardson, anxious to validate Hamlet's moral sense, explained that 'these are not his real sentiments', since Hamlet's 'sense of justice' could never have excused such a 'savage enormity'. So Hamlet invents a motive 'better suited to the opinions of the multitude', 'shelters himself under the subterfuge' (vol. 6, pp. 367 f.). Thomas Robertson rightly objected that this interpretation would imply that 'the pious and noble revenge of Hamlet had something morally blameable in its nature' (vol. 6, p. 488), an unacceptable verdict; thus in trying to solve one problem the critic had created a worse one. For his part Robertson fell back on the earlier concept of Hamlet's gentleness, and argued that he 'was really *imposing* upon himself; devising an excuse for his aversion at bloodshed, for his . . . "craven scruple"' (vol. 6, p. 486). It looks as if the debate should have been about Hamlet's cowardice, not Falstaff's!

All these explanations propose a psychological explanation to a moral problem. Hamlet's speech over Claudius is horrible, they agree, but he doesn't mean it; it is only a rationalization. Yet this psychological end product becomes unsatisfying on different moral grounds. It would give us a Hamlet totally lacking integrity, who deceives himself, and us, about his motives. As well as damaging the wholeness of his character, it would reduce its nobility, in either Renaissance or eighteenth-century terms (the twentieth century does not seem worried about cowardice). Hamlet would now be a coward, 'willing to wound but afraid to strike'. Any critical explanation which both reduces the stature of a character and destroys its coherence is surely unsatisfactory.

The same judgement applies to the other case where a psychological explanation was produced to a moral problem, Hamlet's madness. The orthodox position – of the Shakespeare-lovers, or perhaps we should call them Shakespeare-accepters – was that Hamlet assumes madness to disguise his real feelings from Claudius and the court. Against this was set the objection of neoclassical or formalist critics who judged the play, and the dramatist, in terms of function and economy. George Stubbes, writing the first extended essay on *Hamlet* in 1736, criticized the device for having the opposite effect to that intended: 'so far from Securing himself from any Violence which he fear'd from the Usurper . . . it seems to have been the most likely Way of getting himself confin'd', and thus prevented from pursuing his revenge (vol. 3, p. 55). Mrs Lennox[16] dismissed the madness as 'of no consequence to the principal Design of the play' (vol. 4, p. 129) and was followed by both Johnson, who said that it lacked 'adequate cause', since Hamlet 'does nothing which he might not have done with the reputation of sanity' (vol. 5, p. 161), and Steevens (vol. 5, p. 488).

The formalist critics, then, saw the madness as non-functional, a sign of bad dramaturgy. The character critics of the 1770s and 80s answered that objection by claiming that the madness is not feigned but real. It then becomes an intended effect, not a clumsiness, and must be seen as integral to the psychology of the character. William Kenrick, lecturing in a London tavern in 1774,[17] 'urged that the character of Hamlet was much more moral and consistent' (thus satisfying the twin criteria of neoclassical criticism) 'than his commentators usually allow him; that his madness was *real*,

---

15 Dodd, *The Beauties of Shakespeare*, 2 vols (1752); excerpts in vol. 4, pp. 464–77.
16 Charlotte Lennox, *Shakespear Illustrated*, 3 vols (1753–4); excerpts in vol. 4, pp. 110–46.
17 Kenrick's lectures were reported in many journals: one of the most coherent accounts, with a reasoned reply, appeared in the *Monthly Miscellany*, February–April 1774; reprinted in vol. 6, pp. 115–18. See also Kenrick's *Introduction to the School of Shakespeare* (1774).

at least *essentially* so', caused by Ophelia's inconstancy, 'the blow to his ambition by Gertrude's marriage with Claudius, as well as the unnaturalness of that union' (vol. 6, p. 115). The exponents of Hamlet's sensibility could easily attach this explanation to their own interpretation. Henry Mackenzie occupied a cautious middle ground: Hamlet's madness is assumed, but 'At the grave of Ophelia . . . it exhibits some temporary marks of a real disorder.' His mind 'is thrown for a while off its poise' (vol. 6, p. 277). The anonymous author of an essay in the *London Magazine* for November 1782,[18] had the ingenious idea of confronting, in the after-world, a hero of Shakespeare and a hero of Corneille, Theseus, out of *Oedipe*. Hamlet defends himself from the charge of 'cruel and inconsistent conduct', and claims to have had a mind 'distracted with contending passions', so that he is 'not clear if much of my flighty extravagance was not owing to an imagination really disordered' (vol. 6, p. 318). William Richardson, ever bent on defending Hamlet, discussed the madness and offered some remarks which were 'also intended to justify his moral conduct'. Hamlet's external and internal situation is so fraught that he not surprisingly exhibits 'reason in extreme perplexity, and even trembling on the brink of madness'. Hamlet counterfeits 'an insanity which in part exists', and when he kills Polonius does so 'without intention, and in the frenzy of tumultuous emotion' (vol. 6, pp. 368 f.). The madness was a convenient explanation since it removed Hamlet's responsibility for another moral offence that troubled eighteenth-century critics, the killing of Polonius.

Richardson bases his analysis on Hamlet's 'sore distraction' speech, the apology to Laertes (5.2.225 ff.), and so falls into one of the traps which the play sets its commentators. To accept the literal truth of this speech and to reason back from that point in the play can only lead to seeing Hamlet's madness as real; so that the speech in which he announces his intent to

adopt an antic disposition must have been feigned; or was perhaps a rationalization for what Hamlet knew to be real madness. If, on the other hand, you accept the first speech as true, then the apology to Laertes is at best insincere, and at worst a lie – as Dr Johnson and other critics objected.[19] But the proponents of Hamlet's real madness, attempting to solve both an aesthetic and a moral problem with a psychological explanation, ended up worse than they started off, with a different aesthetic problem – namely what to do with the antic disposition speech – and an equally grave moral problem, namely Hamlet's responsibility for his actions. Only the sane and the adult are morally responsible, as we have known since Aristotle: is Hamlet neither of these? This interpretation, too, would woefully diminish his character.

The composite picture of Hamlet created by the new critics of the 1770s and 80s was a psychological construct designed to answer criticisms of an aesthetic or moral nature. It was not introduced by a new interest in psychology, nor did it arise from a fresh analysis of the text. It was a response within the neoclassical tradition to disparaging criticisms of Shakespeare: his supposed faults in dramatic design were shown to be intentional subtleties of characterization.

18  'A Dialogue between two theatrical heroes of Shakespeare and Corneille', *London Magazine*, 51 (November 1782), 513–15; reprinted in vol. 6, pp. 316–20.
19  Johnson: 'I wish *Hamlet* had made some other defence; it is unsuitable to the character of a good or a brave man to shelter himself in falsehood' (vol. 5, p. 161); Francis Gentleman: 'if it be considered that this madness has been but *assumed*, this appears a mean prevarication to a man whom he has most deeply injured' (vol. 5, pp. 380 f.); George Steevens: Hamlet 'abuses [Laertes] in the grossest manner . . . under the appearance of insanity', and after this 'outrageous violence on Laertes, in his sober senses, descends to the baseness of a serious lye to excuse himself by the plea of his "*sore distraction*"' (vol. 5, p. 488; 'a dishonest fallacy', vol. 5, p. 541); and Thomas Davies: 'Hamlet gives the lie most shamefully' (vol. 6, p. 382).

Hamlet was, and remains, a special case. But a brief report on the conceptions of two other major characters, Macbeth and Falstaff, will show again how critical positions in the discussion of Shakespeare, as of all writers, are affected by the method chosen, and by the reaction to a critical tradition. Thomas Whately, who abandoned Shakespeare criticism to write on modern gardening, juxtaposed Macbeth and Richard III, two characters whose situations – murderers and usurpers – were sufficiently similar to permit extended comparison. If one were making this comparison today, I imagine, it would be in terms of Shakespeare's development as a tragedian, the great enrichment of sensitivity and imagination that it reveals. Whately, however, performed a synchronic, parallel analysis, to expose similarity and difference.[20] It has many intelligent perceptions, such as on Macbeth's humanity, 'his natural feelings of kindred, hospitality and gratitude', his susceptibility to family and social relationships (vol. 6, pp. 410–12). To this picture Whately opposes Richard III, a man destitute of every softer feeling, having no wish for posterity, indifferent to family or house so long as he gains power: 'The possession, not the descent of the crown, is his object' (vol. 6, p. 415). Macbeth vacillates, Richard sweeps on relentlessly. Like other critics of this period Whately is confident that he can infer from represented behaviour how a Shakespeare character would have acted on another occasion. (A dangerous practice, but one which was to persist as long as Bradley!) When Buckingham deserts Richard, his 'determined spirit' never hesitates: 'Had Macbeth been thus disappointed in the person to whom he had opened himself, it would have disconcerted any design he had formed' (vol. 6, p. 419).

Whately's critical model is a sharply antithetical one, and is often justifiable. But in trying to prove his claim that Shakespeare has 'ascribed opposite principles and motives to the same designs and actions' (vol. 6, pp. 409 f.) he allows the antithesis to force him into unreal positions. So he decides that while Richard is fearless, Macbeth has an acquired, though not a constitutional courage (vol. 6, pp. 417–23): he is not truly brave. Whately, we might think, mistakes Macbeth's sense of horror at the moral implications of his actions for mere timidity; indeed, as he pursues the opposition he begins, in effect, to attack Macbeth for not being more manly, or more resolute. The scene with the murderers shows Macbeth's 'weakness of mind', which is one of several 'symptoms of a feeble mind' (vol. 6, p. 425). In the battle scenes Whately criticizes Macbeth for not having fought more efficiently: he is 'irresolute in his counsels, and languid in the execution' (vol. 6, p. 426). Where we might see Macbeth's vacillations as the sign of a deep moral confusion, Whately finds them proof of a weakness in masculine qualities.

Over the last three hundred years any significant attack on Shakespeare has led to a defence. The year after Whately's book was published (posthumously), the young John Philip Kemble came to the defence.[21] Kemble shows that Whately has overlooked the importance in drama – a genre limited in scope and extent – of first impressions. Since Shakespeare describes Macbeth's bravery so strongly at the beginning of the play that must be taken as an essential attribute. There is no sign of fear, Kemble points out, 'while yet the pureness of his conscience is uncontaminated by guilt' (vol. 6, pp. 431 f.). What Macbeth suffers from is not cowardice but a sense of his own evil. To this perception Kemble adds the splendid rider that if Macbeth were indeed as pusillanimous as Whately said, then we would have to 'forego our virtuous satisfaction in his repugnance to guilt, for it arises from mere cowardice'. His remorse would then have no moral signi-

---

20 Whately, *Remarks on Some of the Characters of Shakespeare* (1785); excerpts in vol. 6, pp. 407–29.
21 Kemble, *Macbeth re-considered; an Essay* (1786); excerpts in vol. 6, pp. 430–5.

ficance, but be mere 'imbecility'; instead of feeling for him, we would despise him. Contemporaries noted how Kemble's reply had linked up elements of the play previously dealt with separately. A writer in the *English Review* said that Kemble proves that 'the intrepidity of Macbeth cannot be called in question; and likewise judiciously remarks that the moral effect of the play depends greatly on the intrepidity of his character' (vol. 6, p. 28). Character, moral effect, and audience reaction, are inextricably interconnected.

In this exchange, while much of Whately's criticism is of a high value, and was applauded by his contemporaries,[22] on the issue of cowardice the defender seems to have been stimulated to new and important perceptions. Where Whately gave a psychological explanation, Kemble reasserted the moral one, with unerring rightness, I believe, and located Macbeth's experience in the crucial area of guilt, not fear. The last critical dialogue I shall refer to also opposes psychological against moral criteria, but here the apologist for Shakespeare muddles the issue. I refer to Maurice Morgann's essay,[23] in which he set out to defend Falstaff from the charge of cowardice, a charge that had been made by many critics including the author of a recent anonymous work published about 1774 called *Shakespeare: concerning the Traits of his Characters*.[24] Morgann's essay, which has more than a trace of paradox,[25] belongs to a by now well-established genre, the defence of a Shakespeare character who has been attacked on the grounds of immorality. But whereas other defences of moral criticism resort to a psychological analysis, Morgann's has, rather, moral and aesthetic consequences; that is, it affects our sense of the structure of the play, and challenges Shakespeare's moral judgements. Morgann paints a surprisingly favourable picture of Falstaff, the kind that Falstaff would have approved of, and might have made himself. But while Falstaff might have done it with humour, expecting or challenging a refutation, Morgann

22 Horace Walpole said that Whately had given 'the best comment' on Shakespeare's powers in drawing and discriminating characters, and urged that his essay be 'prefixed to every edition of Shakespeare', where it would 'tend more to give a just idea of that matchless genius than all the notes and criticisms on his works' (vol. 6, p. 407). Malone included a long excerpt from 'these ingenious observations' in his 1790 edition (vol. 6, pp. 538 f.), while both Richard Cumberland (vol. 6, pp. 447–56) and George Steevens (vol. 6, pp. 462–6) also wrote essays comparing the two characters, acknowledging – in part! – their debt to Whately.

23 Daniel Fineman, with *Maurice Morgann, Shakespearian Criticism* (Oxford, 1972), has produced the most meticulous edition yet of any piece of Shakespeare criticism, Dr Johnson's notes not excepted. His dedication and enthusiasm for Morgann do, however, lead at times to a critical imbalance, as I argued in *Yearbook of English Studies*, 2 (1974), 276–9.

24 This tract is undated, but the British Library catalogue dates it 'about 1774'; excerpts in vol. 6, pp. 144–6. On earlier accounts of Falstaff's cowardice see the introduction to vol. 6, p. 21 and note 56, p. 70.

25 Cicero's famous definition of paradoxes: 'sunt admirabilia contraque opinium omnium' (*Paradoxa Stoicorum*, preface: 'these doctrines are surprising, and they run counter to universal opinion'), seems to be echoed by Morgann's description of his work, in which 'the Writer, maintaining contrary to the general Opinion, that, this Character was not intended to be shewn as a Coward . . .' (ed. Fineman, p. 143). The connection with paradoxes was not lost on his contemporaries: Stack described it as 'one of the most ingenious pieces of criticism anywhere to be found', its design being 'in contradiction to the general sentiment of mankind' (vol. 6, p. 470), while Mackenzie described Morgann as 'a paradoxical critic' (vol. 6, p. 443), and a reviewer in the *Critical* described the book as 'a jeu d'esprit, designed to show how much might be said on a desperate subject; how far what seemed incredible might be rendered probable' (vol. 6, p. 71). Towards the end of his life, in a rather plaintive note, Morgann wrote that 'The Writer of this Book was conscious that the End held out to the Reader was almost Nothing. He saw that every Page must compensate by some Entertainment for its own Perusal; critical Amusement became therefore in Truth the sole End tho' regulated and directed by a pretended one of another sort: thus circumstanced it was indifferent whether the vindication of Falstaff's Courage was obtained or no Excepting only that it seemed necessary to seize the object of Pursuit not on its own account but to crown the Pleasures of the Chase' (ed. Fineman, p. 241.).

is deadly serious. He takes all favourable references to Falstaff's fighting at face value, even if these include Doll Tearsheet on his prowess at foining, or those by that real coward, Colevile of the Dale, or Justice Shallow. Again, all that Falstaff says in self-defence is taken *au pied de la lettre*: he really did use 'the utmost speed in his power' to catch up with the army: 'he arrives almost literally *within the extremest inch of possibility*' (ed. Fineman, p. 178). Falstaff's wounding of the dead Percy is described as '*indecent* but not cowardly' (vol. 6, p. 175), and Morgann rejects the suggestion that Falstaff's claim to have killed Hotspur is meant to deceive anyone.

Morgann remains an important critic, but rather, I suggest, for his footnotes, insights made in passing: such as the description of the latent element in Shakespeare's characters, who are 'capable of being unfolded and understood in the whole, every part being relative, and inferring all the rest' (vol. 6, pp. 168–9, notes); or his invention of the concept of 'choric' characters – he instances Enobarbus, Menenius (vol. 6, p. 173 note); or his defence of Shakespeare's puns for their function in characterization (vol. 6, p. 172 note). These and other points – the best footnotes in eighteenth-century criticism – are remarkably intelligent, but his main argument seems fundamentally misguided. It also contradicted the impression of the play which had been universally agreed on for two centuries, and it made Shakespeare's design seem perverse. Dr Johnson's bluff rejection[26] – 'all he should say, was, that if Falstaff was not a coward, Shakespeare knew nothing of his art' (vol. 6, p. 71) – immediately made the point that this moral apologia for a character in fact disvalues both Shakespeare and the play. Those who defended the play, and the dramatist, did so by attacking Falstaff, and thus redressed the balance. Their defence invoked the twin neoclassical criteria of consistency and morality, but it also expressed a more highly developed conception of Shakespeare's dramatic design than we find in the discussion of other plays. Morgann's claims at least pushed the discussion into a more challenging area.

Henry Mackenzie saw characterization in relation to its dramatic function.[27] Shakespeare gives Falstaff the qualities that are needed to attract Hal to him: wit, humour, sagacity in observing men; but to these the dramatist has joined 'a grossness of mind' which Hal 'could not but see, nor seeing but despise' (vol. 6, pp. 441 ff.). Falstaff is at once attractive and repulsive. Mackenzie also gave a sharper definition of Falstaff's character: his evasiveness derives not so much from cowardice as from the wish for self-preservation. Falstaff, like Richard III, is a hypocrite; yet their hypocrisy costs them nothing, since they have no conscience; and both use the weakness of others for their own advantage.

Mackenzie was followed, and excelled, by Richard Stack, in an essay written for the Royal Irish Academy in 1788.[28] Stack refuted Morgann's argument point by point, but I omit many of the details to focus on the issues of consistency and morality. Stack reaffirmed the unity of Falstaff's characterization: his self-defence before Prince John, for instance, is not meant 'to be rational and sober. We find in it the same humorous extravagance as in every other narrative of his exploits' (vol. 6, pp. 476 ff.). For Stack the organizing principle of Falstaff's character is revealed in his counterfeiting death to avoid being killed by Douglas: this shows his constant and 'inexhaustible vein of wit and humour . . . triumphant over every

---

26 Johnson's comment was recorded by Morgann in his own copy of Morgann: Bodleian, Malone 140 (1). Johnson predicted that Morgann would emerge again in defence of Iago: but that step was taken by Richard Hole (vol. 6, pp. 622–6).

27 Mackenzie's essays on Falstaff appeared in his periodical *The Lounger* (Edinburgh), nos. 68 (20 May 1786) and 69 (27 May); excerpts in vol. 6, pp. 440–6.

28 Richard Stack, 'An Examination of an Essay on the Dramatic Character of Sir John Falstaff', *Transactions of the Royal Irish Academy*, 2 (1788), 3–37; excerpts in vol. 6, pp. 469–79.

thing, over calamity, danger and disgrace'. The scene is meant to show not cowardice but the triumph of wit. When Falstaff stabs the dead Percy, however, for Stack this is cowardice, and carried out from motives of self-preservation which are not only base but 'so groundless and improbable' – that Hotspur should rise and attack him – 'that none but a coward's heart could entertain them'.

The great strength of Stack as a critic is his awareness of the consequences of character interpretation for our evaluation of the play as a whole. The stabbing of Hotspur's corpse 'speaks too plainly the poet's design as to the character', Shakespeare's moral evaluation of Falstaff. Secondly, if Morgann's interpretation were adopted, 'a great and delightful portion of Falstaff's wit and humour would be lost' (vol. 6, p. 478), especially in the Gad's Hill robbery and the confrontation scene. Morgann had turned this into a solemn vindication of Falstaff, and tried to discredit Hal, Poins, or anyone else who dared to criticize his hero. Stack showed the consequences of such an overestimation of Falstaff on the relative balance of the other characters:

to accommodate his theory, false opinions of Poins, Lancaster and others, must be resorted to, and systems of malice intermixed in the plot, which certainly the poet never designed. These are not only in themselves mistakes of character, but have a powerful influence on the plot, and such an one as I think takes away a great deal

from both its comedy and its seriousness.

Stack saw the moral design of the play but also its wit, ending by celebrating Falstaff's 'creative fancy, playful wit', and 'his elastic vigour of mind'. The last of the critics of Morgann I shall refer to, William Richardson,[29] is rather more serious. He begins by reaffirming the criteria of morality and consistency, finding the ruling principles of Falstaff in his 'desire of gratifying the grosser and lower appetites': 'upon this his conduct very uniformly hinges', since he lives for his body and

does everything to preserve it (vol. 6, pp. 491 ff.). Richardson divides Falstaff's qualities into good and bad, perhaps too tidily (he was after all Professor of the Humanities, and this is the beginning of academic Shakespeare criticism); but he goes on to relate good and bad qualities more coherently than any previous critic. Falstaff's great talents of wit and eloquence are used 'not merely for the sake of merriment, but to promote some design', such as cajoling or duping other people. He fails in his attempts with the Lord Chief Justice and with Prince John, but succeeds with Hal, with Shallow, and with 'his inferior associates'. What Mackenzie had described in a fairly static way as Falstaff's 'penetration into the characters and motives of mankind' is seen by Richardson in its dynamic function. His 'discernment of character' and 'dexterity in the management of mankind' are great, but are of 'a peculiar and limited species; limited to the power of discerning whether or not men may be rendered fit for his purposes; and to the power of managing them as the instruments of his enjoyment'. Richardson's use of traditional moral criticism leads to some penetrating psychological analysis: thus he notes that Falstaff never laughs himself, wants to appear grave and solemn while making others laugh – for his own manipulations. He says that Falstaff's 'presence of mind never forsakes him', but that, although evidence of a great 'inventive faculty', this also reveals a moral deficiency: 'Having no sense of character, he is never troubled with shame'.

Richardson is unique in seeing that Falstaff does not merely deceive others, but deceives himself. The soliloquy on honour is playful but 'affords a curious example of self-imposition', attempting 'to disguise conscious de-merit and escape from conscious disapprobation'. In

---

29 Richardson, *Essays on Shakespeare's Dramatic Character of Sir John Falstaff, and on his Imitation of Female Characters* (1788); excerpts in vol. 6, pp. 490–9.

analysing Hal's reactions to Falstaff through the two parts of the play Richardson notes Hal's increasingly clear-sighted penetration into Falstaff's designs, and shows how the dénouement arises organically out of the interplay between the characters: 'Thus in the self-deceit of Falstaff, and in the discernment of Henry . . . we have a natural foundation for the catastrophe. The incidents too, by which it is accomplished, are judiciously managed. None of them are foreign or external, but grow, as it were, out of the characters' (vol. 6, p. 498). It is entirely consistent with his characterization of Falstaff, Richardson notes, that Shakespeare should make him relapse into fantasy and self-deception after his rejection by Hal: 'Do not you grieve at this. I shall be sent for in private to him . . . I shall be sent for soon at night.' Richardson has seen the coherence of Falstaff's psychology with his moral sense, being in both beyond 'reformation'.

In this brief survey I have stressed the persistence in the 1780s of traditional critical demands on characterization, that it be morally significant, and internally consistent. Both demands carry on beyond this period: they are found in Hazlitt and Coleridge, and indeed in much of our own criticism. They are, perhaps, universal and perennial expectations of the reader and critic. The writers of this period, in which character criticism began to exist as a critical method, certainly demonstrate some of its weaknesses: some neglect the experience of drama; Morgann is hyper-ingenious; Richardson too heavy-handed and dismissive in his moral judgements. Yet in other places, and in the work of Mackenzie and Stack, the writers who generated character criticism also demonstrate, it seems to me, one of its great values: when, by the examination of individual characters, we are led to a better understanding of Shakespeare's wider design.

# SOCIETY AND THE INDIVIDUAL IN SHAKESPEARE'S CONCEPTION OF CHARACTER

## ROBERT WEIMANN

### I

The social dimension in Shakespeare's conception of character suggests itself perhaps most strikingly when Ulysses, in pursuing his well-devised strategy of 'strangeness' and 'pride' towards Achilles, is made to remark

That no man is the lord of anything,
Though in and of him there be much consisting,
Till he communicate his parts to others.
(*Troilus and Cressida*, 3.3.115–17)[1]

The weight of the passage, over and beyond the immediate scheme of the Greek general, is underlined by Ulysses himself in his earlier reference to that 'strange fellow' who

Writes me that man – how dearly ever parted,
How much in having, or without or in –
Cannot make boast to have that which he hath,
Nor feels not what he owes, but by reflection;
As when his virtues shining upon others
Heat them, and they retort that heat again
To the first giver.                    (ll. 96–102)

Here, at the centre of these utterances, some basic paradox in Shakespeare's conception of character seems to be formulated. The most general implication of the argument is that the identity of a person and the relationships of that person are interconnected and that it is out of their interconnection that each must help to constitute and define the other.

In order to pursue this argument as one basic aspect of my text I cannot do more than mention very briefly some of the current ideas and contemporary contexts against which Shakespeare's conception of character must be viewed at large – ideas, that is, associated with late sixteenth-century faculty psychology,[2] or the *sententia* tradition such as that of the *Nosce Teipsum* topos, reaching from Plato's Alcibiades and Cicero to Montaigne and, finally, John Davies,[3] or, although less apparent in the present text, contemporary religious and philosophical concepts such as '*una*' or 'oneness', according to which the 'little brief authority' of 'man, proud man', tended to be viewed in his 'glassy essence' (*Measure for Measure*, 2.2. 117–20).[4] If no comprehensive treatment of the subject can for a moment afford to set aside this wider context, my present, limited purpose seems justified not only because the social, as distinct from the psychological, dimension of Shakespeare's characterization has in the past been rather neglected but because a study of this one aspect may eventually hope to reveal

---

1 My text, unless otherwise noted, is William Shakespeare, *The Complete Works*, ed. Peter Alexander (London and Glasgow, 1951).
2 Cf. *Troilus and Cressida*, New Variorum edition, ed. Harold H. Hillebrand (Philadelphia and London, 1953), pp. 416–18.
3 *Ibid.*, pp. 411–15.
4 As J. Leeds Barroll (*Artificial Persons: The Formation of Character in the Tragedies of Shakespeare* (Columbia, 1974), p. 70) notes, 'any human's claim to his own "identity" was conditional upon his merging in some measure with a hyper-personality', involving some '"identification" with God, Being, Essence, or Beauty'.

new areas of unity between Shakespeare's thought and his dramatic art.[5]

The language of the passage which I have quoted is particularly indebted to the faculty psychology of Shakespeare's day – as is, even more so, Achilles's reply with his reference to 'the eye itself – That most pure spirit of sense' (ll. 105 f.) together with the whole terminology of 'reflection' (l. 99) and 'speculation' (l. 109). At the same time the language of Elizabethan psychology is here used metaphorically, as a poetic vehicle for social clarifications which are achieved not at all against, but rather through the imagery of contemporary psychological thought. For to say that 'man . . . / Cannot make boast to have that which he hath, / Nor feels not what he owes, but by reflection' is to suffuse a traditional topos with a vision of the social dimension of a character's dramatic identity. The word 'reflection' must be read in the context of the preceding statement, 'That no man is the lord of anything, . . . / Till he communicate his parts to others'. Note the use of the verb 'communicate' which here, I suggest, has a complex meaning, drawing at least in part on the traditional sense of what the *OED* defines as 'To give to another as a partaker, to give a share of, impart', which traditional sense Shakespeare, although intransitively, uses in *The Comedy of Errors*.[6] At the same time, and this is the paradox in question, Shakespeare links the traditional concept of 'communication' with a distinctively modern, not to say revolutionary idea of individuality according to which man potentially can feel 'what he owes', i.e. what he possesses: he *can* be 'lord of anything', he can claim 'to have that which he hath'. The link between the traditional and the individualizing perspectives on personality may still be metaphorically drawn from Elizabethan faculty psychology, but even so the tension involved between the two reflects an awareness (which is no longer psychological) of a new type of contradiction between society and the individual. For whereas the traditional content of 'communication' and 'reflection' stipulates an image of man in his relatedness and his relationships, the other (opposing) assumption seems to grant at least the possibility for a person 'to have that which he hath': in other words, possess and control himself alone, in terms of some potential autonomy or identity.

The point is that in Shakespeare's vision these two differing perspectives on experience, one as socially shared, the other as personally autonomous, are profoundly interrelated. In fact, the degree of a character's relatedness or 'reflection', the extent to which he can 'communicate his parts to others', is viewed as a measure of his identity. To be 'lord of anything' *presupposes* the communication of one's parts to others. The awareness of 'what he owes' is gained 'but by reflection' – 'reflection' in the sense that a character's qualities, when 'shining upon others / Heat them, and they retort that heat again / To the first giver' (3.3.100–2). For a character to be 'author of himself' (*Coriolanus*, 5.3.36) is impossible without relating himself to others. In other words, the achievement of dramatic identity and the poetic mode of the appropriation of social relations coalesce.

This, of course, is the barest of generalizations which must in each case be qualified so as to differentiate the varying forms and levels of characterization, in the plays themselves, from that of the merely typical and purely functional role to that of the more highly individualized image of personality. But irrespective of the psychological dimension of individuality con-

---

5 Since we have in recent years come to make a more critical distinction between traditional ideas and *topoi* and their actual use and embodiment within the work itself, both dimensions, the psychological and the philosophical, can more distinctively be viewed as background than the contradiction, formulated in the thought *and* the composition of the play itself, between images of society and the experience of individuality.

6 'Thou art an elm, my husband, I a vine, / Whose weakness, married to thy stronger state, / Makes me with thy strength to communicate' (2.2.173–5).

ferred, the basic dialectic with which I am concerned can be shown to illuminate those many cases where role predominates over character. As Thomas F. van Laan has recently shown in an analysis of *The Comedy of Errors*, 'all the characters are properly identified . . . only in terms of their links with one another, that is, as husbands, wives, fathers, sons, mothers, masters, servants'. But if this is so, then 'a focus on character reveals . . . that identity consists of the various functions a character acquires through participating in a number of social relationships'.[7] On that level the 'overwhelming importance of external relationships in the composition of identity'[8] in an early comedy must obviously be differentiated from a more highly specified definition of identity through, say, a nexus of several layers of role-playing or through a more highly complex combination between typifying and individualizing features each, in its turn, linked with a certain set of circumstances with which, in the tragedies, the images of individuality are made to interact. It is by the degree of such interaction between self and circumstance that the merely functional definition of dramatic identity may be said to give way to some character 'more dearly parted'.

It is only when these two points of reference – the self and the social – are seen as entering into a dynamic and unpredictable kind of relationship that the most original and far-reaching dimension in Shakespeare's conception of character – the dimension of growth and change – can be adequately understood. This is not the place to discuss the practical amount of change and/or development that some of his characters are subject to; but from within the premises of Shakespeare's conception itself it seems possible to say that the very process of a character's 'reflection' can contribute to the growth of his dramatic identity. If 'reflection' in the context of dramatic characterization is understood as embracing both verbal and non-verbal modes of communicating with and to others, if indeed 'reflection' is based on the

giving and receiving of that 'heat', then the achievement of dramatic identity through the verbal and non-verbal expression of relationships must be a process in time and of the times. In the words of the Duke speaking to Angelo:

> There is a kind of character in thy life
> That to th' observer doth thy history
> Fully unfold. Thyself and thy belongings
> Are not thine own so proper as to waste
> Thyself upon thy virtues, they on thee.
>
> (1.1.27–31)

There is a 'kind of character' in Angelo's life which is taken to unfold his 'history'. The word 'history', in connection with an artificial person's life, should not come as a surprise after Shakespeare, in 2 *Henry IV* (act 3, scene 1), had related the individual's fate and 'progress' (l. 54) to the 'revolution of the times' (l. 46) and 'the main chance of things' (l. 83) by envisioning those many 'changes' (l. 52) and 'necessities' which the individual is faced with. 'Are these things then necessities? / Then let us meet them like necessities' (ll. 92 f.) is King Henry's response to Warwick's words: 'There is a history in all men's lives' (l. 80) – a history by which 'the hatch and brood of time' (l. 86) can be assumed to be a process of great personal consequence to the individual.

Thus, a person's 'history', like Angelo's, is related to, and indeed can be unfolded by, 'a kind of character'. Such 'character', even when it is like an engraving on the image of a person, is nothing external. In fact it is inseparable from what the Duke calls 'Thyself and thy belongings'. 'Belongings', in the language of the Duke, must not be read in any feudal or propertied sense of the world. The editor of the Arden edition of the play quotes the *OED* recorded meaning of 'belongings' as 'qualities pertaining to' and notes that the dictionary cites this as the only use of the word as substan-

---

7 *Role-Playing in Shakespeare* (Toronto, 1978), p. 25.
8 *Ibid.*

tive before the nineteenth century. This parallels, and almost astonishingly so, the highly personalized use of 'lord' in the phrase 'to be lord of anything', in the sense that a character 'without or in' can be said 'to have that which he hath'. To recognize a person's belongings, that is to say his qualities, is one way of acknowledging his identity – what he or she is. In the words of Mercutio: 'Now art thou sociable, now art thou Romeo; now art thou what thou art, by art as well as by nature' (2.4.86–8). Here, again, from one character's particular point of view personal qualities are referred to which are individually significant precisely because they are socially achieved or reflected. But this social dimension of personality is unthinkable in a world where 'Time' is denied 'his customary rights' and where the element of change is not made part of 'a continuing order with expectations and rewards'.[9] To obstruct the flow of time, to upset this 'unknowne order' (Sir Philip Sidney) by refusing to allow, even in 'the revolution of the times', the sequence of the years, the generations and the bearers of the office is to destroy identity:

> take from Time
> His charters and his customary rights;
> Let not to-morrow then ensue to-day;
> Be not thyself.        (Richard II, 2.1.195–8)

It is impossible for a man as an individual to grow (or decay) and be himself unless he relates to the laws of 'Time', the change, the 'sequence and succession' (l. 199). But if the office of the king is traditional and its ceremonies are predictable, the sense of personal identity is not; rather, it results from the expectations and rewards, the relating and the doings of the individual, not from any preordained status, such as degree, inherited possession, or birth. 'And I am I, howe'er I was begot', reflects a new form of self-knowledge and a new kind of pride that results from the Bastard's personally achieved sense of identity (King John, 1.1.175). What finally counts are

not simply a person's belongings, but the use to which they are put in 'the hatch and brood of time'. For such 'belongings / Are not thine own so proper as to waste / Thyself upon thy virtues . . .'. A dramatic personality is wasted until his private qualities are successfully (or otherwise) tested in public. The testing itself (as a process in time), not the qualities as such (as a given condition or heritage), is the dramatic source of character.

The parallels between the Duke's speech and that of Ulysses seem all the more significant since, with one exception, the respective contexts of the two are dramatically so very different. The exception is that in both *Measure for Measure* and in *Troilus and Cressida* these poetic statements on character seem to be ironically counterpointed by what actually happens on the stage. The poetically stated concepts of communication and 'reflection' are as far removed from the scheme-practising egotism of the Greek generals as is the theoretical purity of Angelo's virtues from his actual practice during his 'deputation' (1.1.21). If the context in each case is darkly ironical, how does this affect the meaning and validity of the two texts with which I have been concerned so far? The answer is, that these poetic conceptions are exposed to, though not refuted by, a host of dramatic images of experience and reality. The resulting irony invalidates neither the values in the theoretical position nor the impressions of practical experience but makes their connection precarious and problematic. In that sense, the irony of the context itself is, for Shakespeare, a means to explore the possible and the impossible areas of interaction between idea and experience. The irony, then, is one way of emphasizing the strenuous quality of any attempt at coming to terms with the contradiction between personal autonomy and the outside world of society. The contradiction is there, but even in the process of exploring it,

---

9 Ricardo J. Quinones, *The Renaissance Discovery of Time* (Cambridge, Mass., 1972), p. 313.

the mere juxtaposition of character and society fails to satisfy Shakespeare's immense sense of realism. Merely to confront the idea of personal autonomy with the experience of social relations is not good enough as a definition of character. For Shakespeare the outside world of society is inseparable from what a person's character unfolds as his 'belongings'.

## II

This point needs to be emphasized because it is here that Shakespeare's achievement in the concept and the creation of character most significantly departs from most of the traditional premises of characterization in the literary history of the Middle Ages and the earlier Renaissance. This is not the place to discuss the pre-history of the social dimension of Shakespeare's characterization, but in order to view both the originality and the context of his own achievement in historical perspective let me throw a brief glance at the larger background of the problem in literary history. From a bird's eye view, the most salient difference between Shakespeare and the medieval traditions of, say, allegory or romance is that the latter provided an altogether different mode of relating the individual to the social, the particular to the general. The poet of allegory started out from a previously established notion of the general and the social: his subject was, say, the meaning of virtue or vice, youth or sin, and the figuring forth of these abstractions in the form of sensuous experience precluded that tension between individuality and generality which is so marked an element in Shakespeare's mature mode of characterization. But in dramatic allegory, the individual form or the particular image of human activity, far from helping to define and constitute the generality of ideas and social relations, served as a self-contained medium of the general. And even when the richness and splendour of allegorical form refused to be so functionalized, it was virtue, not the virtuous, youth, not the young, which were represented. Consequently,

the achieved amount of particularization (no matter how elaborate) stood in no interactive relation to the actual meaning of the allegory through which a view of the world was figured forth in poetry or drama.

In contrast to that, the new Renaissance mode of characterization brings forth a new form of interrelating the general and the particular which very soon proves irreconcilable with not only the allegorical mode of characterizing abstractions but also with the epic and romance traditions of characterizing a secular hero. In its most developed form a hero of romance like Tristan or Perceval does undergo changes, but such development is more or less preconceived in whatever degree of growth there is from innocence to maturity. The creative principle on which the mode of medieval epic characterization was based is not that of the exploration of the identity of the individual through his relationships in nature and society. Consequently, the quality of experience in the hero and the nature of his environment do not consistently affect each other. There is only a limited degree of interaction between the hero and the world around him. As John Stevens notes, the character of a romance hero resembles rather 'a rehearsed interior monologue than a meaningful and unpredictable dialogue with the outside world': the medieval hero 'has to realize his potential, not to come to terms with life'.[10]

But in Shakespearian drama, these two aspects (the hero's social relationships and his own identity as a character) no longer form any opposition or alternative. The point that has to be made is that, on the contrary, Shakespeare's heroes, much like contemporary narrative characters such as Panurge, Lazarillo, Jack Wilton, or Don Quixote, do have meaningful and, sometimes, unpredictable dialogues with the image of the outside world. There is an interaction between the way the hero is coming to

---

10 *Medieval Romance: Themes and Approaches* (1973), p. 170.

terms with life and the manner in which his potential as a character is realized.

Here, Shakespeare reflects an advanced Renaissance position which is not confined to the drama. Take, for instance, Sidney's *Arcadia* where a similar conception of character can be shown to develop. According to the narrator, the heroes – after 'having well established' governments in Phrygia and Pontus – 'determined in unknowne order to see more of the world'. The 'unknowne' quality of the order of their experience seems characteristic; it is in many ways connected with their determination 'privately' to set out and to employ their own 'gifts' – 'thinking it not so worthy, to be brought to heroycall effects by fortune, or necessitie (like Ulysses and Aeneas) as by ones owne choice and working'.[11] Sidney's heroes refuse to relate themselves to the standards of previously given norms of heroism and virtue; for they themselves, through 'their doings', their own private 'exercises', seek to act and react upon the conditions upon which to communicate their parts – even when they are far from controlling 'the world' which they set out 'to see'. What Sidney does in fact say is that the 'heroycall effects' are turned into a particularized formula by which the distinctive potential of a character's identity is assessed. And vice versa: these heroes' 'private combats' are fought as 'publike actions'.[12] For Sidney's characters to be lord of their own 'heroycall effects' presupposes a distinctively personal endeavour which cannot be a matter of either fortune or necessity (as was possible for an ancient epic hero, like Ulysses or Aeneas). Pyrocles and Musidorus 'determined . . . to imploy those gifts esteemed rare in them, to the good of mankinde; and therefore would themselves . . . goe privately to seeke exercises of their vertue'.[13] Sidney's hero is determined to convey his 'gifts' to the world; but he has to stand and fall by his 'belongings' and he has to achieve his distinction, which is his character, deliberately and privately, not in reference to any preordained standards or any previously

expended heroical labour but by his 'owne choice, and working'. From now on, the hero himself is called upon to assimilate the conditions of his progress if ever he hopes to be 'lord of anything'.

The 'publike actions' of the Renaissance hero are personally achieved, and for that there is, of course, no greater illustration than the contradiction, in Don Quixote, between his private vanity and his public inefficiency. The hero's travail assumes so towering a stature (and has such devastatingly ironic consequence for the plot) precisely because his personal humour and madness *collide* with an impersonal state of social relationships. Don Quixote quite deliberately, by his own choice and working, endeavours to act and react upon his environment, most of all by his attempt to set up and to revitalize the standards of his own particular version of knighthood. It is through the obstinacy, fortitude, and suffering by which he endeavours to communicate his own parts to others that he builds up his own character and he is what, in fact, he says he is: 'hijo de sus obras'[14] – the son of his own works, the embodiment of his very own labour. The point of the novel is, of course, that the figure which Don Quixote has cut out for himself is a sad one; it is ridiculous, not by his own standards, but in the face of the collision of these standards with those of society.

---

11 Sir Philip Sidney, *The Countesse of Pembrokes Arcadia*, in *The Prose Works*, ed. Albert Feuillerat, 4 vols. (Cambridge, 1912), vol. 1, p. 206.

12 *Ibid.*, p. 204.

13 *Ibid.*, p. 206. Richard C. McCoy (*Sir Philip Sidney: Rebellion in Arcadia* (1979), p. 140) has commented on the peculiar nature of the new hero's 'authority': 'He relies as much on a shrewd understanding and exploitation of human motivation as he does on valour and charisma. Heroic action involves an application of sophisticated political insights and principles. This is the crucial difference between the *New Arcadia* and such chivalric sources as *Amadis de Gaule*.'

14 Miguel de Cervantes Saavedra, *El ingenioso hidalgo Don Quijote de la Mancha*, ed. Clemente Cortejôn, vol. 1 (Madrid, 1905), p. 97.

The conflicting quality of the relatedness between private actions and public results here emerges as brilliantly as in the dramatic work of Shakespeare. As early as *Richard III* the conflict between self-determined passion and 'the main chance of things' looms large. When Gloucester says: 'I am determined to prove a villain' (1.1.30), modern modes of subjectivity and medieval traditions of the allegory of evil almost violently confront each other. As a result, classical and medieval conceptions of the relationship between character and action are profoundly changed. The classical hero's destiny, the fate of Orestes or Hector, was predetermined: his own effort and travail were of no great consequence to the result, and to the way, by which he related to the world. It is only the Renaissance hero who can affect though not control the outcome of events. He must not ignore and he cannot obliterate the conditions of his survival, but he can assimilate them so as to adjust to them or, even, take arms against a sea of troubles. This may – in the case of Hamlet or Don Quixote – lead to madness, but it is not the kind of madness through which the Furies or Eumenides once harassed Orestes. For Hamlet and Don Quixote there is no madness and no folly which is not adumbrated by their own obstinate or antic dispositions. Thus, character is part of their destiny, in the sense that the outcome of events, tragic or comic, reflects both individual disposition and social constellation. It is the dialectic between identity and relationship, between individual action and social circumstance which is at the centre of the greatest of changes in the newly achieved art of Renaissance characterization. The results are almost always tragic: the newly self-determined passions of the human beings can only at great cost, if at all, appropriate the conditions of their existence. The dilemma, so much part of all the success and failure in the appropriation of the world, involves such truth and tragedy as, in *Hamlet*, is worded so simply and so validly: 'Our thoughts are ours, their ends none of our own' (3.2.208). The thinking of the Shakespearian hero is part of his own 'belongings'; his thought is his own, but his destiny is a social one, and as such it remains subject to forces and collisions beyond his control. Indeed, the modern personality in literature can only at the price of his own security undertake to feel 'what he owes'; he cannot securely 'boast to have that which he hath', for the very process of 'reflection' leads to results which are none of his own making. The greatness of man's self-determination and the terrifying limitations in his capacity to communicate his parts to others dramatically collide with 'the main chance of things', and the awareness and the poetry of this collision is with us still.

### III

To consider the relationship between society and the individual is only one way, and admittedly a limited one, of approaching the vast problem of character and characterization in Shakespeare. Having taken Shakespeare's thought as my point of departure, I find it difficult in conclusion not to wish to relate this particular aspect of the study of character to a more comprehensive understanding of the problem of characterization and the tasks of criticism in this respect. The present state of discussion of the problem is marked by the absence of generally received concepts of character and characterization – so much so that it is still possible to use words like character and characterization with or without inverted commas and to have such fine matters of punctuation decide the larger issues of definition and methodology. In the face of so many uncertain and transitional positions (between the formalist and the theatrically oriented types of criticism) there are at least two points that, from the point of view of the present approach, need to be made.

First, it seems virtually impossible at this late date not to react against both the romantic obsession with character and the modernist contempt for it. Shakespeare did not write for a naturalistic stage, where the overriding function of dramatic speech is to provide impressions of personality, nor did he compose the kind of dramatic poem whose structure can be approached mainly or exclusively in terms of image, symbol, or theme. Once the isolation as well as the repudiation of the problem of personality in the drama is overcome, Shakespeare's characters can be viewed functionally, as well as structurally, in the full context of each play. To that, a study of Shakespeare's conception of character may contribute by pointing to the simultaneity of his social and psychological thought and, thereby, shifting the whole problem of characterization to a plane where the dramatist's vision of man in his world can provide some synthesis more effective and comprehensive than any purely psychological or formal analysis. Shakespeare's vision, his unique way of looking at the world, may be taken to be expressed 'in the dramatic situation' as a relationship between characters, involving volition and action,[15] as well as in other forms of dramatic thought and language. But to integrate the study of character into the full complexity of Shakespeare's drama is to go beyond the planes of both mimesis (or dramatic action) and expression (poetic thought through language). What is called for is a perspective on character as reflecting and inspiring the theatrical transaction itself, whereby images of identity and relationship are seen as structured and evaluated through the way in which they are conveyed to, and received by, an audience of spectators. Here, again, character and role should be viewed not in opposition, but as both bordering on that line where one theatrical part is revealed and evaluated in relation to an ensemble of dramatic identities.

Once character is defined not only in terms of mimesis and expression, but as a function of theatrical communication, the social form and quality of the theatrical transaction may be seen to be interconnected with the mode of characterization itself. If all the world is a stage, the stage itself performs a role in the

world: it is both a product of, and an agent in, the social process of which it forms a part. If this is so, then – my second point – Shakespeare's concept of character and his art of characterization cannot very well be considered and reconsidered without taking into account the social needs and historical possibilities of a great theatrical culture at a particular moment in history. But the way in which the thought and language of Shakespeare's characterization tend to express as well as to inspire this culture involves more than technique and dramaturgy. Rather, it appears that the particular social context of the Elizabethan multiple stage has a lot to do with the fact that character in Shakespeare is neither a collective nor, for that matter, an individualistically conceived entity. There must have been some correlation between the civilizing function of that stage in society and the mode of Shakespeare's thought and practice in the creation of his artificial persons. It is at this point that the basic paradox in Shakespeare's conception of character can be viewed in relation to both past history and present meaning: as drawing upon that basic contradiction according to which the individual ultimately, in the course of modern history, does not achieve his particularity and individuality in isolation from, but only in connection with, the social process.[16] Such sense of individuality is unthinkable without those universalizing forms of modern society which one of Shakespeare's most immediate predecessors referred to when he wrote that 'Trafficke and travell hath woven the nature of all Nations into ours, and made this land like Arras, full of devise . . .'[17] It was at this time that, in

---

15 Arthur Sewell, *Character and Society in Shakespeare* (Oxford, 1951), p. 8.

16 Cf. Lucien Sève, *Marxisme et théorie de la personnalité* (Paris, 1972), esp. III. In this as well as in the preceding section I have occasionally drawn on *Realismus in der Renaissance*, ed. Robert Weimann (Berlin, 1977).

17 *The Complete Works of John Lyly*, ed. R. W. Bond, 3 vols. (Oxford, 1902), vol. 3, p. 115.

England, it was possible to comprehend the emerging forms of individuality not as the least, but as the most universalized dimension of character. Like John Lyly or Sir Philip Sidney, Shakespeare perceived the underlying contradiction; but only the greater dramatist was, at least inside the Elizabethan theatre, in a peculiarly fortunate position to explore the contradiction between particularity and universality as a unique source of his shaping powers.[18]

---

18 I wish to thank Leonard Goldstein for his highly perceptive comments on the first section of the essay.

# REALISTIC CONVENTION AND CONVENTIONAL REALISM IN SHAKESPEARE[1]

## A. D. NUTTALL

Can realism have anything to do with reality? I answer, yes, it can, but find that this innocent response now needs a careful defence. In his introduction to the eleventh issue of *Communications*, the issue devoted to *vraisemblance*, Tsvetan Todorov writes, 'A work is described as having verisimilitude in so far as it tries to make us believe that it conforms to the real and not to its own laws; in other words, the *vraisemblable* is the mask in which the laws of the text are dressed up, a mask which we are supposed to take for relation to reality.'[2] We have here an assumption and a thesis. Todorov assumes that conformity to the real and conformity to literary laws are mutually exclusive; if you are doing the one you can't be doing the other. And he asserts that artists in fact do the second; that, even when they claim to be addressing reality, they are really doing something quite different, namely following the laws of literature.

I submit that this assumption is wrong and that the thesis is by consequence also wrong. Reference to the real, so far from being at odds with adherence to convention, actually presupposes it. This is most obviously true at the level of language, which is endlessly formulaic, endlessly conventional. But if language cannot refer to reality we may as well all go home. It is fashionable to speak of the mysterious void which yawns between language and the world, a void constituted by the fatal heterogeneity of words and objects. But if words were indistinguishable from objects they could not be used to

refer or designate. You don't point at a cat with a cat, you use your finger or a stick – or a word.

Of a course a structuralist listening to this would at once point out that Todorov is not the only person who makes assumptions. I have artlessly assumed that the reality to which reference is made is itself truly real. Roland Barthes in *S/Z*[3] argued that the reality referred to by Balzac can be reduced to a set of codes based on conventional maxims and Jonathan Culler similarly observes[4] that 'reality' (which he always places within disparaging inverted commas) is only a tissue of socially agreed conventions as to what is the case; thus the correspondence of a text with reality turns out to be only the correspondence of the one sort of text with another.

We are being told, in effect, that so-called reality is not truly real. We should notice, first, that this proposition evidently presupposes a serious meaning for the word 'real', even while it questions the most obvious paradigm of reality. Presumably, unless it is wholly frivolous,

---

1 The argument of this essay overlaps substantially with that of another essay, due to appear in the third issue of *The History of European Ideas*.

2 'On parlera de la vraisemblance d'une oeuvre dans la mesure où celle-ci essaye de nous faire croire qu'elle se conforme au réel et non à ses propres lois; autrement dit le vraisemblable est le masque dont s'affublent les lois du texte et que nous devons prendre pour une relation avec la réalité' (*Communications*, 11 (1968), 3).

3 Paris, 1970; p. 211.

4 *Structuralist Poetics: Structuralism, Linguistics and the Study of Literature* (1975), p. 139.

33

it purports itself to be connecting with some truth (for example, the truth that discourse is conventional). Therefore some reference to reality (without disparaging inverted commas) is possible. Meanwhile, the contention that socially accepted reality is a distortion must either be supported by the demonstration of specific error (which will presuppose a contrasting possible accuracy) or else – which is much more likely in the present context – will rest on the mere demonstration of conventional ordering or selection. And that is the assumption which *I* question.

This running assumption, itself a simple mistake, that the presence of form or convention can preclude reference to reality, can assume portentous philosophical dimensions. Sartre's attempt to partition the universe into Existence (the dark flux of what really is) and Essence (the world of definitions, concepts, words) foundered on the simple fact that 'Existence' is just as much a word, just as much a concept as 'Essence'. Indeed, language can avenge itself on Sartre by permitting us to say, with perfect justice, that Existence is in Sartre's philosophy the Essence of the world. Barthes has argued[5] that the inclusion of odd circumstantial details like the barometer in Flaubert's *Un Coeur Simple* is not reality but realism and that realism is in turn an ideological stance (essence, not existence). Flaubert's barometer is indeed not a real barometer; but it is offered as an example of what might indeed be found in such a room. We should not linger on the *pons asinorum* of mimetic theory. It is, after all, more than two thousand years since Aristotle explained[6] that literature does not tell us 'what Alcibiades did' but οἷα ἂν γένοιτο, 'the sort of things that would happen'. Of course Flaubert adopted realism as a formal stance, but that very formal stance, so far from insulating him from the real world, at once obliged him to inspect it with especial care.

My argument is essentially conservative. I am saying that the generations of readers who thought they found in George Eliot the very taste of reality were not absurdly deluded by a mere coincidence of ideology. I shall argue in a moment that the taste of reality may even be found in Shakespeare.

To suggest that literature may deal with realistic hypotheses is now unfashionable. The twentieth century has found it much more exciting to consider the effects of nature on art, to explore how social and economic forces may condition the available forms or even – more austerely – how forms themselves beget the forms which follow. But none of this actually precludes cognitive inference. All seeing is from a given perspective but perspectival seeing is still seeing.

But, if I have so much respect for traditional literary responses, must I not acknowledge that the phrase 'merely conventional' has long been used as a disparaging term, implying want of substance? It has indeed, but notice the adverb 'merely', which implies the possibility of convention differently employed. But we must be careful here. The phrase 'merely conventional' is not restricted to passages which, though highly polished, are untrue or improbable. Indeed, it is often applied to truisms. It seems rather that the phrase is used when the formal arrangement of a line obtrusively recalls that of other passages and usurps our attention at the expense of the line's reference. All lovers of literature are familiar with this experience and justly resent its being blandly forced upon them. But I suspect that among professional teachers of literature it can easily get out of hand. The teacher of literature is artificially directed, by the terms of his job, to elicit such repetitions, and then to differentiate author from author, period from period by modifications in the formal character of their work. Thus we come to a line like Sidney's 'Foole, said my Muse to me, looke in thy heart and write' with predisposition to locate its precedents, and to place it in the web of analo-

---

5 'L'Effet de Réel', *Communications*, 11 (1968), 84–9.
6 *Poetics*, 1451a.

gical structure. I question whether even the most literary Elizabethan readers had their attention channelled (for all their love of phrase and echo) in quite this harshly exclusive manner. In fact, it seems to me entirely possible that many of them read the line as I read it in my teens, as another exciting foray out of mere Petrarchan bead-stringing and into the dense reality of love. And with Shakespeare's anti-Petrarchan sonnets, the intuition is stronger still. Shakespeare's Sonnet 21, beginning 'So is it not with me as with that Muse . . .' makes two things quite clear: first that the disparaging concept, if not the actual phrase, 'merely conventional', did figure in his consciousness and, secondly, that his own poem is not offered as merely an alternative convention. Of course it is possible for experts to point out that anti-Petrarchanism is itself a repeated formal posture and it is conceivable that Shakespeare may have intended some such intuition to arise in his reader. But to admit the thought, 'and this also is of course just a convention' is to turn the poem into a wry joke.

I have little doubt that this is just what is done in *As You Like It*, act 2, scene 1. Duke Senior opens the scene with a set speech in praise of their new home in the forest, far from the pomp of court. Virgil in his *Eclogues* praised the uncourtly world as a place of lyric ease: 'Tityre, tu patulae recubans sub tegmine fagi . . .' and in his *Georgics* he praised it on the opposite ground, that it formed character through labour. The Duke's praise rests on grounds more fundamental still. The uncivil world is alone real. When the wind blows till it bites, Duke Senior tells us he can smile and say, 'This is no flattery: these are counsellors / That feelingly persuade me what I am.' But he says all this in an obtrusively formal manner, and at the end of his speech, Amiens, the courtier, pronounces obsequious judgement:

> Happy is your Grace,
> That can translate the stubbornness of fortune
> Into so quiet and so sweet a style.    (2.1.18–20)

The Duke preaches realism and is then praised for his power to transmute reality into *style*. Note that Amiens says 'into' where ordinary usage might have led us to expect 'in'. This all but imperceptible conceptual oddity is of course anticipated in the Duke's own imagery, which presents an almost surrealist transformation of nature into various forms of language, stones into sermons, running brooks into books. At the beginning of his speech the Duke reminded us of Adam. Adam may have named the beasts, but he never thought to translate them into their own names! And the Duke is in no way offended by Amiens's compliment. It does not occur to him that he might be annoyed. We have here a clue to the Duke's dislike (strangely intense for so happy a comedy) of Jaques. As I have said elsewhere,[7] the Duke is a fantasist ineffectively disguised as a realist, while Jaques is a realist very effectively disguised as a fantasist.

My point is that although oppositions of nature and artifice can be reduced to their own formulations either through artistic inadvertency or as a deliberate effect of sophisticated irony, this is not true of every such opposition. Consider 2 *Henry IV*, 2.4.225–84, the episode where Prince Hal and Poins eavesdrop on Falstaff's dalliance with Doll Tearsheet. I offer this first instance as a typically Shakespearian example of *writing against the grain of convention*. I take it that the 'given convention' against which Shakespeare works is roughly as follows: the physically superb young bloods must first eavesdrop on and then expose the folly of the ageing boaster. Shakespeare first makes sure that we are given enough clues to establish this convention in our minds. But then he turns at once to the marvellous and subtle labour of its subversion. To begin with, he gives to Falstaff a golden language but to the Prince and

---

7 In 'Two Unassimilable Men', in *Shakespearian Comedy*, ed. Malcolm Bradbury and David Palmer, Stratford-upon-Avon Studies, 14 (1972), p. 232.

Poins a thin, sour diction. Listen first to Falstaff:

What stuff wilt have a kirtle of? I shall receive money a Thursday. Shalt have a cap tomorrow. A merry song, come. 'A grows late; we'll to bed. Thou't forget me when I am gone.

(2.4.263–7)

And now listen to the Prince and Poins:

*Prince.* Would not this nave of a wheel have his
 ears cut off?
*Poins.* Let's beat him before his whore.

Next he has a lute play softly throughout the conversation of Falstaff and Doll. Next, while the absurdity of the love-making is in no way blurred, it seems that Doll, who weeps to think of Falstaff's passing, may really love the old fraud. W. H. Auden, in his essay 'The Prince's Dog', gives far too little weight to this. He thinks of Falstaff as an *opera buffa* character, a vainglorious boaster who imagines that he has great power over women when really he has none.[8] What Shakespeare shows us is – typically – much more interesting than that: an old man who has very great power over some admittedly pretty seedy women. Lastly and most crucial of all to the subversion of the stereotype, Shakespeare gives to Falstaff, not to Hal or Poins, a truly comprehensive consciousness of what is happening. 'Saturn and Venus this year in conjunction! What says th' almanac to that?' (l. 254) says the Prince, and we laugh, not very *happily*, at the wit. Not happily, because the purging force of the exposure of vice and folly is all lost as soon as we realize that Falstaff himself is fully aware of the ridiculousness of love between those who will soon die: 'Thou dost give me flattering busses . . . I am old, I am old' (ll. 258, 261).

 This time there can be no suggestion that the dramatist hopes for expert appreciation of the way something which appears to be a resistance offered by nature to convention is really an ironically pleasurable contest of conventions. The ways in which the understanding of Fal-

staff and the affection of Doll are conveyed do not present an obtrusively repetitious formal aspect, perhaps because there really is no obvious formal trope involved. The conventions of the English language and of drama are observed, but the detailed content of the scene has no obvious literary or ideological source, but at the same time a blindingly obvious source in nature. Which is exactly what Shakespearian criticism urgently affirmed, when first it found its voice. Indeed, such things as the pathos of old age, the terror of death, the value of love are not so much too *novel* to be counted as tropes, as *too* general, *too* familiar. Although I have said that, more than anything else, it is repetition which produces that usurpation of attention which in turn invites the description 'merely conventional', I must allow that in certain areas of life a sort of running, endless repetition is easily tolerated, becomes once more unnoticeable, so that the mind is freed again to engage with meaning. The word 'and' is not a cliché. The sadness of old age is not a literary trope.

 I have noted the tendency in teachers of literature, confronted with a literary opposition of convention and nature, to react in a reflexive manner, to cry out, in joyous consciousness of their own erudition, that the so-called 'nature' half of the antithesis is itself a conventional trope. And in some highly conscious artists this balletic movement of the sensibility is anticipated, producing a work of ironic self-reference. This, indeed, seems to mark the point of maximum strenuousness in much modern criticism. In Shakespeare it represents an early and (for him) undeveloped phase of his art which he effortlessly outgrew.

 The young man who wrote *Love's Labour's Lost* could turn anything into dapper verse. Where others begin with a problem of poverty,

---

8 In his *The Dyer's Hand and Other Essays* (1963), pp. 184 and 203.

Shakespeare began with a problem of wealth. *Love's Labour's Lost* is in part about the vice of premature articulateness, of the too-swiftly-available formula. The lovers must repent their falsely conventional professions of love, and then subject their very professions of repentance to a fresh purgation:

*Berowne.*
  Henceforth my wooing mind shall be express'd
  In russet yeas and honest kersey noes.
  And, to begin, wench — so God help me, law! —
  My love to thee is sound, sans crack or flaw.
*Rosaline.*
  Sans 'sans', I pray you.          (5.2.412–16)

*Love's Labour's Lost* is a 'happy comedy' and yet it is laced with something like hysteria. The infinite regress of reflexive consciousness whereby each new profession of sincerity can be reduced to its *too-expert* formula becomes a kind of abstract avenging spirit, creating below the surface an accelerating panic in the natural festive process of the comedy, until at last Shakespeare must mortify his own comic conclusion with news of a death and the separation of the lovers, before escaping, through a kind of literary miracle, into the final, immemorial songs of Spring and Winter. This avenging spirit pursues him in other early plays, notably in those which Schlegel called 'the tragedies of thought'. Richard II is plagued not so much by Bolingbroke as by his own capacity for conceptual anticipation: Bolingbroke does not force Richard from the throne; he moves into spaces successively vacated, with elaborately conscious art, by Richard. Hamlet is oppressed by a consciousness which cannot any longer con-

nect with natural events or even natural emotion. Thus, Shakespeare's first recourse was to build his problem of articulacy into the objective emotional economy of the drama; to set the dog which had been hunting *him* upon his hero. Later he learned to convey action and passion without this convulsive intervention of formal consciousness. Often he will avail himself of ancient tropes and deep-laid conventions but without that early restless impulse to register his own consciousness of what is formally involved. The two Henry IV plays mark the new found freedom. In both *Richard II* and 2 *Henry IV* we have an extended comparison of the state of England to a ruined garden. The first is conducted in measured language, which draws attention to its own formal nature, by two emblematic gardeners; the second is (quite properly) not even noticed by critics as an example of the metaphor; I mean the Gloucestershire scenes, broken, discontinuous, almost Chekhovian, in Shallow's decaying orchard, wrinkled apples, old men and the sweet smell of death in the air. He has moved from a mode in which the form is emphatically patterned and asserted to a mode in which the form is broken. And it seems to me wholly appropriate to say that with this fracturing of the more obtrusive symmetries comes an intuition of reality. For — to descend to the utterly simple — people do in fact talk in discontinuous sentences. The fact that an *obtrusive* discontinuity can become, as it has in the hands of the epigoni of Harold Pinter, an obtrusive formal device, should not blind us to the way it is used by Shakespeare, which is to convey the taste of reality.

# ON EXPECTATION AND SURPRISE: SHAKESPEARE'S CONSTRUCTION OF CHARACTER

## HERBERT S. WEIL, JR

I

For Grigori Kozintsev, writing the journal about his film, *Karol Lir*, that turned out so splendidly, Lear surprises us with everything he says and does: 'From the very first moment his every action is unexpected: it is impossible to guess what he will do next, what tricks he is capable of . . .'[1] For Stephen Booth in his provocative essay, each sequence in *Hamlet* should surprise us: 'From its very first lines, *Hamlet* frustrates and fulfills expectations simultaneously. . . . The audience's sensation of being unexpectedly and very slightly out of step is repeated regularly.'[2]

Yet these statements can be reversed, in effect, and the alternative perspectives seem to me valid as well, even though it is difficult to find careful, probing discussion of the ways in which what we expect shapes how we interpret. Unless we anticipate, however wrongly, there can be very little surprise, no frustration, no fulfilment. Most of us 'know' or all-but-know from the first scene of *The Merchant of Venice* that none of Antonio's ships will return quickly and safely. Later we feel sure that Shylock will not manage to gain his pound of Antonio's flesh. Probably none of us expects Benedick to carry out Beatrice's command: 'Kill Claudio.' And when we read *Measure for Measure*, do we for long expect Angelo to succeed in killing the other Claudio?

These examples of commonly shared expectations and of the surprises proposed by Kozintsev and Booth are not as diametrically opposed as they might seem. Especially in comedies and in plays based upon familiar historical or mythical characters, most readers will confidently expect the ultimate resolution. Yet even for the most familiar plays this confidence will combine with surprises and discoveries along the way. I want to propose that the better we know a play by Shakespeare and the more attentively we observe it, the greater, richer, more resonant will be our surprise. If we try to recapture our pre-conscious awareness rather than explicit, consciously formulated expectations, we should be able to discover striking examples of where our foresight has guided us well and of where it has led us astray. We shall want to attend closely to some of the varying intensities and pressures we feel while we watch or read – but often we can avoid distortion only by reflecting in retrospect, because during particularly rich dialogue (as when Isabella and Angelo debate) we are probably too busy following the arguments to think much about where they will lead the action.

Even a glance at our critical vocabularies – whether we discuss the 'anticlimax' or the 'problematic' in the play itself, or the qualities

---

1 *King Lear: The Space of Tragedy* (Berkeley, 1977), p. 188.
2 'On the Value of *Hamlet*', in *Reinterpretations of Elizabethan Drama: Selected Papers from the English Institute*, ed. Norman Rabkin (New York, 1969), p. 139.

of our responses to it, our 'surprise', our 'frustration', our 'satisfaction', our 'delight' and 'sympathy' – will indicate that we need more sophisticated and careful ways of evaluating the design and the accomplishment of the dramatist in arousing his audiences to participate. What E. H. Gombrich has discussed as the 'beholder's share' in responding to a painting or a sculpture has been less adequately applied to drama where it might well prove even more apt.[3] Perhaps because of the unfolding temporal quality of a play, perhaps because of its extreme variations in performance from cast to cast, stage to stage, original language to translation, even from night to night – always under the same title as if each performance remained *Hamlet* or *Richard III* or *Much Ado About Nothing* – we deal with an art form compared with which the changes that are caused by decay, restoring or re-hanging a master painting may seem relatively mild.

Shakespeare's construction of character provides a particularly suitable focus for such a discussion because there has been little emphasis upon 'the beholder's share' in the creation of character. Even though one cannot assume universal agreement about basic traits in many of Shakespeare's greatest creations, the vital questions for our purposes concern not what makes up a character, but how effects are created.

Most important is the beholder's share in Shakespeare's control of timing and emphasis. When do we discover, when do we first suspect, essential matters about a character? Does Lear or Edmund change – or does the spectator instead discover qualities that were always there? Do these questions themselves mislead? If a trait is potential in the character, does he or she change when that trait is realized – or is the proposed dichotomy between our discovery and the character's integrity really one that ignores an overlapping of creation and of spectator?

We may all recognize, in principle, how different must be the construction of a charac-

ter for the spectator (or for the reader, who imagines himself as a spectator at his ideal production) from the strategies of those who are trying to create effects – the dramatist, the director, the actor – and those trying to interpret the effects – the critic, the scholar. But in practice I have found few who distinguish successfully how it differs to be the spectator at a drama – a live performance of a 'finished' script – as opposed on the one hand to a spectator at a film or the reader of a book (the completed script), and on the other hand to the spectator at, say, a football game or a cricket match, where there is no script but where someone must win and someone must lose – unless the rules permit a draw. Yet whether or not there is a script, the more knowledgeable the spectator the more he will predict and the more fully he will appreciate the reversals and variations.

Before looking more closely at the four plays – *Richard III, Much Ado About Nothing, King Lear, Antony and Cleopatra* – that will be our primary concern, it should help to clarify the direction of this paper to mention two paths *not* taken – two significant emphases that could well be subjects for other papers, but which might distract the audience from this one. Another paper might well focus upon the surprises felt by the naive, innocent spectator who is viewing the play for the first time, or upon one's own surprises during particular performances.

Readers of this paper rarely come to a play with an uninfluenced attitude. Even the first time we see a new play or film, we almost certainly respond to apparent conventions, to advertisements, and to word-of-mouth comments. And I think it most likely that Shakespeare's audiences – at least after his first nights – responded in similar ways to analogous reports. The 'naïve' spectator poses even greater problems of subjectivity. Any teacher

---

3 In part 3 of *Art and Illusion* (1960) and repeatedly in analyses of specific paintings and drawings.

can no doubt readily add his or her examples, but while teaching an advanced class of university undergraduates – most of them English majors who had completed at least one course in Shakespeare (and who therefore were hardly an innocent group) – I discovered that many did *not* expect Cressida to betray Troilus. And some did not expect the Trojans to lose the war. ('Didn't you know the story of the Trojan horse?', 'Yes, but how should we know that these were the *same* Trojans?') Lest this degenerate into typical professional lamenting the ignorance of today's students, I would like to suggest by a comparison based upon responses to a contemporary film how unpredictable in any one audience is the awareness of conventions and the application of their relevance. Advance descriptions of Robert Altman's *Nashville*, which employs many of the expository strategies of Shakespeare's histories, mentioned, almost in passing, an assassination. Apparently the director's choice of the killer in a very large cast was meant to surprise most of the spectators, for there was no preparation from his dialogue, no foreshadowing expressed in his motivation, no overt insanity or violence. (Altman declared later, 'The moment you take surprise away, there is no art.') Yet many of those students who did not apply the Trojan horse to the Trojan war did identify the assassin in advance because they responded to a group of extremely unobtrusive conventions – essentially summarized by his frequently carrying a locked guitar case in the home of country music.

One example of the surprise that had the most extreme impact on any performance that I have seen may indicate why I consider this a less fertile aspect than my primary examples. (Furthermore, although it is repugnant to me to describe my own experiences as some sort of model, the audience at a paper on expectation and surprise deserves at least one personal example – not as a model but more as an echo of Alfred Hitchcock when he briefly appears and trundles across the screen so that we can stop

looking for him and get on with the main action.)

At Stratford, Ontario, in the midst of the energetic and effective battle scenes from *1 Henry IV*, one of the anonymous soldiers who were charging up the broad ladders that were constructed to look like railroad-ties fell (as intended) but apparently hit his head or neck and rolled over to a recessed gutter before the main stage. He lay absolutely still, visible from our seats in the balcony though not from the orchestra. After a brief dim-out for all the corpses to leave the stage, the lights came on. And this soldier lay there, still – through all the speeches about courage and mock-courage, about honour and death. Through the fights between Douglas and Blunt, Douglas and Falstaff, Hotspur and Hal, through the scene with Falstaff pretending to be a corpse near the 'real' corpse of Hotspur, we sat distracted from lines and action by what seemed to be the corpse of an actor – an actor we normally would probably not have noticed and surely would not then be remembering.

Thus accident doth distract us all. The experience seemed to tell us that mere chance (one that might well, however, have been easily simulated again) could surprise or move us so extremely as to overwhelm the fictive dramatic action. Perhaps this example is not quite fair, because the next morning I learned from the hospital that the actor was recovering from a hangover and some bad bruises, and that after observation he would be released. Gradually the accident that had overwhelmed the text receded; the text from which we had been so sorely distracted became once again far more resonant and evocative than the still-nameless actor.

This example is consistent with my fundamental hypothesis about the nature of very strong surprise for those who 'know' a play quite well. Quantitative measures are unlikely to prove particularly informative because such surprise is more likely to come either from an accident of performance or from perverse exaggeration by a critic or a director than from a deeper, more subtle understanding.

## II

From outrageous accident, I want to turn to designed outrage: the scene (act 1, scene 2) when Richard, Duke of Gloucester, woos the Lady Anne. That Anne would so quickly change from her hatred for Richard to accept the demonic villain has aroused the incredulity of generations of students. In the film Olivier, despite his flair for close-ups, would not trust the energies and inevitability of the scene but interpolated an episode with Clarence to provide time for Anne's affections to mature.

If the wooing scene is to work during the play, however, Anne's surrender, like Richard's unscrupulous – and wildly shifting – claims, must shock us; the resolution, upon first exposure, must astonish us. From the virtuous, wailing widow who curses her tormentor, calls him the Devil, and spits in his eye, there must be a great leap to the coy woman who takes Richard's ring with the near-cliché (in this context so utterly unconvincing), 'To take is not to give' (l. 202), and who concludes, 'Imagine I have said farewell already' (l. 224).[4] Even though we need not recapitulate in detail here all the brilliantly clear steps by which Shakespeare and Richard impose their will upon Anne, let us recall Richard's superb timing. At line 91 he lies, 'I did not kill your husband.' When Anne completes the line, 'Why, then he is alive', Richard glibly lies again, 'Nay, he is dead, and slain by Edward's hands.' Within moments, his next speech admits the crime, but claims the provocation of slander and concludes with 'upon my guiltless shoulders'. After this three-step about his murder of Anne's husband, Richard varies the rhythm and rhetoric of 'this keen encounter of our wits'. When Anne concludes her next strong direct refutation, 'Didst thou not kill this king?', Richard simply replies, 'I grant ye.' From Richard's 'I did not kill your husband' to his 'I grant ye', he and Anne have managed

seven separate speeches in eleven lines. One of the many effects of this quick repartee may be to create the temporary illusion that Anne thus far controls the scene – that she firmly, forcefully, and virtuously refutes every lie and excuse of Richard.

In relatively low-keyed casual sparring, Richard then argues on sound political and theological grounds that the dead king 'was fitter for [heaven] than earth' and that Anne's beauty is as blameful as was the executioner. In response Anne, who has been losing her advantage even by continuing to prolong the argument, makes the first of those vaunts which she will not carry out:

If I thought that, I tell thee, homicide,
These nails should rent that beauty from my cheeks.
(ll. 125–6)

But she does forcefully reject Richard's claims – spitting at him, cursing, insulting – in ever less charitable terms:

Never hung poison on a fouler toad.
Out of my sight! Thou dost infect mine eyes. . . .
Would they were basilisks to strike thee dead!
(ll. 147–8, 150)

Only then does Richard have his first long speech of the scene. In it he overwhelms Anne, largely with his timing. His pauses mark three clear stages: after more flattery – now overtly sexual – and a final appeal to forgiveness, he offers Anne his sharp-pointed sword, '[I] humbly beg the death upon my knee'. When Anne does not answer or strike, Richard knows that he has her: 'Nay, do not pause: for I did kill King Henry. . . ./But 'twas thy heavenly face that set me on.' And climactically, 'Take up the sword again, or take up me' (ll. 178–83).

In some ways Shakespeare's brief sketch for Anne must have brilliantly created a naturalistic credible character – for how else can we explain the great resistance of so many to the

---

4 All quotations from Shakespeare's works come from *William Shakespeare: The Complete Works*, ed. A. Harbage (Baltimore, 1969).

inevitable logic of the scene? The moment Anne accepts Richard's definition of a world with only two alternatives, 'Take up the sword again, or take up me', she is lost. He can toy with her in the next two steps which by logic seem to clinch his case. To Anne's 'Arise dissembler: though I wish thy death, / I will not be thy executioner' (ll. 184–5) – a reply almost heartbreaking in both its futility and its drawing in the sympathetic participation, I suspect, of almost every spectator – Richard can with absolute assurance and overt, generous humility answer, 'Then bid me kill myself, and I will do it.' Anne's 'I have already' by now can only be feeble and futile – as Richard knows, so that he can respond with his evocative definition of her character, 'That was in thy rage.' This both masterfully clinches his now inevitable argument and seems to give us the *impression* of a full character for Anne – a changing personality that in her rage has wandered from a strongly implied essential nature. The true Anne (he argues) cannot be vengeful – and for all her fears, all her insights that Richard lies, she is reduced to a tease, a weak evasive lost object, as these brief exchanges show:

*Gloucester.* But shall I live in hope?
*Anne.* All men, I hope, live so.
*Gloucester.* Vouchsafe to wear this ring.
*Anne.* To take is not to give.      (ll. 199–202)

*Gloucester.* Bid me farewell.
*Anne.*                'Tis more than you deserve;
   But since you teach me how to flatter you,
   Imagine I have said farewell already.

                        (ll. 222–4)

Let us ask ourselves first just what we knew and what we expected during this scene – and then how such a sequence tends to increase or reduce the integrity of its characters.

Probably we all – on some level – sense where this scene is heading: that Anne will *not* accept Richard's first offer which would require her to stab him in cold blood, that she will not accept his next offer to kill himself. Less firmly, we recognize that the sequence is building to

some ultimate triumph by Richard. If Richard is *not* to overcome Anne's strong emotional and moral resistance, why is the scene here? Clearly it is a magnificent *tour de force* that allows Richard to 'creep in favor with myself', whether or not we follow convention and believe his claim in the closing soliloquy 'I do mistake my person all this while!' Why then does our submerged recognition apparently have so little reassuring effect for many of us? What sort of character do we expect Richard to become in the remainder of the play? And what do we expect Anne to do or to suffer after this wrenching assault?

Do not your answers to my questions somewhat distort your responses as you read or watch this scene? The dynamism of this sequence works largely because we do *not* apply our expectations about where the scene is heading and its place in the whole drama.

We might call this an example of suspended expectation. We probably do not bring to the surface our strong pre-conscious feeling of direction and shape – and certainly we do not apply these controlling senses of function *during* the action.

This suspension fits well with another aspect of its economy. Our pre-conscious knowledge applies to the ways in which the personality or traits of each character must be subordinated to his or her role – as manipulating hero–villain and as grieving victim. Such phrasing may not direct the actor and actress, but within this frame many have found cues for superb invention and performance. In the fine production at Stratford, Ontario in 1977, Brian Bedford and Martha Henry varied their physical gestures from night to night as their own energies fluctuated and as did those they felt from their audiences.

One can describe some of the qualities or roles any performer must capture in Richard – as wit, actor, director, creator, unscrupulous manipulator – even though this leaves a great range for interpretation. But what of Anne? What essence or integrity is left if we reject that which was 'in thy rage' for this heroine who never again appears with her tormentor and who comes on stage again only once, briefly, before her death?

In her one big scene she may be played as holy, as sanctimonious, as a conscious lover of flattery, as an unconscious lover of flattery, or even as a machiavel conniver (so one student argued, claiming that she actually stage-manages Richard in order to retain power). Even though later references to Anne, I think, eliminate the final option and some of the others seem highly unlikely, refutation comes from one's interpretation of larger contexts, not from the lines of the scene itself. The delayed effect will come when we recognize that here apparent independence or freedom of character must recede to achieve a necessary ending.

## III

Anne is a forerunner of many Shakespearian characters who are so vivid in early appearances on stage that we tend to think that they will prove much more important to the action and have much more personality than turns out to be the case. Mowbray, both Claudios, even Angelo and Lear's fool are among the most memorable examples. That actors have made them so effective in such various ways should help reinforce our argument that the sequence of our delayed recognition is vital, that the subordination of character (in the sense of personality) should not detract from effectiveness during playing or imaginative reading.

It seems appropriate to move from a scene about which apparently few consciously apply their sense of where the action will go and how the characters will develop, to a play where, quite early in the action, all major obstacles seem to have been overcome, or promise safely to be overcome in the near future, with the result that many readers relax and may miss refinements of character.

By mid-play in *Much Ado About Nothing* few readers doubt that Hero will marry Claudio and Beatrice will wed Benedick. Those for whom the play is new may vary a bit more in the timing of their recognition: some will see or guess from Beatrice's first line, many within the first scene, others only when each character admits his or her *own* feelings in asides – but to no one else. Clear evidence of how greater individualizing of the lovers helps make our expectation more confident and more accurate will come if we try to imagine exchanges in the pairings of these four lovers such as those attempted by Proteus in *Two Gentlemen of Verona* or by Demetrius and by the Puck-afflicted Lysander in *A Midsummer Night's Dream*.

For many well-attuned auditors, the very absence of significant obstacle combines with the sketching of Don John's slanders to lead us to expect some sort of 'much ado' before the wedding, but it seems unlikely that many would foresee how extreme and passionate would be the vindictiveness of Claudio's 'Give not this rotten orange to your friend' (4.1.31).

A somewhat similar combination of the expected and the unexpected comes to the fore when Beatrice answers Benedick's offer 'Come, bid me do anything for thee' with 'Kill Claudio' (4.1.286–7). Anyone who thinks of the shape of the play would expect Benedick to pass some test to win Beatrice (although we might well ask what test we expect for Beatrice and whether she does in fact ever have to prove herself dramatically in order to win *her* love). But despite some need for testing the hero, the critical literature confirms every reader's surprise at 'Kill Claudio' – especially because Beatrice, Benedick, and the audience all know at this moment that Hero is alive.

No doubt none of us expected Benedick actually to kill Claudio: he promptly answers Beatrice's command with, 'Ha! not for the wide world!' But it does seem worth asking what such a command tells us about the character of Beatrice – especially in light of its power mingled with our near-certainty that the killing will *not* take place – a vivid contrast with our knowledge in Richard's wooing scene of what *will* take place.

Perhaps our knowledge tends to inhibit our applying Beatrice's explosive line to our understanding of the speaker. This critical silence toward some aspects of her character has echoes in treatment of the final passages of the play. Very few have commented upon the relative subordination of Beatrice as well as of Hero. After the scene in which she bids Benedick, 'Kill Claudio', Beatrice does not appear for four hundred lines, which are largely devoted to the comic bumbling of the watch and then to the rude insults Claudio inflicts upon Leonato, Antonio, and Benedick. Probably more noticeable (as well as more significant) than this absence of Beatrice from the stage is her silent presence on stage during the play's final two sequences.

Could even good readers have predicted the final treatment of Beatrice? Her last speech seems surprisingly flat, 'I would not deny you; but, by this good day, I yield upon great persuasion, and partly to save your life, for I was told you were in a consumption' (5.4.94–6). After Benedick responds, 'Peace; I will stop your mouth',[5] Beatrice does not speak again; this throws all focus upon the repartee among the men. Benedick dominates the pair of conclusions that remain – the first a strange return to the forced, almost humourless repartee in which Benedick slips back into his earlier banter with Pedro, Claudio, and Leonato. It may be stretching a point too far if we question the appropriateness of Benedick's most memorable line in this sequence, 'For man is a giddy thing, and this is my conclusion', in light of his growth and richness so unusual for a hero in Shakespeare's comedies. More disturbing is Benedick's apparent final statement with its gross return to the horn jokes, 'Prince, thou art sad. Get thee a wife, get thee a wife! There is no staff more reverent than one tipped with horn.'

Then the action comes to a full stop. We may not attend to the implications of this feigned closing because in the brief coda we receive a much more satisfying conclusion for a comedy. When the messenger reports to Don Pedro that his brother John is captured and brought back to Messina, Benedick deflects all comment, 'Think not on him till tomorrow. I'll devise thee brave punishments for him. Strike up, pipers!'

Even though this ending effectively supersedes Benedick's earlier one with its 'tipped with horn' we still might consider why Shakespeare stressed the cuckold joke at this time so near the end of the play. Partly, I am sure, to contrast with the final line – but partly, as well, to show us something about Benedick.

His jesting phrase seems especially inconsistent in light of the dialogues among the men between 'Kill Claudio' and this vigorous, festive, resolution. We recall that Benedick changes from his immediate rejection of 'Kill Claudio' with the final speech of the long focal scene: 'Enough, I am engaged. I will challenge him. . . .' And then, strangely, 'Go comfort your cousin. I must say she is dead' (4.1.326, 329–30). Benedick now uneasily yokes his challenge with its cause – the treatment of Hero. Here Dogberry and Verges enter with their prisoners and we have a visual paradigm of the plot in which events will turn out well – but hardly because the characters, especially Claudio, have earned their success.

In act 5 the confrontation of Benedick with Claudio, like the latter's immediately preceding insensitive dialogue with Leonato and

---

5 Benedick is given this line in every modern edition. In the First Quarto (followed by the Folio), this speech goes to Leonato – suggesting all sorts of challenges to directors' ingenuity – and evoking that delightful argument for his emendation by Theobald, 'What can Leonato mean by this? . . . This mode of speech preparatory to a salute is familiar to our poet in common with other stage-writers.' Ever since his edition audiences can watch Benedick stop Beatrice's mouth with a kiss instead of ponder Leonato's obscure, perplexing threat.

Antonio, tells us much more about the accusers of Hero than about Benedick. Claudio and Pedro both insist upon treating Benedick's righteous anger as mere inexplicable jest. This should make any observant spectator uneasy. But for just what design – either of rhetorical effect or in terms of character construction – remains, I think, less apparent, particularly when Don Pedro concludes the sequence by belittling the challenge – while rightly identifying the romantic cause – 'What a pretty thing man is when he goes in his doublet and hose and leaves off his wit!' (5.1.191–3).

The next meeting of Benedick and Claudio should reinforce the suspicion of the perceptive auditor that he is being given very strange options for understanding Shakespeare's construction of character. In the brief intervening scenes Claudio has discovered Hero's innocence, admitted his own guilt, humbly apologized to Leonato, and started his ritual of penance. The final scene begins with the Friar reminding us that he insisted all along that Hero was innocent, only to be quickly supplemented by Leonato's forgiving (if less necessarily convincing), 'So are the Prince and Claudio, who accused her.' When we are all prepared for the final reconciliation, the ensuing exchange between Benedick, Pedro and Claudio should startle us.

Still believing that Hero is dead, Claudio and Don Pedro nevertheless cannot understand why Benedick should 'have such a February face, / So full of frost, of storm, and cloudiness' (5.4.41–2). We may or may not be expecting Benedick to carry out his challenge in some way, but the context of Claudio's imminent marriage makes it difficult for us to imagine a satisfying resolution to this plot. If the attitudes of Pedro and Claudio echo their heartless jibes when they believed Hero both guilty and dead, what are we to make of this later pair of speeches when Claudio now knows her innocent, but still believes her dead (while the angry Benedick knows that she lives)? Claudio needles his former friend:

> I think he thinks upon the savage bull.
> Tush, fear not, man! We'll tip thy horns with gold,
> And all Europa shall rejoice at thee,
> As once Europa did at lusty Jove
> When he would play the noble beast in love.

Benedick finds no wit or humour, but angrily reacts:

> Bull Jove, sir, had an amiable low,
> And some such strange bull leaped your father's cow
> And got a calf in that same noble feat
> Much like to you, for you have just his bleat.
>
> (ll. 43–51)

At this moment the ladies enter, so this conflict remains unresolved, Claudio responding only, 'For this I owe you. Here comes other reck'nings. / Which is the lady I must seize upon?'

I want to propose that Shakespeare has not been careless in constructing this scene but that he has gone out of his way to create harshly discordant rhetorical and moral effects that we may or may not attend to – especially because they do not change in any way what happens, what by now, we most confidently expect to happen. The final silence of Beatrice after 'Peace; I will stop your mouth' functions in much the same way because one would expect some harmonious dialogue between Beatrice and Benedick. Even if we do think about this atypical conclusion, Shakespeare's purpose remains far from certain. My own preference would be that Benedick, even though here reduced to the crude insult – 'some such strange bull leaped your father's cow . . . for you have just his bleat' – through the final acts manages to communicate a sensitivity that rejects this sort of joking about death, rape, and sexual violence found in 'all Europa shall rejoice at thee, / As once Europa did at lusty Jove / When he would play the noble beast in love' – spoken by the man who thinks his chaste beloved newly dead, essentially because of his own sexual slander.

I am only too aware of the problem raised for this interpretation of Benedick's character by his penultimate speech to Don Pedro, 'Get thee a wife', with its concluding poor horn joke. Perhaps the most convincing explanation in terms of mimetic construction is that Benedick cannot completely escape the triviality and cruelty of his friends, that, once Hero is publicly restored, he is willing to admit the sort of joking that he must reject in the context of the 'dead' Hero. 'To play the noble beast in love' can be accepted in the world of a villain like Don John, made of such cardboard that comedy can leave him with 'think not on him till tomorrow'. But Benedick's loyalty and his love remind us how much more he and Beatrice can recognize and feel than can Claudio, Leonato, or Pedro. Although this comedy has repeatedly insisted that the true lover at least temporarily 'leaves off his wit', Benedick – to an extent unparalleled among the male leads in Shakespeare's romantic comedy – has grown and transformed the typical graffiti about love to an attitude that does not deny them but rises far above their limitations.

## IV

Perhaps the most striking and significant of Shakespeare's lines that reveal new aspects of a character but do not lead to changes in the action show the transformation of Edmund in *King Lear*. After he sees the dead bodies of Goneril and Regan, Edmund, dying, surprises us:

> I pant for life. Some good I mean to do,
> Despite of mine own nature.     (5.3.244–5)

The immediate effects of this evocative assertion are muted. Quite properly we are distracted from wondering just what he means and whether he can accurately describe his own nature by our sudden concern about the efforts to save Lear and Cordelia and then by the entry of Lear carrying her body. The ordering of values that so quickly moved us away from attending to the implications of this

speech seems reinforced when the messenger enters to report, 'Edmund is dead, my lord', and Albany replies, 'That's but a trifle here' (l. 295).

I think that Edmund's forceful, if apparently gratuitous, definition of his own nature is meant by Shakespeare to encourage us to ponder *in retrospect* the relation of individual character and especially of unexpected virtue to the vision of the whole play and the complex character of its hero. Because we are swiftly deflected from considering the implications of Edmund's statement, because his good intentions so quickly prove futile, and because he receives no reward or praise, we are left to interpret his 'nature' for ourselves. Whether or not we accept Albany's view (and it is the final comment in the play concerning Edmund), we can recognize how important 'the beholder's share' must be if we are to understand his character. That our first impressions of him do not prepare us for this final sequence and that an apparently choric figure cannot appreciate his nature suggests that Shakespeare followed a deliberate strategy in raising questions about the possible unexpected emergence of virtue in such a character.

Shakespeare's treatment of Edmund epitomizes a procedure that he has used throughout *King Lear*, especially in dramatizing those secondary characters with whom Edmund increasingly associates. That Albany and Edmund suggest unexpected moral growth while Cornwall, Goneril, and Regan never do seems more significant for raising problems about their natures (and subsequently about Lear's) than for any influence upon the action. But Shakespeare constructs his play so that we should *not* notice too quickly the differences between these sisters and their husbands. For example, the very first line, Kent's 'I thought the King had more affected the Duke of Albany than Cornwall', with Gloucester's accord, presents information that we cannot evaluate upon first exposure to the play. Only after Albany and Cornwall cease to act in concert can we appreciate how they differ and therefore how significant are Kent's comparison and Lear's earlier preference. Shakespeare gradually leads the beholder to notice that the similarity of personal traits and roles of the evil sisters becomes much less consequential than their differences, especially when each describes Edmund and her feelings for him. Spectators may have expected such sisters to destroy themselves, but the actual agent and manner of murder and suicide should not be predictable early in the play any more than were the ways that Cornwall and Edmund die. If the killings by the anonymous servant, by the formerly gullible brother, and by the passionate eldest sister do not surprise and shake us, many important effects will be diluted.

However great our participation as we discover unsuspected aspects of Edmund, Goneril, and Regan, Lear's entrance carrying the dead Cordelia overwhelms us. Before this 'promised end' or 'image of that horror', our share becomes circumscribed. Albany's harsh 'That's but a trifle here' helps ensure that we do not exaggerate our place in interpreting the action. The ending of *Lear* dwarfs the incipient repentance of Edmund, the growth in vision of Albany and Edgar, and even the transformation of Lear himself.

V

After such a wrenching ending, how could one expect the dramatist to develop? It seems quite appropriate that when Shakespeare next decided to construct major characters upon the lines I have been suggesting, he should turn from less to more familiar history. Nor should we be surprised that the rhetorical action in *Antony and Cleopatra* should move from an initial satiric external commentary to an overwhelming realization (or perhaps near-realization) as the play ends. Philo's opening speech echoes the tone of the title of *Much Ado About Nothing* when he describes the 'triple pillar of the world' and the Queen as unsympathetically as Goneril and Regan had

described their father. Philo – or Shakespeare – quickly and confidently moves from critic of the famous lovers to carnival barker to puppet-master: 'Behold and see.' But again and again through the play we see that this cynical Roman view of Antony and Cleopatra tells us part of the truth; again and again we feel its partial and inadequate nature.

Antony and Cleopatra themselves repeatedly and explicitly grapple with the problem of their own characters as essences that can be gained and lost: 'But since my lord is Antony again, I will be Cleopatra' (3.13.186–7) suggests a momentary ability to capture a spark in a scene where Enobarbus never lets us forget its heart-rending brevity. On how many levels of sincerity, of pretending, of hoping, does such an idea reiterate Richard's conception of character when he told Anne 'that was in thy rage' – that was not the true Anne, the real character? However devious was Richard, however transparent (in some ways) to the audience, however ambivalent are Cleopatra and Antony, each stresses a dynamic, fluctuating, surprisingly optimistic attitude toward character. You are *yourself* only at your best. Anne's revenge, Antony's cruelty, Cleopatra's cowardice are only temporary veils that hide their true selves.

For me, the epitome of such groping toward one's essence comes most economically and forcefully in act 3, scene 11. After Antony laments 'I have fled myself, and have instructed cowards', Cleopatra tries to restore him. She humbly apologizes:

> O my lord, my lord,
> Forgive my fearful sails: I little thought
> You would have followed.

Antony refuses to accept her claim, correcting her:

> Egypt, thou knew'st too well
> My heart was to thy rudder tied by th' strings,
> And thou shouldst tow me after.     (ll. 54–8)

How do we expect Cleopatra to respond? Can the apparent conflict be resolved? As in *Much Ado*, we are very much aware of how the action will end, but can we – any more than with Benedick and Beatrice – now distinguish which qualities the lovers share or how they differ from each other?

Cleopatra answers humbly and briefly 'O, my pardon!' – acknowledging the rightness of Antony's apparent refutation. She thereby wins him again. This brief scene of less than seventy-five lines ends with Antony's buoyant:

> Fall not a tear, I say: one of them rates
> All that is won and lost.

What a vast distance in a few moments from Antony's first lines in the scene:

> Hark! the land bids me tread no more upon 't,
> It is ashamed to bear me . . . I
> Have lost my way for ever.

Do we believe in the essential validity of Antony's joy? Do we expect it to last? Can Cleopatra's humility and their mutual trust survive their defeat and death? Our answers will surely vary, but if I read their speeches correctly, Antony's seeming victory – like Philo's earlier description – proves but superficial. That Cleopatra thrice begs Antony's pardon, and says nothing else, does not mean that she lied or even erred when she told him: 'I little thought you would have followed.' Nor does she reverse herself or become hypocritical when she accepts his reply: 'Egypt, thou knew'st too well / My heart was to thy rudder tied by th' strings.' Part of the essence of these two characters may well be captured here and Cleopatra's rapid instinctive comprehension shows her at her most worthy – and challenges the audience to respond in kind. Cleopatra does not lie: she did not *consciously think* that Antony would follow, but on some deeper level she *knew* she would tow him after.

We all know how ambivalent are Cleopatra,

Antony, and our responses to them – especially when they are at their best. Such a peak – if peak it be – cannot last. Like Benedick, Antony himself by his next appearance cannot maintain his joyous grasp of what his beloved feels. But our scepticism is, I think, essential both to Shakespeare's construction of his characters and to our own feelings. When Cleopatra finally describes her dead Antony to Dolabella, she concludes 'Think you there was or might be such a man / As this I dreamt of?' (5.2.93–4). We, like Dolabella, are meant to respond, 'Gentle madam, no.' Yet I think a superb actress on her best night – or our imagination at its most refined – can transform our scepticism, as Cleopatra's impassioned imagination wins from Dolabella the truth about Caesar's deceiving intention.

I want to conclude briefly with a very familiar speech from the play performance of which evoked my own most surprised moments. Now instead of the accidental fall of an anonymous extra, let us think once again of Hal's first soliloquy. How little upon first reading or watching could we have expected it – as how little could we have expected Cressida's first soliloquy which is identically placed and similarly reverses the rhetoric of the first scene in which she appears.

I eagerly await an actor and a production that will take full advantage of the thrust stage. After all Hal's companions have left by rear and side exits – and last not Falstaff, but Poins – Hal will step forward and address us in the audience. We all think we know the speech well. We expect Hal's promise and his rejection of his drinking fellows. But the true Shakespearian surprise comes not through accident or through idiosyncratic original interpretation, but through a fuller realization of the lines and the character expressed by them. No doubt most of Shakespeare's earlier audiences too came primarily to see Falstaff, to escape their cares, and to be entertained. It is perhaps those audiences – and ours – who become Hal's 'foul and ugly mists' when he

steps forward and speaks not to Falstaff – but to
us – to ask from us the beholder's share:

> I know you all, and will awhile uphold
> The unyoked humor of your idleness.

Yet herein will I imitate the sun,
Who doth permit the base contagious clouds
To smother up his beauty from the world. . . .

(1.2.188–92)

# SHAKESPEARE AND THE VENTRILOQUISTS

## LEO SALINGAR

Relatively early in Shakespeare's career the minor poet John Weever affirmed the devotion of 'thousands' of spectators or readers to Romeo, Richard and others of Shakespeare's characters, his 'children' as the heavy-handed eulogist dubs them.[1] In the movement of opinion that established Shakespeare as the supreme dramatic poet in the course of the eighteenth and early nineteenth centuries, progressively clearing him of reproach for offending against the neoclassical rules of construction, his gift of character portrayal was the outstanding theme for praise and wonder, and character study became the leading occupation of criticism. And the Elizabethan's metaphor of fatherhood, biological creation, re-emerged as an accepted critical fiction, almost a critical doctrine. Pope had repeated that Shakespeare was an instrument of nature, not a mere copier, and had said that each of his people was as distinct as an individual in real life; Johnson added, with a different emphasis, that this lifelikeness was not the result of any searching after personal idiosyncrasies but of Shakespeare's truth to typical human nature; others, like Morgann, began to treat the plays like psychological case-books, probing the depths of separate characters as if they were independent human beings. What impressed the commentators so forcibly was not merely the wealth of observation revealed by Shakespeare's people but their air of spontaneity, of free-standing autonomy, uninhibited by theatrical contrivance. Hazlitt says, for example, enforcing what had become an approved commonplace, that in *Antony and Cleopatra* 'the characters breathe, move, and live'; Shakespeare, he goes on, 'does not stand reasoning on what his characters would do or say, but at once *becomes* them, and speaks and acts for them'; and again, in *Hamlet*, 'the characters think and speak and act just as they might do, if left entirely to themselves. There is no set purpose, no straining at a point. The observations are suggested by the passing scene – the gusts of passion come and go like sounds of music borne on the wind.'[2] That simile, with its suggestion of an Aeolian harp, is a reminder of the romantic bias of Hazlitt's period. We can no longer, as reflecting critics, attribute such spontaneity to Shakespeare's characters, and we are cautious about the illusion of their separate personalities. Indeed, when Hazlitt was lecturing, Schlegel and Coleridge were already sketching out a theory of organic unity in Shakespeare, which might have led interpreters to subordinate character study to the latent governing idea within each play as a whole. On the other hand, it is possible that in large measure the enthusiasm of the Romantics for creative freedom and psychological intuition was caused by, and not simply transferred to, their admiration for Shakespeare. And the illusion that each of his

---

1 John Weever, *Epigrammes in the Oldest Cut and Newest Fashion*, 1599 (Stratford-upon-Avon, 1922), p. 75.
2 Hazlitt, *Characters of Shakespeare's Plays* (1817); ed. Catherine MacDonald Maclean (1964), pp. 228, 233.

characters is a separate being with thoughts and impulses of his own cannot simply be argued away; the actors in every performance are there to revive it.

Belief in the spontaneity of Shakespeare's characters, as separate centres of consciousness, is closely allied to an interest in their capacity for self-awareness and introspection, an interest which Coleridge did a great deal to encourage. In this paper I shall try to examine some aspects of Hamlet, the favourite subject for this interest of the Romantics. I shall not set out to reinvestigate the details of Coleridge's faded portrait of the melancholy prince, but I think there are still important questions to consider in his general statements about Shakespeare's methods of characterization.

'Shakespeare shaped his characters out of the nature within', says Coleridge: 'but we cannot so safely say, out of *his own* nature, as an *individual person . . .*' And, to bring home this elusive concept, Coleridge points, as he often does, to a radical contrast between Shakespeare and other playwrights: 'There is no greater or more common vice in dramatic writers than to draw out of themselves. How I – alone and in the self-sufficiency of my study, as all men are apt to be proud in their dreams – should *like* to be talking king! . . . Shakespeare in composing had no I but the I representative.'[3] Other stage poets, then, according to Coleridge, are not creators, endowing characters with an independent life; they are essentially 'ventriloquists', projecting themselves through the mouths of all their puppets. Coleridge repeats this criticism several times. For example, in a play by Beaumont and Fletcher, 'the scenes are mock dialogues, in which the poet solo plays the ventriloquist, but cannot suppress his own way of expressing himself'. And even Jonson, for all his 'erudition', is guilty in *Sejanus* of 'an absurd rant and *ventriloquism*' such as can be found 'in no genuine part of Shakespeare' – 'ventriloquism, because Sejanus is a puppet out of which the poet makes his own voice appear to come'.[4] The figures in other writers' plays are one-sided, uniform, subjected to the author's voice, overshadowed by his self-importance, whereas Shakespeare's are abundant, varied and free. Or, to use Hazlitt's wording again, Shakespeare '*becomes*' his characters, whereas other playwrights 'stand reasoning' about them, are straining to make a point.

Now, if we apply this contrast to the Elizabethans in general, it is clear that there is a share of injustice in it. Coleridge simplifies stage history; he ignores, or takes for granted, the new impulse in that assertive rhetoric that brings their characters to life. The 'high astounding terms' of Marlowe's Tamburlaine are still recognizably akin to those of medieval stage figures, Herod in the Coventry *Slaughter of the Innocents*, for instance, but they carry a new dynamic force. Herod boasts to the audience of what he is, or believes himself to be – 'the myghttyst conquerowre that eyuer walkid on grownd!';[5] but although he is certainly 'talking king' (and comic villain as well), there is no personal inflection in his voice. He simply lists his magical attributes, as in a herald's proclamation:

> To reycownt vnto you my innevmerabull substance,
> Thatt were to moche for any tong to tell!
> For all the whole Orent ys vnder myn obeydeance,
> And Prynce am I of Purgatorre, and Cheff Capten of Hell!

Tamburlaine, by contrast, boasts not of what he is so much as of what he wills himself to become:

> I am a Lord, for so my deeds shall prove,
> And yet a shepherd by my Parentage.
>
> *(Part 1, 1.2.34–5)*

---

3 Coleridge, Lecture VII, 1818; in *Miscellaneous Criticism*, ed. T. M. Raysor (1936), pp. 43–4.

4 *Miscellaneous Criticism*, pp. 54, 90; see M. M. Badawi, *Coleridge: Critic of Shakespeare* (Cambridge, 1973), pp. 58, 103–8.

5 Coventry *Slaughter of the Innocents*, ll. 487, 500–3, ed. J. Q. Adams in *Chief Pre-Shakespearean Dramas* (Cambridge, Mass., 1924).

His will creates a role, which is at once a commanding stage presence and a programme for action.

Again, to glance at another innovative role, consider these typical lines from Hieronimo's soliloquy at a crisis in *The Spanish Tragedy*:

Thus therefore will I rest me in unrest,
Dissembling quiet in unquietness.

(3.13.29–30)

No doubt the author's voice is audible here, imposing a heightened self-consciousness on the speaker; and further, they are keynote lines, summarizing the conduct of every active personage in the play. But without such inner tension, and such projection and magnification of tension, there would be no Elizabethan tragic drama, not simply at the level of *The Spanish Tragedy*, but at the level of *Richard III* or even *Macbeth*.

Nevertheless, there is strength in Coleridge's generalization. The will-to-power in Marlowe's heroes is always much the same will-to-power, and very few expressions of feeling are allowed to his characters out of the range of its magnetic attraction. Ben Jonson is much more subtle and on the surface more varied; but when, for instance, Volpone says, 'I glory / More in the cunning purchase of my wealth / Than in the glad possession', we recognize the note that is common to all his active characters, the note of intellectual self-congratulation which blends together their otherwise discordant humours and also motivates the plot. Although he is a profound critic of manners, Jonson is only at one remove from 'talking king' in his own person. Webster dwells on the subjective sensations and the mental quirks of his characters; but when, for example, Flamineo exclaims,

We endure the strokes like anvils or hard steel,
Till pain itself makes us no pain to feel,

(*The White Devil*, 3.3.1–2)

he conveys the essential experience of all of them. Angry, feigning or resigned, they all come to life principally as victims, and the tragedy is a parade of their sufferings. None of Shakespeare's contemporaries can confer on their actors that degree of self-consciousness, or that capacity for self-questioning, that makes us feel completely that the speaker is a living person in his own mind and so, consequently, for us. A partial exception is Middleton (who may, of course, have learned from Shakespeare); and – to offer one more brief typifying extract – we seem to hear the tones of a natural self-consciousness in speeches like Livia's soliloquy in *Women Beware Women*, when she has made up her mind to engineer the liaison between her brother and their niece:

I am the fondest where I once affect,
The carefull'st of their healths, and of their
  ease, forsooth,
That I look still but slenderly to mine own;
I take a course to pity him so much now
That I have none left for modesty and myself.

(2.1.65–9)

She knows herself, and does not know herself, like a living individual; and this kind of confident self-deception, which reveals the inner mind of the characters, is the guiding thread in Middleton's main tragedies. However, all Middleton's tragic characters are subject to much the same form of self-deception and follow it along much the same course. And, although Middleton shows us that each of them has in mind an 'I', a separate identity, he does not develop that consciousness beyond the discovery of self-deception, and he invites us to respond to it mainly in a critical spirit, from the outside.

As Coleridge emphasizes, Shakespeare writes from an altogether different level of understanding. He 'shaped his characters out of the nature within' – which implies that he could share the subjective, the experiencing side of their feelings; 'but we cannot so safely say, out of *his own* nature as an *individual person*' – which implies his freedom from emotional self-interest. And 'Shakespeare in composing had no *I* but the *I* representative.' In effect, this reconciles Pope's view of the individuality of Shakespeare's characters with Samuel Johnson's sense of their common humanity. At the same time, Coleridge suggests a view of the impersonality of great writing more positive and inclusive than the definitions put forward by Joyce and the early T. S. Eliot. And it comes very close to the insight Leavis expresses, with regard to tragedy, when he says that tragedy 'undermines and supersedes' self-centred and 'self-boosting' emotional attitudes:[6]

[Tragedy] establishes below them a kind of profound impersonality in which experience matters, not because it is mine – because it is to me it belongs or happens, or because it subserves or issues in purpose or will, but because it is what it is, the 'mine' mattering only in so far as the individual sentience is the indispensable focus of experience.

Leavis's distinction between the possessive and the impersonal aspects of experience in tragedy supplements Coleridge's distinction between the personal 'I' of the poet and his 'I representative'. But Leavis's statement also suggests that in genuine tragedy we are made aware of both sides of the distinction, personal and impersonal or representative, together, and that in the experience which 'matters' for us we cannot have one without the other. And this reflection in turn, I think, has a bearing on what Coleridge says about Shakespeare's characters. I mean that in his leading tragic characters Shakespeare makes us aware of a gap between a character's image of himself and an image of a more complete humanity that could be described as an 'I representative'. No individual could embody such a representativeness, or even define it. But on the other hand it is not simply a poetic mirage. A sense of what such complete humanity might be, or might require, emerges in the course of Shakespeare's mature tragedies, partly in the speeches of the leading characters and partly through the interplay of the action as a whole. It is partly

indicated by negatives. But Shakespeare is the only Elizabethan dramatist to convey a sense of what Coleridge calls 'the *I* representative', while at the same time and by the same token he distinguishes it from a character's personal 'I'. And the deep-lying interest within his mature tragedies springs somewhere within that distinction, or gap. At the centre, or point of origin, is the way Shakespeare brings about the hero's perception of a division within himself.

This is not the same as speaking of a 'tragic flaw', because that seems to imply that apart from the flaw in question the hero would approach perfection – which is not what Shakespeare intimates. Nor would it help to return to Coleridge's speculations about Shakespeare creating such a character as Hamlet by meditating upon some inner quality of his own carried to excess,[7] if only because those speculations lead away from the impact and movement of drama. The notion of a gap within the hero's image of himself gives a better pointer, I think, to Shakespeare's method – a notion well brought out by Peter Ure in his essay on 'Character and Role from Richard III to Hamlet', where he argues that the central interest in the tragic plays is the 'gap', the lack of 'consonance', between 'the hero's inward self' and his office or role, as king, for instance, or avenger. A role is both a social and a theatrical concept, and hence for the audience as well as the character a provisional guide to the line the action will follow. But, as Ure points out, 'it is the character faced with his role, forced to decide about it, the quality of his response, that Shakespeare shows us, not just his performance in the role'.[8] In brief, the effective guid-

---

6 F. R. Leavis, 'Tragedy and the "Medium"', in *The Common Pursuit* (1952; Harmondsworth, 1962), p. 130.

7 Coleridge, *Shakespearean Criticism*, ed. T. M. Raysor, 2 vols (1960), vol. 1, p. 34, vol. 2, p. 85; cf. *Miscellaneous Criticism*, pp. 43–4.

8 Peter Ure, 'Character and Role from Richard III to Hamlet', in *Hamlet*, ed. John Russell Brown and Bernard Harris, Stratford-upon-Avon Studies, 5 (1963), p. 10.

ing line within the psychological movement of the play is the hero's efforts to close the gap. In Shakespeare's mature tragedies, this brings the hero's inward self into question besides his attitude towards his role.

*Hamlet* is the first play in which Shakespeare develops this method of characterization at length. Many of the outstanding characters in his early plays, the figures who hold the stage and seem typically Shakespearian, are not notable for self-questioning but rather for self-assertive, humorous energy, like Richard III and Faulconbridge, Petruchio and Falstaff. Richard III only doubts himself for a moment, under the belated blows of conscience. And although Shakespeare makes dramatic use of introspection very early, he does not bring it to the centre of interest even with Richard II or Brutus, who question their roles more than themselves. Something new in Shakespeare seems to be afoot when *The Merchant of Venice* opens with Antonio's 'In sooth, I know not why I am so sad'; but this puzzlement is left undeveloped in the play. In contrast, Hamlet's part begins with his reference to the mystery of his own state of feeling, and this mystery complicates Hamlet's reponse to his imposed duty of revenge until very near the end. Hamlet is agitated by the problem of himself, not only as a son, a prince, a lover and a revenger, but as a human being, a man among men. This conception of the hero is closely linked with two other features of the play which, together with it, give considerable substance to Coleridge's thought about Shakespeare and the '*I* representative'. One is the explicit concern of the play with speech, style, speaking out, communication through words. The other is the frequency of attempts to describe what a complete or authentic man would be like. These features are principally related to Hamlet, but they also belong to the construction of the play as a whole.

The play begins, of course, with a challenge, a question about identity: 'Who's there?'[9] The setting is supposed to be dark and cold, as we soon learn, and suggests the wearing of large cloaks, like military greatcoats. There is an additional touch of nervous excitement in this military formula, since it comes from the wrong soldier, as we gather from the reply of the other sentinel, Francisco: 'Nay, answer me. Stand and unfold yourself.' This tiny exchange sets going far-reaching currents. *Unfold* – reveal yourself, come out of concealment, declare your allegiance and who you are. In this play Shakespeare is going to use the stage with an approximation to unity of place, since all the actors will be seen at Elsinore or nearby. Again and again we shall witness newcomers to the stage, or hear of strangers approaching Elsinore – Horatio, the Ghost, young Fortinbras, Rosencrantz and Guildenstern, the Players, and then Laertes and finally Hamlet himself returning – whose reasons for coming there will be questioned somewhat as Francisco questions his comrade. This is one dramatic basis for the emphasis the dialogue gives to the theme of speaking out. The verb *to speak* is heard fifteen times in the six acting minutes or so of the opening scene, together with related terms such as *answer, inform* and *impart*, implying the sharing of a secret.

Nearly all the characters have something to hide or to explain, from the King to the Gravedigger; most conspicuously, Hamlet. But his first speeches, beginning with an aside, amount to a refusal to answer questions, to discard his 'inky cloak' and 'unfold' himself, and even to a hint that no explanation is possible. His first two lines – 'A little more than kin, and less than kind', and 'Not so, my lord, I am too much in the sun' – contain a riddle about family relationships which touches his own identity (of what 'kind' is he, if not Claudius's kinsman?) and a hint of clinging to the shade. His first reply of any length, pouncing on his mother's word, 'seems', not only contrasts his inward state with 'customary'

---

9 Quotations and references from *The Riverside Shakespeare* (Boston, 1974).

demonstrations of grief, which he compares to play-acting, but implies that he cannot even clarify it to himself. 'I have that within which passes show' may mean that I have more grief than I wish to show here, or more grief than custom and external shows can express, but again it may mean that what I have within is beyond the reach of expression at all, like the peace of God which passeth understanding. And that inwardly Hamlet is wrestling with the inexplicable comes out very soon, in his first soliloquy, where it appears that he not only cannot bear his mother's remarriage but cannot understand how her incest, as he thinks of it, can have been humanly possible, and cannot bear, or understand, the insistence of his own reaction: 'Must I remember? . . . Let me not think on't!' Unlike Shakespeare's other heroes, Hamlet is shown at once at the deepest point of despair, and a part of his despair is precisely the difficulty of stating clearly to himself what he is feeling. Neither Richard II nor Brutus has had to encounter a similar conceptual difficulty in their moments of introspection:

> I have been studying how I may compare
> This prison where I live unto the world
>
> (5.5.1–2)

or,

> Since Cassius first did whet me against Caesar,
> I have not slept.                    (2.1.61)

These are apparently statements of fact, in the indicative mood; the speaker himself knows what has been happening. But Hamlet at first can only express wishes, and negative wishes, in the mood of the subjunctive:

> O that this too too sallied flesh would melt, . . .
> Or that the Everlasting had not fix'd
> His canon 'gainst self-slaughter! (1.2.129,131–2)

and the rest of his soliloquy, apart from one assertion that the world is 'an unweeded garden', moves forward through exclamations, elliptic sentences circling around his mother, broken up and overlaid with interjections, and

then a noun clause with an infinitive verb ('to post / With such dexterity to incestious sheets'), before settling for a moment into a plain statement ('It is not, nor it cannot come to good'), but only to lurch into another subjunctive: 'But break my heart, for I must hold my tongue.' Holding his tongue, then, is for the moment the only determination Hamlet can arrive at, and he arrives at it against his will.

The only account Hamlet gives of himself in this soliloquy is an incidental and dismissive contrast with the typical hero ('. . . no more like my father / Than I to Hercules'). But he compares his father to a god; and even in his inclusive expression of disgust with life ('How weary, stale, flat, and unprofitable / Seem to me all the uses of the world!') – which incidentally contradicts his recent statement to his mother that he '[knows] not "seems"', – there is still a corner of his mind from which the world could appear beautiful and his own reaction not conclusive but pitifully and puzzlingly abnormal. Similarly, later, in his outburst of guarded candour to Rosencrantz and Guildenstern – 'What a piece of work is a man' – he keeps his cool description of his own unexplainable listlessness separate and distinct from his praise of man in the abstract. Man's intellect and 'faculties' – the amazing co-ordination of the human 'machine' (to apply the term so strangely inserted by Hamlet in his letter to Ophelia)[10] – can still impress Hamlet vividly in spite of and by contrast with his private experience. And during the middle scenes he re-

---

10 'Thine evermore, most dear lady, whilst this machine is to him' (2.2.123). Had Giordano Bruno's *De gli eroici furori* (1585) found its way into Hamlet's reading? Arguing that the soul should not repudiate the things of the senses, Bruno writes: 'Soccorrassi al corpo con la materia e soggetto corporeo, e l'intelletto con gli suoi oggetti s'appaghe; a fin che conste questa composizione, non si dissolva questa macchina, dove per mezzo del spirito l'anima è unita al corpo' ['Let the body help itself with matter and bodily subject, and the intellect be content with its own objects; in order that this combination should hold firm, that this machine wherein soul is united to body by means of the spirit

turns repeatedly to reflections on such human completeness, or symbolic tokens of it: in his wonder at the First Player's professional self-command and in his advice to the actors; in his praise for Horatio, whose 'blood and judge-ment are so well co-meddled' that he is not 'passion's slave'; in his effusion over his father's picture during the closet scene; and in his soliloquy on how 'rightly to be great' in action when he contemplates Fortinbras and his army.[11] These reflections pull against his 'wild' aberrations in his 'antic disposition', his fits of rant and fury when he could 'drink hot blood', and his acid reduction of mankind to 'this quintessence of dust'. They are sketches describing a state of health and human integrity, rather than reachings-out towards any remote ideal.

Other speakers supplement these sketches; for instance, Ophelia, in her lament for the 'noble mind' and harmonious accomplishments of Hamlet in the past. Even Claudius adds a significant touch, during the scene where he is hooking Laertes to his side, when, in a crafty digression within a digression, he alludes admiringly to the 'witchcraft' on horse-back of the Norman visitor to Elsinore, who 'grew unto his seat, / . . . As had he been incorps'd and demi-natur'd / With the brave beast' (4.7.81–90); a fleeting but classically evocative glimpse of the unity between mind and instinct in a man. Altogether, these various speeches constitute a line of poetic thought that Shakespeare was to develop further, especially in *Macbeth*, culminating in Macbeth's soliloquy on 'To-morrow, and to-morrow'. In that soliloquy Macbeth, who has been driven deep into unreality, seems to be asking himself what reality in human experience would be like: something tangible and immediate, for example, not elusive; free and composed, unlike a bad actor; clear, authentic, lasting and coherent. Although it works through negatives, that soliloquy is a concentrated example of what, I take it, Leavis means by the experience in tragedy that matters

because it is what it is and not because it is 'mine', and of what Coleridge means by speaking of the '*I* representative' in Shakespeare. There is nothing in the tragedy of *Hamlet* to equal it. But in the character of Hamlet Shakespeare has for the first time portrayed a mind that raises such questions about human authenticity, and raises them out of an inward need.

Hamlet's reflections on the nature of man do not lend themselves to sequential dramatic treatment, or at any rate Shakespeare does not treat them that way. But he makes an important guiding-thread out of Hamlet's preoccupation with the act of speech, which affects both his attitude towards his role and his conception of his innermost self. 'But break my heart, for I must hold my tongue' was the upshot of his initial monologue. And the trajectory of his part brings him back repeatedly

---

should not be dispersed'] (*Opere italiane*, ed. Giovanni Gentile, Bari 1927, vol. 2, p. 386). In classical usage a *machine* was always a material construction (I owe this point to a letter from Professor W. S. Allen), and *OED* cites this passage from *Hamlet* as the first English example of a figurative use, 'Applied to the human and animal frame as a combination of several parts'; (the only other possibly, though not certainly, Shakespearian instance of the noun comes in 'this machine, or this frame', meaning the device of the morris dance, in *Two Noble Kinsmen*, 3.5.113). In his next paragraph, Bruno continues (the Soul is addressing its own thoughts): 'Ondi vi è nato questo malencolico e perverso umore di rompere le certe e naturali legge de la vera vita che sta nelle vostri mani, per una incerta e che non è se non in ombra oltre gli limiti del fantastico pensiero?' ['Whence springs this melancholy and perverse humour of breaking the certain and natural laws of the true life dwelling within your grasp, for the sake of one uncertain and non-existent unless in the shadow beyond the limits of fantastic thought?'] This passage also invites comparison with Hamlet. In his letter to Ophelia, Hamlet, like Bruno, is commenting on a poem he has just written, in extravagantly worded prose; and finally, the poem itself contains a faintly Brunoesque speculation about the stars. All in all, it seems very possible that Bruno suggested Hamlet's unique use of the word *machine*.

11 2.2.303–7, 551–7; 3.2.5–7, 16–19, 63–74; 3.4.55–62; 4.4.33–9, 53–6.

to a similar place of deadlock between heart and tongue. Almost at once, he is rushed through a cycle of opposites. 'I'll speak to it though hell itself should gape', he exclaims when he hears of the coming of the Ghost, but only to enjoin 'silence' upon his informants – 'Give it an understanding but no tongue' (1.2.244–9). And again, 'I will speak to thee', when he meets the Ghost (1.4.44), followed swiftly by a renewed injunction to his friends to be silent, with an elaborate mimicry of the 'doubtful phrase' or 'ambiguous giving out' they might be tempted to lend themselves to but for his express prohibition (1.5.140–87). Act 1 is virtually rounded off with 'And still your fingers on your lips, I pray' – transposing the tension from Hamlet's soliloquy.

After these expository scenes Shakespeare carries Hamlet's concern with speech through what may be described as three more waves or cycles. The first begins in his reported visit to Ophelia, when he appeared to her 'As if he had been loosed out of hell / To speak of horrors' (2.1.80–1), but did not utter a word. It rises through the relaxed moments of his exchange with Rosencrantz and Guildenstern – 'to speak to you like an honest man', he says at one point (2.2.268) – and it advances to a peak in his praise for the 'speech' he asks the First Player to repeat and then his appreciation of the Player's delivery (2.2.434–557). But here Hamlet reaches a limit. When he had boasted 'I have that within which passes show', contrasting his own feelings with the play-acting of public grief, he had been caught unawares in a paradox, which only now rises to the surface of his mind. That is the paradox that a man who feels what he does not 'show' resembles an actor, no less than the man who shows what he does not feel; but that a professed actor can exhibit a passion in its integrity although or even because he does not share it. A gap yawns for Hamlet between sincerity and communication. So he finds the Player's unmotivated expressiveness 'monstrous' by reference to his own condition, and falls steeply back towards the deadlock of his first soliloquy, castigating himself for 'say[ing] nothing' in his 'cause' and yet for 'unpack[ing his] heart with words', 'like a whore' (2.2.550–87). He hopes to break out of his deadlock by means of the acted play, which may provoke Claudius to 'proclaim' his guilt,

> For murther, though it have no tongue, will speak
> With most miraculous organ.

This sounds like a desperate remedy for Hamlet's inhibition, but it points a way forward, if only 'by indirections'.

He is still close to deadlock in his next sequence, the 'To be' soliloquy and the nunnery scene. Then what I may call the second wave (after the exposition) begins at a high point, in his instructions to the Players:

> Speak the speech, I pray you, as I pronounc'd it to you, trippingly on the tongue, . . . for in the very torrent, tempest, and, as I may say, whirlwind of your passion, you must acquire and beget a temperance that may give it smoothness . . . [And] suit the action to the word, the word to the action, with this special observance, that you o'erstep not the modesty of nature . . .                    (3.2.1–19)

This advice may very well convey the professional views of the actor–poet, William Shakespeare, but it is also dramatically appropriate to Hamlet's mind and present purpose. His desire for speaking out, making the truth known, unburdening his heart and achieving revenge, can only be fulfilled adequately with a concern for style, for full and apt expression and hence resolution of feeling, neither too little nor too much;[12] and this matters acutely for his intentions in staging *The Murder of Gonzago*. This statement about lucid, significant speech shows Hamlet at the height of his collected thought, but it is a lucidity at a distance from himself, projected in a

---

12 Cf. Maurice Charney, *Style in* Hamlet (Princeton, 1969); R. A. Foakes, 'Character and Speech in *Hamlet*', in *Hamlet*, ed. Brown and Harris; J. M. Newton, '*Hamlet* and Shakespeare's Disposition for Comedy', *The Cambridge Quarterly*, 9 (1979), 39–55.

work of art. As soon as the performance begins he breaks his own rules, and the excitement of triumph carries him far beyond the pitch of 'temperance'. 'I will speak daggers to her, but use none', he assures himself when preparing to meet his mother; 'My tongue and soul in this be hypocrites' (3.2.396–7). He is back, therefore, to his initial self-contradiction; so that after the heated accusations in the closet scene he is obliged to urge his mother to put out of her mind the thought 'That not your trespass but my madness speaks' (3.4.146). Satisfactory utterance, 'a temperance that may give it smoothness', is still beyond his reach.

His soliloquy on his way to England ('How all occasions do inform against me', 4.4.32–66) shifts to doing rather than saying, and to the public reverberation of events; it is 'occasions' now that 'inform'. But this is Hamlet's last soliloquy and self-interrogation. In the closing cycle of the tragedy he is in an altered frame of mind after his actions at sea, and this shows itself in a change in his attitude towards speech. He is more free. 'I have words to speak in thine ear will make thee dumb', he writes to Horatio (4.6.24–5), in pointed contrast to his injunction after meeting the Ghost. He is a sharp critic, varying in mood but objective, about the language spoken by the Gravedigger, Laertes and then Osric.[13] Before the fencing match, he can 'proclaim' his wrongs done to Laertes (5.2.232), in his first open statement at the Danish court, directed, ironically, against himself. And then, as he is dying, his thoughts are with public 'report' of his 'cause'. 'O, I could tell you', he begins, and only breaks off to entrust the duty 'to tell my story' to Horatio.

But by now he has only enough energy left to give his 'dying voice' for the Danish throne on behalf of the newly-arrived Fortinbras, and beyond that, 'the rest is silence'. He has come back full circle to his first soliloquy, but with something like acceptance instead of frustration. At the same time, he has changed places with Horatio completely as regards silence and speaking. It will fall to Horatio to become his deputy, apologist and storyteller and 'speak' in his stead 'to th' yet unknowing world / How these things came about'.

There are strong temptations in Hamlet's plight and temperament for a student of the play to identify himself with the hero as Coleridge did, and I have been suggesting that the methods of character presentation Shakespeare has adopted contain further temptations of the same sort. But there are contrary impulses throughout the play, towards a more detached view, coming to rest on something like Coleridge's representative 'I', and these continue to the very end. For instance, there is a fresh trace of the paradox about acting in Shakespeare's giving the office of Hamlet's ultimate spokesman to the devoted but unimpassioned Horatio. And there is a touch of subdued irony, but of something more constructive as well, in giving to the impulsive Fortinbras the delivery of Hamlet's epitaph and the utterance of the last line of all in the play, 'Go bid the soldiers shoot'. That is an order to give a command. This introspective tragedy ends, as it had begun, with a gesture of military ritual.

---

13  5.1.117, 137–41, 254–7, 283–4; 5.2.112–94.

# THE RHETORIC OF CHARACTER CONSTRUCTION: 'OTHELLO'

## GIORGIO MELCHIORI

'Zounds, a dog, a rat, a mouse, a cat, to scratch a man to death', says Mercutio mortally wounded before being led off stage; and Hamlet, at the climactic point of the graveyard scene, faces Laertes in Ophelia's grave with 'Swounds, show me what thou't do'. Modern producers are uncertain whether to keep the old-fashioned strong oaths (Christ's wounds), or to accept the weak replacements suggested by the Folio versions, 'What' and 'Come' respectively, though there is no need today to take those precautions that the King's Men took in their time. If the 1606 Act imposing a ten-pound fine on the actors each time a swear word or even mildly blasphemous expression was used on the stage were still in operation now, the contemporary London stage would be one of the major contributors to the British economy, and comfortable prospects would open up for professional informers, who were rewarded with half of the fines collected. I am not advocating a re-enactment of that law; on the contrary, I deplore that it was enforced, because it has deprived us of what I consider an important element in assessing one of Shakespeare's most relevant rhetorical devices: the gradation in the use of oaths and interjections. Apart from Fluellen's ''Sblood' in *Henry V*, 4.8.9 (but that's Welsh, anyway), only the bastard Faulconbridge's 'Zounds' in *King John*, 2.1.466, escaped Heminges and Condell's overcareful expurgation of the texts – overcareful because the act applied only to performances and not to the printed page: but being actors themselves, it is

likely that they had suffered personally from it. We shall never know whether any character in *Macbeth* or in other plays surviving only in the Folio ever pronounced 'Zounds' or ''Sblood'. Fortunately the publishers of the Quartos even after 1606 did not scruple to reproduce the original strong oaths – at times, especially in reported play-scripts, one may suspect they actually added some. And it is from the evidence of the surviving Quartos that it can be assumed that Shakespeare had a very clear sense of the propriety and use of oaths. The mild ones, such as 'marry', 'faith', or those involving the name of God, he generally treated as discursive interjections, while strong oaths he used very sparingly and always to a precise purpose: as basic supports of an over-all linguistic structure, what I would call the rhetoric of character construction.

I will start – at the cost of some dangerous generalization – from a definition of the use of the word 'rhetoric' in this paper. If it is true that the purpose of language is communication – and therefore we must extend the conception of language from word communication to gestures and any number of other signs and signals through which we communicate – rhetoric is the *art* of creating consensus through linguistic communication, and not simply (as is generally assumed) a classification of the forms of merely verbal expression into figures, tropes and schemata; I am rather taking it back to the Renaissance idea that considered Rhetoric as the first of the seven liberal arts. In this sense it is quite proper to speak of a rhetoric of fiction as the art of writing convincing stories by the appropriate arrangement of word structures. If rhetoric is the art of creating consensus, that is to say of carrying conviction, in fiction, drama needs it even more. The effectiveness of communication between the stage and audience relies in the first place on the creation of audience consensus, a consensus that must extend from the overall pattern of the play to each single actor in it – even the villain must secure the audience's consensus to and belief in his villainy, otherwise the very foundation of drama, which is conflict, does not hold.

Hence the necessity of a rhetoric of drama, and more specifically a rhetoric of character construction. In this paper I shall try to test only one instance of Shakespeare's use of this rhetoric, but my assumption is that each play has its own rhetorical structure and is keyed as a whole to a dominant figure or mode. Obviously, in Shakespeare's tragedies, the prevailing figures are those of contrast or conflict: *Lear* is constructed on a gigantic metaphor, the predominant figure in *Macbeth* is antithesis, that in *Hamlet* is oxymoron, *Romeo* rehearses the rhetorical patterns characteristic of love poetry. The Roman plays on the other hand privilege the more specifically oratorical figures: the traditional *dispositio* in *Julius Caesar*, hyperbole in *Antony and Cleopatra*, invective in *Coriolanus*. These are very general statements which I would need volumes to substantiate (and recent criticism has been doing excellent work in that direction[1]); I have deliberately left out from this list *Othello* because I am going to use it as my test case.

I must insist on one distinction between the rhetoric of drama and, say, that of fiction: while in considering a work of literature the rhetorical features are limited to its word structures, in the case of a play they extend to the totality of its language, that is to say to the gestures implicit in its word textures. In other words, what the old rhetorical treatises called 'action' (an essential part of oratory and elo-

quence in general) has greater importance.[2] Under the heading of 'action' we can include the implicit stage directions in the speeches and all those expressions, exclamations, demonstrative pronouns and adverbs and other deictic parts, which are not really part of a rational argument but verbal gestures, or, as I prefer to call them, action pointers. This leads back to my beginning. Such expressions as 'Zounds' or ''Sblood' have no rational meaning in themselves except as manifestations of feelings, they are visual more than aural, they are in fact the strongest possible action pointers. A study of their use by Shakespeare is instructive. It is in itself significant that they never appear in his comedies, even those that have survived in Quarto versions, and this is in contrast with the practice of most of his contemporaries, who use them freely to provoke easy laughs. Shakespeare reserved their use for moments of ex-

---

1 I am thinking of such seminal works as Sister Miriam Joseph, *Shakespeare's Use of the Arts of Language* (New York, 1947), K. Muir, 'Shakespeare and Rhetoric', *Shakespeare Jahrbuch*, 90 (1952), M. M. Mahood, *Shakespeare's Wordplay* (1957), H. Hulme, *Explorations in Shakespeare's Language* (1962), and more recently T. Hawkes, *Shakespeare's Talking Animals* (1973), M. Doran, *Shakespeare's Dramatic Language* (Madison, 1976), and R. Berry, *The Shakespearean Metaphor* (1978). Among studies devoted to single plays I wish to mention as of particular methodological relevance: J. Fuzier, 'Rhetoric versus Rhetoric: A study of Shakespeare's *Julius Caesar*, III.i', *Cahiers Elisabéthains*, 5 (1974), M. Pagnini, *Shakespeare e il paradigma della specularità* (Pisa, 1976), P. Gullì Pugliatti, *I segni latenti – Scrittura come virtualità scenica in 'King Lear'* (Messina – Florence, 1976), and several essays by A. Serpieri: 'La retorica della politica in Shakespeare', *Il piccolo Hans*, 13 (1977), 'Il crollo della gerarchia medievale in *King Lear*', *Il piccolo Hans*, 19 (1978), and the introduction to his Italian translation of *Hamlet* (Milan, 1980).

2 In modern theatrical parlance, the equivalent of 'action' is 'stage business', but that 'action' was used exactly in this sense in Elizabethan times is testified, for instance, by Munday's marginal note 'action' on fo.4ᵛ of the manuscript *Booke of Sir Thomas Moore*, a direction for the actor to introduce at this point the appropriate 'business'; cf. *The Book of Sir Thomas More*, ed. W. W. Greg (Oxford, 1911), p. 9.

treme indignation or exasperation in a character like Hamlet, who uses both ''Sblood' and
'Zounds' twice, or to characterize the impulsive
temperament of the Bastard in *King John* and
Hotspur in *1 Henry IV*. But there are other
occurrences: the fullest use of these words is
made by Falstaff in the same play, ''Sblood'
seven times and 'Zounds' five – they are
obviously Falstaff's conception of a soldier's language, and he has recourse to them especially
when he feels that his martial image is called
in question, and Bardolph, Gadshill and Poins
(once each) follow suit. Other instances occur
in earlier plays, where 'Zounds' is found in the
mouth of even more questionable characters:
Aaron the Moor in *Titus* and, a more interesting case, *Richard III*, where 'Zounds' is used
first by the two murderers of Clarence, then by
Buckingham, when he pretends to persuade a
most willing Gloucester to accept the crown of
England: 'Zounds, I'll entreat no more', he
says in false exasperation, to which Gloucester's suave reply is 'O, do not swear, my lord of
Buckingham'. But in the last act, in the early
dawn at Bosworth Field, it is Richard himself
who exclaims: 'Zounds, who is there?' taking the faithful Ratcliff for another visiting
ghost. Altogether 'Zounds' twenty times and
''Sblood' eleven in all the plays written before
and including *Hamlet*.

These oaths reveal two basic functions. First,
they are part of a conventional linguistic code,
that of the soldier or the man of action, for
whom swearing is a natural form of expression
– such is the case of the Bastard and Hotspur;
Falstaff, the *miles gloriosus*, feels therefore
bound to use them even more generously in
order to show his 'valour'. As such they belong
to the rhetoric of character construction, giving
to the characters concerned a professional con-
notation; the murderers in *Richard III* use the
oaths to encourage each other in their horrid
action. The oaths' second basic function – and
this is the case with Mercutio and Hamlet – is
more specifically that of action pointers, an
attempt at going beyond words to express

an excess of indignation: they belong to the
overall rhetorical patterns of their respective plays, marking the points of maximum
tension.

But, apart from *1 Henry IV*, the play with
the largest number of strong oaths is *Othello*,
with ten occurrences, and these deserve particular attention. It is significant that the very
first word pronounced by Iago in the play is
''Sblood': a soldier's oath, expressing indignation at Roderigo's doubts about his behaviour.
Such is the first impression, reinforced by his
repeated 'Zounds' shortly afterwards (ll. 87 and
109), when Brabantio refuses to believe that his
daughter has run away. Here the interjections
contribute to the creation of character, and full
advantage is taken of the ambiguous function
of these strong oaths. Professor Sprague, as far
back as 1935,[3] pointed out the slowness in the
discovery of the real roles of the characters in
*Othello*, a discovery which is complete only by
the end of act 1. At first Iago may well appear
as, in Sprague's words, the good frustrated
soldier, embittered by the promotion of a mere
'arithmetician', one Michael Cassio, a minor
courtier with no experience of the battlefield.
These oaths are a part of Shakespeare's
strategy in his character construction, together
with the indirect presentation of Othello
through Iago's words, throughout the first
scene, as simply a reincarnation of the devil.
We are not informed of his name till 1.3.48,
and significantly the word 'Othello' is pronounced for the first time by the highest authority in the play, the Duke himself, while in
the first scene we must accept Iago's sarcastic
title of His Moorship. It is a strategy of reversal
of roles to which I will return later.

When Iago's role of blunt soldier turns,
especially through the final monologue of the
first act, into that of vulgar machiavel or diabo-
lical casuist, he no longer needs to use soldier's
oaths, which are replaced by a debased barrack

---

3 A. C. Sprague, *Shakespeare and the Audience* (Cambridge, Mass., 1935).

language bristling with bawdy innuendos grafted on to the logician's sophistry. He says 'Zounds' only once more in the play, in the very last scene, when Emilia reveals his real role in the killing of Desdemona: 'Zounds, hold your peace' (5.2.221). In this case it is not the soldier's oath but the inarticulate cry of the trapped animal, the villain unmasked, like Richard's 'Zounds, who is there?' in his tent at Bosworth Field, or Aaron's 'Zounds, ye whore! Is black so base a hue?' when his intrigue with Tamora – foreboding the fall of another machiavel – is discovered.

In *Othello*, the soldier's oath 'Zounds' is heard twice in the quarrel scene (act 2, scene 3), shouted by Cassio (but only when he is completely drunk) pursuing Roderigo, and grunted by the wounded Montano, a soldier unwillingly involved in a drunken brawl. And it is this drunken brawl, Iago's first move in his machiavellian plan, that for the first time discomposes Othello's equanimity, introducing a harsh note in the language of a noble commander:

> Now, by heaven,
> My blood begins my safer guides to rule . . .
> Zounds if I stir
> Or do but lift this arm, the best of you
> Shall sink in my rebuke.   (2.3.196–7, 199–201)

Up to this point, in spite of his protestation to the Venetian Senate,

> Rude am I in my speech,
> And little blest with the soft phrase of peace,

Othello had been a master in the rhetoric of speech-making: his speeches were perfectly constructed, not the artificial exhibitions of the courtier wanting to show off his accomplishments, but the natural expressions of a believer in the art of rhetoric as the only means of civilized communication. 'Zounds if I stir' is the first crack in Othello's noble rhetorical armour. A crack that there is hardly time to mend, since he next appears in the temptation scene (act 3, scene 3), when Iago instils the poison in his mind. It all begins with another

pointer, 'Ha!', this time Iago's:

> *Iago.* Ha! I like not that.
> *Othello.* What dost thou say?
> *Iago.* Nothing, my lord; or if –   (3.3.35–7)

In her 'Iago's "if"': an Essay on the Syntax of *Othello*,[4] Madeleine Doran has identified in Iago's 'if' the tragedy's central point, the basic syntactical device on which it all turns. I am indebted to her as well as to the more recent detailed study by Alessandro Serpieri, *Otello, l'Eros negato*,[5] in which, moving from syntax to rhetorical figures, he identifies in the litotes (understatement) and its cognate figures of negation, reticence, and suspension the main features of Iago's language in particular, and, together with hyperbole, of the play as a whole.

But in a play, besides all these, one should also take into account action pointers. Iago's 'Ha' is as important as his 'if' in disgregating Othello's ample rhetorical schemata; and in fact, not long after in the same scene (l. 158), Othello interrupts Iago's tortuous insinuations with: 'Zounds, what dost thou mean?'; and again later with the inarticulate interjection 'Ha!' (l. 169). Othello's subjection to Iago even on the linguistic level is shown by his exit line in 3.4.99, after Desdemona has been unable to produce the incriminating handkerchief; this exit speech is only one word, 'Zounds' (though many editors prefer the rather pointless Folio reading 'Away'). Othello's linguistic and rhetorical disintegration is complete by 4.1.35–7, his fainting fit:

Lie with her – lie on her? We say lie on her when they belie her. Lie with her. Zounds, that's fulsome. Handkerchief – confessions – handkerchief!

All grammatical or syntactical connections are severed. The linguistic disintegration had begun two lines before with the single word

---

4  1970; included, under the title 'Iago's If – Conditional and Subjunctive in *Othello*' in her *Shakespeare's Dramatic Language*, pp. 63–91.

5  A. Serpieri, *'Otello': L'Eros negato – Psicoanalisi di una proiezione distruttiva* (Milan, 1978).

'Lie –' said by Iago, which broke the already uncertain sequence of iambic pentameters by beginning a new line that was never completed, in so much as that word caused a kind of semantic dissociation in Othello, not knowing by what preposition he should complete the meaning of Iago's verb: 'Lie *with* her?' Faced with Iago's sarcastic reply 'With her, on her; what you will', Othello loses all powers of semantic discrimination. It is not only disintegration but linguistic degradation: the pun on *lie* is the most obvious and hackneyed in the English language, and so it was already in Shakespeare's time and on the Elizabethan stage in particular. It is a clown's pun, and in fact the Clown, in the second of his two brief appearances in the tragedy, had elaborated on exactly that very weak pun in reply to Desdemona's question: 'Do you know . . . where the Lieutenant Cassio lies?' It is only logical that this very rapid process of disintegration – first of the verse petering out into prose, then of the semantic functions, and lastly of the syntactical and grammatical structures (a reduction of the words to mere action pointers) – should be followed by the Quarto's neat stage direction: *He falls down*, elaborated by the Folio into *Falls in a Traunce*, an 'action' that has been the torture and delight of generations of actors, with their different renderings of all possible forms of epileptic fit. I remember seeing a great Italian actor recently deceased rolling and crawling right across the stage in inarticulate passion, and, from Henry James's account, the famous Ernesto Rossi's rendering of this cannot have been very different.[6] My feeling is that the rest of Othello's speech, appearing only in Folio and Q2 before the modified 'trance' stage direction, and which is no more than an extended resumption of the last phases of the same verbal disintegration process, is merely in the nature of an addition for the benefit of an actor who wanted to exploit to the full the histrionic potentialities of the speech, wanted in fact to provide an encore to an entranced audience. The short first Quarto version is self-sufficient, a masterly example of the use of action pointers as an integral part of the rhetoric of character construction.

From this point on, for most of the last two acts, Othello's world of rhetorical order is disrupted. The art of Rhetoric, which he had mastered, represented for him his greatest achievement: it represented the civilization of the Venetian Republic, which he had the honour of serving and of which Desdemona had become the living emblem, his personal conquest. Desdemona's supposed betrayal was the betrayal of Venice, and this is reflected in Othello's inability to construct ample and articulated sentences: his speeches are now questions, exclamations, expostulations, invective.[7] Even the monologue at the beginning of the last scene ('It is the cause, it is the cause, my soul') is a sequence of short sentences held together by disjunctives ('yet', 'if', 'but') and punctuated by action pointers ('one more, one more'). And again and again his speeches are reduced to simple 'Ha's' or even 'O! O! O!', not meaningful words but rather theatrical notations suggesting adlibbing for the actor.[8]

But after Othello learns the truth, his faith restored in the innocence of Desdemona, what is reflected in his words is not so much the

---

6  James's account of Rossi's performance in 1873 was included in a revised form in his *Italian Hours* (1909), and can be found in H. James, *The Scenic Art*, ed. A. Wade (1949), which includes also glowing accounts of Salvini's rendering of the part in Boston (1883) and London (1884); cf. M. Rosenberg, *The Masks of Othello* (Berkeley, 1961).

7  His most sustained speech in this part of the play is the famous oath of revenge at 3.3.457–66, ten lines developing a single formal figure of comparison, pedantically classical in structure ('like to . . . Even so . . .') and in content (the first term of the comparison is borrowed almost literally from Holland's translation of Pliny). It is a last attempt at disguising an alien passion in a classical pattern.

8  For 'O! O! O!' see 5.2.201 and 285, but compare 'O! O! O! O!' added to Hamlet's dying speech in the Folio *Hamlet* (5.2.350), and 'O! O! O! O! O!' in Q1 and Q2 of *King Lear* (5.3.310–11), both rejected by modern editors as reporters' additions or substitutions.

feeling of his own guilt (that appears from the 'action', his final suicide) as the recovery of the old values, of his faith in Venetian civilization. Othello's last great speech has been seen as essentially a piece of play-acting, either in good or in bad faith, and hardly in good taste, so that F. R. Leavis felt able to speak of a 'brutal egotism' and a 'habit of self-approving self-dramatization' in him.[9] I would like to call attention to the rhetorical structure, the *dispositio*, of Othello's last speech, 'Soft you; a word or two before you go.' The structure is a replica on a smaller scale of that of the great double speech to the Venetian Senate in act 1, scene 3. It opens with a *captatio* not of the benevolence but of the attention of the representatives of the Venetian Republic, less ceremonial than that addressed to the Duke and Senators; there follows an *excusatio* which is in fact, as in the previous speech, a plea for fairness in judging his acts. The main body of the speech, the relation of his past behaviour, has exactly the same anaphoric disposition as the previous one: '. . . of one that lov'd not wisely, but too well . . . Of one not easily jealous . . . of one whose hand, /Like the base Indian, threw a pearl away . . . of one whose subdu'd eyes . . .' – they correspond to the 'catalogue' made to the Senate: '. . . of moving accidents . . . Of hair-breadth scapes . . . Of being taken . . .' And again: 'of antres vast and deserts idle . . . And of the Cannibals that each other eat . . .'. The *ornatus* is also of the same kind in both speeches: the evocation of the exotic element which is part of Othello's own nature – in one case the antres, deserts, rocks, the Cannibals and the Anthropophagi, in the other the base Indian (surely not the Folio's *Iudean*!), the Arabian tree, the turbaned Turk at Aleppo. While in the speech to the Senate the long peroration centred on Othello's relationship with Desdemona, here the theme of the short peroration, a mere coda to the previous relation ('and say besides . . .'), turns on his relationship to the Venetian State. We cannot miss the significance and appropriateness of the substitution: for Othello, Venice and Desdemona are one and the same thing. Both speeches close with action pointers, extended to a whole line in the first case: 'Here comes the lady; let her witness it'; limited to one word in the second: 'thus' (there is no need of the stage direction *stabs himself* to know what that means). Othello's last speech is no histrionic exhibition: it is the recovery of his real self through the return to the rhetoric that he had made his own.

To follow Shakespeare's strategy in the rhetorical construction of his characters provides safer guidance to the reading of his intentions than the Bradleyan or even the more sophisticated psychological approaches of recent, and not so recent, years. I have chosen *Othello* as a test case as being, among Shakespeare's tragedies, the one constantly cited as a model of dramatic construction, in spite, or perhaps *because*, of the coexistence in it of three separate time-scales, and also because of its stylistic unity. The praise is well-deserved; but to insist on this unity of style tends to blur the quality of the component parts of the total stylistic pattern, that is to say the 'styles' of the different characters. The predominance of Iago and Othello is such (together they speak over 56 per cent of the words in the play),[10] and they are, stylistically, so obviously complementary, that all the other characters are seen as mere contributors to the pattern established by protagonist and antagonist, with hardly any distinction in their individual contributions. This obscures the subtlety of Shakespeare's art, or rather of his extreme linguistic sensitivity, and impoverishes the meaning itself of the tragedy. Let us take for instance the light exchanges and bawdy innuendos between Iago and Desdemona waiting for the arrival of Othello at Cyprus

---

9 F. R. Leavis, 'Diabolic Intellect and the Noble Hero' (1937), in *The Common Pursuit* (1952), pp. 141–6.

10 According to Spevack's *Complete and Systematic Concordance to the Works of Shakespeare* (Hildesheim, 1968–70), Iago speaks 32.58 per cent and Othello 24.09 per cent of the total number of words in the play.

(act 2, scene 1). Distressed moralists in order to justify them have invoked the conventions of the Elizabethan stage with their unaccountable mixture of comedy and tragedy, bawdy and solemnity, high and low styles, and have underlined Desdemona's attitude, pathetically taking refuge from her anxiety in Iago's cheap jokes. It is true that a boy Desdemona enjoyed much greater freedom of speech than a demure nineteenth-century lady actress, but the problem does not even arise if one considers the language of the two interlocutors. Iago has assumed the role of the court jester with his characteristic extemporizing, and Desdemona's language is that of the *chatelaine* who bandies words with her fool. Iago's bawdy and malicious allusions are taken by her as a homage to her status: in Cyprus she is indeed the wife of the supreme authority in the island.

Throughout the play Desdemona's language, the way in which her few longer speeches are constructed, exhibits a constant simplicity and propriety of grammatical and syntactical patterns that reveal a proper education in the art of speaking. This is apparent from her very first words, where the idea of her 'divided duty' is reflected in the neatly balanced articulation of the one long sentence contrasting the duty to a father with that to a husband. Her rhetorical skill, with nothing of the over-studiousness apparent in Othello's great speeches, is at its best in the declaration of her love for the Moor, when she pleads to accompany him to Cyprus:

That I did love the Moor to live with him,
My downright violence and storm of fortunes
May trumpet to the world. My heart's subdu'd
Even to the very quality of my lord.
I saw Othello's visage in his mind . . .

(1.3.248–52)

where she models her language on the military images appropriate to the figure of Othello: the storm of fortunes is not so much an anticipation of the events on the journey to Cyprus and

in Cyprus itself, as the evocation of military feats, the storming of a besieged city.

Desdemona's is the rhetoric of the natural aristocrat and remains such throughout, uncontaminated (unlike that of Othello) by Iago's influence. Her moment of weakness comes when she pretends not to have lost her handkerchief, but even that is justified by the scepticism of a person with a different cultural background toward the magic lore attributed by Othello to the handkerchief – a scepticism that prompts a fearful evasion of his irrational request. The social status of Desdemona, governing her powers of verbal expression, is confirmed in the willow song scene (4.3), which is a resumption in a more subdued key of the Desdemona–Iago exchanges in act 2 scene 1. The waiting woman replaces the court jester, and the lady condescends to her familiar chattiness.

It is in this scene that Emilia emerges as a fully rounded character, especially in her last speech, the best example of the rhetorical pattern that Shakespeare assigned to her role. In its sequence of blank verse closed by a rhymed couplet, it looks at first sight modelled on the formal pattern of the other long speeches in the play, notably Iago's soliloquies at the end of act 1, scene 3 and act 2, scenes 1 and 3 – and in fact in her previous speeches Emilia's diction seemed to share some of Iago's characteristic tricks, such as the sudden breaking out of 'low' allusions through the veneer of polite address. But Iago's soliloquies were perfect applications of all the figures of formal logic, while Emilia's speech (a very effective piece of oratory, perhaps the first feminist manifesto) is a straight sequence of statements followed by a simple catechism and concluded by a gnomic couplet which has nothing of the formal *sententiae* in the couplets of Brabantio or the Duke, but savours of the proverb or popular saw:

Then let them use us well; else let them know
The ills we do their ills instruct us so.

(4.3.100–1)

Within this framework the words used are plain

abstract words taken in their simplest meanings: affection, frailty, sport, duty, jealousy, restraint, revenge; and what imagery there is, is concrete and physical like that so effectively employed by her on a previous occasion:

'Tis not a year or two shows us a man.
They are all but stomachs, and we all but food:
They eat us hungerly, and when they are full,
They belch us. (3.4.104–7)

It emerges that Emilia uses a completely different linguistic code from Desdemona or any other character in the play, and the distinction between the codes is essentially a social distinction.

What I wish to underline is that the impression of a unified style conveyed by the tragedy of *Othello* as a whole is achieved though the extreme precision with which each character has been endowed with a personal linguistic code and, over and above it, with different rhetorical habits in the construction of their respective speeches. The over-all pattern suggesting the stylistic unity is provided by the recurrent use of keywords and grammatical, syntactical, and rhetorical constructions which are not the personal property of any one character but occur in the speeches of most of them. The obvious example of the second sort of recurrence is the use of 'if' and of the conditional and subjunctive clauses so acutely studied by Madeleine Doran, while in the case of keywords, William Empson's analysis of 'Honest in *Othello*'[11] inaugurated a method of critical enquiry to which we are all indebted; but we should not forget such words as *abuse, beguile, approve, proof*, which appear in *Othello* more frequently than in any other play and which contribute to create the dialectic of seeming versus being, that web of deception in which not only the characters on the stage, but we, the audience, are all caught. The recurring words and rhetorical patterns are effective only in so much as they appear each time in a different context, like balls tossed from character to character in an intricate game of skill. Their effectiveness depends on their constant reappearance within different lexical and rhetorical codes. And such codes in turn are determined by the social and cultural status of the different characters. There is certainly something to be learned from the fact that Shakespeare in his character construction had this extreme awareness of the influence of social condition on the language of each in all its nuances.

I hope that what I have said about the rhetoric of the character of Othello, with its internal movement from the ample rhetorical patterns of one who has passionately studied and acquired the most noble expressions of an alien civilization, to a more and more frequent recurrence, in the second part of the play, of action pointers in his broken speeches, and the final return to his original pattern – all this should warn us against those one-sided interpretations that see in Othello either the noble general *or* the mere savage.[12] It supports rather Ernst Honigmann's contention that 'the same speeches suggest that the noble and the savage Moor are more intimately one than either Bradley or Leavis were willing to allow', with the proviso that it is Iago who reawakens the savage in him by goading him to accept an alternative linguistic code. From a comparative analysis of Othello's rhetoric in the first act and that of the representatives of the old Venetian nobility (Brabantio, the Duke and the Senators) there would emerge a clear distinction in quality: the deliberate elaboration in Othello's speeches is in no way less genuine and sincere than the naturalness with which the Venetian lords manipulate the devices of classical rhetoric.

---

11  *The Structure Of Complex Words* (1951).
12  See R. A. Foakes, 'Iago, Othello and the Critics', in *De Shakespeare à T. S. Eliot: Mélanges offerts à Henri Fluchère* (Paris, 1976), pp. 61–72; and E. A. J. Honigmann, 'Recent Trends in the Discussion of Shakespeare's Characters, with special reference to *Othello*', *Handlingen van het 29e Vlaams Filologencongres* (Belgium, 1974), pp. 173–83. Also, for Iago, S. E. Hyman, *Iago: Some Approaches to the Illusion of his Motivation* (1971).

Without going into this I must draw attention to the Shakespearian rhetoric in the construction of one more character. It is the character that for number of words in the play comes fourth after Iago, Othello, and Desdemona: Cassio. I have noticed a trend in recent criticism to revalue the character of Cassio, not simply an indispensable wheel in the plot mechanism, not just Iago's dupe, but somebody with a personality of his own. Support for this evaluation of Cassio has been found in the text and above all in the conclusion of the play: even before Othello's death, it is proclaimed that 'Cassio rules in Cyprus', and to him, the new lord governor, is deferred, in the last lines of the play, the task of doing justice and finding a suitable punishment for Iago, 'the time, the place, the torture'. Starting from these unquestionable facts, there has been a growing tendency to consider Cassio either as a projection of the positive side of Othello's character, or as the personification of the ideal good ruler; indeed, as a recent study of this role proclaims in its title, a 'Mirror of Virtue'.[13] Let us test this claim by trying to identify his linguistic code. On his first appearance on stage, his language is that of the zealous messenger:

> The Duke does greet you, General;
> And he requires your haste-post-haste
>     appearance
> Even on the instant,

perhaps a little over-fussy:

> It is a business of some heat: the galleys
> Have sent a dozen sequent messengers
> This very night at one another's heels . . .
>         You have been hotly call'd for;
> When, being not at your lodging to be found,
> The Senate hath sent about three several quests
> To search you out.     (1.2.36–8, 40–2, 44–7)

Cassio comes really into his own upon his landing at Cyprus; when Montano asks him 'is your general wiv'd?' Cassio can give free rein to his linguistic propensities:

> Most fortunately: he hath achiev'd a maid
> That paragons description and wild fame;

> One that excels the quirks of blazoning pens,
> And in th'essential vesture of creation
> Does tire the ingener.     (2.1.61–5)

And again

> Tempests themselves, high seas, and howling
>     winds,
> The gutter'd rocks, and congregated sands,
> Traitors ensteep'd to enclog the guiltless keel,
> As having sense of beauty, do omit
> Their mortal natures, letting go safely by
> The divine Desdemona.     (2.1.68–73)

And after having wished that Othello may soon 'Make love's quick pants in Desdemona's arms', he greets her landing with:

> O, behold,
> The riches of the ship is come ashore!
>     (2.1.82–3)

Talk of figures and tropes, the 'quirks of blazoning pens'! Cassio has certainly mustered as many as he could in his few lines. Is this the language of the man of *virtù*, the courtier, soldier, statesman, the Sir Philip Sidney of Othello's Venice? It is enough to compare this with the language of the truly noble Venetians to realize what an abyss divides them. Cassio is fond of hyperbole, but if we put his hyperboles side by side with those of Othello, we realize that, while the latter's are the high points of ample rhetorical constructions passionately believed in, those of Cassio are at best the enthusiastic rehearsal of the conventional devices of the aspiring court poet. Such language 'places' Cassio as not even the accomplished courtier, but rather the apprentice. A man who, in order to express his trust that Othello will ride the storm safely, must go about it this way:

> His bark is stoutly timber'd, and his pilot
> Of very expert and approv'd allowance;
> Therefore my hopes, not surfeited to death,
> Stand in bold cure     (2.1.48–51)

---

13 E. Z. Cohen, 'Mirror of Virtue: the Role of Cassio in *Othello*', *English Studies*, 57 (1976), 115–27.

sounds to me not very unlike young Osric in *Hamlet*. That Cassio is still a very immature aspiring courtier is shown also by his incredibly gauche remark to Iago after kissing Emilia on her arrival in Cyprus:

> Let it not gall your patience, good Iago,
> That I extend my manners; 'tis my breeding
> That gives me this bold show of courtesy.
>
> (2.1.97–9)

This punctilious but frequently misplaced show of courtesy (if by courtesy we mean the external ornament of speech) is the hall-mark of Cassio's language throughout the play; it is a veneer that wears off when he gets drunk: we have already noted his 'Zounds' during his brawl with Roderigo and Montano, and when the shock of his dismissal sobers him up, his one preoccupation is 'reputation'. Reputation is a word seldom used by Shakespeare, and always with a very specific meaning: the opinion that others have of us. When Cassio exclaims:

> Reputation, reputation, reputation! O, I have lost my reputation! I have lost the immortal part of myself, and what remains is bestial. My reputation, Iago, my reputation!                    (2.3.254–7)

it is the courtier who speaks, the courtier who is concerned not so much with the true feeling of honour, but identifies his immortal part, his soul, with the figure he will cut in society. The serenading of Othello, the elaborate compliments to Desdemona, the impatient condescension to Bianca, casually addressed as 'sweet love' or simply 'sweet', or even 'woman', confirm him in this role. Only in the very last scene, carried in wounded in a chair, his few statements are unadorned, tinged with astonished pity.[14] But at no point is he a paragon of virtue: his rhetorical structures are unequivocally those of conventional court poetry, the same used by Romeo when in love with Rosaline, but Romeo (or rather Shakespeare for him) succeeded in transforming them into stronger lyrical modes when his love for Juliet

acquired a tragic stature.

There remains the other argument: Cassio inherits the rule of Cyprus. Why choose such a weak character for this function? In *Hamlet* Fortinbras had hardly been present on the stage before the last scene and we may be prepared to believe all the good that had been said of him, and accept him as a restorer of the state. But, alas, we have seen and heard Cassio throughout the play. Shakespeare takes the precaution of giving the final speech not to him but to Lodovico. Lodovico is the voice of the Venetian republic, the representative of real power – a far-away power, though, from this outpost of civilization, and arbitrary enough, or, if we prefer, inscrutable: before Othello's fall it had chosen Cassio as his successor, and no reason given. The simple fact is that it does not matter who is going to rule in Cyprus. The formal closing speech is a stage necessity; what matters is the experience of the two hours' traffic on the stage, the representation of a conflict which has no conclusion because it is part of the human condition. *Othello*, like *Hamlet*, like the dark comedies, like *Lear*, is an open-ended play. I can sympathize with Richard Levin's impatience, in his *New Readings versus Old Plays*,[15] with the modern critics' and producers' reading into Shakespeare's plays completely unwarranted meanings, with their practice, as he calls it, of 'refuting the ending'. But I think that a consideration of Shakespeare's strategy in the rhetoric of character construction helps us to see that some of Shakespeare's endings cannot be taken literally. What is, in fact, the meaning of Lodovico's final couplet? –

---

14 See the comments on Cassio's behaviour in the last scene, when 'at most, the lesson of experience induced him to get rid of the outworn formulas of court rhetoric, and strengthened his "sympathy" . . . but did not give him a more mature political consciousness' in Maria Rosa Colombo's book *Le utopie e la storia: Saggio sull' 'Othello' di Shakespeare* (Bari, 1975), pp. 140–1.

15 Chicago, 1979.

Myself will straight aboard; and to the state
This heavy act with heavy heart relate.

(5.2.374–5)

It underlines that what matters is not the ending, but the *act*, and the relation of the act, or of the action, that is to say the 'show', the performance that we have been witnessing. The message is the action itself, and the action of a play is the conflict of characters, indeed, of actors. The task of the dramatist is that of creating characters through words and action; his art is rhetoric, the art of endowing each character with the power of securing our consensus, our recognition and acceptance of his message, transmitted through his individual linguistic code.

What holds together this plurality of individual linguistic codes (which are at the same time social codes, since all human conflict is also social conflict) is an over-all design, a secret rhetorical pattern that does not reconcile or conclude the conflict, but presents it as an aesthetic whole. Critics have remarked that the prevalent rhetorical figures in *Othello* are litotes, or understatement – mainly connected with Iago – and hyperbole – mainly related to Othello himself. I would suggest that over and above these contrasting figures there is a third that includes them both – the sort of figure that would come instinctively to the Elizabethan mind hearing the story of a Moor, perhaps partly savage but undoubtedly noble, being deceived by a perfidious Christian: the reversal of the traditionally accepted view. Even by Shakespeare the word Moor had always been used in a totally negative sense. *Titus Andronicus* provided, in the character of Aaron, the prototype, a 'barbarous Moor', irreligious and damned, or indeed, as he is called in the play, an 'incarnate devil', an 'accursed devil'. And we remember Hamlet's double-edged words to Gertrude, when he shows her the portraits of her two husbands:

Could you on this fair mountain leave to feed,
And batten on this moor? (3.4.66–7)

In fact, throughout the first scene of *Othello*, the Moor is presented in the traditional way. Iago calls to Brabantio:

an old black ram
Is topping your white ewe. Arise, arise;
Awake the snorting citizens with the bell,
Or else the devil will make a grandsire of you.

(1.1.89–92)

But in the last act, when Iago's perfidy is discovered, it is Othello who says of him:

I look down towards his feet – but that's a fable.
If that thou be'st a devil, I cannot kill thee.

(5.2.289–90)

The fair Iago is the devil, the foul fiend. It is a translation on to the ethical level of the aesthetic paradox current at the time in lyrical poetry: black is fair, white is ugly – a paradox harking back to the Biblical Song of Songs, *nigra sum sed formosa*, and that Shakespeare himself had played with at length in *Love's Labour's Lost* (4.3.243–65):

No face is fair that is not full so black.

The King counters Berowne's words with:

O paradox! Black is the badge of hell,
The hue of dungeons, and the school of
night . . .

In *Othello* the exit lines of the Duke in 1.3. 289–90 were addressed to Brabantio:

If virtue no delighted beauty lack,
Your son-in law is far more fair than black.

And Iago had recalled the paradox with a bawdy innuendo in the scene which I have already mentioned, when he plays the part of the fool to Desdemona:

If she be black, and thereto have a wit,
She'll find a white that shall her blackness fit

(2.1.132–3)

– the sort of joke that induces Desdemona's remark:

These are old fond paradoxes to make fools laugh
i' th' alehouse.

Paradox, then, is the hidden rhetorical principle governing the tragedy of *Othello*. It is as if the arch-villain in *Titus Andronicus*, Aaron the Moor, had split into two separate persons: something barbaric and instinctual remains in the character of Othello, but the diabolic element is transferred wholly to fair Iago.

The colour paradox extends beyond the ethical field to become the expression of the ambiguity of human nature within the context of the dialectical contrast between seeming and being, appearance and reality, which is the central theme, or rather the supporting structure, of most of Shakespeare's tragedies – and comedies.

*Postscript*

When I wrote the present paper I had no access to at least two books which would have made my task much easier. Only after reading the paper at the Nineteenth International Shakespeare Conference in Stratford-upon-Avon did I discover that the first section, on the use of oaths, covers ground much more extensively explored by Frances A. Shirley in her thorough study of *Swearing and Perjury in Shakespeare's Plays* (1979), especially pp. 110–24 on *Othello*. I can only regret that I was unable to acknowledge her admirable work, and find comfort in the extraordinary coincidence of approach to the subject in our two independent treatments of it. The other book which I wish to mention is *Shakespeare's Styles – Essays in Honour of Kenneth Muir*, edited by Philip Edwards, Inga-Stina Ewbank and G. K. Hunter (Cambridge, 1980); the essays by L. C. Knights, 'Rhetoric and insincerity', R. A. Foakes, 'Poetic Language and dramatic significance in Shakespeare', E. A. J. Honigmann, 'Shakespeare's bombast', and G. Bullough, 'In defence of paradox', are all very relevant to the present paper, which is certainly indebted to the previous work of their authors.

# CHARACTERIZING CORIOLANUS

## MICHAEL GOLDMAN

I

The trouble with characterization is that we think we know what character is, or rather we think we know where it is and what kind of discourse best describes it. We think, or at least we generally speak as if we think, that it is to be found inside people, and we answer questions about character with summaries of inner qualities. This is a reasonable procedure and, it should be stressed, not a recent one. Nevertheless, it is true that in the past 150 years or so the description has tended more and more to stress the problematical and the psychological; character is seen as elusive, a subject for puzzle and argument, depending on the difficult and never entirely satisfactory attempt to chart the way someone's mind works. And debate about dramatic character is likely to turn on whether it is reasonable to expect this kind of novelistic presentation of character from plays, especially plays written before the nineteenth century.

It is at this point that the discussion of character in drama becomes dangerously tangled, through the operation of hidden assumptions. For the implication in the typical debate I have described is that the psychological discourse of novels and novelizing psychology is the most accurate form for describing character in what we helplessly refer to as real life. But does our experience of other people correspond more to the helpful summaries of a novel or to the un-narratized encounters of a play?

I do not mean to argue for any presumed metaphysical superiority of drama to the novel; what I wish to bring out is the potential for error in assuming that the original, as it were, of character is discursive and that drama must thus constitute a translation of that original into more foreign terms. It should be noted that my distinction applies not only to nineteenth-century novels and modern psychology, but to all discursive accounts of character, including Aristotle, Burton, or whom you will. By comparison with any mode of discursive analysis, it can at least be argued that our experience as members of a theatre audience comes closer to the way in which we apprehend character in our daily encounters. Surely our efforts to characterize our friends and enemies – even the effort to characterize them as friends and enemies – follows, and always to a degree haltingly, after our experience of them, experience which, in the first instance, we approach through what Francis Fergusson calls the histrionic sensibility, the art, as it were, of finding the mind's construction in the face.

The notion of characterization as description may well have had a significant influence on the study of character in drama. I think it explains why, beginning with Aristotle, critics frequently maintain that character is somehow of secondary importance in drama, the implication clearly being that it is more important elsewhere, presumably in real life. With the conception of character, as with so much else, the hidden assumptions behind our normal critical vocabulary tend to make drama parasitic on narrative, and thus to distort our understanding of the effects and methods of the dramatist from the start.

I bring up these matters because they bear very interestingly on the play I have chosen to discuss. *Coriolanus* submits the whole question of character to a remarkable analysis. To begin with a point to which I would like to devote some extended attention, it exhibits a concern unique in the Shakespearian canon with discursive characterization of the kind we recognize as distinctly modern and familiar – the nice and argumentative discrimination of psychological qualities. It contains many passages in which Coriolanus is discussed in this manner by other characters, and the effect of these characterizations is to strike the audience as increasingly inadequate to its own unfolding dramatic experience of the man.

In no other Shakespearian play do people analyse another character in the fashion they repeatedly employ in *Coriolanus*. I have in mind not disagreement or uncertainty over motivation, as in *Hamlet*, but perplexity over what we would call a character's psychological makeup. In Shakespeare we often feel the presence of such complexity, but his characters almost never comment on it. The type of question Othello raises about Iago at the end of his play – what makes him do such things? – is almost never explicitly addressed, and of course in *Othello* no answer is even hazarded, except the suggestion, immediately rejected, that Iago is a devil. Iago's own motive-hunting is just that, statements of particular reasons for enmity, rather than analysis of his mental constitution.

*Hamlet* is the play that seems most concerned with the subject, but even there one finds no clear-cut example. When Hamlet asserts that he has that within which passes show, he is referring to an inarticulate depth of feeling rather than some hidden aspect of his character. There is much concern with ambiguous givings out in the play, and it may well point to inner ambiguity, but no character explores the question explicitly. When Claudius says, 'There's something in his soul / O'er which his melancholy sits on brood' (3.1.164–165), his language may suggest the elusiveness to description of a complex personality, but the explicit content is either that something is bothering Hamlet or that he is up to something which, like love or ambition, is capable of simple definition and explicable as the product of an external situation, for example his father's death and his mother's hasty marriage. Perhaps more could be made out of 'I have something in me dangerous' (5.1.256), or 'Pluck out the heart of my mystery' (3.2.356), but again these are matters, at most, of resonance and implication, not explicit statement. And the examples I have just cited are the closest we ever come in Shakespeare to the discussion of character as a complex and problematic psychological essence, with the exception of *Coriolanus*.

There the discussion begins with the opening scene. Like many of Shakespeare's tragedies, *Coriolanus* opens with the eruption of a dangerous force. The mob that rushes on stage carrying staves and clubs is meant to be felt as a threat; these 'mutinous' citizens are on the verge of extreme violence. Yet suddenly, even before Menenius appears, the rebellion loses momentum. Within moments of their first appearance, the rebels pause – to discuss Coriolanus's character.

This is the issue the second citizen has on his mind at line 12, 'One word, good citizens.' He is answered in a well-known speech by a comrade who first says of Marcius that he is proud and, after an interruption, continues:

Though soft-conscienc'd men can be content to say it was for his country, he did it to please his mother and to be partly proud . . .

The phrase has an air of simplicity and of caricature as well, caricature both of the subject and the speaker, but it is also very much a qualification of the speaker's original confident analysis. And the uneasiness of the formulation, 'to be partly proud', which has provoked emenda-

tion and extensive commentary, suggests a difficulty in characterizing Coriolanus, even by an
angry enemy who is none too scrupulous about
his speech.

This kind of difficulty recurs at many moments in the play. Again, I am not talking
about simple disagreement over Marcius's
character, but about passages which have this
habit of qualification, of instability, of attempts
to specify a complex essence. The most striking
example occurs in Aufidius's soliloquy at the
end of act 4:

> First he was
> A noble servant to them, but he could not
> Carry his honors even. Whether 'twas pride,
> Which out of daily fortune ever taints
> The happy man; whether defect of judgement,
> To fail in the disposing of those chances
> Which he was lord of; or whether nature,
> Not to be other than one thing, not moving
> From th' casque to th' cushion, but commanding
>   peace
> Even with the same austerity and garb
> As he controll'd the war; but one of these –
> As he hath spices of them all – not all,
> For I dare so far free him – made him fear'd,
> So hated, and so banish'd. But he has a merit
> To choke it in the utt'rance.

Aufidius first poses three reasons for Coriolanus's failure to 'carry his honors even'. This
latter formula, with its obscure suggestion of a
difficult balancing act, initiates a meditation
that keeps sliding away from fixity and clarity
of analysis. Aufidius presents his three explanations as if they were mutually exclusive,
but they are not. 'Pride' is the old accusation of
the Tribunes, 'defect of judgement' means
perhaps political miscalculation or a deeper-
seated inability to calculate shrewdly, and
'nature', of course, can include the first two.
But Aufidius quickly limits the application of
nature to a specific failing:

> or whether nature,
> Not to be other than one thing, not moving
> From th' casque to th' cushion, but commanding
>   peace

> Even with the same austerity and garb
> As he controll'd the war . . .

Then, as if he felt that none of his reasons was
quite sufficient, Aufidius goes on to complete
his thought in a tangle of qualifications:

> but one of these –
> As he hath spices of them all – not all,
> For I dare so far free him – made him fear'd,
> So hated, and so banish'd.

It is the passage's sole point of certainty that
most gives it a feeling of bewilderment. Why is
Aufidius so sure that *but* one of these causes is
responsible, 'not all,/For I dare so far free him'?
There can be no logical reason; Aufidius simply
feels that it would be too much to accuse
Coriolanus of all three failings. Why? A sense
of his character, of course, which underlies the
entire speech and which Aufidius has been unable to articulate. And a further sense of it
seems to rise at this very point, to comment on
the difficulties Aufidius is finding:

> But he has a merit
> To choke it in the utt'rance.

This is another line that gives editors problems. The primary meaning, I think, is that
Coriolanus's merit breaks in and chokes back
the account of his faults, but the 'it' is ambiguous; there is a clouding suggestion that his
merits choke themselves. And of course
Aufidius's own emotions seem to be registered
in the verse. Coriolanus and his merits are
certainly a bone in his throat. The main effect
is that the attempt to characterize becomes
tangled and chokes on itself.

What has been evoked here, too, is the
complexity and elusiveness of the very notion
of character itself. The speech delicately
catches the way innate predisposition, training,
feeling, and choice come together and respond
to external circumstance, the shifting changes
of politics, and the feelings and actions of the
public world – and also how, being a public as
well as a private quality, one's character is
modified, in a sense created, by the responses of

other people, as Marcius's is by Aufidius. Coriolanus's character has something to do with the way other people choke on it. It exists somewhere between Coriolanus and his audience.

The paradoxical impact of Coriolanus on his society is felt strikingly in Aufidius's final speech:

> My rage is gone,
> And I am struck with sorrow. Take him up.
> . . . Though in this city he
> Hath widowed and unchilded many a one,
> Which to this hour bewail the injury,
> Yet he shall have a noble memory.
>
> (5.6.147–8, 151–4)

*Yet* is the important word. Though Marcius has done hateful things, nevertheless he will be loved. We have with Aufidius the sensation we have with so many of Shakespeare's tragic characters – but never with Coriolanus – that it is difficult to tell where play-acting leaves off and authentic feeling begins. Is Aufidius shifting gears for political reasons here? Or is he suddenly abashed? Is he asserting that Coriolanus manages, perplexingly, to be nobly remembered, or that he will see to it that Coriolanus is so remembered, in spite of his desert? All these notes mingle in the very believable compound of envy and awe that characterizes Aufidius whenever he contemplates his great rival.

This is not the only point in the play where the notion of noble memory is associated with perplexity about characterizing Coriolanus. Many less elaborate passages have helped develop the idea. When the servingmen at Antium try to explain the mysterious quality they claim to have detected in the disguised Marcius, their language goes comically to pieces:

*Second Servingman.* Nay, I knew by his face that there was something in him; he had, sir, a kind of face, methought – I cannot tell how to term it.

*First Servingman.* He had so, looking as it were – Would I were hang'd, but I thought there was more in him than I could think.

(4.5.154–7)

Of course this is a joke, whose point is that the servingmen had noticed nothing, but this only refines the question of how a noble character is constituted. The language of the servingmen calls attention to the 'something' in Coriolanus over which his friends and enemies quarrel. Even the play's repeated use of 'thing' to describe Coriolanus suggests not only his inhumanity, as is commonly argued, but the resistance of his nature to characterization.

In the last act, Aufidius, on the verge of denouncing Coriolanus to the lords of Antium, offers to his fellow conspirators – apparently in all frankness – a further interpretation of his character, which only adds to our sense of elusiveness:

> I rais'd him, and I pawn'd
> Mine honour for his truth; who being so heighten'd,
> He watered his new plants with dews of flattery,
> Seducing so my friends; and to this end
> He bow'd his nature, never known before
> But to be rough, unswayable, and free.
>
> (5.6.21–6)

Aufidius describes Coriolanus as having changed and become politically manipulative. He has no reason to deceive his listeners at this point, but his account does not square with the Coriolanus we have seen, though we understand how Aufidius may have arrived at it.

There is, moreover, a tendency in the play to keep before us the whole issue of how we characterize people – whether it be by internal attributes or external ones, by simple epithets or puzzled formulas. The three scenes of act 2, for example, have a very distinct parallel structure. This is the act in which Coriolanus, newly named, returns to Rome; and each scene begins with a prelude in which his character is debated by the people who await him. In act 2, scene 1, conversation about Marcius between Menenius and the tribunes becomes a war of rather Overburyan character descriptions, Menenius topping the tribunes by offering two 'characters', as he calls them, first of himself and then of his opponents. In the second scene of the act, the officers argue as to whether or not Coriolanus is proud and disdainful. Finally, the third scene begins with the citizens arguing over whether Coriolanus should have their voices; this prelude ends with words which sum up the aim of so much of the play's dialogue, 'Mark his behavior'. Heightening the parallelism, each scene ends with a conversation between Brutus and Sicinius in which they decide how to make political capital out of Coriolanus's impact on the people.

## II

What does this interesting emphasis on character mean? Surely it suggests that the character of Coriolanus is meant to be seen as problematic, and beyond this it raises the possibility that the idea of character itself may be under scrutiny – that the play may force us to confront the question of what character is and how it is perceived. Here we must pause to examine further the peculiar relation of character and drama. Let me say a few words about how we perceive character in performance. First of all, the fictitious person we watch on stage, Hamlet, or Hal, or Othello, is not an object, but a process. He is something we watch an actor making, not the result of making but the making itself. Hamlet, in performance, is not a tenth-century or sixteenth-century prince, not even a twentieth-century one; he is in no way physically separable from the actor who plays him. Yet we perceive him as a self, a character, rather than a series of physical actions. Where is that self? It is there, on the stage; it, too, is inseparable from the actor we are watching. Yet it is not the actor's everyday self, his biographical personality. It is something he is accomplishing by acting. A character, in a play, is something an actor *does*.

We are all too likely to think of an actor's characterization as an object, a presented mask, something produced and built up by the actor's preparation, as makeup or a dossier on the character might be. Such a product might well be described by a discursive summary. But a dramatic character is an action that goes on throughout the play.

I have shifted to another meaning of the word character – that of imagined person in a drama. But the two conceptions are linked. What is the character of a dramatic character? Clearly it, too, must spring from what the actor does. And what an actor does, first of all and ceaselessly, is perform. Performance is inseparable from dramatic character. It is true that sometimes in our discussion of a play we separate the performance from the character – as for example when we object that the actor has spoken more than is set down for him. But in that case we are simply imagining a better performance, for all the words he should speak – all the words Shakespeare has written – are meant as performed words. Thus, our view of dramatic character will gain by a consideration of the performance qualities built into the role, the necessary creative action of the actor called for by the script in order to project the part.

In the case of Coriolanus, certain problems of character have always been recognized, and I think they are illuminated by attention to some of the problems of performance. That is why the play, in proper performance, gives us an impression of its hero rather different from that conveyed by a bare recital of his deeds or a bare account of his language and behaviour. We should start with the observation, particularly striking because of the great amount of discussion the character of Coriolanus receives in the play, that of all the mature tragedies this is the one whose hero seems simplest in inner constitution, a relatively narrow or immature self. Indeed, by virtue of the apparent ease with which he can be manipulated, he runs the risk of being interpreted as comic. Furthermore, many critics feel that the play's rhetoric is chill, and that this corresponds to something uninviting about both the play's ambience and its hero – a lack of warmth or generosity.

Now, though I do not think these comments give a complete picture of the response a fully imagined performance of *Coriolanus* provides, there is a degree of truth in them, and they help define a major acting problem of the role. This might be described as finding what Coriolanus means when he refers to his own 'truth' as something he is afraid of ceasing to 'honour'. Is there more to this truth than doing what his mother wants, or fighting fearlessly, or hating compliments? That is, does the role suggest a freedom and depth of personality to which the audience can sympathetically respond? To keep Coriolanus from being simply comic means finding the passion hidden in the chill rhetoric, the richness of spirit beneath the many signs of poverty.

To indicate one or two ways in which the play addresses this problem, I would like to draw attention to some qualities of performance that are required by the language of the role. Much of Coriolanus's language requires of the actor a kind of grip, a domination over complexity which is exactly the opposite of comic predictability. This grip depends on an emotional and intellectual penetration by means of which the actor maintains focus on a goal that is delayed and hidden by the movement of his speech. The histrionic action is rather like that of Coriolanus the warrior penetrating to the centre of Corioles, thrusting ahead in battle, except that it cannot be rendered as a blind pushing forward; it is not like Macbeth's 'Before my body I throw my warlike shield.' It constitutes an important part of the action which is the character of Coriolanus.

The quality of performance I am describing is largely determined by syntax. A good example may be found in act 3:

> I say again,
> In soothing them we nourish 'gainst our Senate

> The cockle of rebellion, insolence, sedition,
> Which we ourselves have ploughed for, sow'd,
>     and scatter'd
> By mingling them with us, the honor'd number,
> Who lack not virtue, no, nor power, but that
> Which they have given to beggars.

> (3.1.68–74)

If this sentence were diagrammed, one would see that it is the final pair of subordinate clauses – syntactically very subordinate indeed – which define its energy and direction. Coriolanus is primarily agitated by the idea that the patricians have given their power and virtue to beggars, and it is this which governs the notion of soothing them and is developed as sowing the seeds of rebellion. The actor must be gripped by this idea and render its presence in the speech articulate, even as he must suspend stating it till the very end. Thus the felt movement of the speech is not simply accumulative – this thing, that thing, and another – but a pursuit toward a syntactically buried point.

I think I can make this clearer by comparing another passage from act 3 with a speech from *Othello*. This is Coriolanus's climactic outburst that goes from 'You common cry of curs' to 'I banish you' (3.3.122–5). It is a swift and frightening forecast of revenge, but how different in its movement from Othello's:

> Like to the Pontic sea,
> Whose icy current and compulsive course
> Ne'er feels retiring ebb, but keeps due on
> To the Propontic and the Hellespont;
> Even so my bloody thoughts, with violent pace,
> Shall ne'er look back, ne'er ebb to humble love,
> Till that a capable and wide revenge
> Swallow them up.          (3.3.457–64)

The Othello actor must start out his passage with a desire for revenge large enough to be measured against the scope and flow of the Pontic sea. But the movement of sweep and obstruction is grandly simple. The Coriolanus actor, by contrast, must struggle forward toward the instigating idea, *You corrupt my air*, which informs the three preceding lines of imagery and comparison, and which prepares the springboard for 'I banish you':

> You common cry of curs, whose breath I hate
> As reek o' th' rotten fens, whose loves I prize
> As the dead carcasses of unburied men
> That do corrupt my air – I banish you.

The intricacy here can be expressed yet another way. The opening lines of the passage appear to set up a neat symmetry: 'whose breath I hate / As reek o' th' rotten fens, whose loves I prize / As the dead carcasses of unburied men', but the following phrase, 'That do corrupt my air', unbalances this symmetry and, thus, to keep the passage alive there has to be an emotional thrust through the symmetries, which allows the crucial half-line to refer back to the earlier, 'You common cry of curs'. This problem occurs repeatedly in the role. A lot of the apparent coldness of Coriolanus's rhetoric resides in the balance and opposition he is constantly striking, but very often these balances get disturbed as the speech moves on, demanding a grip that keeps the balances clear and yet enlivens them by something not at all cool or settled.

A variation on this structure occurs when an apparently concluding phrase kicks off new images, requiring a supplementary charge of energy at a position normally felt to be subordinate or merely, as it were, passive:

> What would you have, you curs,
> That like nor peace nor war? The one affrights
> you,
> The other makes you proud.     (1.1.166–8)

Here, the subordinate 'that like nor peace nor war' cannot be thrown away. The actor must pursue it with an articulation which makes coherent the balanced opposition of 'The one . . . the other'. And if we were to extend the analysis to his whole great concerto-like first appearance, in which Marcius enters at full tilt with what is in effect a long speech over and against the interjections of the First Citizen and Menenius, we would see how the larger structure echoes the tendency of the smaller and in

so doing prevents our first impression of the hero from being comic. After all, what is it that keeps Marcius, with his repeated 'Hang 'em's and 'What's the matter's, from playing as a young Colonel Blimp? It is the presence of a source of emotion which governs the entire speech, pursued by Marcius through all kinds of syntactical complications and shiftingly balanced reflections on the Roman populace, and which does not surface till the very end of the sequence, when we learn that the people have been given five tribunes, which Marcius correctly sees as a source of future insurrection.

So, repeatedly, we have this construction, in which the delayed phrase may be modifier or object or even a piece of information. But the effect is regularly that what is delayed is a central source of energy and we feel it radiating through earlier phrases. Or, to put it more accurately, if even more impressionistically, we feel its radiance being pursued by the speaker down branching corridors which blaze and echo with its force. The pursuit helps establish for us a great quality of the hero – the quality of attacker. In the speeches I have described, the sense of attack comes from the pursuit of the delayed idea, the buried trigger. If it were not buried, the pursuit would not feel like attack, or at least not that magnificence of attack we associate with Coriolanus.

In the great final outburst before he is murdered, the trigger is the word 'Boy':

> Cut me to pieces, Volsces; men and lads,
> Stain all your edges on me. 'Boy'! False hound!
> If you have writ your annals true, 'tis there
> That, like an eagle in a dove-cote, I
> Flutter'd your Volscians in Corioli.
> Alone I did it. 'Boy'!     (5.6.112–17)

The method I have been attempting to describe explains why that speech does not play simply as a confirmation of the Tribunes' and Aufidius's theory that Coriolanus is a manipulable figure: call him certain names and you've got him. Nor does it allow us to accept the explanation the play itself seems at times to put forward – that Coriolanus is, in fact, a boy of tears. The stimulus does not set off a mere raving reaction, but a pursuit, a kind of branching plunge, in which the whole being of the performer attacks the insult. Every phrase, 'Men and lads', 'Cut me to pieces', 'Alone I did it', 'Like an eagle', responds, separately, to 'Boy!' Each bears *toward* the word, presses in on it, ranges pieces of a multiple attack that bursts into the clear only as the offending word is finally snapped in place.

Awareness of this technique will help us with at least one crucial passage which has often been misinterpreted:

> Though I go alone,
> Like to a lonely dragon, that his fen
> Makes fear'd and talk'd of more than seen . . .
>
> (4.1.29–31)

Most readings focus on the dragon but the fen is the point. What makes Coriolanus most like a dragon is his isolation; indeed it is not even simply the fen that is at the centre of the speech, but the power of fen-dwelling to make someone feared and talked of and hence lonely. It is not, then, a definition of his inhumanity Coriolanus gives us here, but of his felt distance from others. The dragonish qualities seem most to derive from being feared and talked of. They are, at least in part, an aspect of how society characterizes Coriolanus.

'Alone' is of course an important word in the play. But it varies greatly in meaning as Coriolanus pronounces it, and these variations are histrionic – that is, they represent differences in the way the actor projects a character through his performance of the word. In the passage just cited, 'alone' suggests isolation, but it also is coloured here, as elsewhere, by loneliness. By contrast, when Coriolanus turns on his accusers in the last act, crying, 'Alone I did it', the word means 'unaided, singling oneself out'. This is mingled with an implied insult: 'The Volsces can be beaten by one man', and a provocation: 'I take full responsibility.' It

is a challenging statement of personal strength.

Now, there is another moment when the word is used in a very different sense, which is of the greatest importance for the performance of the role. And it is very different both in syntax and mood from any of the examples we have been considering. This occurs when Marcius addresses Cominius's troops after the successful assault on Corioles and before the battle with Aufidius. He asks for volunteers to follow him, and *'They all shout and wave their swords, take him up in their arms, and cast up their caps.'* At which point, he cries:

> O, me alone! Make you a sword of me?
>
> (1.6.76)

This wonderful and startling line is not that of the isolated attacker, or the automaton, or the scorner of the crowd. It has a rush and a surprised pleasure we hear nowhere else from Coriolanus. It is his happiest moment in the play.

Significantly, it is presented by Shakespeare as one of a series of stage images which intricately comment upon each other. It reverses the group of images we have had a few minutes earlier, first of Coriolanus scorning the soldiers as they flee, then deserted by them, then scorning them again as they pause to loot; and it will be partially reversed, restated dissonantly, one might say, a few minutes later when he angrily denounces the same crowd as it cheers him again. Finally, it will be most emphatically reversed in the assassination scene, the only other moment in the play when Marcius allows a group of men to touch him. But now in act 1 he is elated, he accepts the praise and the physical contact of the crowd, and the word 'alone' here means singled out by others, uniquely valued by people with whom he feels a bond. He is the sword of a courageous community – and the attacking hardness of the image of the sword is modified by the moment of joyous physical contact and celebration. This is the aloneness Coriolanus has felt himself bred up for, to be truly a limb of his country, a healthy limb of an heroic society; and for an instant his dream appears to come true.

### III

We can appreciate some of the play's distance from Plutarch if we compare the variable implications Shakespeare gives to 'alone' with the idea of 'solitariness', which Plutarch, in North's translation, borrows from Plato to describe Coriolanus. In Plutarch, solitariness is simply a vice, an inability to deal with others, the opposite of 'affability'. Shakespeare's use of 'alone', as we have seen, suggests not only a different and far more interesting character, but a far more complex notion of how character is to be understood. In the concluding portion of this paper, I would like to focus on how the idea of aloneness in the play illuminates two closely related themes. The first is Coriolanus's own conception of character – that is, not only what kind of person he wishes to be, but also how he understands character to be created and possessed. The second is the critique of this conception of character that emerges in the course of the drama. Taken together, I think they help us understand more clearly the complex appeal of *Coriolanus* as a theatrical creation and perhaps something of Shakespeare's intention in writing the play.

Most of Shakespeare's tragic heroes entertain peculiar ideas about the relation of the self and its acts, ideas which poignantly reflect our own troubled sentiments on this bewildering subject. Coriolanus's version of this peculiarity is his notion that a man may be 'author of himself'. It is a phrase that evokes many of the same associations as his use of 'alone', and it stimulates us especially because, while it plainly reflects his gravest folly, at the same time it seems fairly to express the very authority that makes Coriolanus so much more interesting than a fool.

Perhaps no passage in the play has produced such troubled critical discussion of character as the scene in which he announces his decision to go over to the Volsces. His soliloquy seems in the most literal sense an attempt at self-authorship, at rewriting his play in the face of facts well known to the audience. Critics have frequently noted that it is an odd speech for what it fails to say, but it is equally odd for what it says:

> Friends now fast sworn,
> . . . shall within this hour,
> On a dissension of a doit, break out
> To bitterest enmity; so fellest foes,
> Whose passions and whose plots have broke their sleep
> To take the one the other, by some chance,
> Some trick not worth an egg, shall grow dear friends
> And interjoin their issues. So with me:
> My birthplace hate I, and my love's upon
> This enemy town.           (4.4.12,16–24)

For Coriolanus to describe his banishment, the hatred of the Tribunes, and the accusation of treachery as 'a dissension of a doit' or 'some trick not worth an egg' is nearly incredible and suggests how far he has distanced himself from his feelings. The same may be felt in the overly neat conclusion, 'So with me', and the flat and unconvincing assertiveness of:

> My birthplace hate I, and my love's upon
> This enemy town.

This distance from feeling is one of the perils of self-authorship. And in *Coriolanus*, as in *Macbeth*, the relation between feeling, action, and full humanity becomes very important. Certainly the moment of silence with Volumnia in act 5 is reminiscent of Macduff's pause. It comes about because in act 4 Coriolanus has failed to feel his banishment as a man. He has attempted to violate the natural relation between feeling and action, and like other Shakespearian heroes he must pay for it. If it is true that the defining problem for the actor in this play is to suggest an inner action deeper than the reflexive manipulable response seen by his enemies, it is interesting that Coriolanus's crisis comes when he tries to manipulate himself. To assert that one can do anything one wants is as humanly insufficient as to assert that one is completely predictable. The creature who will acknowledge no obedience to instinct is as subhuman as the gosling.

But even more than in one's relation to one's feelings, the fallacy of self-authorship may be felt in one's relation to the outside world. Like many of Shakespeare's heroes, Coriolanus must be tutored in the connections between theatricality and life, between the private individual and the social theatre in which he plays his part and finds his audience. The lesson he learns, however, is unique to his play. If Hamlet must discover that a connection exists between play-acting and the heart of one's mystery, Coriolanus is forced to explore the relation between one's character and one's audience. We can feel this even at the very beginning of the play. Most, if not all, Shakespearian heroes initially hold back from the opportunities for action that are first presented to them, and this is usually linked to a rejection of theatre, though it is not always so plain as Hamlet's 'I have that within which passes show', or so fearful as Macbeth's 'Why do you dress me in borrowed robes?' At first glance, Coriolanus appears not to conform to this pattern, plunging with his opening words into a denunciation of the crowd. But his opening line contains a refusal which precedes this eager engagement:

*Menenius.*
 . . . Hail, noble Marcius!
*Marcius.*
 Thanks. What's the matter, you dissentious
    rogues . . .                                    (1.1.161–2)

What is Coriolanus holding back from? I would describe it as the authority, the authorship, of an audience. Menenius offers him a name, praise, a characterization: 'Noble'. It is a term Coriolanus values – in the last act, nobleness will be the quality he prays that the gods give his son. And the word 'noble' occurs more frequently in *Coriolanus* than in any other Shakespeare play. But while he may readily

pray to the gods for nobility, he will not consent to be called noble, even by Menenius.

In the same way, Coriolanus seems regularly to reject *our* interest in him. And this contributes to our perception of his character as cold or unsympathetic. The problems of his act 4 transition to revenge, for example – the 'break' in characterization, the lack of transition, the flagrant inappropriateness of his remarks – constitute a defiance of the theatre audience comparable to his regular defiance of his on-stage audience. Nevertheless he retains his power over both audiences – and it is clear that he *needs* them. Just as we feel an invitation to the audience in the actor's mastery of those syntactically difficult passages, or in 'O, me alone!', or the moment of silence, or the moment of assassination, or the physical release of battle – just as there are solicitations of sympathy here, enactments of aloneness which carry us along with the actor – so in his relation with the on-stage audience we see that the apparent defiance is far from complete. How else explain, for example, Coriolanus's repeated appeals to Aufidius to note how honourably he is behaving? As at Corioles, Coriolanus needs an audience to give him the name he has won. He cannot author himself alone.

This dependence of character on audience is echoed in the story of the benefactor whose name Coriolanus forgets. The point is similar to the one Shakespeare makes in *Romeo and Juliet* about the way in which names, fate, and society are interwoven. The romantic attitude is that names do not matter; what one is counts. But our name reflects a real connection between our past, present, and future, between our selves, our acts, and our social being. Romeo *is* a Montague, and his name soon becomes that of the man who has murdered Tybalt. It matters quite as much as whether the name of the bird one hears is lark or nightingale. In the benefactor scene, Marcius has just become Coriolanus, a name which will permanently fix his relationship with Aufidius and lead to his death, and his poor friend has become a non-person because Coriolanus cannot remember his name.

Now, the relation between one's character and the behaviour of audiences is of troublesome resonance to any great artist, and I imagine Shakespeare was aware of this. At any rate, he seems as he reaches the end of the great cycle of tragedies to become specially interested in the ironies of an artistic career. In *Antony and Cleopatra*, he tells the story of a man whose gifts have equipped him for the greatest success in the practical world and who instead casts his lot with a greatness that depends wholly on the imagination, on the splendours of gesture, passion, self-dramatization – an achievement as materially insubstantial as black vesper's pageants, and which the practical world will always associate with the arts of the gypsy and the whore. In *Coriolanus* he tells the story of another man whose ruling passion suggests the situation of the artist, a man who wishes to be the author of himself, an ambition, one would think, not only artist-like, but particularly theatrical – who but an actor can change his being every day? Certainly it is an ambition easily associated with the appeal of high creativity. Who more than a great poet can make a claim to spiritual independence? Yet the theatre is, of course, the most social of the arts. Indeed, it presents in its most unpalatable and least disguised form the fact that no artist is the author of himself, but a dependent part of an inconstant multitude, which is always in some sense interpreting him. Among playwright, actors, and audience, who is the belly, who the members?

There is, it should be noted, another side to the story of the poor benefactor with the forgotten name. For it also projects a version of Coriolanus's fantasy of unconditioned power which is similar to the artist's fantasy of self-authorship. Perhaps one thinks that by being best warrior (or poet) one will gain absolute power over names – that one can command people by giving names or destroy them by forgetting them, that one can be free of the

common cry, can stand outside of society, banish the world at will, that moving others one can be oneself as stone. This is an illusion, as any poet discovers, and as Marcius discovers when he tries to forget his own name and that of friend, mother, wife, and child.

You will by now have grown tired of my saying, with Aufidius, 'And yet'. And yet I must say it again. For to end on the self-deluding aspect of Coriolanus's desire to stand alone would be to distort the play. The project of self-authorship, however mistaken, is bound up with the power and magnetism – indeed with the sympathetic appeal – of Coriolanus as a dramatic character. I think the issue here has to do with the nature of tragedy. In a sense all tragic heroes are authors of themselves. I am certain that the writer of a tragedy feels more intensely than in any other form the struggle between what he wants to make happen and what his chief character wants to do. It is true of course that any tragedy exhibits a severe sense of scriptedness, but the play would be flat and tame if we did not feel that its hero had an equally exigent sense of the script *he* wants to write, of his own authorial power. Faced with some terrible contingency, the tragic hero makes it his own necessity. Like a great actor, he makes the part he is given his own. And I think that when we argue over whether Coriolanus the character is cold and uninviting, when we ask whether his nature is fully expressed by the facts of his upbringing and the reflexes of his temper, we are asking whether he has the authority, the inspiriting freedom, of a tragic figure.

That is why the play must end, and why I wish to conclude, with Aufidius's 'Yet he will have a noble memory.' As with both Romeo and Juliet, and as with the self-authorizing ambitions of great poets, there is in Coriolanus something cherishable and indeed social about the lonely impulse which drives him. We return a last time to what I have called Coriolanus's truth. What did Shakespeare see in Plutarch's life of Coriolanus? He found there a great warrior firmly characterized as intemperately angry and hence given over to solitariness, and he accepted almost everything about him except the characterization, which is to say he accepted everything except what mattered most to his play. Shakespeare seems to have looked at Plutarch's story of the choleric superman and said, 'And yet'. Here was a man whose whole life seemed to have been devoted to a notion of character; he was, in Menenius's Overburyan sense, the very character of a Roman warrior. And yet he could decide to betray Rome. And yet, being able to betray Rome, he again could give in fatally – more than fatally, embarrassingly – to his mother's plea. Shakespeare added complexities which show Coriolanus to be determined and manipulable in the most psychologically credible way – all that family history and revealing imagery. But he also added all the details which make him less easily characterized – his moments of unexpected response, the exciting complexity of his speeches, the range of meanings he gives to the notion of aloneness, and, always, that chorus of friends and enemies inadequately, perplexedly explaining him.

To sum it up, Shakespeare insists on the problematics of characterization in *Coriolanus* because he is there peculiarly concerned with a paradox: that the distinctive quality of an individual is at once incommunicably private and unavoidably social. As such, it is situated neither entirely within our grasp or the grasp of our fellows but, fascinatingly, between us – rather like the meaning of a poem or a play – between us in our encounters on the stage of the world. Character lies in the interpretation of the time, as Aufidius puts it, and is thus susceptible to change and falsehood. And yet it is the most enduring thing about us. Perhaps this is what tragedy is about – that there is such a thing as human character. Perhaps it is only in tragedy that we feel that character as a personal possession really exists, in spite of the contradictions which surround it as a philosophical conception. At the end of *Coriolanus*, I feel that strange response which a less apologetic age would simply call tragic exaltation. And if I interpret the significance of that mood correctly, it means we feel, in spite of everything, that there is in the end something about Coriolanus which is truly his, that it characterizes him, and that for us to have shared his character, by participating in it through the process of the actor's performance, has been an experience of immense value to ourselves.

# THE IRONIC READING OF 'THE RAPE OF LUCRECE' AND THE PROBLEM OF EXTERNAL EVIDENCE

## RICHARD LEVIN

For some time now we have watched the ironic critics working their way through Shakespeare's canon, demonstrating that his major characters must not be 'taken at face value', which invariably means that they must be taken at a good deal less than face value. One by one, thanks to their 'new readings', the heroes and heroines who seemed to be presented sympathetically have been exposed as ridiculous or reprehensible figures meant to evoke our antipathy. There was no reason to expect that Lucrece would escape this fate, and we now have several studies of the poem named for her which assert that she is not supposed to be viewed as an admirable model of chastity and fidelity, or even as a pathetic victim, but as one of the guilty parties.[1] Although the authors of these studies differ in their indictment of her (one calls her crime 'a little beyond forgiveness', another finds it is 'reciprocal' with Tarquin's), and in their manner of proving it, they usually claim to base their case, or at least a substantial part of it, upon historical grounds – upon a contemporary 'perspective' or 'world view', as they call it, which would have predisposed Shakespeare and his readers to condemn Lucrece. As evidence for this 'perspective' they cite a number of authoritative texts that stated or embodied it, including Petrarch, Landino, Fabrini, Tyndale, several books of the Bible, and above all St Augustine, whose attack on Lucrece (*City of God*, I, xix) they regard as decisive. But none of them cites a single contemporary response to

the poem itself, except for Gabriel Harvey's remark (in his copy of Speght's *Chaucer*) that it and *Hamlet* 'haue it in them, to please the wiser sort', which does not reveal any attitude toward Shakespeare's heroine.

This silence on the part of critics who claim to be reconstructing the historical meaning of the poem is rather strange, to say the least, since a number of references have come down to us which indicate very clearly how members of Shakespeare's audience actually did view Lucrece, almost all of which are easily available in *The Shakspere Allusion-Book* and Chambers's *William Shakespeare*.[2] I propose, therefore, to rectify the omission by surveying them, in order to see how they bear upon the arguments of these new ironic readings. The following list contains all such references that

---

1 See especially Don Cameron Allen, 'Some Observations on *The Rape of Lucrece*', *Shakespeare Survey 15* (Cambridge, 1962), pp. 89–98, reprinted in *Image and Meaning: Metaphoric Traditions in Renaissance Poetry* (rev. edn., Baltimore, 1968), and Roy Battenhouse, *Shakespearean Tragedy: Its Art and Its Christian Premises* (Bloomington, 1969), pp. 3–41, as well as the briefer (and milder) versions in J. C. Maxwell's edition of the *Poems* (Cambridge, 1966), pp. xxii–xxiv, and in Michel Grivelet's 'Shakespeare's "War with Time": The Sonnets and *Richard II*', *Shakespeare Survey 23* (Cambridge, 1970), pp. 76–7.

2 John Munro (ed.), *The Shakspere Allusion-Book: A Collection of Allusions to Shakspere from 1591 to 1700* (1932), vol. 1, pp. 8, 14–15, 23–4, 51, 71, 123, 125, 245; E. K. Chambers, *William Shakespeare: A Study of Facts and Problems* (Oxford, 1930), vol. 1, p. 443; vol. 2, pp. 189–90, 192–3, 195, 199, 220.

have been discovered up to now, including a few doubtful ones that may not allude to Shakespeare's poem, or to his heroine, but cannot be left out if we are to cover all of the possible evidence.

1. This anonymous commendatory poem[3] was prefixed to *Willobie His Avisa; or, The True Picture of a Modest Maid, and of a Chaste and Constant Wife*, which was published in 1594, the same year as *The Rape of Lucrece*:

> IN Lauine Land though Liuie bost,
> *There hath beene seene a* Constant *dame*:
> *Though* Rome *lament that she haue lost*
> *The* Gareland *of her rarest fame*,
>> *Yet now we see, that here is found,*
>> *As great a* Faith *in* English *ground.*
>
> *Though* Collatine *haue deerely bought,*
> *To high renowne, a lasting life,*
> *And found, that most in vaine haue*
>> *sought,*
> *To haue a* Faire, *and* Constant *wife,*
>> *Yet* Tarquyne *pluckt his glistering grape,*
>> *And* Shake-speare, *paints poore* Lucrece
>> *rape.*
>
> *Though* Susan *shine in faithfull praise,*
> *As twinckling Starres in Christall skie,*
> Penelop's *fame though* Greekes *do raise,*
> *Of faithfull wiues to make vp three,*
>> *To thinke the* Truth, *and say no lesse,*
>> *Our* Auisa *shall make a messe.*
>
> *This number knits so sure a knot,*
> Time *doubtes, that she shall adde no*
>> *more,*
> Vnconstant Nature, *hath begot,*
> *Of* Fleting Feemes, *such fickle store,*
>> *Two thousand yeares, haue scarcely*
>> *seene,*
>> *Such as the worst of these haue beene.*
>
> *Then* Aui-Susan *ioyne in one,*
> *Let* Lucres-Auis *be thy name,*
> *This* English Eagle *sores alone,*
> *And farre surmounts all others fame,*
>> *Where high or low, where great or*
>> *small,*
>> *This* Brytan Bird *out-flies them all.*

*Were these three happie, that haue found,*
*Braue* Poets *to depaint their praise?*
*Of* Rurall Pipe, *with sweetest sound,*
*That haue beene heard these many daies,*
*Sweete* wylloby *his* AVIS *blest,*
*That makes her mount aboue the rest.*

(A4ʳ–A4ᵛ)

Clearly, the author believes that Shakespeare's depiction of Lucrece is entirely favourable, and is in this respect equivalent to the depiction of Susanna in the Apocrypha, and of Penelope in the *Odyssey*, and of Avisa in Willobie's poem.

2. The following lines appear at the beginning of *Epicedium: A Funeral Song upon the Virtuous Life and Godly Death of the Right Worshipful the Lady Helen Branch* by 'W. Har.',[4] which was also published in 1594:

> YOu that to shew your wits haue taken
>> toyle,
> In registring the deeds of noble men:
> And sought for matter in a forraine soyle,
> (As worthie subiects of your siluer pen)
> Whom you haue rais'd from darke obliuions
>> den.
> You that haue writ of chaste *Lucretia*,
> Whose death was witnesse of her spotlesse life:
> Or pend the praise of sad *Cornelia*,
> Whose blamelesse name hath made her fame so
>> rife:
> As noble *Pompeys* most renoumed wife.
>> Hither vnto your home direct your eies:
>> Whereas vnthought on, much more matter
>> lies.                    (A2ʳ)

This author, too, obviously believes that Shakespeare's Lucrece is presented as an object of unqualified admiration, comparable to the

---

3 It is signed '*Contraria Contrarijs: Vigilantius: Dormitanus*', which Chambers notes is an 'apparent allusion to St Jerome's *Contra Vigilantium*, in which he calls his opponent Dormitantius' (*William Shakespeare*, vol. 2, p. 192). I have modernized titles but have reproduced the passages themselves as they appear in the original texts, except for the long *s* and a few obvious errors.
4 Chambers suggests that he may be William Harvey (*William Shakespeare*, vol. 2, p. 190).

presentation of Cornelia in Thomas Kyd's tragedy (published in the same year), and of Lady Helen Branch in his own poem.

3. In a tract entitled 'England to Her Three Daughters, Cambridge, Oxford, Inns of Court, and to All Her Inhabitants' which William Covell appended to his *Polimanteia*, published in 1595, this marginal note is printed:

*All praise worthy. Lucrecia Sweet Shakspeare. Elo- quent Gaueston. Wanton Adonis. Watsons heyre. So well graced Anthonie deserueth immortall praise from the hād of that diuine Lady who like Corinna contēding with Pindarus was oft victorious. Sir Dauid Lynsay. Matilda honorably honored by so sweet a Poē. Diana.* (R2ᵛ–R3ʳ)

It is of course possible that 'All praise worthy' applies to Shakespeare's poem instead of his heroine, but this is rendered unlikely by the form of the name 'Lucrecia' and by the fact that Covell usually is referring to characters rather than works in the rest of this note and in the adjoining portion of the main text, which reads

And vnlesse I erre, (a thing easie in such simplicitie) deluded by dearlie beloued *Delia*, and fortunatelie fortunate *Cleopatra*; *Oxford* thou maist extoll thy courte-deare-verse happie *Daniell*, whose sweete refined muse, in contracted shape, were sufficient amongst men, to gaine pardon of the sinne to *Rose- mond*, pittie to distressed *Cleopatra*, and euerliuing praise to her louing *Delia*: Register your childrens petegree . . .

4. At the end of act 2 of the anonymous play *Edward III* (published in 1596 and usually dated between 1590 and 1595), King Edward abandons his pursuit of the Countess of Salis- bury, having been converted by her heroic de- fence of her honour, and exclaims:

Arise true *English* Ladie, whom our Ile
May better boast of then euer Romaine
    might,
Of her whose ransackt treasurie hath taskt,
The vaine indeuor of so many pens.  (E1ʳ)

If this play was written after the publication of Shakespeare's poem in 1594, then it seems

very likely that his pen is one of those referred to, which would mean that the author thought he had depicted a praiseworthy Lucrece. The passage takes on additional interest when we realize that this author might possibly have been Shakespeare himself, since some critics have argued that he had a hand in this portion of the play. If they are right, we would have here a very authoritative refutation of those ironic readings.

5. This is the fourth and final stanza of Richard Barnfield's 'A Remembrance of Some English Poets', published in 1598 in his *Poems in Divers Humors* (the preceding stanzas are devoted to Spenser, Daniel, and Drayton):

And *Shakespeare* thou, whose hony-flowing
    Vaine,
(Pleasing the World) thy Praises doth obtaine.
Whose *Venus*, and whose *Lucrece* (sweete, and
    chaste)
Thy Name in fames immortal Booke haue plac't.
    Liue euer you, at least in Fame liue euer:
    Well may the Bodye dye, but Fame dies
        neuer.  (E2ᵛ)

Here it is more likely that the adjectives refer to the poem rather than to Lucrece herself, and it should be noted that the second stanza speaks of Daniel's 'sweet-chast Verse'.

6. This is epigram 22 in the fourth section (or 'week') of John Weever's *Epigrams in the Oldest Cut and Newest Fashion*, published in 1599:

Honie-tong'd *Shakespeare*, when I saw thine
    issue,
I swore *Apollo* got them and none other,
Their rosie-tainted features cloth'd in tissue,
Some heauen born goddesse said to be their
    mother:
Rose-checkt *Adonis* with his amber tresses,
Faire fire-hot *Venus* charming him to loue her,
Chaste *Lucretia* virgine-like her dresses,
Prowd lust-stung *Tarquine* seeking still to proue
    her:
*Romea-Richard*; more whose names I know
    not . . .  (E6ʳ)

The sonnet continues for five more lines, which

are not relevant. Here obviously it is Lucrece who is 'Chaste' and 'virgine-like', and who is regarded as the innocent victim of Tarquin.

7. The following stanza appears in the section on 'lewde Lecherie' in *Tom Tell-Troth's Message and His Pen's Complaint* by John Lane, published in 1600:

> VVhen chast *Adonis* came to mans estate,
> *Venus* straight courted him with many a wile;
> *Lucrece* once seene, straight *Tarquine* laid a baite,
> VVith foule incest her bodie to defile:
>    Thus men by women, women wrongde by
>     men,
>    Giue matter still vnto my plaintife pen.   (F2ʳ)

Although Shakespeare is not mentioned, the juxtaposition of the two examples suggests that this is an allusion to his poems, and that it is his Lucrece who, again, is seen as an innocent victim 'wrongde' by Tarquin.

8. In 1603 Henry Chettle wrote *England's Mourning Garment, Worn Here by Plain Shepherds in Memory of Their Sacred Mistress Elizabeth, Queen of Virtue while She Lived, and Theme of Sorrow, Being Dead*, in the course of which he complains that several noted poets (each given a classical pseudonym) have failed to memorialize the death of Elizabeth. The following lines presumably refer to Shakespeare:

> Nor doth the siluer tonged *Melicert*,
> Drop from his honied muse one sable teare
> To mourne her death that graced his desert,
> And to his laies opend her Royall eare.
>    Shepheard remember our *Elizabeth*,
>    And sing her Rape, done by that *Tarquin*,
>    Death.         (D3ʳ)

The analogy, of course, means that Chettle regards Shakespeare's Lucrece, like Elizabeth, as a virtuous and blameless victim.[5]

9. The second stanza of *Saint Mary Magdalene's Conversion* by 'I. C.', published in 1603,[6] reads

> Of *Helens* rape, and *Troyes* beseiged *Towne*,
> Of *Troylus* faith, and *Cressids* falsitie,
> Of *Rychards* stratagems for the english crowne,

> Of *Tarquins* lust, and lucrece chastitie,
> Of these, of none of these my muse nowe
>    treates,
> Of greater conquests, warres, and loues she
>    speakes.        (A3ʳ)

Here (as in item 7) the selection of examples suggests that the passage may be alluding to Shakespeare's *Troilus and Cressida*, *Richard III*, and *The Rape of Lucrece*. If it is, then this is further evidence that his Lucrece was seen as chaste and innocent.

10. This is epigram 92 in *Run, and a Great Cast*, which is the second part (or 'bowl') of Thomas Freeman's *Rub, and a Great Cast*, published in 1614:

> SHakespeare, that nimble *Mercury* thy braine,
> Lulls many hundred *Argus*-eyes asleepe,
> So fit, for all thou fashionest thy vaine,
> At th' *horse-foote* fountaine thou hast drunk full
>    deepe,
> Vertues or vices theame to thee all one is:
> Who loues chaste life, there's *Lucrece* for a
>    Teacher:
> Who list read lust there's *Venus* and *Adonis*,
> True modell of a most lasciuious leatcher . . .
>                (K2ᵛ)

(The remaining six lines of the sonnet are not relevant.) Even if '*Lucrece*' refers to the poem rather than the character, it is obviously the latter who is envisaged as 'Vertues . . . theame' and the 'Teacher' of 'chaste life'.

11 and 12. There are, finally, two other contemporary versions of the Lucrece legend which appear to have been influenced by Shakespeare's poem and which therefore could be regarded, in a sense, as responses to it.

---

5 The metaphor is also used in John Quarles's *The Banishment of Tarquin* (1655), where Collatine says that Lucrece is 'Ravish'd by death, nay, and by *Tarquin* too' (F8ᵛ). Since this poem was written as a continuation of Shakespeare's, and states that his Lucrece represents 'virtue . . . opprest by violence' (F7ᵛ), it could have been cited as further evidence against the ironic readings, although it cannot be called a contemporary response.

6 No place of publication is indicated in this book, which probably comes from a Catholic exile on the Continent.

Thomas Middleton's *The Ghost of Lucrece*, published in 1600, adopts Shakespeare's stanzaic form and takes up the story of Lucrece, in the manner of a continuation, at the point where he left off. And Thomas Heywood's play, *The Rape of Lucrece*, although not published until 1608, may have been written as early as 1594,[7] and may contain some vague echoes of Shakespeare. In both of these works Lucrece is presented as wholly innocent and wholly admirable.[8] This does not, of course, prove that Middleton or Heywood saw Shakespeare's Lucrece in that light, but it would seem more likely than not that they did, if they were in fact influenced by him.

This completes our survey of the evidence. It should be emphasized that I have not simply selected material which supports my thesis. These are *all* the contemporary responses known to us that could possibly shed any light on how Shakespeare's heroine was regarded by his audience. And they all indicate very clearly that she was accepted 'at face value' as a praiseworthy character. There is no evidence that anyone at the time thought that this portrayal of her was 'ironic', or that it was qualified in any way. We should note, moreover, that none of the authors quoted attempts to argue the question; each of them treats this conception of Shakespeare's Lucrece as a well-known fact which is perfectly obvious to him and will be just as obvious to his own readers, as if it had not occurred to him that there could possibly be any other view of her. And this assurance is underscored by the manner in which she is employed in comparisons with other women, both real and fictional, whom the author also regards as models of their sex – the biblical Susanna, Homer's Penelope, Willobie's Avisa, Kyd's Cornelia, Lady Helen Branch, the Countess of Salisbury, and Queen Elizabeth.

What conclusion, then, may be drawn from this survey? Although the number of responses is not very large, we can scarcely suppose that they come from an atypical minority, and that most of Shakespeare's readers actually had a negative impression of Lucrece. Unless there was some special reason (and I cannot

7 The principal evidence for this date is the sixth stanza of Michael Drayton's *Matilda* (published later in 1594), where the heroine complains:

> *Lucrece*, of whom proude Rome hath boasted long,
> Lately reuiu'd to liue another age,
> And here ariu'd to tell of *Tarquins* wrong,
> Her chast deniall, and the Tyrants rage,
> Acting her passions on our stately stage.
> She is remembred, all forgetting me,
> Yet I as fayre and chast, as ere was she.     (B2ʳ)

Allan Holaday claims that this refers to an earlier version of Heywood's play, which was written and produced shortly after the publication of Shakespeare's poem (entered in the Stationers' Register on 9 May), and then revised around 1607. For his arguments on this point and on Heywood's indebtedness to Shakespeare, see his edition of the play in *Illinois Studies in Language and Literature*, 34 (1950), 5–23. (Although Drayton seems to be describing a play, some people have taken the stanza as an allusion to Shakespeare's poem, which would make it another piece of evidence against the ironic critics.)

8 One of the critics we are dealing with tries to prove that Middleton's poem also presents a condemnation of Lucrece, but his argument rests on a few verses wrenched out of context and ignores the body of the poem, as well as Middleton's dedication, which begins '*Castissimo, purissimoque Lucretiae Spiritui*' and ends '*Castissimo Spiritui tuo addictissimus*' ('to the most chaste and most pure spirit of Lucrece . . . in devotion to your most chaste spirit'). In the British Library copy of the first edition of Heywood's play the following lines are written at the end, in a seventeenth-century hand:

> Thus ended is the rape of fayre Lucrece
> Rebuke and shame hath Tarkin, Rome hath peace;
> But though some men commend this Act
>     Lucretian
> She shewd her selfe in't (for all that) no good
>     Christian
> Nay eu'n those men yᵗ seeme to make yᵉ best ont
> Call her a Papish good, no good Protestant.
> Of this opinion Grendon John was the
> Nine and fiftyeth of June one thousand
>     hundred thirty and three.

But Grendon, of course, is not saying that this was the attitude of Heywood's play; he is objecting because it was not. Unlike the ironic critics, he feels no need to reverse the meaning of the work in order to make it conform to his own 'opinion'.

imagine what it could be) why those negative views were never recorded, or why the records of them never survived, the odds against such a possibility are astronomical. We must assume that the responses we have constitute a representative sample, and, therefore, that the overwhelming majority, if not all, of the people for whom Shakespeare was writing found his Lucrece entirely sympathetic and admirable.

If this conclusion is granted, we can proceed to ask how it will bear upon the new ironic readings of *The Rape of Lucrece*. The most obvious result, it seems to me, will be to invalidate the 'historical' dimension of their argument. For their contention that an 'Augustinian perspective' on the poem would have been 'inescapable', and would have determined the 'meaning a man of the Renaissance might find in it', is directly contradicted by our survey, which shows that men of the Renaissance could very easily escape from such a perspective and form a very un-Augustinian judgement of Lucrece. No matter how many respected authorities are cited to establish the existence of this perspective, they can never outweigh the only evidence we have (or are ever likely to get) as to how the poem actually was understood in its own time. Because the ironic readings not only ignore this evidence, but are diametrically opposed to it, they must surrender any claim to historical support. They are in fact antihistorical.

This does not disprove the ironic readings, of course, for it is still possible that Shakespeare meant Lucrece to be antipathetic. But if they are right about this, then I am afraid we would have to conclude that his poem is an utter failure, since, so far as we can tell, it did not convey its intended meaning to the audience for whom it was written. And that is a judgement few ironic critics would care to endorse. They have a way around this, however, a standard gambit of the ironic approach adopted by two of the studies we are concerned with, which is to divide that audience, and hence the poem, into separate components. According to

them, Shakespeare built into *The Rape of Lucrece* a 'double perspective' or 'double understanding': it contains one meaning (variously described as 'outward' or 'overt' or 'superficial' or 'simplistic' or 'literal') which is favourable to Lucrece and is supposed to be taken in by 'surface readers' (or to take them in),[9] and a second meaning ('inner', 'covert', 'deep', 'profound', 'symbolic') which is unfavourable to her and is aimed at 'knowing readers'. And as evidence for this we are given Gabriel Harvey's remark, quoted at the outset, about the 'wiser sort'. The trouble is that Harvey never suggests that the wiser sort interpreted the poem differently from ordinary folk; he simply says that they were pleased by it. But since the authors of the passages in our survey seem to have liked the poem, they should qualify as the wiser sort, by his definition. Indeed they should qualify by anyone's definition, for they all certainly appear to be men of some education and culture, so that a few of them, at least, should have seen this 'inner' meaning, if anyone did. Therefore, whether we accept the ironic critics' division of the audience or deny it, we are forced to the same conclusion: if their reading is correct, then the poem is a failure.

This still does not prove that their reading is incorrect, however, since no evidence drawn from contemporary responses can establish Shakespeare's conception of Lucrece, or any other aspects of his intended meaning. The only way to do that would be to examine the poem itself, and the various devices employed by these critics to turn it on its head – a task I cannot undertake here.[10] But there is another kind of external evidence which might shed some light on his conception, and which is also completely ignored by the

---

9 If this were a play, they would of course be the 'groundlings', who have proved so useful in ironic readings of Shakespeare's other works.

10 I discuss the typical devices of the ironic approach, using other examples, in *New Readings vs. Old Plays: Recent Trends in the Reinterpretation of English Renaissance Drama* (Chicago, 1979), ch. 3.

ironic readings – namely, the references to Lucrece in his other works. One can easily understand why they pass over this evidence, because it, too, directly contradicts their thesis. The canon contains nine such references in all. Two of them, in *Twelfth Night*, do not reveal any particular attitude toward Lucrece (the 'impressure her Lucrece' and the 'Lucrece knife' in 2.5.86, 98),[11] but each of the remaining seven presents an entirely favourable view of her, as either a model of chastity or an innocent victim. Petruchio, enumerating the virtues he claims to find in Kate, says that 'For patience she will prove a second Grissel, / And Roman Lucrece for her chastity' (*The Taming of the Shrew*, 2.1.294–5); and Orlando's poem in praise of Rosalind attributes to her 'Sad Lucretia's modesty' (*As You Like It*, 3.2.142). In *Titus Andronicus* Aaron assures Chiron and Demetrius that 'Lucrece was not more chaste / Than this Lavinia' (2.1.108–9), and both Titus and Marcus compare the rape of Lavinia to that of Lucrece (4.1.64, 91). Macbeth, as he goes to kill Duncan, thinks of 'wither'd murder' that 'thus with his stealthy pace, / With Tarquin's ravishing strides' moves 'towards his design' (*Macbeth*, 2.1.52–5); and Iachimo, emerging from the trunk in Imogen's bedchamber, is reminded that 'Our Tarquin thus / Did softly press the rushes ere he waken'd / The chastity he wounded' (*Cymbeline*, 2.2.12–14). These last comparisons, of course, require us to envisage a Lucrece as guiltless as Lavinia, Duncan, and Imogen.

I think we must be very cautious in applying this type of evidence, since we have no right to assume that the speeches of any given character will embody the author's own attitudes,[12] or, even if they did, that this attitude will remain constant in other kinds of works produced by him at other times. But when we find the same attitude expressed by so many different characters, both sympathetic and antipathetic, in so many different works, covering almost all of his genres and almost the entire span of his writing career, and find no suggestion of any

other attitude anywhere in the canon, then surely we are justified in concluding that it represents Shakespeare's view of Lucrece (and the view he assumed in his audience), and hence that it should also appear in *The Rape of Lucrece*, unless there was some special reason for him to depart from it. Consequently, until the ironic critics come up with such a reason (and, again, I cannot imagine what it might be), we will have to maintain that these references greatly increase the probability that their reading of the poem is wrong. And that seems to be as far as any external evidence can take us.

I think it might be interesting to see what would happen if the ironic readings of Shakespeare's plays were also confronted with this argument from external evidence. The second kind of evidence would not apply to most of them, of course, since we find relatively few references to the characters in plays where they do not appear. In this respect, Lucrece is something of a special case. But we do find many references to the plays scattered throughout the literature of the period, and some of these express a definite view of the major characters. I do not recall seeing any of these references cited by the ironic readings, even by those which claim to be based (as many of them do) upon 'Elizabethan attitudes' or 'ideas of the time'. Like the ironic readings of *The Rape of Lucrece*, they are very generous in quoting from the moral and religious authorities in order to establish the contemporary attitude that they wish to impose on the play, but they never seem to mention the contemporary responses to the play itself, which could

---

11 The edition of Irving Ribner and George Lyman Kittredge (Xerox College Publishing, 1971) is used for quotations and citations.

12 One of our critics quotes the reference to Nestor in *3 Henry VI*, 3.2.188, to prove that 'Shakespeare's own estimate' of him was negative, so that he can use this to score a point against Lucrece (by reinterpreting l. 1401 of the poem); but he never mentions any references to Lucrece herself. Nor does he mention any of the other references to Nestor, some of which are much more positive (e.g. *1 Henry VI*, 2.5.6).

tell us whether or not that attitude actually did affect the audience's conception of the characters and their actions. And I suspect the reason for this silence will turn out to be the embarrassing fact that this kind of external evidence does not corroborate any of these historical claims, or any of the ironic readings of Shakespeare.

# THE UNITY OF 'ROMEO AND JULIET'

## T. J. CRIBB

Dryden thought Mercutio was Shakespeare's rather ill-bred idea of a Gentleman.[1] Coleridge thought he was a man possessing 'all the elements of a Poet'.[2] Between them they may be taken to establish the two poles of preference, the one for the realistic, the other for the poetic, between which criticism has since oscillated. Many critics have settled the dilemma by sacrificing the play, for example Duthie, who agreed with Charlton that 'as a pattern of the idea of tragedy [the play] is a failure'.[3] Such critics excuse it as prentice work and concentrate on deciding whether it is trying to be mainly a medieval tragedy of the stars and Fortune, or a social tragedy, or a tragedy of character. The most sophisticated attempt to reconcile the poetry to the realism in defence of the play's unity is by Nicholas Brooke, who argues: 'The play depends, then, very much on formal patterning, like a sonnet; but explored, criticized, and penetrated, so that the formal surface not only restrains but also reveals the inner experience.'[4] I say 'sophisticated', for the argument, brilliant and illuminating though it is, verges on the sophistical in the way it recruits the play's poetry against itself and so, in the last resort, into the service of a kind of realism. My own view is that the play is indeed a unity, but a unity founded not on 'poetry' as such, whatever that might be, and still less on realism, another vexed term, but on a particular set of values or ideas principally embodied in the lovers, values which may indeed appear to be highly poetical. It is these which are the

source of doubts about the play's responsibility to reality and viability in the theatre.

I can best begin my exposition of these ideas by calling attention to Romeo's language in the balcony scene, the scene to which T. S. Eliot paid remarkable tribute, and to which Harold Mason, seeking to explain the predominance in it of a 'sense of the sacred', has also devoted a sensitive if inconclusive study.[5] Romeo begins:

> But soft, what light through yonder window breaks?
> It is the East, and *Juliet* is the Sun.  (2.2.2–3)

If we follow this image through we find that Romeo associates or actually identifies Juliet once with the moon, once with the stars, four times with the sun, and twice, climactically, with an angel. The effect is of a light shining through darkness with steadily increasing

---

All quotations from *Romeo and Juliet* are taken from the 1599 Second Quarto, ed. Greg (Oxford, 1949), except for 1.4.54–91, where I introduce verse lineation; 2.2.16, where I adopt the First Quarto's *do* instead of *to*; 4.3.58, where I adopt Dr Johnson's emendation; and 5.3.102–3, where I delete the redundant 'I will beleeve' and relineate accordingly.

1 John M. Aden, *The Critical Opinions of John Dryden* (Nashville, 1963), p. 237.
2 R. A. Foakes (ed.), *Coleridge on Shakespeare* (1971), p. 78.
3 G. I. Duthie and J. D. Wilson (eds), *Romeo and Juliet* (Cambridge, 1955), p. xxvi.
4 Nicholas Brooke, *Shakespeare's Early Tragedies* (1973), p. 87.
5 H. A. Mason, *Shakespeare's Tragedies of Love* (1970), pp. 42–55.

splendour. We must remember that in the context of the original performance in an outdoor theatre the play of reference between the audience's reality – day – and the imagined reality of the scene – night – would be peculiarly bewildering and disorienting, and contrived indeed to refer us to another reality beyond both – and that is Juliet. The logic of the syntax works to the same end, for Romeo's references to the sun, the moon, her eyes, the stars, lamps, her cheeks, daylight and darkness, earth and heaven are presented in a subtly confused structure of hypothetical statements, later taken as assumptions for further statements based on them. The subtlety is insidious, for the opening assertion that Juliet is the sun is not maintained, but changes to almost its opposite, as the thought of the moon being lost in the light of the sun makes Romeo think of Juliet's virginity as one of Diana's handmaidens. The idealizing transformation of Juliet is then renewed in:

> Two of the fairest starres in all the heaven,
> Having some busines do entreate her eyes,
> To twinckle in their spheres till they returne
> (2.2.15–17)

and this time Romeo interrupts the fancifulness by his half-question, 'What if her eyes were there, they in her head'. Yet in the very act of dismissing the fancy he creates a new one, which, supported and as it were established by a lengthening of the phrasing, is even more transforming:

> The brightness of her cheek wold shame those stars,
> As day-light doth a lampe, her eyes in heaven,
> Would through the ayrie region streame so bright,
> That birds would sing, and thinke it were not night.        (2.2.19–22)

All is governed by the hypothetical condition, but at the end of the conceit that control is lost sight of and Juliet once again is the sun, transforming and vivifying all nature with her radiance. The cumulative effect of these liber-

ties with logic and metamorphoses of imagery is to pass on us as real what begins as frank hyperbole or mere fancy.

All this is too specific, too insistent and too extraordinary to be encompassed in naturalistic terms, whether of atmosphere and scene-setting or of adolescent psychology. As Nicholas Brooke says of a sequence of images in *Macbeth*, it 'emerges from an acute psychological speech, but transposes into a mode that cannot be accounted for in psychological terms'.[6] When Romeo says that Juliet is the sun, since it is unsatisfactory to take him psychologically or pictorially and clearly impossible to take him literally, what then does he mean? In only one intellectual context do his images become intelligible, his feelings become principled, and his words make sense. Take for instance of that context the following:

> The passion of a lover . . . desires the splendour of the divine light shining through bodies, and is amazed and awed by it . . . Certainly it is not a human passion which frightens them, which seizes and breaks them . . . but that glow of divinity, shining in beautiful bodies, like an image of God, compels lovers to awe, trembling, and reverence.[7]

The speaker is Giovanni Cavalcanti in Ficino's commentary on the *Symposium*. Awe and amazement are a good description of the feelings portrayed and evoked at the climax of Romeo's soliloquy:

> Oh speake againe bright Angel, for thou art
> As glorious to this night being ore my head,
> As is a winged messenger of heaven
> Unto the white upturned wondring eyes,
> Of mortalls that fall backe to gaze on him,
> When he bestrides the lazie puffing Cloudes,
> And sayles upon the bosom of the ayre.
> (2.2.26–32)

Early on in his explanation of the difficult pas-

---

6 Brooke, 'Myth and Naturalism: *Merchant* to *Macbeth*' in Bevington and Halio (eds), *Shakespeare, Pattern of Excelling Nature* (Newark, 1976), p. 141.

7 Sears R. Jayne (trans.), *Marsilio Ficino's Commentary on Plato's 'Symposium'* (Columbia, 1944), p. 140.

sages in Petrarch, Castiglione rather defensively admits that 'Many will say I want to make out that our poet was a Platonist, against his will.'[8] Such an attribution is not what is at issue here. We can rest content that our English poet is a poet and not a philosopher. However, as J. V. Cunningham observed of St Augustine, 'Experience never comes together except when ordered by some principles, implicit or explicit, and the principles are describable.'[9] Since Shakespeare's ordering principles in *Romeo and Juliet* are certainly implicit, the issue is whether or not we find Renaissance Platonism offers a satisfactory explication of the evident features of the play. In the instance before us, the master image of light, the peculiarly ideal nature of the description and the climactic idea of beauty as a theophany are all consistent and meaningful in the terms provided by the passage from Ficino. Analysis couched in purely intellectual terms, however, would omit the main quality, which is the feeling. Edgar Wind pointed out long ago that the distinguishing feature of the attitude to the world that Ficino represents is that the divine may be attained by a *via amoris* that begins in passion.[10] It is true that at the end of the way the world is left behind so that the divine may be contemplated in pure intellection, but this, in its measure of compatibility with traditional *contemptus mundi*, is not the novel feature of the doctrine. What is striking is that the original motive to this progress is love, and love of another, not for another, *eros* not *caritas*. This revaluation of desire is quite explicit. Pico interprets the figure of Janus to mean that some natures can contemplate both intellectual beauty and the corporeal beauty that communicates with it.[11] Indeed, the only way out from the deceptions of matter is 'the amatory life, which by sensible beauties, excites in the soul a remembrance of the intellectual . . . by the flame of love refined into an Angel'.[12] Castiglione, following Plato, presents the same idea in the myth of the two Venuses, the vulgar leading to the heavenly.[13] Such an attitude to life, with its emphasis on

emotion and subjectivity, can be called psychological, but it is a highly spiritualized psychology, combining intense idealism with intense emotion founded on real desire, and such is the quality of feeling demonstrated in Romeo's speeches.

Guided by this peculiar orientation to life we can turn from the language of the soliloquy to Romeo's role in the play and what he represents. In her very interesting monograph on Shakespeare's play in the context of the sonneteers Inge Leimberg has shown how the revaluation of *eros* by the Florentine Academy led to a reinterpretation of classical myths.[14] Hence Bruno can take the goddess Diana to mean the beauty of the world reflecting 'the light shining through the obscurity of matter and so resplendent in the darkness'.[15] Consequently, Actaeon's seeing of Diana naked is not an act of presumption or of reprehensible lust, as it had been interpreted in the moralized Ovids of the Middle Ages, but a theophany achieved by an eager hunter after beauty. His transformation into a deer pursued by his own hounds is not a punishment but an apotheosis, because 'he comes to apprehend that it is himself who necessarily remains captured, absorbed, and united'.[16] To make of love rather

---

8  Giovanni Battista da Castiglione, *I Luoghi Difficili del Petrarcha nuovamente dichiarati* (Venice, 1532), p. 5ʳ.

9  J. V. Cunningham, *Tradition and Poetic Structure* (Denver, 1960), p. 22.

10  Edgar Wind, *Pagan Mysteries of the Renaissance* (rev. edn, 1967), 'Virtue Reconciled with Pleasure', pp. 81–96.

11  Giovanni Pico della Mirandola, *A Platonick Discourse upon Love*, trans. Thomas Stanley (1651), ed. Edmund Gardner (1914), p. 45.

12  *Ibid.*, p. 17.

13  Castiglione, *I Luoghi Difficili*, pp. 44ᵛ–45ʳ.

14  Inge Leimberg, *Shakespeare's 'Romeo und Julia'. Von der Sonnettdichtung zur Liebestragödie* (Munich, 1968). The reinterpretation is shown to have been accomplished by the sonneteers in England by 1590. Daniel's *Complaint of Rosamund* is echoed at 5.3.92–6 and 112–15.

15  Giordano Bruno, *The Heroic Frenzies*, trans. Paul E. Nemmo (Chapel Hill, 1964), p. 225.

16  *Ibid.*, p. 225.

than reason the determining factor in one's account of the world has the natural consequence of making a hero of the lover, and this is what Bruno does with Actaeon. However, although 'there is no man who does not have God within him'[17] yet 'very few are the Actaeons to whom destiny gives the power to contemplate Diana naked'.[18] To judge by his language Romeo would seem to be a member of this elite, the new category of the heroic lover. Previous critics have remarked Shakespeare's originality in taking the unhappy story of the two young lovers as suitable for a serious stage tragedy, but without perceiving the principles and implications.[19] In the context of Renaissance Platonism the lovers and their fate have the dignity of heroes *par excellence*.

Their fate, like Actaeon's, is death, and the manner in which it is presented is as distinctively ideal, emotional and unnaturalistic as their love. Inge Leimberg amply demonstrates from the sources in Ficino and Pico and from the practice of the sonneteers in France and England how widely diffused was the idea that death was a symbol for the highest form of love or, as Edgar Wind has shown, to be identified with love itself. In this latter case it was symbolized by the kiss. Pico comments on Benivieni's poem that 'He who would possess her [the heavenly Venus] more intimately . . . must be separated from the body by the total separation of the second death, and then . . . transfusing their souls into each other by kisses . . . they will unite themselves together in perfection.'[20] This is the meaning of Romeo's final pun: 'O true Appothecary: / Thy drugs are quicke. Thus with a kiss I die' (5.3.120–1). The whole of his speech in the tomb is as surprising in the circumstances as his speech in the garden. It is full of images of light, marriage, triumphs, lanterns, feasts, laughter, lightning, love and beauty, all reminiscent of earlier scenes in the play, particularly the one in which he first met Juliet. This light shines through an opposite series of images of darkness – the death of Paris, the pale flag, Tybalt's

corpse and the palace of night. Like the speech in the balcony scene, the climax to the structure is a kind of theophany. Just as Juliet there became an angel, so here death becomes her lover:

> Ah dear *Juliet*
> Why art thou yet so faire? shall I beleeve
> That unsubstantiall death is amorous,
> And that the leane abhorred monster keepes
> Thee here in darke to be his parramour?
>
> (5.3.101–5)

This grisly medieval version of Pluto would triumph were it not that Romeo proves himself a more heroic lover than Orpheus by going to the extreme of death. The true climax is in Romeo's resolution 'For fear of that I still will stay with thee', and action. Juliet recapitulates the theme, language, and symbolically erotic act in her last words:

> I will kisse thy lips
> Happlie some poyson yet doth hang on them
> To make me dye with a restorative. . .
> O happy dagger
> This is thy sheath, there rust and let me dye.
>
> (5.3.164–6, 169–70)

The effect therefore of the death of the lovers is not one of frustration or accident, but of the triumph of life in death, or of consummation.[21]

So much as this may perhaps be granted readily enough, for it concerns only the lovers

---

17 *Ibid.*, p. 165.

18 *Ibid.*, p. 225.

19 E.g., H. B. Charlton, '*Romeo and Juliet* as Experimental Tragedy', British Academy Shakespeare Lecture (1939); Harry Levin, 'Form and Formality in *Romeo and Juliet*', *Shakespeare Quarterly*, 11 (1960), pp. 3–11; Paul N. Siegel, 'Christianity and the Religion of Love in *Romeo and Juliet*', *Shakespeare Quarterly*, 12 (1961), pp. 371–92.

20 Quoted by Wind, *Pagan Mysteries*, 'Amor as a God of Death', p. 155, n. 7.

21 This is Leimberg's well supported conclusion, in flat contradiction to D. R. C. Marsh, *Passion Lends Them Power* (Manchester, 1976), pp. 83–8.

and their values. It is when one turns to the play as a whole that disagreement is more likely. The most popular interpretations of the tragedy ascribe it either to society or, more commonly, to the stars, and both of these are of course deterministic readings.[22] It is my intention to argue that both are wrong, or at best partial, and I can best show this through an extended study of the role of Tybalt, since he is obviously crucial to the plot. If *Romeo and Juliet* is the tragedy of two young victims of social circumstances, then Tybalt is necessarily the agent of those circumstances. There are numerous objections to such an interpretation. The first is his complete lack of detailed characterization. He consequently offers absolutely no purchase for an attempt to relate him to a social background. Moreover, the feud between the families is explicitly renounced by old Capulet at the feast and Tybalt's rebellion against this prohibition is given no context of social causation beyond his own wilfulness. Again, at no point in the play are we able to connect its personae to any set of relations that could be called social process, however much we make of the realistic detail particularly associated with Capulet's household. Lastly, if the lovers are rebels against an oppressive society of which Tybalt is the voice, then we might expect them to refer to society in general terms, such as we find in *Titus Andronicus* or *Julius Caesar*. Instead, their references to the feud are summary, and in Juliet's famous reflections on Romeo's name the lovers immediately translate family relationships into the more abstract terms of nominalism and realism.[23]

Since the feud is clearly a prominent factor in the action of the play, and Tybalt is clearly a part of it, then we are still to seek a meaning for it, unless it is to be taken as a mere *donnée* of the story, having no tragic meaning in itself. Before accepting so trivializing a reading, let us turn to that other view of the play which sees it as the story of two lovers crossed by the stars. If *Romeo and Juliet* is a tragedy of this kind of

fate, then, again because of his role in the plot, Tybalt must again be its agent. I cannot myself see the play quite in that way, but it does, I think, bring one closer to the truth; accordingly I shall now play devil's advocate for the view that the stars predominate, but, having done so, return to Tybalt, and try to show how his true role rises out of and above this particular pattern of meaning. J. W. Draper long since pointed out that Shakespeare is noticeably at pains to particularize the time of year, day, and days of the week when the events take place. His thoroughgoing astrological reading of the play can in fact be taken even further.[24] Juliet's birthday is on Lammas Eve, that is 31 July, and the play occurs a fortnight and odd days before then. Juliet was therefore born under Leo and the play takes place under Cancer and very likely during the dog-days. According to almanacs of the period the summer period of 23 June to 23 August is associated with youth, fire and yellow choler, which is hot and dry. In July one should avoid lechery, because 'then the braine and the humours are always open' while the dog-days are 'of great daunger and perill'.[25] The other sign governing this season is Virgo and the organs affected by the three signs are the breast, lungs, back, ribs, heart and stomach. Love, violence, misfortune and hot weather are to be expected, therefore, at this period. In this context of medieval–Renaissance natural science the fiery Tybalt

22 E.g., Duthie (ed.), *Romeo and Juliet*; Irving Ribner, '"Then I denie you starres": A Reading of *Romeo and Juliet*' in *Studies in English Renaissance Drama*, ed. J. W. Bennett (New York, 1959); Virgil Whitaker, *The Mirror up to Nature* (San Marino, 1965).

23 See James L. Calderwood, *Shakespearean Metadrama* (Minnesota, 1971), pp. 81–91.

24 J. W. Draper, 'Shakespeare's "Star-Crossed Lovers"', *Review of English Studies*, 15 (1939), pp. 16–34. In contrast Whitaker judges that 'the metaphysics of the play is not particularly sophisticated, and it is nowhere clear whether the stars symbolize blind fate or chance or . . . natural forces', *The Mirror up to Nature*, p. 111.

25 'Erra Pater', *A Prognostication for ever* (n.d., c. 1565), Bodleian Library, Douce A 55(4), Sigs. A7ᵛ, B2ᵛ.

and his 'wilful choler' might perhaps signify the determining influence of the stars, which is indeed Draper's unqualified conclusion.

The fullest commentary on the zodiac which we know Shakespeare read is Barnabie Googe's translation of Palingenius, many phrases from which lodged themselves in his memory.[26] We there find that the book on Cancer or summer begins with a hymn to the sun, the 'starre divine' who 'partes in foure the yeare' and that the book is devoted to the subject of love – Venus, Cupid's rule, fire and social love.[27] The book of Leo asks why so few are wise and finds an answer in the subjection of most men to Nature by confluence of the stars or by genetically transmitted accidents of birth. Book VI moves into Virgo, opens with a grim description of Hell and Death, and deals with the troubles of man's estate, the chief of which is mortality. The three books may therefore be seen as corresponding to the three phases of the play: ardent love, rash error, and death, all presided over by the stars, although if Shakespeare did have such a scheme in mind he would have been conflating an astrological time-scale of four months with his own time-plot of four days. Palingenius lays as much emphasis on material causes as any author we know Shakespeare to have read and this, in addition to his anti-clericalism, may have been a heterodoxy that resulted in *The Zodiake of Life* being placed on the Index. Yet however materialist and determinist some of the arguments, the overall attitude to man's lot is traditional enough, if eclectic in a typically Renaissance way. The three books mentioned all conclude with the mind rising superior to adversity in a fashionably Stoic manner, which is consistent with the concern of the whole work to show how rationality can triumph over ignorance and matter. Thus book IV in fact opens with two hymns to the sun, first as governor of times and seasons and all things engendered in time, and second as source of the holy spirit which inspires the minds of poets to rise to immortal fame beyond time.[28] Simi-

larly, two Venuses are distinguished, one a physical principle determining, for instance, erotic dreams, the other a spiritual principle preserving the world in harmony, like God's love for Creation.[29] There is thus already present in *The Zodiake* an incipient Platonism, as is explicitly avowed in the preface.[30]

Against this background we can perhaps get a clearer view of the parts played by determinism, chance and will in the play. When Romeo exclaims 'O I am fortunes foole' (3.1.141), he realizes that by killing Tybalt he has delivered himself over to a world of consequence and law which he had seemed triumphantly to surmount in his union with Juliet. When he later says 'Then I denie you starres' (5.1.24), he resolves to shake off that yoke by joining Juliet in the tomb. When in act 1 his mind misgives 'Some consequence yet hanging in the stars' (1.4.107) his dream appears to be ironically reversed by his then meeting and falling in love with Juliet, yet the meeting does eventually lead as it happens to the bitter consequence of death. When in act 5 his dreams presage 'some joyful newes at hand' (5.1.2) they seem to be ironically reversed with the news of Juliet's 'death', yet this news does in fact cause him to return from separation and exile to lie with her that night. The marked prophetic symmetry of the two dreams calls attention to the central paradox of the play, that their love is both destiny and choice. It is both presaged, and hence independent of individual will, and embraced, so that in fulfilling their love they rise superior to circumstances, including the stars. Pico expresses this metaphysically when he says that 'Every Creature consists of two

26 See T. W. Baldwin, *William Shakspere's Small Latine and Lesse Greeke*, 2 vols. (Urbana, 1944), vol. 1, pp. 652–81, and John Erskine Hankins, *Shakespeare's Derived Imagery* (Lawrence, 1953), passim.

27 [Marcellus Palingenius Stellatus,] *The Zodiake of Life*, trans. Barnabie Googe, new edn (1588), pp. 40–1.

28 *Ibid.*, p. 41.

29 *Ibid.*, pp. 46–8, Sig. D2ʳ (mispaginated as p. 62).

30 *Ibid.*, π4ʳ.

Natures, Material, the imperfect (which we here understand by Necessity), and Formal, the occasion of perfection' and he makes the same point in mythical terms when he explains that Venus is said to command Fate because 'temporal, corporeal things only are subjected to Fate; the Rational Soul, being incorporeal predominates over it'.[31] A similar paralogical double standard may lie behind the seeming self-contradiction in Palingenius when he proceeds from an emphatic assertion that love is a mystery of destiny to the more mundane proverb that there's no love without luck.[32] Tybalt, then, is an agent not merely of the stars, but of the metaphysical paradoxes which present the lovers both as star-crossed by 'misadventur'd pittious overthrowes' (Prologue, 7) and as heroes of love who triumph over the stars through love itself, for Tybalt is the principle opposite to love: Tybalt is hate.

If we consider his role in the play from this point of view, character and plot unite in meaning. If we see him not as an intrinsically insignificant part of the mechanics of plot but as arising from the principles of the play, then a covert parallel between him and Romeo becomes apparent. He is equally youthful, equally impetuous – Mercutio considers him equally fantastic (2.4.20). The same night and feast that reveal Juliet to Romeo reveal Romeo to Tybalt and he chooses Romeo for his enemy as immediately and absolutely as Romeo chooses Juliet for his love. His voice is insistently counterpointed against that of the lovers. We think of him in the orchard when Juliet tells Romeo the place is death if any of her kinsmen find him there. Directly after the Friar leaves to arrange the marriage we learn of his challenge, and directly after the marriage the challenge is effected. His name alternates bewilderingly with Romeo's as Juliet gathers the news of the duel from the Nurse, and she equivocates with the two names to her mother just after Romeo has left for Mantua. Capulet refers to him in conversation with Paris. Perhaps most striking of all are Juliet's references

as she plucks up courage to take the potion. There are three, all coming after the thoughts of Romeo in the first part of the speech. As her imagination grows more fevered and the relatively ordered syntax disintegrates, he is displaced by Tybalt. 'Where bloudie *Tybalt* yet but greene in earth, /Lies fest'ring in his shrowde' (4.2.42–3) suggests a sinister life in him. A few lines later she thinks she may 'pluck the mangled *Tybalt* from his shrowde' and shortly after that he appears, together with Romeo:

> O looke, me thinks I see my Cozins Ghost,
> Seeking out *Romeo* that did spit his body
> Upon a Rapiers poynt: stay *Tybalt*, stay:
> *Romeo, Romeo, Romeo*, I drinke to thee.
> $$(4.2.55–8)$$

The ghost rises as an hallucination on the realistic psychological basis of her fear, but its role in the scene and its relation to Romeo in the structure of the speech go beyond realism. It is almost as if Romeo were metamorphosed into Tybalt. Juliet's words and action at the end anticipate Romeo's 'Heeres to my Love' (5.3.119) when he drinks the poison in the tomb. There is a further point of resemblance in the startling and unexpected way that Tybalt occurs here too, this time in Romeo's description of Juliet:

> Thou art not conquerd, bewties ensigne yet
> Is crymson in thy lips and in thy cheeks,
> And deaths pale flag is not advanced there.
> *Tybalt* lyest thou there in thy bloudie sheet?
> O what more favour can I do to thee,
> Then with that hand that cut thy youth in
>     twaine,
> To sunder his that was thine enemie?
> Forgive me Couzen.          $$(5.3.94–101)$$

---

31 Pico della Mirandola, *A Platonick Discourse*, pp. 39–40.

32 Palingenius, *The Zodiake of Life*, p. 49. There may be interesting echoes in Romeo's speeches at 2.2.82–4 and 5.3.116–18 of the comparison in this passage between merchant-venturers and lovers when crossed by stars. Muir links Romeo's imagery here to Sidney and (following Whiter) Brooke, in *The Sources of Shakespeare's Plays* (1977), pp. 43–5.

Once Tybalt is dead these continuing references to him cannot be said to further a sense of doom gathering over the lovers' heads; rather, Tybalt's role in the play is akin to that of an image or theme as well as that of an agent or character. The curious association with Romeo weaves plot and poetry together as varying aspects of a single imaginative vision, and the principle uniting both is of course the *discordia concors* of Platonic theology. Bruno explains it psychologically:

The human heart contains two summits, which rise progressively from one root; and in the spiritual sense, from a single passion of the heart proceed the two contraries of hate and love. For Mount Parnassus has two summits rising from one foundation.[33]

Pico explains the same principle in aesthetic terms:

Beauty arises from contrariety, without which is no composition; it being the union of contraries, a friendly enmity, a disagreeing concord. . . . Thus in the Fictions of the Poets, Venus loves Mars: this Beauty cannot subsist without contrariety.[34]

Spenser pictures it iconographically when in the Temple of Venus Concord is mother of the two brothers Love and Hate, Hate the elder but Love the stronger.[35] It is typical of Florentine idealism that it is love which subsumes hate in the end. So the feud, and Tybalt's role as agent of the feud, should be understood ultimately in the context not of social causes, nor even of the stars, but of a metaphysic of opposites that informs both of these secondary causes, and indeed all of the human and natural world. Study of chance, destiny and Tybalt's role in the plotting of the play leads one to reaffirm that the death of the lovers is to be seen as a strange kind of triumph rather than defeat, and their status as a special kind of heroes is also confirmed.

From observation of the strange affinity between Romeo and Tybalt, then, follows the conclusion as to the meaning of Tybalt's role in the play and the subsidiary status of material causes. Once again such an interpretation may

perhaps be conceded, as with the interpretation of Romeo's love, but this time on the ground that Tybalt is, after all, a character who makes relatively little impact on audience or reader. Now this is odd in itself, for there is something wrong about a play that does not make its dramatic emphases coincide with the main lines of its meaning. We are in fact returned to the critical disagreements about the play which were my point of departure, for, apart from Romeo and Juliet themselves, and indeed sometimes despite them, the characters who do make an impact on audiences and readers are surely Mercutio and the Nurse. Indeed, the question now arises as to what such robust realists can possibly have to do with a dramatic poem so idealistically Ficinan. I shall offer an answer to this presently, but, and this is the critical point, it is not necessarily an answer that will convince in the theatre. I am myself convinced of its intellectual coherence and that it answers to Shakespeare's design in this particular play, but that design, by its very supraphysical idealism, goes beyond the inherent possibilities of theatre. An actor playing Romeo has to overcome an audience's sense of mundane reality and the main resource he is given is the power of words; an actor playing Mercutio is given words that happily reinforce that sense of everyday reality. The one strives against natural limitations, the other revels in them – an unequal contest, although a Romeo who manages to win should sweep the board. This dramatic difficulty about the play is not a matter of one or two characters only, for a good deal of the texture of it is essentially realistic and comic.

The play's first scene begins comically with gross punning and although the entry of Tybalt makes a sudden change of tone and tempo, it is resolved in a serio-comic way. Montagues and Capulets slink off with their

---

33 Bruno, *The Heroic Frenzies*, p. 86.
34 Pico della Mirandola, *A Platonick Discourse*, p. 26.
35 Spenser, *The Faerie Queene*, 4.10.31–6.

tails between their legs, very much like re-
buked schoolboys, and it is an easy modulation
from the self-consciously 'moved prince' who
has to shout to get himself heard to old Capulet
asserting his authority over young Tybalt:

What goodman boy, I say he shall, go too,
Am I the master here or you? go too.

(1.5.79–80)

Capulet and his household are the source and
location of a good deal of the comedy in the
play, a comedy that maintains itself not only in
the face of the furious Tybalt, cutting him
down to size, but also against choplogic Juliet in
her 'peevish selfewield harlottry' (4.2.15). All
his servants are comic, from Peter, played by
Will Kemp, to the one who wants the porter to
'let in Susan Grindstone, and Nell, Anthonie
and Potpan' at the same time as the gentlefolk,
to, above all, the Nurse. Outside the household, she is reinforced by Mercutio, and the
two of them supply the mixture of simple
earthiness and cynical obscenity for which the
play is also well known. Each of the two
romantic lovers is pointedly coupled with a
satiric counterpart embodying an attitude remote indeed from lyricism: 'This driveling
love is like a great naturall that runs lolling up
and downe to hide his bable in a hole' (2.4.95–
7). An important part of the play's tone and
atmosphere is determined by domestic
arrangements, bedrooms, adolescent joking,
potmen, nurses, orchard walls, truckle beds,
people sitting up late talking or returning from
parties, cooks, parental tantrums and family
scenes, worms pricked from the lazy fingers of
maids. Proverbs are ready for every occasion
and the busy surface of domestic normality is
confidently maintained, supported in turn by
the novella elements of the plot. The effect of
all this is to set the Romeo and Juliet story, and
also Tybalt's, in a world where Jove laughs at
lovers' perjuries, because they have all happened before and are no more than youth and
sex.

Now it is possible to reconcile all this to the
ideals of the play by a simple reiteration of the
principle that while such things as the stars,
adolescent desire, comic family life and tragic
family feuds do indeed have a standing in the
play, their physicality is ultimately subsumed
in a metaphysic which works in and through
the natural towards the spiritual: *serio ludere*.
Equally simply, however, a sort of Occam's
razor of the theatre automatically applies, for
all these physical elements are, as far as theatre
goes, sufficient in themselves, and do not need
the support of ulterior meanings to be enter-
taining, vivid and moving. Nor is such a view
of the play a case of *Hamlet* without the Prince,
for an audience may well be content to accept
the story of Romeo and Juliet as simply a very
sad and very human one, on a level with what
one might read in the papers. That such a view
is sensational, sentimental and indifferent to
matters of intellectual and aesthetic coherence
need be no obstacle to the play's success in the
theatre. As I now turn, then, to analysis of the
principal comic figures in relation to that aesthetic and intellectual coherence, it should be
understood that it is something which exists at
a poetic level that may not be fully appreciable
on stage. In other words, in this play poet and
playwright are not perfectly united.

It was H. C. Goddard who pointed out the
interesting symmetry between Mercutio, the
Nurse and the Friar as both advisers and opposites to the hero and heroine.[36] Inge Leimberg
takes the idea a good deal further and reveals a
quite elaborate system of parallelisms between
characters, although she leaves her analysis at a
purely formal level.[37] Taking up the analysis
from this point, then, it is easy to see that just
as Mercutio and the Nurse are supplanted as
guides and confidants by the Friar, so he in turn
is abandoned for the Apothecary, and the similarity of function is pointed up by verbal
echoes. The effect of this can only be to divert

---

36 H. C. Goddard, *The Meaning of Shakespeare* (Chicago,
1951), pp. 120–4.
37 Leimberg, 'Romeo und Julia' in *Das englische Drama*,
ed. Dieter Mehl (Düsseldorf, 1970), pp. 60–78.

our attention beyond the characters in themselves and towards the patterns, ironic correspondences and unconscious motives that they represent. Within the Ficinan scheme of things, the physicality of sex is not so much antithetical to ideal intellection as the first crude and yet indispensable impulse towards it. The bawdry for which the play is noted is not so much antithetical to the elevated lyricism for which it is famous as a lower version of the same thing. This was because, as André Chastel says of the arts in general:

The new idea which triumphed through the teaching of Ficino was that of the fundamental unity of all human activity . . ., and this affirmation of an *impulsus* common to all . . . transformed the mental horizons of the age.[38]

Ralegh gives a physical version of the same idea in the preface to his *History of the World* when he says that 'all things worke as they do . . . by an impulsion, which they cannot resist; or by a faculty, infused by the supremest power'.[39] Not everyone was prepared to go much further, or even so far. Burton, for example, sharply separates the perturbing passions from reason and prefers materialist explanations when they are to be had. He nonetheless faithfully reports the more heady and exciting doctrine, quoting Leone Ebreo to the effect that God's beauty 'draws all creatures to it' through the 'habit infused' into them, and he ruefully acknowledges of Eros that all must 'doe homage to him . . . and sacrifice to his altar'.[40]

Now the idea that Shakespeare had to kill Mercutio off to prevent him from stealing the play has proved a popular one ever since Dryden first gave it currency, but against the background of erotic theology we can see that his death has a meaning. His method is to 'be rough with love . . . and you beate love downe' (1.4.27–8) and that is what he does in his famous speech.[41] Strangely, however, the very virtuosity with which he mocks dreams, dreamers and lovers and attempts to belittle them produces the opposite effect. He picks up

a piece of idle superstition or rustic fancy to argue that dreams express merely the preoccupations of the dreamer, but having picked it up he seems unable to let go and the very circumstantiality with which he miniaturizes Queen Mab's state serves to authenticate and establish it. When he moves from charming description of her appearance to reporting her actions as she 'gallops night by night', the wheels begin to take fire from their own motion, the pace quickens, Mab reveals more and more powers, the syntax becomes disordered, and we begin to feel that the fancy embodies something real:

> Sometime she driveth ore a souldiers neck,
> And then dreames he of cutting forrain
>   throates,
> Of breaches, ambuscados, spanish blades:
> Of healths five fadome deepe, and then anon
> Drums in his eare, at which he starts and
>   wakes,
> And being thus frighted, sweares a praier or
>   two,
> And sleeps againe.                    (1.4.82–8)

By this stage we have lost sight of the supposed argument, that men's dreams are merely the twitches of habitual thoughts during sleep. Such an interpretation of our impression of the speech seems as superficial as Theseus's of that other Dream:

> Or in the night, imagining some feare,
> How easie is a bush supposed a Beare?
>                                       (5.1.21–2)

We have already seen that the play espouses the Platonic belief that dreamers may propheti-

---

38 André Chastel, *Marsile Ficin et l'art*, Travaux d'humanisme et renaissance 14 (Geneva and Lille, 1954), p. 61.
39 Ralegh, *The History of the World* (1614), Preface, Sig. C3$^r$.
40 Burton, *The Anatomy of Melancholy*, 'Religious Melancholy', III.4.i.1. and 'Love Melancholy', III.2.v.5.
41 I am encouraged in my reading of this speech by my closeness to the analysis by Brian Gibbons in his new Arden edition (1980), pp. 67–8.

cally dream 'things true' (1.4.53).[42] Mercutio professes a robust disbelief in such claims, yet the racing uncontrolledness of this speech, and the suddenly dashed, veering rhythm of the one following, undermine his position. The Mab he mocks is a domestic, folkloric version of Titania–Diana, goddess of the moon, childbirth and death. It is in *A Midsummer Night's Dream* that Shakespeare gives us English folklore developed on Renaissance principles of comparative mythology, but *Romeo and Juliet* may anticipate it in this, as it is well known for doing in other ways.[43] If Mab is Diana, to whom Mercutio bears unconscious witness through the diminishing-glass of his scepticism, then his conscious intentions are dangerously hubristic. The book of the *Metamorphoses* in which Diana is called Titania is also the book telling the stories of Pentheus, Semele, Narcissus and Actaeon, and Diana is shown to be a jealous goddess.[44] Mercutio's scorn for her mystery is paralleled by his scorn for Tybalt: 'The Pox on such antique lisping affecting phantacies' (2.4.29), and this is a kind of madness. The *pulsus* of the world, then, which exalts the lyrical rhythms of the lovers, also beats in Mercutio's speeches, but dangerously *à travers*. Nicholas Brooke finds a shocking insensitivity when Romeo continues to speak in verse while Mercutio is dying in prose, and from a modern humanistic point of view this may be so.[45] The play, however, is not imagined from that point of view. It is much closer to the analysis of Mercutio offered by its most recent editor, who concludes that it is 'as if some unacknowledged premonition like Romeo's were inducing [his] train of thought'.[46] In its own Platonistic context, how appropriate that he should die in prose and that, according to Robert O. Evans, Mercutio's distinctive figures of speech are chiasmus and anaphora, whereas the characteristic figure for the rest of the play is oxymoron, ironically concealing truth behind apparent contradiction.[47] Mercutio is bound to die. Similarly the Nurse is bound to be excluded from the play's consummation, and excluded in the very definite terms that Juliet uses: 'Auncient damnation' (3.5.235).

Any doubts about Shakespeare's comprehensive espousal of the Ficinan tradition in this particular play may be assuaged by comparing it with two other treatments of the same material, Arthur Brooke's in 1562, Shakespeare's main source, and Luigi Groto's in 1578. Brooke asserts that his purpose is to deter people from yielding to the excesses of passion by showing them the pitiful things that happen to those who do. He therefore represents the lovers as continually torn between the dictates of reason and the impulses of desire. This yields one of the principal interests of the poem, that is, a detailed psychological realism and a touching pathos as the lovers wallow in their conflicting feelings after their successive misfortunes. Brooke, like Fenton later, thus helps to bring England up to date with the interests of the Italian novellas. There is a further conflict between Romeus who, as a man, can sometimes muster a degree of rational self-restraint, and Juliet who, as the weaker vessel, has to be lectured by Romeus: 'Wherfore represse at once, the passions of thy hart'.[48] At the end, Romeus kneels in the tomb and prays to Christ:

---

42 'Dream', *New Catholic Encyclopaedia* (Washington, D.C., 1967), vol. 4, p. 1054b. Marjorie Garber's discussion of *Romeo and Juliet* in *Dream in Shakespeare* (New Haven and London, 1974), does not grasp the issues.

43 See Frank Kermode, 'The Mature Comedies' in *Early Shakespeare*, ed. J. R. Brown and B. Harris, Stratford-upon-Avon Studies, 3 (1961), and Glynne Wickham, *Shakespeare's Dramatic Heritage* (1969), pp. 180–90.

44 Ovid, *Metamorphoses*, III.1.173.

45 Brooke, *Shakespeare's Early Tragedies*, p. 83.

46 Gibbons (ed.), *Romeo and Juliet*, p. 69.

47 Robert O. Evans, *The Osier Cage. Rhetorical Devices in 'Romeo and Juliet'* (Lexington, 1966). See also Leonid Arbusow, *Colores Rhetorici* (Göttingen, 1963), p. 88.

48 Arthur Brooke, *The Tragicall Historye of Romeus and Juliet* in G. Bullough (ed.), *Narrative and Dramatic Sources of Shakespeare*, 8 vols. (1957–75), vol. 1, p. 329, l. 1683.

Take pitty on my sinnefull and my poore afflicted mynde.
For well enough I know, this body is but clay,
Nought but a masse of sinne, to frayle, and subject to decay.[49]

In contrast, Shakespeare introduces Tybalt at the beginning, omits the long complaints to Fortune, and above all discards the rational, moralizing framework to concentrate on the lovers' passion as an end and value in itself. To discard rationality of the moralizing kind as an ultimate criterion was, in the English context, a poet's radical stroke.

Where Brooke's poem is interesting but not informed by any principle grasped comprehensively enough to confer unity on the work, Groto's drama is boring but systematically elaborate. As such it shows what the learned of the age were capable of seeing in the story. The social status of the lovers is elevated to royalty, thus underlining the doctrine of heroic love that the celestial arrow strikes only 'materia alzata ad alto'.[50] The Friar becomes a Magus and the presence of a Chorus shows that the story is to be treated on the level of classical tragedy. The lovers are self-consciously compared with the classical myths of Orpheus, Persephone and Cupid and Psyche, which Shakespeare hauntingly assimilates by subtle echoes. The two forces of love and hate are developed by setting the love story in a city under siege and the Magus gives an exposition of how frequently marriage is the father of war, changing the pipe to the trumpet, invoking Mars instead of Hymen, changing garlands to helmets, and torches to swords – all simultaneously and emblematically present in the tomb scene of Romeo and Juliet. Hadriana dies asserting the union of the lovers in death: 'O stay, husband, that I may follow thee',[51] thus demonstrating the Prologue's equation of the arrow of 'Amor' with the arrow of 'Morte',[52] just as Ronsard had asserted in his final sonnet that 'l'Amour et la Mort n'est qu'une mesme chose'.[53] In sum, Groto's version is academic and frigid, but he does display the meanings his age found in the story and may thus alert us to many details of Shakespeare's treatment.

*Romeo and Juliet*, then, is up-to-date, perhaps even avant-garde in the English theatre of its day. Both in over-all design and local detail it is informed by a 'single energy', which Coleridge detected in his notes on the play but did not follow through in his lectures.[54] To say this is to accept the play on its intellectual, ideal and poetic level. In the physical medium of theatre, concreted in the personalities of actors and responding to an audience in all its humanity, the Ficinan aspirations may well fade in the light of common day, or haunt the play with a sense of the strained and unachieved. This however is not because of something lacking in its design but more because of an excess of purpose, almost an overdetermination of meaning. Those who mislike, for example, the death of Mercutio, or the dismissal of the Nurse, or the unrealistic elevation of the language, should not explain these features as the accidental immaturities of an apprentice writer, but rather fasten their objections on the principles of which the features are consequences. It was a kind of religion and a very unorthodox one. Having strong feelings and principles of his own about such matters, Dr Johnson grasped this in one of his notes, which, thwart and opposite to the yearning beauty of the play though it may be, is of the essence:

Juliet plays most of her pranks under the appearance of religion; perhaps Shakespeare meant to punish her hypocrisy.[55]

---

49 Ibid., p. 354, ll. 2678–80.
50 Luigi Groto, La Hadriana. Tragedia nova (Venice, 1599 edn), p. 6v.
51 Ibid., p. 70r.
52 Ibid., Prologo, p. 5v.
53 Ronsard, Sonnets Pour Hélène, ed. M. Smith (Geneva, 1970), p. 195, cited by Leimberg, Das englische Drama, pp. 73–4.
54 Coleridge, Shakespearean Criticism, ed. T. M. Raysor, 2 vols (1930; repr. 1960), vol. 1, p. 5.
55 Quoted from Johnson on Shakespeare, ed. Arthur Sherbo, 2 vols (New Haven and London, 1968), vol. 2, p. 953.

# NO ABUSE: THE PRINCE AND FALSTAFF IN THE TAVERN SCENES OF 'HENRY IV'

## J. McLAVERTY

Bradley's disquiet at the new King's rejection of Falstaff at the end of 2 *Henry IV*[1] continues to be suggestive because it raises so vividly questions about dramatic presentation and construction. Bradley is constantly bringing us up against the problem of how personal relations in the plays are constituted: How do the Prince and Falstaff communicate? How do we understand their relationship? Does the Prince have any affection for Falstaff? How would such affection be displayed? And alongside these are questions of structure: How is the conclusion prepared for? Which movements in the play culminate in this cruel confrontation? One way of approaching these problems is by looking at those of Bradley's remarks which draw attention to the structure of the plays by suggesting that Shakespeare might have written them differently.

Bradley considers two ways in which Shakespeare might have tried to improve the plays. First, he might have strengthened sympathy for the Prince, or at least have provided him with some protection against charges of coldness and cruelty. This would not have been too difficult because it is obvious where Hal went wrong: 'He ought in honour long ago to have given Sir John to understand that they must say good-bye on the day of his accession' (p. 254). Without such prior communication the rejection is unsatisfactory; with it, we might even have been able to accept the ten-mile banishment: 'These arrangements would not have prevented a satisfactory ending: the

King could have communicated his decision, and Falstaff accepted it, in a private interview rich in humour and merely touched with pathos' (p. 253). Secondly, Shakespeare might have withdrawn sympathy from Falstaff and so made the rejection palatable. As Bradley sees it, he did make some effort to change our feelings towards Falstaff, but the devices he employed were inadequate; he was not willing to 'cloud over Falstaff's humour', and that alone would have done it.

In imagining possible new scenes between the Prince and Falstaff, Bradley is drawing us towards an important point, though he seems unaware of it himself. Towards the end of the essay he acknowledges (really for the first time) that we are dealing with two plays, and that in the second Shakespeare separates the Prince and Falstaff as much as he can: 'In the First Part we constantly see them together; in the Second (it is a remarkable fact) only once before the rejection' (p. 271). The parenthesis, 'it is a remarkable fact', gives him away: it is not something his reading notices. Bradley is unwilling either to regard these two plays as separate dramatic entities,[2] or to treat the scene

---

1 A. C. Bradley, 'The Rejection of Falstaff' in *Oxford Lectures on Poetry* (1909, repr. London, 1950), pp. 247–75.

2 Whatever the relationship between the parts, they clearly constitute two dramatic units. See G. K. Hunter, 'Henry IV and the Elizabethan Two-part Play', *Review of English Studies*, n.s. 5 (1954), 236–48; H. Jenkins, *The Structural Problem in Shakespeare's*

as the essential dramatic unit; instead he tries to fuse the two plays into a single extended narrative. While, in the theatre, the one scene in which Hal and Falstaff meet in Part 2 will build and control the audience's understanding of their relationship, for Bradley it seems chiefly another source of information. He invents more scenes (or toys with them) because that would help to dissolve the distinction between the two plays. He doesn't see that in the second play Shakespeare wrote one Prince–Falstaff scene, and one only, because that was the way to create the right understanding of relations between the Prince and Falstaff.

In Part 1 we regard Hal and Falstaff as intimates, as men whose lives are intertwined, not because of information from other characters or because of tenderness in their conduct towards one another, but because we see them together so often. In all, they appear together in eight scenes, and in four of them they are to be found alone together on stage. There is only one scene of importance in which one appears without the other, and that, significantly, is the scene in which Harry is reconciled with his father (act 3, scene 2). Through these shared scenes their relationship comes to be an important contrasting strand in the structure of the play. The business of their scenes is largely that of the relationship itself; they are not dependent on the introduction of material (such as plots and rebellions) from outside. Together they can generate a dialogue which in its conflicts, harmonies, and rhythms satisfies the audience; and the ease and vitality of their communication sets them apart from the rest of the play, which is riddled with failures of communication (most notably between Hotspur and the King).

The first appearance of the Prince and Falstaff (act 1, scene 2) provides a good example of how Shakespeare focuses on the intimacy between them. The prose medium provides an immediate relaxation from the tensions of the first scene, and we are quickly taken up by the immediacy of response, and the shared language and metaphorical habit which we now encounter. Falstaff's initial question, 'Now, Hal, what time of day is it, lad?', provokes from the Prince a reply which sketches a whole way of life and shows how intimately he is acquainted with it:

What a devil hast thou to do with the time of the day? Unless hours were cups of sack, and minutes capons, and clocks the tongues of bawds, and dials the signs of leaping-houses, and the blessed sun himself a fair hot wench in flame-coloured taffeta, I see no reason why thou shouldst be so superfluous to demand the time of the day.[3]

This is the way Falstaff talks too (repetition of small syntactic units, forced yoking of disparate material – decent and indecent – the final quibble on 'superfluous'), as his following speech shows:

Marry then sweet wag, when thou art king let not us that are squires of the night's body be called thieves of the day's beauty: let us be Diana's foresters, gentlemen of the shade, minions of the moon; and let men say we be men of good government, being governed as the sea is, by our noble and chaste mistress the moon, under whose countenance we steal.                    (1.2.23–9)

Here the yoking asks for acceptance rather than rejection, and the quibbles are more insistent ('good government', 'countenance', 'steal') but the whole set of mental and linguistic habits is shared. Our sense of their relationship, then, depends not so much on what is said as on the interchange, its assurance and rapidity. Paradoxically, it is when the Prince and Falstaff are most in conflict, when they are exchanging abuse, that we are most aware of how close they are and how much they share. In their efforts to

---

'Henry IV' (London, 1956); and Muriel C. Bradbrook, 'King Henry IV' in Stratford Papers on Shakespeare 1965–67, ed. B. A. W. Jackson (Hamilton, 1969), pp. 168–85.

3 The First Part of King Henry IV, ed. A. R. Humphreys, new Arden edition (1960), 1.2.6–12. All references to Henry IV are to this edition and its companion, The Second Part of King Henry IV (1966).

cap insults they reveal their familiarity with, and dependence on, one another. There is a good example in the tavern scene when they engage in a ferocious 'rhyming' of insults.

*Prince*. This sanguine coward, this bed-presser, this horse-back-breaker, this huge hill of flesh, –
*Falstaff*. 'Sblood, you starveling, you eel-skin, you dried neat's-tongue, you bull's-pizzle, you stock-fish . . .                    (2.4.237–44)

It is the tavern scene in the first play which staff arrives and they, so accomplished in the relationship between the Prince and Falstaff. The centre of the scene, the culmination of the Gad's Hill episode, is generated exclusively by the world of Eastcheap and is sustained by Prince–Falstaff dialogue. Moreover, the scene begins and ends with a casual mockery of the action outside it: in its self-confidence and contempt for outsiders it seems temporarily to command the play. At the beginning of the scene, the Prince and Poins tease the drawer, Francis. Some critics have found the episode pointless and distasteful, but the parallel between Francis and Hotspur (whom we have seen with his wife in the previous scene) is clear enough. Both are shown as uncommunicative, obsessed with business, called away from conversation. It is quite natural for the Prince to move directly from Francis to a discussion of Hotspur, ridiculing his defects as a conversationalist. He plans a fuller ridicule when Falstaff arrives and they, so accomplished in the realms of language, can act out a scene between Hotspur and his wife. That small play doesn't materialize (it has in a sense been completed by the Prince already) but we find as a substitute a mockery of the play's next important scene, the confrontation between King and Prince. It is not necessary to analyse the successes of that episode here, but it is worth noting in passing that the Prince does give Falstaff the warning Bradley asks for:

*Falstaff*. . . . Banish plump Jack, and banish all the world.
*Prince*. I do, I will.                    (2.4.473–5)

The father–son relationship which is being satirized finally asserts its strength against that of the comic dialogue.

The confrontation over Gad's Hill at the centre of the scene is in essence a Prince–Falstaff dialogue writ large. The suspense and the repetition which build up the unit have been analysed admirably by Emrys Jones,[4] but it is worth stressing that the comic climax is generated by the interaction between Hal and Falstaff. Falstaff sets the conflict in motion with his opening provocation, 'A plague of all cowards' (2.4.111), and reaps the appropriate insults; he then builds up his story (the men in buckram) in collaboration with Hal, who marks the stages by repeating the numbers (four, seven, eleven) and displays the incredulity to be felt by the audience. This climaxes in a free exchange of insults (part of which I have already quoted), and then the tempo is changed by the Prince, who tells the truth coolly, 'Mark now how a plain tale shall put you down' (2.4.250–1). But even now Falstaff is able to respond in kind; he and the Prince are on a level as he responds, 'I knew ye as well as he that made ye' (2.4.263). I take the tavern scene, therefore, to be the epitome of the presentation of the Prince and Falstaff in Part 1; it is built from their fellowship, their ability to utilize and resolve conflicts through a shared command of language; it shows their verbal facility in command of the world of the play.

I think Shakespeare had this central scene very much in mind when he came to write Part 2. We may recollect the possibilities Bradley thought open to Shakespeare: he might allow the Prince to warn Falstaff, possibly in an intimate and pathetic scene; he might distance these two characters; he might change our feelings for Falstaff by clouding his humour. I hope it is now clear that the first and most important decision was to keep Hal and Falstaff apart; unless they were together the relationship of Part 1 could not be maintained. But,

---

4 *Scenic Form in Shakespeare* (Oxford, 1971), pp. 30–2.

of course, Shakespeare did not keep them completely apart, he allowed them to meet once, and in that one meeting he must have tried to present the audience with whatever understanding of the relationship was necessary. And to do so he chose to write another tavern scene, not, I think, in an attempt to repeat a former triumph, but so that he could define the present relationship against the past.

Before turning to details of the scene, we must notice some general points of structure and atmosphere. In Part 1 the tavern belongs to the Prince: he is there at the beginning and end of the scene; Falstaff arrives late and is sleeping at the end. In Part 2 the tavern is Falstaff's and the Prince arrives late and leaves early; moreover, about three-fifths of the scene is occupied by Falstaff and Pistol with the Hostess and Doll; new comic relationships have been established; Hal is not necessary to the comic world of this scene. In Part 1 we wait for Falstaff, but here we can do without the Prince. The atmosphere of the tavern has changed too. For all their bawdy talk, the Falstaff and Hal of Part 1 occupy an adolescent, pre-sexual world; now we encounter a prostitute, Doll, and a marriageable Hostess. This shift in sexual emphasis, present in the insistent images of corruption in the scene, can be focused on explanations of Falstaff's size: in Part 1 he is fat because of his diet (as the bill found in his pocket confirms), in Part 2 he is diseased, 'You make fat rascals, Mistress Doll' (2.4.41).

In writing the Prince section of the second tavern scene Shakespeare deliberately calls on the knowledge and expectations of an audience which has experienced the first; he deliberately reminds us of the first scene by parallels and echoes. The central episode of the first scene (Gad's Hill) had been planned in advance (Poins tells us that our chief amusement will be the lies the fat rogue will tell at supper), so this episode is planned too: the Prince and Poins are to spy on Doll and Falstaff, disguised as drawers. To remind us of the drawer comedy of Part 1, the Part 2 scene begins with Francis and another drawer in conversation, repeating the arrangements for the plot against Falstaff. Later, at two vital points, Shakespeare brings in echoes of Part 1. When the Prince and Poins step forward to reveal themselves to Falstaff, they do so with Francis's catch-phrase of Part 1:

Falstaff. Some sack, Francis.

Prince.⎫
⎬ [Coming forward] Anon, anon, sir.
Poins. ⎭
(2.4.278–9)

And later, when they are pressing Falstaff about his abuse of the Prince, the Prince says, 'Yea, and you knew me, as you did when you ran away by Gad's Hill' (2.4.303–4). The audience is deliberately invited to consider the attempts to trap Falstaff side by side, and to define the one against the other.

The second tavern scene as a whole is very much concerned with the past, with age, regret, and diminishment of powers. As the relationship between Hal and Falstaff of Part 1 is evoked, we become conscious of how that too has been diminished. The paralleling of the tricks against Falstaff shows what has been lost: shared life, ease of communication, the intimacy which makes abuse innocuous. And through the workings of the scene the audience experiences this change; it expects one sort of comedy (from one sort of relationship) but finds another in its stead. The encounter between the Prince and Falstaff over Gad's Hill depends from the start on conflict and interrogation; but at the start of this episode the Prince is confined to the role of observer. This diminishes to some degree the comic possibilities open to the scene; admittedly Emrys Jones does show how in the duping of Malvolio an interplay between soliloquizer and observers can create an intensely satisfying comic rhythm (pp. 24–7), but here Shakespeare deliberately avoids even that degree of interplay. The Prince and Poins are not allowed to maintain the necessary continuous commentary on Falstaff's conversation because Shakespeare moves him to territory where they will not venture. Although Falstaff begins as we expect by insulting the Prince (fit only for a pantry boy) and Poins (wit as thick as Tewkesbury mustard), he soon moves to describing them in such a way that we become aware of his sense of exclusion from their society of youth and energy.

*Doll.* Why does the Prince love him [Poins] so, then?

*Falstaff.* Because their legs are both of a bigness, and 'a plays at quoits well, and eats conger and fennel, and drinks off candles' ends for flap-dragons, and rides the wild mare with the boys, and jumps upon joint-stools, and swears with a good grace, and wears his boots very smooth like unto the sign of the Leg . . . for the which the Prince admits him: for the Prince himself is such another, the weight of a hair will turn the scales between their avoirdupois. (2.4.240–52)

From this we move to the franker avowals, 'I am old, I am old'. This is comic, but it is a comedy mingled with pathos; it is not what the audience has been led to expect. The passing of time Falstaff discusses has changed his relations with the Prince, and that means a change in the nature of their dramatic interaction.

When the Prince and Poins finally confront Falstaff with his slanders, we still expect a full conflict with a frank exchange of abuse; but we are disappointed. Falstaff will not confront the Prince; he can no longer generate comedy from any antagonism between them. He continually backs away, 'No abuse, Hal, o'mine honour, no abuse' (2.4.310). His escape from the ambush they have mounted this time is to turn back again to Doll, 'I dispraised him before the wicked that the wicked might not fall in love with thee' (2.4.315–17). In Part 1 Falstaff produces a splendid and outrageous falsehood ('I knew ye as well as he that made ye') which caps the dialogue with the Prince and suggests the power of the imagination to transform the whole episode. But on this occasion he is defensive and hesitant; he satisfies neither the Prince nor the audience. He turns towards Doll

because with her he is at his ease; she is his companion now.

As soon as Falstaff has made his excuses, Shakespeare disrupts the scene. In Part 1 a messenger comes from the King but the Prince will not speak to him; instead, Falstaff sends him away. This time the Prince responds to the message immediately by leaving the tavern. His final words to Falstaff (the last before the rejection) are 'Falstaff, good night' (2.4.363). A. R. Humphreys remarks that these are the only civil words he addresses to him throughout the scene, but from my standpoint it is the very civility which chills. We have come a long way from the familiarity of Part 1. This is only the second time in the two plays that he addresses Sir John as 'Falstaff'; in the scenes of intimacy it is nearly always 'Jack'. In an earlier scene the Prince has said to Poins, 'What a disgrace is it to me to remember thy name' (2.2.12–13). 'Falstaff' is a significant step to 'I know thee not, old man' (5.5.47).

I would argue that in the tavern scene of Part 2 Shakespeare does much that Bradley suggests, but he does it with a skill which is essentially dramatic. The comedy is clouded, not by making Falstaff dull, but by removing the conflict and familiarity which characterized it at its brightest. The audience knows that the relationship has changed because it experiences the change as an adjustment from one kind of comedy to another. It is an intimate scene, and in a profound sense Falstaff has learnt that he has lost Hal: his talk to Doll of his isolation, and his inability to confront the Prince, acknowledge it. His greeting of the King at the end of the play, 'God save thy Grace, King Hal, my royal Hal', is foolish and inappropriate; we see it as a gross self-deception.

I should like to conclude by noting one displaced echo. In the first tavern scene we suddenly become aware that it is morning and that the night has been passed in Falstaff's company:

*Sheriff.* Good night, my noble lord.
*Prince.* I think it is good morrow, is it not?

*Sheriff.* Indeed, my lord, I think it be two
  o'clock.                                    (2.4.516–18)

In the second play the tavern scene ends before morning and is followed by the King's soliloquy on sleep. That in turn is followed by this exchange:

*Warwick.* Many good morrows to your Majesty!
*King.* Is it good morrow, lords?
*Warwick.* 'Tis one o'clock and past.    (3.1.32–4)

In passing from the first play to the second, we have moved from the sleeping Falstaff and the tavern to the bedchamber of the sleepless King. It is an essential part of the experience of the play that we understand this as the Prince's movement also. Even if we wish to recapture the warmth and vitality of the past, we cannot; we find the loneliness and responsibilities of kingship instead.

# 'TWELFTH NIGHT': THE EXPERIENCE OF THE AUDIENCE

## RALPH BERRY

Let the claret which Shakespeare drank, as we know, on expense account[1] symbolize the general experience of *Twelfth Night*. The taste of this play has the same tension between sweetness and dryness, which translates easily into the indulgent reveries of the opening and the realities of rain, ageing, and work, in Feste's final song. To analyse this tension is surely the business of criticism. The experience of *Twelfth Night* blends our sense of the title metaphor with the growing magnitude of the joke that goes too far, and with it our grasp of the relation between the gulling and romantic actions. It is a matter of changing expectations, of a modified sense of the initial *données* of the play. *Twelfth Night* is played out, as it were, on a metaphysical revolving stage, which slowly rotates through half a revolution: the profiles that were presented to us at the beginning are not those of the end. The heads remain the same, the presented view is much altered. In the end the audience is asked to revise its judgement, not simply of people, but of a convention, 'festive' comedy itself. And that is bound to be disturbing.

Let us sketch in the initial experience of an audience not closely acquainted with the text. *Twelfth Night* is advertised and known as a comedy; the audience expects to be amused and entertained. At once it encounters a romantic and lovesick Duke. In the second scene an attractive young lady emerges from a shipwreck, who determines to enter the Duke's service. We can see the future there clearly enough. In scene 3 we meet the comics, Sir Toby Belch and Sir Andrew Aguecheek: why, this is the best fooling, when all is done. The form is now clear. A romantic main action, with some comic relief from a bibulous knight, two varieties of fool, and an intolerable bureaucrat who is obviously to be done down. We have it. The play can run on metalled lines into the future.

And for some time yet, there is no need to rethink this position. The revels of act 2, scene 3 will secure the sympathy of the audience, and the great confrontation between Sir Toby and Malvolio does at the time seem like the life-force challenging the powers of repression and sterility: 'Dost thou think, because thou art virtuous, there shall be no more cakes and ale?' As presented, there is no chance of an audience denying this affirmation. (Or critic, one might add. There is an all but universal convention for commentators to stand up and be counted as in favour of cakes and ale.) And if *Twelfth Night* stopped at act 2, scene 3, there would be no need to modify C. L. Barber's view of the matter, 'The festive spirit shows up the kill-joy

---

1 'One quart of sack and one quart of claret wine' is recorded as the refreshment with which Shakespeare entertained the visiting preacher at New Place, and for which he was reimbursed. See S. Schoenbaum, *William Shakespeare: A Compact Documentary Life* (Oxford, 1977), p. 280.
   Citations are to *The Complete Works of Shakespeare*, ed. David Bevington, third edn (Glenview, 1980).

vanity of Malvolio's decorum. The steward shows his limits when he calls misrule "this uncivil rule" . . . Sir Toby uses misrule to show up a careerist.'[2] But that verdict is slowly phased out by the play itself. Not at first: the garden scene is pure delight. Here we yield absolutely to the pleasure of the gulling. One has to stress the point, for in the later stages the ultimate theatrical effect of guilt requires that we should have participated fully in the garden scene. There is a certain moral responsibility, even culpability, which the audience assumes in *Twelfth Night*: I don't think the play can be understood without it.

The scene in which Malvolio makes a fool of himself before Olivia (act 3, scene 4) begins to insinuate unease into the audience's consciousness. It is a scene we have been prepared for, and kept waiting for, and it is an unholy delight; yet the thought is emerging that Malvolio has committed an irreversible *bêtise*. The activities of Sir Toby, Fabian, and Maria begin to look like open sadism, and we may make the subliminal connection between Malvolio and bear-baiting, mentioned earlier (1.3.92, 2.5.8). Sir Toby's 'Come, we'll have him in a dark room and bound' contributes to the unease, and so does its continuation:

My niece is already in the belief that he's mad. We may carry it thus, for our pleasure and his penance, till our very pastime, tir'd out of breath, prompt us to have mercy on him; at which time we will bring the device to the bar and crown thee for a finder of madmen.                                    (3.4.138–43)

The inexorable line of development holds into the cell scene of act 4, scene 2, and however this is played, the audience is now conscious that the affair is much less funny than it was. The joke has been taken too far, and we know it. Let us hold on to that formulation, and cast back to the beginning of the play. The entire construct prepares us for our realization in the later stages. (One cannot point to a precise moment in act 3, or even 4, when the audience becomes aware of its own queasiness; but it

must surely happen.) The hints start, of course, with the title. Twelfth Night is a festival that has already been going on too long. Twelve days and nights of overeating and overdrinking, little or nothing done in the way of useful work: the Elizabethans were not so different from ourselves. By 6 January they were ready enough for one more party, and then back to work. The experience of satiety is confirmed in Orsino's opening words. They stem from a condition, '*If music be the food of love, play on . . .*' that itself indicates an uncertainty about the festive mood. The terms that follow are *excess, surfeiting, appetite may sicken and so die. Enough, no more, 'Tis not so sweet now as it was before.*

This last is the motto-statement, and it should stand not only before the play as a whole but before act 2, scene 3. This scene, more than any other, evokes the experience of Twelfth Night. That is because it is a revel, which goes on too long, and because Sir Toby actually hints at a seasonal festivity in his song 'O' the twelfth day of December' (2.3.84).[3] The opening and closing sections of the scene are worth pausing over. Sir Andrew would clearly be happy to go to bed, but Sir Toby insists on keeping the party going. He is the moving spirit in what is not simply a revel, but rather a revived and maintained revel – against the pressures of those who feel that enough is enough. The scene moves up from the lyric nostalgia of 'O Mistress mine' to the bar-room catch, 'Hold thy peace', and so to the intense climax of the confrontation: it then is stepped down to the lesser excitements of the projected plot, and finally reverts to the mood of the *piano* opening. Bottom is hit, apparently, with Sir Andrew's Chekhovian 'I was adored once too.' A moment's silence, a grunt, then 'Let's

---

2  C. L. Barber, *Shakespeare's Festive Comedy: A Study in Dramatic Form and its Relation to Social Custom* (Princeton, 1959), pp. 249, 251.

3  See John Russell Brown, 'Directions for *Twelfth Night*', in *Shakespeare's Plays in Performance* (Harmondsworth, 1969), pp. 222–34.

to bed, knight.' The scene has ended now, and with it the party? No. Sir Toby, needing more money from Sir Andrew, presses him to send for it; then he changes his mind about going to bed. 'Come, come, I'll go burn some sack, 'tis too late to go to bed now. Come, knight, come, knight.' And those four monosyllables, which seem to symbolize the energy needed to lug a sack of potatoes from a room, close the scene. Who is there who has not shared and understood this episode? Whatever one's temperament, there is a time to move off and to bed. Someone else prefers to stay and keep things going, though the fire has died out of the occasion. It is a fault of taste, this failure to judge the natural life of a party, and someone always commits it.

I put it, then, that Sir Toby's interpretation of the Twelfth Night spirit prepares us for, as it is analogous to, his pursuit of the gulling action. Both impulses spring from the same mind. And this leads us to a concept which we have, I think, to contemplate in this play: the likeableness of the *dramatis personae*.

Likeableness, for obvious reasons, is not a critical concept. It looks like an invitation to the untrammelled subjectivities of all readers and playgoers – an abdication of critical decorum. All the same, we need the term here. That is because Shakespeare, as I view it, sets up a design in which we are to begin by liking certain characters and disliking others, and to end with reversing these judgements.

It is all focused on Sir Toby and Malvolio, though other characters can affect matters marginally. First, let us place Sir Toby, without preconception. I think C. L. Barber's 'gentlemanly liberty incarnate'[4] hopelessly over-romanticized, just as I would think 'parasite' a misleading importation of modern values concerning employment. It is better to take Sir Toby as a dramatized case-history, with the implied caption 'This is the sort of person certain social conditions yield.' Sir Toby is a knight; he has no substance, no land or money;

he lives with and upon his wealthy kinswoman. The order of relationship was familiar and sanctioned. Having no employment, he is endemically short of things to do, and his activities emerge as drinking, the pursuit of practical jokes, spectator sports, conversation. What else could be expected? Sir Toby is gripped by that ennui which is the condition of the unemployed, at all social levels. More, to base any dramatic system of festive values on Sir Toby is self-evidently absurd, for 'holiday' is a meaningless concept save to those who work. Sir Toby does not work, and therefore usurps the values of 'play'.

His revealed characteristics become steadily less appealing. His drunkenness is nicely poised: in act 2, scene 3 it can appear as a tribute to the good life, but in act 1, scene 5 his brief appearance is all but incoherent. (Perhaps the most telling comment on his state is Olivia's 'By mine honour, *half* drunk' (l. 113). What was the finished product like?) Stage drunkenness is always an ambivalent affair, for the sufficient reason that it is in real life. A drunk is funny, an alcoholic is not. The human mind contains diverse views of the matter, and its responses are generally mixed. So in *Twelfth Night*. On the whole, our experience of Sir Toby is in this respect probably analogous to our reception of anyone who, like the immortal Captain Grimes, 'puts in some very plucky work with the elbow': we warm to him more in the earlier than the later stages of the acquaintance.

Sir Toby's other characteristics are similarly disenchanting. His relationship with Sir Andrew emerges as contemptuous and exploitative. The comic glow protects his name for a while, certainly. Ask anyone who said 'Thou hadst need send for more money', and he will probably answer 'Iago', and he will be wrong. It is in the gulling actions that Sir Toby appears at his least appealing. There are two main points here. He pursues the Malvolio

---

4 Barber, *Shakespeare's Festive Comedy*, p. 250.

affair with a relentlessness that is disturbing: 'I would we were well rid of this knavery. If he may be conveniently deliver'd, I would he were, for I am now so far in offence with my niece that I cannot pursue with any safety this sport to the upshot' (4.2.67–71). Not remorse, but fear of the consequences for himself, inhibits 'gentlemanly liberty incarnate' here. No wonder this unattractive little speech is so often cut in performance. The other matter is the gulling of Sir Andrew and the arranged duel between him and Cesario. Here I stress the force of pattern, so often Shakespeare's way of imparting personality and being. One joke is inconclusive; two suggest a mind obsessively addicted to making sport out of others. It comes back to the ennui of the unemployed, and therefore to the social attitudes that condition Sir Toby's cast of mind.

'Art any more than a steward?' Everyone quotes the great tribute to cakes and ale; fewer recall, or perhaps in the audience even register, the words that immediately precede it. The greater quotation drives out the lesser. It is typical of this play's strategy that the reservation is set into the record, before being overtaken by the main tenor of the play's surface statement. Yet the question summarizes much of this play's concerns and tensions. All Shakespeare's plays exhibit some social tensions, if only within the same class. *Twelfth Night*, more than any other comedy of this period, reveals a discreet awareness of these tensions. Three of its personages marry upwards (Sebastian, Viola, Maria), and two seek to (Sir Andrew, Malvolio). This movement upwards is caricatured in Malvolio, but the others demonstrate it too. There is a general blurring of social frontiers in Olivia's household, and this contributes to the friction and resentments of the play. Malvolio is the administrator, formally in charge, and he has to deal with people who are or feel themselves to be socially superior to him. It recalls the resentments that Drake identified years before: 'I must have the

gentleman to haul and draw with the mariner, and the mariners with the gentleman.' These resentments, dramatized most forcefully in the encounters of Malvolio and Sir Toby, are in fact most subtly expressed through Maria.

Maria need not be seen and played as the bouncy, vital soubrette of stage history.[5] Her pattern is one of social resentment, a willingness to stir up trouble for others (while usually exiting rapidly from the scene of the crime), and a remorseless drive towards her postcurtain apotheosis: Lady Belch. (Her route there is charted via the subtextually unimpeachable 'do not think I have wit enough to lie straight in my bed', and whatever the director wants to make of 'Come by and by to my chamber'). With Maria, conversations tend to turn into threats to others. Sir Toby is in trouble; Feste may be fired; Cesario should be shown the door; Malvolio will come; Malvolio is mad. Maria's 'perfectly selfless tact'[6] is invisible to me. As with Sir Toby, we must reach out for a type from the characteristics of the individual. Maria endures the classic ambivalences of the lady-in-waiting, above the servants but not ranking with the great. Who is Maria? 'My niece's chambermaid' is Sir Toby's description, in her presence. It is not what we should term an introduction: Sir Toby is speaking to Sir Andrew, presumably just out of earshot of Maria. The editorial glosses are unanimous in their assurance that 'My niece's chambermaid' means 'lady-in-waiting' or 'lady's maid'. But the *OED* does not confirm this certitude. The fact is that *chambermaid* did also, at this time, mean (as we should expect), 'female servant', roughly the usage of today. Interestingly, the *OED* marks the 'lady's maid' sense of *chambermaid* as obsolete: the latest reference cited is Swift's, in 1719. In other words, the editors limit the word to a sense destined to become historically moribund

---

5 The alternatives need not be confined to the RSC orthodoxy of the 1970s, the presentation of Maria as an elderly spinster.

6 Barber, *Shakespeare's Festive Comedy*, p. 252.

(perhaps, already so), while rejecting a perfectly healthy sense that has survived to our present day. I don't, of course, doubt that the editorial gloss substantially identifies the position Maria holds in Olivia's household. (Olivia herself refers to Maria as 'my gentlewoman', 1.5.160.) I suggest that the 'servant' sense is present, and in Maria's mind; which is why Sir Toby does not speak the word to Maria's face. *Chambermaid* indicates a historic trap, out of which the most socially agile clambered – upwards. Why they should wish to is touched in during act 1, scene 5. Maria receives a deadly thrust from Cesario: her nautically-phrased intervention is met with 'No, good *swabber*, I am to hull here a little longer' (ll. 199–200), after which no more is heard from Maria. *Swabber* is one who swabs down decks – and is therefore pure metaphor – but contains the lingering hint that Maria was engaged in a similar activity, as *chambermaid*. The social insult is all part of what the play identifies as the fluid and shifting lines of social demarcation.[7]

In the collisions of aspiration and resentment Malvolio stands, or seems to stand, for an absurd and affected species of folly. That is the unmistakable verdict that we are required to arrive at in the first half of *Twelfth Night*. Yet the play's strategy is to pivot the *dramatis personae* around on their revolving stage, and the second half is insistent that we reconsider Malvolio. Notoriously, this poses problems for the actor. It is fairly easy to play the Malvolio of the first few scenes; it is fairly easy to play the Malvolio of the later scenes; it is difficult to knit the two halves into a whole, which is one reason why Malvolio is a star part. There are difficulties for the audience, and for the critic, too, since all are engaged in revising a settled position. As we look back on the early scenes, a few obvious points can be ticked off. Malvolio is a charmless and humourless bureaucrat, but honest and able, and Olivia thinks well of him. ('I would not have him miscarry for the half of

my dowry', 3.4.64–5.) It cannot be easy to get Sir Toby to behave – Olivia cannot – and the functional opposition between them slips easily into antagonism. Then, the drinking scene (act 2, scene 3) is presented entirely from the view of the partygoers. We, the audience, are at the party, and we want it to go on. Yet everyone has had the experience of being woken up in the small hours by a crowd of late revellers, and of feeling precisely the rage that Malvolio puts words to (acting on behalf of Olivia, and Malvolio would never lie on a matter like that). That rage is the greater if one needs to get up to *work* – unlike the revellers, who can sleep it off. In the theatre there is only one case, that of the partygoers. In real life there is a quite different case, and our backward glance recognizes it. Malvolio, then, is not the simple anti-life stereotype that he is cast for in act 2, scene 3. But the on-stage case for Malvolio does not emerge until act 4, scene 2.

The cell scene is crucial. On the one side, we begin to detach ourselves from the sustained animosity of Feste, and from the self-interested sadism of Sir Toby. On the other, we recognize a 'different' human being emerging from the darkness. It is a rebirth, almost. I do not wish to support some of the excesses of stage history. Henry Irving, for instance, used to play the scene all out for pathos, with much weeping and an appeal to the 'poor man' response.[8] What happens to Malvolio has nothing to do with pathos. It is a matter of human identity emerging, and it is all in the words. Take, as a simple comparison, Malvolio's opening lines, 'Yes, and shall do, till the pangs of death shake him. Infirmity, that decays the

---

7 These lines are touched again in Sir Toby's advice to Sir Andrew, concerning a socially explosive term: 'If thou thou'st him some thrice, it shall not be amiss' (3.2.43–4).

8 Irving's own prompt copy, now lodged in the Folger Library (call-mark TN, 13), notes 'crying' during the cell scene. Madeleine Bingham states that Irving 'turned comedy into tragedy, especially in the last scenes, where he was deeply tragic', *Henry Irving and The Victorian Theatre* (1978), p. 207.

wise, doth ever make the better fool . . . I marvel your ladyship takes delight in such a barren rascal' (1.5.72–81). It is impossible to speak these lines without giving in some form the impression of an affected dolt. And now take:

I say this house is as dark as ignorance, though ignorance were as dark as hell; and I say there was never man thus abus'd. I am no more mad than you are; make the trial of it in any constant question . . . I think nobly of the soul, and no way approve his opinion. (4.2.46–56)

Unless one strains intolerably against the directions of the words, it is impossible to speak them in the manner and accent of a fool. They express a being of sense, and human worth. The words must be respected, and thus the speaker. Above all, the words express an identity, individual and social.

And what is this identity? It is that of a gentleman. The first phase of the cell scene, the dialogue with Sir Topas, shows Malvolio at bottom. This is the dark night of the soul, the communion with madness and (apparently) clerical imbecility. The second phase, with Feste speaking in his own voice, records Malvolio's struggle out of the pit and towards the light. The themes are communication, relationship, ways and means. Phase two starts with the calls of 'Fool!' (which Feste affects not to hear) and, after 'Who calls, ha?', modulates into 'Good fool'. What follows is decisive:

Good fool, as ever thou wilt deserve well at my hand, help me to a candle, and pen, ink, and paper. As I am a gentleman, I will live to be thankful to thee for't. (ll. 80–3)

The identity which Malvolio discovers for himself in the cell, and which he imparts to us, is the backing for his promise: 'As I am a gentleman.' Not, be it noted, 'steward'. The identity of functional authority is rejected in favour of a term whose core of meaning lies outside, as well as within, social rank. The *OED* does not commit itself to a categorization of Malvolio's word here – neither does Schmidt or Onions –

but I judge sense 3 to be the nearest: 'A man in whom gentle birth is accompanied by appropriate qualities of behaviour; hence, in general, a man of chivalrous instincts and fine feelings.' *Gentleman*, of all social terms, casts the widest net. The word contains the ideas of birth, education, wealth, behaviour, and values; yet it allows no single aspect to dominate, nor can any element insist on its presence. *Gentleman*, that uniquely English invention, is at bottom the principle of 'tolerance' within the social structure, the moving part that takes the strain of fixed relationships.[9] It is also, in dramatic terms, a variable, and it permits a case to be re-opened and the standing of Malvolio to be reconsidered, very late.[10] The term accounts for Malvolio's changed address to the Fool. Malvolio does not offer him a crude bribe, but a form of words that combines the hint of material reward with the understatements of

---

9 Lawrence Stone's chapter on 'The Peerage in Society' contains many illuminating instances of attitudes towards the gentleman (*The Crisis of the Aristocracy 1558–1641* (Oxford, 1965), pp. 21–64). On the blurring of lines, for example, he quotes Philip Stubbes (1583): 'such a confuse mingle mangle of apparell . . . that it is verie hard to know who is noble, who is worshipfull, who is a gentleman, who is not; for you shall have those . . . go daylie in silkes, satens, damasks, taffeties and suchlike, notwithstanding that they be both base by byrthe, meane by estate & servyle by calling. This is a great confusion & a general disorder, God be merciful unto us' (p. 28). But: 'Despite the blurring of the line by the devaluation of the word "gent.", despite the relative ease with which it could be crossed, the division between the gentleman and the rest was basic to Elizabethan society' (p. 50).

10 By coupling the term with Malvolio as late as act 4, scene 2, Shakespeare imparts to the audience that it has got an important judgement wrong on him. Nor can Malvolio's claim be dismissed: it is confirmed explicitly by Viola and Olivia (5.1.274, 277). The insidious force of the revelation is the greater if we consider the word's history in *Twelfth Night*. There are twenty-two references to 'gentleman', more than in any other play in the canon: the term occupies significant space in the play's consciousness. And all sixteen of the references that precede Malvolio's claim are to Cesario. 'Gentleman', then, is dramatically validated by its main illustration: a gentleman is what Cesario is.

courtesy. 'I will live to be thankful to thee for't . . . It shall advantage thee more than ever the bearing of letter did. . . . Fool, I'll requite it to the highest degree.' (4.2.82–3, 111–12, 118) Under all is the implied admission of fellowship with the Fool. Not 'fellow', that socially ambivalent word Malvolio mistook from Olivia, but fellowship, is Malvolio's discovery. The man who would be 'Count Malvolio', fantasy's alternative to 'Steward', now founds himself on the truth of 'gentleman'.

Shakespeare admits the claim, for Malvolio at the end speaks the language of a gentleman. Before his final irruption occurs the intermezzo of the letter. This episode throws some light on the dramatic origins of Fabian. Commentators have often wondered as to the point of this nondescript character, who appears, as few characters in Shakespeare do, to have been less created than manufactured.[11] Of the functional reasons for his existence, the most important that I can detect is his reading of Malvolio's letter. We need Fabian for the same reason that we need a newscaster for news: we require a fairly neutral and objective tone for the delivery of potentially explosive information. By universal assent, a too emotional, personal delivery distracts one's reception of the message. Feste's hatred of Malvolio bars a neutral reading, and he obviously mimics Malvolio's voice; hence Olivia orders Fabian to read the letter. His colourless delivery is exactly the right medium, and the message comes through with undisturbed clarity. Malvolio's deep sense of injury is expressed with both passion and control, and the Duke's comment ratifies its inner decorum: 'This savours not much of distraction.' (This line is a perfectly-formed cell in the structure of the final scene: the aesthete's word, 'savour', confronts a reality outside the world of aesthetic contemplation.) Malvolio's is a well-filed message, and by dramatic convention it is, like almost all letters, expressed in prose.

Hence the way is paved for Malvolio's entry, and his climactic statement of injury. The tone and quality of that last speech are obvious to all. What matters formally is that the speech is in verse. For the first time in the play, Malvolio speaks in the language of the rank to which he had aspired. It is his ultimate irony, that in the moment of humiliation and disgrace he speaks in the tongue of social elevation and human dignity.

That final speech, leading to the appalling 'I'll be reveng'd on the whole pack of you', is the climax of everything that happens in *Twelfth Night*. The experience must be confronted, and neither denied nor indulged. 'Malvolio: a Tragedy' is a sentimentalization of this play. But equally, one is struck by the large number of critics who, on this issue, seem bent on repressing instincts which, outside the theatre of *Twelfth Night*, they would surely admit. I cite a few instances, though my point could easily be illustrated at far greater length. To Joseph Summers, 'Malvolio is, of course, justly punished.'[12] Barbara K. Lewalski concurs in the natural justice of the affair: 'Since he so richly deserves his exposure, and so actively cooperates in bringing it upon himself, there seems little warrant for the critical tears sometimes shed over his harsh treatment and none at all for a semi-tragic rendering of his plight in the "dark house".'[13] For C. L. Barber, Malvolio is 'a kind of foreign body to be expelled by laughter, in Shakespeare's last free-and-easy festive comedy'.[14] Most certainly he is to be expelled, if *Twelfth Night* is a 'free-and-easy festive comedy'; but supposing the intruder belongs in the play, what then?

How can one explain this critical imperviousness to the ending? One comes to view the critics here as a representative sampling of

---

11 Hugh Hunt sees him as 'a second clown – a rival to the ageing Feste', *Old Vic Prefaces* (1954), p. 77.

12 Joseph Summers, 'The Masks of *Twelfth Night*', *University of Kansas City Review*, 22 (1955), 25–32.

13 Barbara K. Lewalski, 'Thematic Patterns in *Twelfth Night*', in *Shakespeare Studies*, 1 (1965), 171.

14 Barber, *Shakespeare's Festive Comedy*, p. 257.

the human mind. They *want*, as we all do, a comedy; they do not want a disturbance to the agreeable mood created in *Twelfth Night*; it is easiest to find a response based on 'Serve Malvolio right: he asked for it: anyway, Olivia and Orsino will do their best to smooth things over.' They seek a formula that helps to suppress the disquiet one inevitably feels. In this they faithfully embody certain tendencies within the mind, and thus – as Shakespeare well knew – of his audience.

Even so, it is a failure of criticism. Hardin Craig catches the essence of the position I have illustrated, commenting that the reading of Malvolio's last line 'is by many modern actors so passionate and revengeful as to spoil the effect of the comedy; this cannot have been Shakespeare's intention'.[15] Precisely: but it is only necessary to extend the thought an inch further, and ask: was it not Shakespeare's intention to 'spoil the effect of the comedy', and was not that the goal to which the entire dramatic enterprise was directed? Why not? Where is it laid down that a dramatist may not build into his design a threat to its own mood?

In the final stages, that threat all but destroys the mood of *Twelfth Night*. The minor action bids to overwhelm the major. The Illyrian world of fulfilled romance, genial comics, and harmless pranks metamorphoses into an image of the real world, with its grainy texture, social frictions, and real pain inflicted upon real people. Malvolio must bear the burden of the real world, as he did its festive release. The disposable person of part one has become the victim of part two, and thus the agent for showing up the festive spirit itself. The Duke's last nine lines exactly measure the play's attempt to pull together the vestiges of the mood of comedy. But this time the party, barring a last song from Feste, is really over. It is balm of a sort, and the audience needs it, for it has to recover from a climax in which it participated, to the origins of which it was privy. It is necessary for the mind's defences to re-group. They have, after all, to deal with shock.

'I'll be reveng'd on the whole pack of you.' The theatrical dimension of the line is all-important, and we need the historical imagination to grasp it. At *pack*, the subliminal metaphor discloses itself. It is a bear-baiting. The audience becomes spectators, Malvolio the bear. The theatrical voltage of the shock is immensely increased if we accept that bear-baiting actually occurred within the same auditorium.[16] It is, however, unnecessary for me to argue here that theatres were 'multi-use auditoria'. The essential point is that the original audience would have witnessed enough bear-baitings, whether in the specific theatre of *Twelfth Night* (Globe), in other theatres such as the Hope, or elsewhere. The connections between theatre, bear-baiting, and festivity were well established.[17] And the awareness of those connections would have governed the audience's experience of Malvolio. So would the delivery of the line. We see a Malvolio who must address his stage tormentors, roughly at

---

15  *The Complete Works of Shakespeare*, ed. Hardin Craig (Glenview, 1951), p. 642.

16  'Probably the variety of the entertainment at the Hope seemed nothing new to Londoners. All London public playhouses appear to have accommodated more miscellaneous spectacle than we are accustomed to associate with theatres, and the bear-garden tradition had long been one of variety.' G. E. Bentley, *The Jacobean and Caroline Stage*, 7 vols. (Oxford, 1941–68), vol. 6, p. 209. Oscar Brownstein views more sceptically the relationship between theatres, and bull- and bear-baiting yards, in 'Why Didn't Burbage Lease the Beargarden? A Conjecture in Comparative Architecture', in *The First Public Playhouse: The Theatre in Shoreditch 1576–1598*, ed. Herbert Berry (Montreal, 1979), pp. 81–96.

17  They govern other variants of the bear metaphor, such as Ursula in *Bartholomew Fair*. Joel Kaplan sees her as 'a roaring ursuline devil, like the comic bear-demons in *Like Will To Like* or *Mucedorus*, particularly at home in Jonson's Hope Theater used on alternate days for stage plays and bear baitings', 'Dramatic and Moral Energy in Ben Jonson's *Bartholomew Fair*', *Renaissance Drama*, n.s. 3 (1970), 144–5. Note also Macbeth's apotheosis as bear:

> They have tied me to a stake; I cannot fly,
> But bear-like I must fight the course.   (5.7.1–2)

right angles to the sight lines of the audience. He is addressing Orsino and company, not us. Imagine a Malvolio in the centre of the platform stage,[18] addressing others downstage: he is surrounded on three (or all) sides by tiers of spectators, who are still perhaps jeering at him, and turns on his heel through at least 180 degrees to take in 'the whole pack of you'. That way the house, not merely the stage company, is identified with the 'pack'. It is theatre as blood sport, theatre that celebrates its own dark origins. That, too, is 'festive' comedy. What the audience makes of its emotions is its own affair. I surmise that the ultimate effect of *Twelfth Night* is to make the audience ashamed of itself.

18 Bernard Beckerman, in his discussion of Globe staging, makes the point that 'without a ranking figure . . . an object of ridicule, accusation, or pity serves as the focal point', *Shakespeare at the Globe 1599–1609* (New York, 1962), p. 171. Whatever the variable geometry of the final grouping, Malvolio must be its focus during his brief appearance, after which it reverts naturally to Orsino – who, among other things, is a metamorphosis of Bear.

# PLAYS AND PLAYING IN 'TWELFTH NIGHT'

KAREN GREIF

'The purpose of playing,' says Hamlet, is 'to hold as 'twere the mirror up to nature: to show virtue her feature, scorn her own image, and the very age and body of the time his form and pressure.'[1] Hamlet himself employs 'playing', in various guises, as a means of penetrating false appearances to uncover hidden truths, but he also discovers how slippery illusions can be when their effects become entangled in the human world. Like *Hamlet*, but in a comic vein, *Twelfth Night* poses questions about 'the purpose of playing' and about whether illusion is perhaps too deeply embedded in human experience to be ever completely separated from reality.

Virtually every character in *Twelfth Night* is either an agent or a victim of illusion, and often a player will assume both these roles: as Viola is an impostor but also a prisoner of her own disguise, or as Sir Toby loses control of the deception he has contrived when he mistakes Sebastian for his twin. Illyria is a world populated by pretenders, which has led one critic to describe the action as 'a dance of maskers . . . for the assumption of the play is that no one is without a mask in the serio-comic business of the pursuit of happiness'.[2] In the course of the story, many of these masks are stripped away or willingly set aside; but illusion itself plays a pivotal yet somewhat ambiguous role in this process. While Viola's masquerade serves to redeem Orsino and Olivia from their romantic fantasies and ends in happiness with the final love-matches, the more negative aspects of de-

ception are exposed in the trick played against Malvolio, which leads only to humiliation and deeper isolation.

Role-playing, deceptions, disguises, and comic manipulations provide the fabric of the entire action. So pervasive is the intermingling of illusion and reality in the play that it becomes impossible at times for the characters to distinguish between the two. This is not simply a case of illusion becoming a simulated version of reality. 'I am not that I play', Viola warns her fellow player (1.5.184); but, as the subtitle suggests, in *Twelfth Night* one discovers that 'what you will' may transform the ordinary shape of reality.

The fluidity of the relationship between 'being' and 'playing' is indirectly illuminated at the beginning of act 3, in the play's single face-to-face encounter between Viola and Feste, who share the distinction of being the only pretenders in Illyria who do not wear their motley in their brains. They match wits in a contest of wordplay, which moves the Fool to sermonize: 'To see this age! A sentence is but a chev'ril glove to a good wit. How quickly the wrong side may be turn'd outward!' (3.1.11–13). According to Feste, words have become like kidskin gloves, pliable outside coverings readily yielding to manipulation by a good wit.

---

1 3.2.20–4. Quotations from Shakespeare are from *The Riverside Shakespeare*, ed. G. Blakemore Evans *et al.* (Boston, 1974).

2 Joseph H. Summers, 'The Masks of *Twelfth Night*', *The University Review*, 22 (1955), 26.

Viola's response echoes this sense; those who know how to play with words 'may quickly make them wanton' (l. 15). Men may expect words to operate as constant symbols of meaning, faithfully reflecting the concrete outlines of reality; but, in fact, words prove to be flighty, untrustworthy mediators between human beings and experience:

*Clown.* But indeed, words are very rascals since bonds disgrac'd them.
*Viola.* Thy reason, man?
*Clown.* Troth, sir, I can yield you none without words, and words are grown so false, I am loath to prove reason with them.          (ll. 20–5)

Rather than serving as a medium for straightforward communication, words have become bent to the purposes of dissembling. Feste declares himself a 'corrupter of words' (l. 36), and throughout the play he demonstrates how chameleon-like words can become in the mouth of an expert dissembler like himself. Yet Feste is also recognized by his audience and many of his fellow players as a kind of truth-teller; under the guise of fooling and ingenious word-play, he reminds those around him of truths they have blocked out of their illusion-bound existences. The Fool's dialogue with Viola suggests that 'since bonds disgrac'd them', words have fallen under suspicion within the world of *Twelfth Night*, at least among those who admit their own dissembling. But for those who possess wit and imagination, the protean nature of words also affords an exhilarating form of release. Dexterity with language becomes a means of circumventing a world that is always shifting its outlines by exploiting that fluidity to the speaker's own advantage.

The same ambiguity that is characteristic of words pervades almost every aspect of human experience in *Twelfth Night*. Illyria is a world of deceptive surfaces, where appearances constantly fluctuate between what is real and what is illusory. Out of the sea, there comes into this unstable society a catalyst in the form of the disguised Viola, who becomes the agent re-quired to free Orsino and Olivia from the bondage of their self-delusions. Equilibrium is finally attained, however, only after the presence of Viola and her separated twin has generated as much error and disturbance as Illyria could possibly contain.

Moreover, this resolution is achieved not by a straightforward injection of realism into this bemused dreamworld, but by further subterfuge. 'Conceal me what I am', Viola entreats the Sea Captain after the shipwreck (1.2.53), setting in motion the twin themes of identity and disguise that motivate so much of the action in *Twelfth Night*. Identity, it is important to bear in mind, includes both the identity that represents the essence of one's being, the 'what I am' that separates one individual from another, and also the identity that makes identical twins alike; and the comedy is concerned with the loss and the recovery of identity in both these senses.

Viola's plan to dissemble her true identity proves to be ironically in keeping with the milieu she has entered. But the fact that Viola, left stranded and unprotected by the wreck, assumes her guise as Cesario in response to a real predicament sets her apart from most of the pretenders already dwelling in Illyria. Surfeiting on fancy, they endlessly fabricate grounds for deceiving others or themselves. Orsino and Olivia are foolish, in part, because it is apparent that the roles of unrequited lover and grief-stricken lady they have chosen for themselves spring more from romantic conceits than from deep feeling or necessity. The games-playing mania of Sir Toby Belch and his cohorts carries to comic extremes the Illyrian penchant for playing make-believe. Just as words, in Sir Toby's hands, are rendered plastic by his Falstaffian talent for making their meaning suit his own convenience, so he manufactures circumstances to fit his will.

The kind of egotism that stamps Sir Toby's perpetual manipulation of words and appearances, or Orsino and Olivia's wilful insistence on their own way, is far removed from

Viola's humility as a role-player. Although she shares Feste's zest for wordplay and improvisation, Viola never deludes herself into believing she has absolute control over either her own part or the actions of her fellow players. Musing over the complications of the love triangle into which her masculine disguise has thrust her, Viola wryly concedes 'O time, thou must untangle this, not I, / It is too hard a knot for me t'untie' (2.2.40–1). Viola's outlook is unaffectedly realistic without the need to reject imaginative possibilities. Her own miraculous escape encourages her to hope her brother has also survived the wreck, but throughout most of the play she must continue to act without any certainty he is still alive. She accepts the facts of her dilemma without self-pity and begins at once to improvise a new, more flexible role for herself in a difficult situation; but she also learns that the freedom playing permits her is only a circumscribed liberty. For as long as the role of Cesario conceals her real identity, Viola is free to move at will through Illyria, but not to reveal her true nature or her love for Orsino.

The first meeting between Cesario and Olivia creates one of the most demanding tests of Viola's ability to improvise. She meets the challenge with ingenuity, but Viola also insists, with deliberate theatricality, on the disparity between her true self and the role that she dissembles:

*Viola.* I can say little more than I have studied, and that question's out of my part. Good gentle one, give me modest assurance if you be the lady of the house, that I may proceed in my speech.
*Olivia.* Are you a comedian?
*Viola.* No, my profound heart; and yet (by the very fangs of malice I swear) I am not that I play.
(1.5.178–84)

In her exchanges with Olivia, Viola is able to treat the part she plays with comic detachment; but the somewhat rueful tone underlying her awareness of the ironies of her relation to Olivia turns to genuine heartache when this separation between her true identity and her

assumed one comes into conflict with her growing love for Orsino.

Unable to reveal her love openly, Viola conjures for Orsino the imaginary history of a sister who

> lov'd a man
> As it might be perhaps, were I a woman,
> I should your lordship. (2.4.107–9)

As long as Orsino clings to his fancied passion for Olivia and she herself holds on to her disguise, Viola can vent her true feelings only by more dissembling, so she masks her secret love for the Duke with the sad tale of this lovelorn sister. Yet her fiction also serves to present her master with a portrait of genuine love against which to measure his own obsession for Olivia. 'Was this not love indeed?' she challenges him:

> We men may say more, swear more, but indeed
> Our shows are more than will; for still we prove
> Much in our vows, but little in our love.
> (ll. 116–18)

Her story is a touching one, and for once Orsino's blustering is stilled. He is moved to wonder 'But died thy sister of her love, my boy?'; but she offers only the cryptic answer 'I am all the daughters of my father's house, / And all the brothers too – and yet I know not' (ll. 119–21). Viola's veiled avowal of her love is perhaps the most delicate blend of imagination and truth in the play, and this fabrication will finally yield its reward when Cesario is free to disclose 'That I am Viola' (5.1.253).

Role-playing, whether it be a deliberate choice like Viola's disguise or the foolish self-delusions that Orsino, Olivia, and Malvolio all practise upon themselves, leads to a general confusion of identity within Illyria. In the second encounter between Olivia and Cesario, this tension between being and playing is given special resonance:

*Olivia.* I prithee tell me what thou think'st of me.
*Viola.* That you do think you are not what you are.

*Olivia.* If I think so, I think the same of you.
*Viola.* Then think you right: I am not what I
am.
*Olivia.* I would you were as I would have you
be.
*Viola.* Would it be better, madam, than I am?
I wish it might, for now I am your fool.

(3.1.138–44)

Like a tonic chord in a musical passage, Viola's riddles always come back to the idea of 'what you are' and 'what I am', the enduring truth of one's real identity. But this note of resolution is never a stable one. Viola warns Olivia that she has deluded herself into acting out fantasies with no basis in reality, first in her vow of celibacy to preserve her grief and then in her pursuit of the unattainable Cesario. In turn, she herself admits that 'I am not what I am.' Olivia, meanwhile, is obsessed with 'what thou think'st of me' and what 'I would have you be'. She is less interested in the truth about Cesario or her own nature than in making what is conform to what she would like it to be. On the one hand, the facts of nature ensure that she will be frustrated in her wooing, and yet her beloved will indeed be transformed into what she would have him be when the counterfeit Cesario is replaced by the real Sebastian.

The compression of so many levels of meaning within this passage suggests how complicated and paradoxical the relationship is in *Twelfth Night* between what actually is and what playing with reality can create. Viola's exchange with Olivia follows directly upon her encounter with Feste, and the second dialogue translates into terms of identity and role-playing the same attitudes towards words appearing in the first. The Fool claims that 'since bonds disgrac'd them', words have no static nature – that no unchanging identification between the-thing-itself and the word symbolizing it is ever possible – and the condition of being, the identity belonging to 'what I am', is in a comparable state of flux throughout most of the action.

The separation between being and playing,

like the disjunction between words and concrete reality, may lead to a sense of disorientation closely akin to madness. This is the condition that the release of imagination creates in Malvolio. When he exchanges the reality of what he is for the make-believe part he dreams of becoming, he begins to act like a madman. Viola's charade as Cesario produces a welter of mistaken identities that so disorient her fellow players no one is quite certain of his or her sanity. Yet another variation of the madness which springs from unleashing the effects of imagination upon reality is seen in the escapades of Sir Toby Belch. His reign of misrule is fuelled by his refusal to allow reality to interfere with his desires, and this unruliness drives his associates to wonder repeatedly if he is mad.

Yet, just as Feste finds means of communicating truth by playing with words, so does the unstable relationship between being and playing allow at least a few of the players in Illyria to discover a more flexible sense of identity that can accommodate both enduring truths and changing appearances. The same loosening of the bonds governing identity that can lead to bewildering confusion may also open up a fresh sense of freedom in shaping one's own nature. What you will may indeed transform what you are.

The point at which all these attitudes converge is in the recognition scene of the final act. At the moment when Viola and Sebastian finally come face to face upon the stage, the climactic note of this motif is sounded in Orsino's exclamation of wonder:

One face, one voice, one habit, and two persons,
A natural perspective, that is and is not!

(5.1.216–17)

For the onlookers, who are still ignorant both of Viola's true identity and of the existence of her twin, the mirror image created by the twins' confrontation seems explicable only as an optical illusion of nature. Yet the illusion proves to be real; this 'natural perspective' is the stable reality underlying the mirage of shifting appearances caused by mistaken identity.

This dramatic revelation of the identity that has been obscured by illusory appearances, but is now made visible in the mirror image of the twins, is deliberately prolonged as Viola and Sebastian exchange their tokens of recognition. Anne Barton has drawn attention to the fact that the recognition scene provides

a happy ending of an extraordinarily schematized and 'playlike' kind. Viola has already had virtual proof, in Act III, that her brother has survived the wreck. They have been separated for only three months. Yet the two of them put each other through a formal, intensely conventional question and answer test that comes straight out of Greek New Comedy.[3]

The recognition of identity is at first an experience involving only the reunited twins; but, as the facts of their kinship are brought forth, the circle of awareness expands to include Orsino and Olivia. They appreciate for the first time their shared folly in desiring the unobtainable and both discover true love in unexpected forms by sharing in the recognition of the twins' identities. As Orsino vows,

If this be so, as yet the glass seems true,
I shall have share in this most happy wrack.

(5.1.265–6)

The reflections of identity that have been present throughout the play are now openly acknowledged and sealed by the bonds of marriage and kinship. The similarities between Viola and Olivia, for example – the lost brother, the unrequited love, the veiled identity – which are echoed in the names that are virtually anagrams, are now confirmed by the ties of sisterhood when each wins the husband she desires.

Paradoxically, what allows this dramatic moment of epiphany[4] to occur at all is the same loss and mistaking of identities that caused the original confusion. It is the separation of the twins and Viola's subsequent decision to 'Con-

ceal me what I am' which gives emotional intensity to the moment when identity is recognized and regained. This final scene, moreover, makes it clear that the regaining of lost personal identity – the individuality that distinguishes Viola from Sebastian – is closely tied to the recognition of the likeness that makes the twins identical. The recognition scene, with its ritual-like ceremony of identification, suggests that men and women must recognize how much they are identical, how much alike in virtues and follies and in experiences and desires, before they can affirm the personal identities that make them unique.[5] These twin senses of identity converge in the final act, dramatically embodied in the reunited twins who share 'One face, one voice, one habit, and two persons'.

But at what point do the reflections stop? Beyond the onlookers upon the stage who behold this ceremony of recognition is the larger audience of the illusion that is *Twelfth Night*. The play itself is 'a natural perspective, that is and is not': a mirror held up to nature intended to reflect the contours of reality and simultaneously a work of imagination that incarnates the world of being in a world of playing. What the audience encounters in the mirror of the play is its own reflected identity

---

3 '"As You Like It" and "Twelfth Night": Shakespeare's Sense of an Ending', in *Shakespearian Comedy*, ed. Malcolm Bradbury and David Palmer, Stratford-upon-Avon Studies, 14 (1972), p. 175.

4 It is relevant to recall that the festival of Twelfth Night, in addition to its popular associations with the holiday release of Misrule festivities, was also a religious celebration of the Feast of Epiphany.

5 Discussing the use of identical twins in *The Comedy of Errors*, Northrop Frye argues: '. . . I feel that one reason for the use of two sets of twins in this play is that identical twins are not really identical (the same person) but merely similar, and when they meet they are delivered, in comic fashion, from the fear of the loss of identity, the primitive horror of the döppelganger which is an element in nearly all forms of insanity, something of which they feel as long as they are being mistaken for each other.' (*A Natural Perspective* (New York, 1965), p. 78)

in the characters who play out their experiences upon the stage. In sharing the experience of *Twelfth Night*, we come to recognize the ties of identity that link our own world of being to the imagined world of the play; and, on a more personal level, we identify our private follies and desires in our fictional counterparts upon the stage. In acknowledging this kinship of resemblance, we too gain a fresh awareness of the nature of 'what I am', the true self concealed beneath the surface level of appearances. Moreover, having witnessed how deeply life is ingrained with illusion within Illyria, we may awake from the dreamworld of the play to wonder if 'what we are' in the world outside the playhouse is perhaps less static and immutable than we once believed. At this point, imagination and truth may begin to merge in our own world: 'Prove true, imagination, O, prove true' (3.4.375).

If art possesses this creative power, however, there remains the problem of dealing with the more troubling issues raised by the gulling of Malvolio. The plot contrived to convince the steward of Olivia's passion for him is enacted with deliberately theatrical overtones, and the conspirators employ deception to feed and then expose Malvolio's folly in much the same way that a playwright manipulates illusion and reality upon the stage. Yet Malvolio's enforced immersion in the world of make-believe in no way reforms him. Nor does it enable him to gain a more positive understanding of either his own identity or the ties that bind him to his fellow men. Malvolio remains isolated and egotistical to the end. What is more, the mockers who have seen their own follies reflected in Malvolio's comic performance are no more altered by the experience than he is.

The plot against Malvolio is originally planned along the traditional lines of Jonsonian 'humour' comedy: the victim's folly is to be exposed and purged by comic ridicule to rid him of his humour. Maria explains the scheme in such terms to her fellow satirists:

. . . it is his grounds of faith that all that look on him love him; and on that vice in him will my revenge find notable cause to work. . . . I know my physic will work with him.    (2.3.151–3; 172–3)

But there is also a strong dose of personal spite in their mockery. The pranksters are really more eager to be entertained by Malvolio's delusions of grandeur than they are to reform him. Maria guarantees her audience that 'If I do not gull him into an ayword, and make him a common recreation, do not think I have wit enough to lie straight in my bed' (ll. 134–7). It is certainly in this spirit that the revellers take the jest. 'If I lose a scruple of this sport', Fabian pledges as the game begins, 'let me be boil'd to death with melancholy' (2.5.2–3).

Maria plants the conspirators in the garden box-tree like spectators at a play, bidding them: 'Observe him, for the love of mockery; for I know this letter will make a contemplative idiot of him' (ll. 18–20). Malvolio, who 'has been yonder i' the sun practising behavior to his own shadow this half hour' (ll. 16–18), is a natural play-actor; and he immediately takes the bait of this improvised comedy. The megalomania suppressed beneath his Puritan façade is comically set free by the discovery of Maria's forged letter, and he is soon persuaded to parade his folly publicly by donning the famous yellow stockings.

Maria's letter cleverly exploits Malvolio's conceit, but he himself manufactures his obsession. With only the flimsiest of clues to lead him on, Malvolio systematically construes every detail of the letter to fuel his newly liberated dreams of greatness, never pausing to consider how ludicrous the message really is:

Why, this is evident to any formal capacity, there is no obstruction in this. And the end – what should that alphabetical position portend? If I could make that resemble something in me!. . . M.O.A.I. This simulation is not as the former; and yet, to crush this a little, it would bow to me, for every one of these letters are in my name.

(ll. 116–20; 139–41)

The deception deftly juggles appearances to prompt Malvolio to his own undoing, but there is always the danger inherent in such games of make-believe that the dupe will no longer be able to cope with reality once his self-fabricated fantasies are stripped away from him. 'Why, thou hast put him in such a dream', Sir Toby laughingly tells Maria, 'that when the image of it leaves him he must run mad' (ll. 193–4). But no such qualms disturb these puppet-masters. When Fabian echoes this warning, Maria replies 'The house will be the quieter' (3.4.134).

Although it is the letter that persuades Malvolio to play out his fantasies in public, his audience has already been treated to a display of his fondness for make-believe. While the conspirators impatiently wait for him to stumble on the letter, Malvolio muses on his dream of becoming the rich and powerful 'Count Malvolio'. As he paints the imaginary scene of Sir Toby's future humiliation and expulsion, the eavesdroppers find themselves unexpectedly drawn into the performance they are watching. Sir Toby, in particular, becomes so enraged at this 'overweening rogue' (l. 29) that Fabian must repeatedly warn him to control his outbursts: 'Nay, patience, or we break the sinews of our plot!' (ll. 75–6). Malvolio's audience prove to be as uncertain as their gull about the boundaries separating fiction from fact, as will be made comically evident in the miscalculations and confusions that result from the duel contrived between Sir Andrew and Cesario. Taken unawares by Malvolio's tableau of future triumph, the three spies inadvertently become participants in the comedy they are observing.

Malvolio's private playlet of revenge and his discovery of the letter are staged in a deliberately theatrical manner, played before the unruly audience of Sir Toby, Sir Andrew, and Fabian. His play-acting exposes Malvolio's folly to comic perfection; but it also, in its own topsy-turvy fashion, holds the mirror up to nature for both the spectators in the box-tree and the audience beyond the stage. It is a glass more like a funhouse mirror than the symmetry of a 'natural perspective', but in Malvolio's absurd performance the pranksters are presented with a comically distorted image of their own follies and delusions. Malvolio's folly is made more ludicrous by the charade that openly exposes the overweening ambition and conceit normally held within respectable bounds by the sanctimonious steward, but the difference between the performer and his audience is simply one of degree.

If Malvolio is treated by these practical jokers as a puppet on a string, a 'trout that must be caught with tickling' (2.5.22), Sir Andrew is no less Sir Toby's own 'dear manikin' (3.2.53). His auditors deride Malvolio's pretensions to his mistress's love; but Sir Andrew's wooing of Olivia is equally preposterous, and his hopes are based entirely on Sir Toby's counterfeit assurances. Sir Toby may ridicule Malvolio's determined efforts to 'crush' the letter's message to accommodate his own desires, but the assertion of imagination over concrete reality is no less a characteristic trait of Sir Toby himself, who has earlier insisted that 'Not to be a-bed after midnight is to be up betimes' (2.3.1–2). The only difference in their dealings with words is that Malvolio uses logic as a crowbar to twist and hammer meanings into a more gratifying form, while Sir Toby chooses to suspend logic altogether. The steward's obsessive instinct for order is simply the inverted image of Sir Toby's own mania for disorder. Even their plot to put an end to Malvolio's authority is dramatized for the spectators in a parody version supplied by Malvolio's own dream of revenge.

The spectators are in their own ways as much drowned in excesses of folly and imagination as their gull. But as they mock the woodcock nearing the gin, the onlookers fail to realize that the 'play' itself is an imaginary snare for the woodcocks in its audience. Sir Andrew's reaction to Malvolio's fictive dialogue with a humbled Sir Toby exemplifies the fatuity of his fellow auditors:

*Malvolio.* 'Besides, you waste the treasure of your
  time with a foolish knight' –
*Andrew.* That's me, I warrant you.
*Malvolio.* 'One Sir Andrew' –
*Andrew.* I knew 'twas I, for many do call me fool.
                    (2.5.77–81)

Sir Andrew makes the correct identification but
remains oblivious to the intended reprimand.
In the same fashion, all the members of Malvolio's audience observe their reflected images in
the mirror of the comedy without recognition,
thus comically fulfilling Jonathan Swift's
famous dictum that 'Satyr is a sort of Glass,
wherein Beholders do generally discover every
body's Face but their own.'[6]

By the time Malvolio encounters Olivia
again after reading her supposed declaration of
love, his perceptions have become completely
mastered by his delusions. To those around
him who are unaware of the deception, Malvolio appears quite mad. 'Why, this is very midsummer madness', (3.4.56) cries Olivia in
response to the incoherent ramblings of this
smiling, cross-gartered apparition. From his
own perspective, however, he is unquestionably
sane, and it is the rest of the world that is
behaving strangely. Unlike Viola or Feste,
Malvolio has no talent for improvisation.
His rejection of a rigidly defined identity,
although it gives him a temporary release
from social bonds, affords Malvolio no room
for flexibility.

Faced with the fluidity of the world of
playing in which he suddenly finds himself,
Malvolio insists on trying to marshal shifting
appearances back into regimented formation:

Why, every thing adheres together, that no dram of
a scruple, no scruple of a scruple, no obstacle, no
incredulous or unsafe circumstance – What can be
said?                   (3.4.78–81)

But Malvolio's efforts to control the flux are
like trying to sculpt water into solid shapes; the
material itself refuses static form. His obstinate insistence that the words and actions of
those around him should conform to his will

makes him appear mad to his fellow players,
while they seem equally insane to him.

The quandary over who is mad and who is
sane becomes even more entangled in the dialogue between the incarcerated steward and the
Fool, disguised as Sir Topas. Malvolio is entirely
just in his charge that 'never was man thus
wrong'd. . . . they have laid me here in
hideous darkness' (4.2.28–30). From his perspective, the darkness is tangible and his madness the fantasy of those around him. Yet it is
also true, as 'Sir Topas' insists, that the darkness is symbolic of the shroud of ignorance and
vanity through which Malvolio views the
world:

*Malvolio.* I am not mad, Sir Topas, I say to you this
  house is dark.
*Clown.* Madman, thou errest. I say there is no darkness but ignorance, in which thou art more
  puzzled than the Egyptians in their fog.
*Malvolio.* I say this house is as dark as ignorance,
  though ignorance were as dark as hell; and I say
  there was never man thus abus'd. I am no more
  mad than you are.           (4.2.40–8)

His 'confessor's' riddles seem designed to
force Malvolio to a new understanding of his
identity as a fallible and often foolish human
being. But 'Sir Topas' is himself a fake – a
self-avowed corrupter of words whose disguised purpose is not to heal Malvolio's imagined lunacy, but to drive him deeper into
madness. Feste juggles words with ease
because he understands that they are 'very
rascals since bonds disgrac'd them', but Malvolio stubbornly insists on making rascal words
behave with as much decorum as he believes
they should. Throughout this scene, Malvolio
returns to his claim 'I am not mad' with the
same tonic emphasis as Viola reverts to 'what I
am' in her dialogue with Olivia (act 3, scene 1).
But being incapable of Viola's playful attitude,
Malvolio rejects any imaginative interpretation of his dilemma.

6 *A Tale of a Tub, With Other Early Works, 1696–1707,*
  ed. Herbert Davis (Oxford, 1957), p. 140.

His rigidity toward both language and experience leaves him incapable of comprehending any truth beyond the concrete limits of reality. 'I tell thee I am as well in my wits as any man in Illyria' (4.2.106–7), Malvolio insists with absolute justice; but how far from madness are the other inhabitants of Illyria? In a very ironic sense, Malvolio gets what he deserves when he is imprisoned in his cell. Having persisted in imposing his arbitrary order upon capricious words and appearances, he is himself confined in a guardhouse for his own caprices.

Whatever his deserts, there is nonetheless considerable justice to Malvolio's charge that he has been much abused by the deceivers who have made him 'the most notorious geck and gull / That e'er invention play'd on' (5.1.343–4). Ironically, Malvolio's absurdly inflated ego and his isolation are only hardened by his satiric treatment. Even in making his defence, Malvolio stubbornly maintains yet another delusion, that Olivia is personally responsible for his torment. Humiliated beyond endurance, Malvolio stalks off the stage with a final ringing assertion of his vanity and alienation: 'I'll be reveng'd on the whole pack of you' (l. 378). Malvolio stands as an isolated figure in a festive world from beginning to end because never once does he honestly perceive his own nature, the true identity of 'what I am', or the corresponding ties of identity that bind him to his fellow players.

The pranksters, in spite of their fondness for 'fellowship', do not fare much better. They have already demonstrated a failure to detect their own follies in Malvolio's pretensions, and it is therefore appropriate that the beguilers as well as their gull should be missing from the witnesses at the recognition scene and the subsequent revelations. Sir Toby, in particular, suffers for his failures of identification. After having challenged Sebastian to a fight in the mistaken belief he was the timorous Cesario, Sir Toby rages onto the stage with a bloody head, angrily spurning the comfort of his friend Sir Andrew: 'Will you help? – an asshead and a coxcomb and a knave, a thin-fac'd knave, a gull!' (5.1.206–7).

Whereas the mistaken identities and role-playing in the romantic plot centring on Viola ultimately lead, in the recognition scene, to a renewal of identity and the human bonds of kinship and marriage, Malvolio's immersion in a world of make-believe yields no such beneficial rewards. The ironic counterpart to the recognition scene with its unravelling of identities is Malvolio's dungeon scene. There, Malvolio is literally enclosed in darkness in a cell cutting him off from all direct human contact, and he is bedevilled by tricksters who would like to drive him into deeper confusion. Nor does his audience there or in the garden scene gain any greater insight into their own characters. This failure of imagination, set against Viola's own miraculous success, reflects ironically on the supposedly therapeutic value of 'playing' and the dubious morality of the would-be satirists as much as it does on Malvolio's own recalcitrance. Malvolio's final words and his incensed departure add a discordant note to the gracefully orchestrated harmonies of the final act.

Malvolio's response to his comic purgatory stirs unresolved questions about the value of playing with reality. Whereas Viola's part in the comedy reveals how the release that playing allows can lead to a renewed sense of identity and human bonds, Malvolio's role exposes the other side of the coin, the realm in which release of imagination leads only to greater isolation and imperception. Fabian's jest about Malvolio's absurd play-acting, 'If this were play'd upon a stage now, I could condemn it as an improbable fiction' (3.4.127–8), like the theatrical overtones of Viola's improvisations and the playlike quality of the recognition scene, deliberately opens up the vistas of the play by reminding us that we are witnesses of a play, 'a natural perspective, that is and is not'. But amusing as Malvolio's surrender to playing is, it raises the most disturbing questions in the play. Can men, in fact, ever perfectly distinguish what is real from what is imagined or intentionally spurious? Can they ever come to know the truth about themselves, the identity appearances have concealed from them?

*Twelfth Night* itself offers no pat solutions. In a comic world devoted to playing and yet mirroring the actual world of being, in which identities are both mistaken and revealed, in which deception can both conceal truths and expose them, and in which bonds have disgraced the words on which men are depen-

dent for communication, no permanent resolution of these ambiguities is ever possible. Shakespeare himself shrugs off the task of providing any final illumination with delightful finesse. As the play draws to a close with Feste's epilogue song and the world of playing begins to dissolve back into the world of being, the Fool concludes:

> A great while ago the world begun,
>   With hey ho, the wind and the rain,
> But that's all one, our play is done,
>   And we'll strive to please you every
>     day.

# SCEPTICAL VISIONS: SHAKESPEARE'S TRAGEDIES AND JONSON'S COMEDIES

RUSS McDONALD

Two masters of the stage, writing mostly for the same actors and the same audience, achieving their full artistic powers in the same decade in the greatest age of English drama, would seem to invite, even to demand, simultaneous consideration.[1] But received opinion holds that Shakespeare and Jonson resist comparison, that the search for resemblance is a waste of time. The disposition of authors in the normal university English curriculum reflects the conventional point of view: Shakespeare is given one course, 'contemporaries of Shakespeare' another. Modern reluctance to consider their work together is probably a function of the clumsy, tendentious way such comparisons have been conducted in the past. Dryden innocently established the terms of discourse when he confessed that he admired Jonson but loved Shakespeare, and since then, particularly in the first half of this century, Jonson has frequently been called in merely as evidence of the superior artistry and especially the deeper humanity of Shakespeare. The manifest impropriety of this practice seems to have generated a powerful backlash against outright comparison: most critics hesitate to put the two playwrights side by side, and some proclaim openly the perils of doing so. Gabriele Bernhard Jackson's excellent study of Jonson contains only two references to Shakespeare, one of them devoted to the posting of such a notice: 'Jonson has had much to bear from critics irresistibly tempted to set him against his greatest contemporary. . . . Apart from date, however, there is very little similarity in the intention or achievements of their work to make such comparisons fruitful.'[2] Hers is an admirable summary of the commonplace I wish to dispute.

---

1 Since this topic is usually considered unworthy of attention, comment is sparse. In searching for statements of the traditional view, one can do little more than select a sentence from this author or that. George Parfitt, for example, asserts that Jonson is Shakespeare's greatest contemporary but 'the most consistently unlike Shakespeare in dramatic method'. *Ben Jonson: Public Poet and Private Man* (1976), p. 132. The attitude expressed by David L. Frost in the opening chapter of *The School of Shakespeare: The Influence of Shakespeare on English Drama 1600–1642* (Cambridge, 1968) is representative: insulted at the suggestion that Jonson could have been considered more important than Shakespeare in the seventeenth century, Frost attacks G. E. Bentley's study of allusions to both playwrights and then dismisses Jonson from his own analysis of Shakespeare's influence with the remark that 'their activities were not parallel' (p. 20). Maurice Charney offered to investigate the topic in 'Shakespeare – and the Others', *Shakespeare Quarterly*, 30 (1979), 325–42. He begins with some of the same observations that I do, although we part company in our approach to the subject. I should add, in claiming that these plays were written mostly for the same audience, that two of them, *Epicoene* and *Bartholomew Fair*, were not written for the King's Men.

2 *Vision and Judgment in Ben Jonson's Drama*, Yale Studies in English, 166 (New Haven, 1968), p. 93. Peter G. Phialas takes a similar stand concerning the two playwrights' comedies, insisting that Shakespeare and Jonson adopt different methods in order to 'dramatize two different responses to the human situation'. See 'Comic Truth in Shakespeare and Jonson', *South Atlantic Quarterly*, 62 (1963), 80.

131

Comparative study of Shakespeare and Jonson has fallen into disrepute because it has produced few significant insights, a failure attributable to the narrow focus employed. Investigation is normally confined to the comedies, particularly to the definition of two distinct comic modes and to the articulation of differences in artistic aims and effects. Once it has been established that Shakespearian comedy is typically romantic, gentle, and reassuring, Jonsonian comedy critical, hortatory, and pessimistic, little remains to be said. Although the rigidity of this schematization and the firmness with which it has taken hold are open to question – and some such questions have been raised – the accuracy of its principal tenets is unexceptionable. Evidence of difference overwhelmingly asserts itself; few resemblances are to be found in comic subject, method, or vision. The topic is abandoned.

We will do better to examine Jonson's great comedies and Shakespeare's major tragedies under the same lens. It is true that the obvious distinctions, most of them a function of the differences in mode, are initially formidable. Shakespeare dramatizes weighty historical subjects, while Jonson is original, topical, and 'modern'. At the same time there is the matter of Jonson's ancient allegiances, his devotion to the classical conventions in which Shakespeare exhibited little interest. Jonson's early practice seems to have given to his major middle plays a residual satiric tone, a quality absent from Shakespearian tragedy. The dramatic effects sought by the two playwrights often differ radically, particularly their manipulation of sympathy, irony, suspense, and distance. Finally, Jonson's self-proclaimed didactic impulses seem to sharpen the distinction between him and his less hortatory rival. But with generic considerations taken for granted, this fresh perspective on the comedies of one and tragedies of the other reveals visions of human experience that are arrestingly similar.

Herschel Baker, in summarizing the 'new philosophy' of the seventeenth century, speaks of its two principal forms, 'Baconian empiricism' and Cartesian 'mechanical philosophy': 'as strategies for interpreting man's place in nature both were radically incompatible with the sacramental view of nature which the Renaissance had inherited from the Middle Ages, and both resulted from the fracturing of that uneasy synthesis which had subsumed the tradition of Christian humanism.'[3] Jonson and Shakespeare were witnesses, and their greatest works testify, to the first stages of this collapse. The death of Elizabeth – chronologically appropriate as a monument to the dissolution of Elizabethan optimism, authority, and rationalism – also roughly marks the emergence of a new and darker vision in the work of the two greatest playwrights of the day. Gone are the confident progressivism of Shakespearian romantic comedy and the sense of corrigibility implicit in Jonson's comical satires. The visions that displace them reflect the tensions of the philosophical transition, but they are similarly negative, and the central feature of each is the inevitability of human error, limitation, and failure.

The most telling way to compare these visions is to study the authors' visionary characters, those figures whose conflicts with the world lead them to imagine 'a world elsewhere'. It is unusual, certainly, to link such characters as Othello, Antony, Lear, Coriolanus, Hamlet, and Macbeth with Volpone, Morose, Sir Epicure Mammon, and Zeal-of-the-Land Busy, and yet these memorable figures share certain fundamental traits: they are imaginative, solipsistic, inflexible, larger than life. The better lives they envisage, for all the variations in detail, are similarly impressive and unattainable. The worlds they seek to alter or escape are likewise of a piece. In each of the plays containing such a character, his conception of an ideal underscores the im-

---

3 *The Wars of Truth: Studies in the Decay of Christian Humanism in the Earlier Seventeenth Century* (Cambridge, Mass., 1952), pp. 354–5.

perfection of the actual against which the ideal is set. The attitude of each playwright toward this collision between a harmonious vision and a corrupt world produces the two kinds of dramatic action: Shakespeare regards the clash as tragic, while Jonson conceives of it comically.

What is even more interesting, however, is the ambivalence that both authors display toward their imaginists' visions. Shakespeare, although insisting finally upon the impossibility of attaining such an ideal, emphasizes its beauties. Jonson, admitting the potential attractions of another world, firmly repudiates the fool who clings to it. Yet Jonson portrays the unreal world in highly sensual terms, even lingering over its seductive beauties, and Shakespeare fiercely destroys any hope of sustaining the ideal. Beauty and grandeur may be found in the fantasies of a mad knight, folly and delusion in the dreams of a sensitive prince. Investigation of these visions, characters' and creators', will reveal the near connections between the tragic and the ridiculous, between the sublime and the absurd, between human heroism and foolishness. Critics have often wished for, or thought that there ought to be, a kinship between Shakespeare and Jonson. This essay suggests that there is.

The major characters in Jonson's comedies and Shakespeare's tragedies are created on a similarly grand scale. All are magnificent creatures, superb in their strength or error or folly. The 'greatness' of the Shakespearian hero, so familiar that it hardly requires additional comment, is a property he shares with all genuinely tragic figures, especially those of contemporary playwrights: Tamburlaine, Faustus, Bussy D'Ambois, and the Duchess of Malfi. Jonson created his two great villains, Sejanus and Catiline, according to similar proportions. Such tragic magnitude has its comic equivalent in the enormous scale on which Jonson's rogues and fools exhibit their wit or folly or delusion. If Othello is larger than life, then so is Sir Epicure Mammon. Although Jonsonian comedy does not focus, as does Shakespearian tragedy, upon the experience of a single great personage, it nevertheless presents certain grand figures, such as Volpone and Busy, who stand out from the rest of the *dramatis personae* and who compel our attention by virtue of their elaborate speech, forceful personality, obsession, solipsism, or intransigence. In short, they attract notice for many of the same reasons that the Shakespearian hero fascinates his audience. In them, Jonson depicts trickery or foolery on a heroic scale.

Shakespeare's most effective means of signifying a heroic nature is the idiom he creates for his protagonist. Each speaks a language that is expansive, hyperbolic, and immediately identifiable.

> Let Rome in Tiber melt, and the wide arch
> Of the ranged empire fall! Here is my space.
> Kingdoms are clay.
> (*Antony and Cleopatra*, 1.1.33–5)[4]

Antony's declaration is representative of the grand style. And though each figure exhibits particular verbal turns that individualize him and reflect his distinctive nature, such as Othello's exotic diction or Lear's propensity to curse, the heroic voice is common to all. The vocabulary, rhythms, syntax, and sound indicate strength of will and breadth of vision. Maynard Mack goes to the heart of the matter when he identifies the tragic hero as an 'overstater'.[5] So familiar is this idiom that detailed description or illustration would be

---

4 I quote throughout from *The Complete Pelican Shakespeare*, gen. ed. Alfred B. Harbage (Baltimore, 1969).

5 'The Jacobean Shakespeare: Some Observations on the Construction of the Tragedies', in *Jacobean Theatre*, ed. John Russell Brown and Bernard Harris, Stratford-upon-Avon Studies, 1 (London, 1960; New York, 1967), p. 13. On the same subject, see Madeleine Doran, *Shakespeare's Dramatic Language* (Madison, 1976), especially the chapter entitled 'The Language of Hyperbole in *Antony and Cleopatra*', where she discusses the connection between Antony's language and his 'large and generous imagination' (p. 155).

superfluous: it is a style that we tend to think of as distinctively Shakespearian and distinctively tragic.

And yet Jonson is capable of writing in Ercles' vein. Morose rises to it: 'O, the sea breakes in upon me! another floud! an inundation! I shall be orewhelm'd with noise. It beates already at my shores. I feele an earthquake in my selfe, for't' (*Epicoene*, 3.6.2–5).[6] At an especially calamitous moment Mosca also overstates:

> if my heart
> Could expiate the mischance, I'ld
>     pluck it out!
> Will you be pleas'd to hang me? or
>     cut my throate?
> And I'le requite you, sir. Let's die like
>     *Romanes*,
> Since wee have liv'd, like *Grecians*.
>
> (*Volpone*, 3.8.11–15)

The sound of these outbursts is much the same as in those spoken by Shakespeare's heroes, but the difference, of course, is in the nature of the speakers, their circumstances, and their absurd causes. An obsessed old miser and a clever servant lament their misfortune as if it were the stuff of tragedy: Morose seeks cosmic equivalents for the chatter of the Collegians, and Mosca, placing the failure of Volpone's lustful scheme in an exalted historical tradition, determines that he and Volpone should put an end to their miseries 'after the high Roman fashion'.

What Jonson offers here and elsewhere is a ridiculous version of Shakespearian eloquence. He is aware that the extravagance upon which the grand style depends is potentially ludicrous. Professor Mack points out that the Shakespearian idiom 'depends for its vindication – for the redemption of its paper promises into gold – upon the hero, and any who stand, heroically, where he does'.[7] In Shakespeare, consciousness of the protagonist's greatness ensures the audience's acceptance and appreciation of his speech. Since Jonson does not admit heroes into his comic universe, the lan-

guage he creates in this vein properly strikes the audience as inflated, empty, and overwrought. And this is precisely the point. By assigning a grandiose dialect to a race of impostors, the playwright exposes the great distance between what the characters say and what they are. Shakespeare, on the other hand, employs such eloquence to establish the distance between the hero and the ordinary men around him. Yet this opposition of technique ought not to be oversimplified. Shakespeare often allows a note of bombast to sound in his heroes' speeches, as even a cursory acquaintance with *Othello* (or *Othello* criticism) reveals; and Jonson's raging fools, absurd though they be, occasionally achieve a grandeur not easily dismissed, as the arguments about generic classification of *Volpone* suggest.

This exalted language, in both its Jonsonian and Shakespearian forms, attests to the speaker's extraordinary vision. Hamlet and Sir Epicure and Antony all possess an active imaginative faculty. They speak differently from their fellows, at least in part because they see differently. Even such a figure as Othello, often considered the least sensitive of the major tragic heroes, conceives of and therefore speaks of his military experience and his marriage in a style that may be called imaginative, idealized, or even artistic. He demands perfection of his wife, his officers, and himself, and this vision of perfection is representative of the dreams of the Shakespearian hero. It is also germane to the imaginative designs of the Jonsonian fool and rogue. The undeniable tendency of their speech to mock itself, which depends upon its relation to the genuine article, does not cancel the imaginative appeals that it sets forth. Jonson allows the verse or prose to forecast the eventual collapse of this vision of delight – he twits the speaker in mid-career – but the

---

6 Quotations from Jonson are taken from the edition of C. H. Herford and Percy and Evelyn Simpson (Oxford, 1925–52). I have modernized *v* and *i*.

7 'The Jacobean Shakespeare', p. 14.

hyperbolic quality testifies also to the imaginative fertility of the dreamer's mind. Each of Shakespeare's and Jonson's imaginists invents and seeks to realize an ideal state of being. Although each vision originates in personal desire, such as Morose's insistence upon quiet and Hamlet's reverence for truth, the dreamer's solipsism and strength of will lead him to generalize, to expand that wish into a great silent empire or a Denmark, indeed a world, set right. The most important feature common to each vision is that it is unattainable, and the imaginist's commitment to it brings about his undoing.

The imagination of an ideal world, or at least the hankering after a better lot in this one, is a constant and fruitful topic in Jonsonian comedy, and the touchstone for such activity is found in the ruminations of Sir Epicure Mammon:

I will have all my beds, blowne up; not stuft:
Downe is too hard. And then, mine oval roome,
Fill'd with such pictures, as TIBERIUS tooke
From ELEPHANTIS: and dull ARETINE
But coldly imitated. Then, my glasses,
Cut in more subtill angles, to disperse,
And multiply the figures, as I walke
Naked betweene my *succubae*. My mists
I'le have of perfume, vapor'd 'bout the roome,
To loose our selves in; and my baths, like pits
To fall into: from whence, we will come forth,
And rowle us drie in gossamour, and roses.
(*The Alchemist*, 2.2.41–52)

These roses are without thorns, of course, for this is Sir Epicure's conception of an earthly paradise, of the way life ought to be lived. Yet the private chamber here described is only one province in the 'novo orbe' the lubricious knight promises Surly, the 'free state' he imagines for Dol. Although the details reflect Sir Epicure's personal obsession with physical pleasure, the passage essentially represents the desires shared by all the clients in *The Alchemist*. They wish for something novel, for liberation from the mundane, for distinction, for transformation.[8] 'The tongues of carpes' and 'camels heeles' are to Mammon what customers are to Drugger or knowledge of the duello to Kastril, and each dreamer regards the 'cunning man' as a source of secret knowledge, power, and change. Sir Epicure's highly developed fantasy is the most elaborate expression of Jonson's concern, here and everywhere, with human aspiration.[9] Nor is this vision of a better world limited to *The Alchemist*. Volpone's appeals to Celia are based upon similar impulses – he offers her the milk of unicorns – and Morose will model his household after the court of a Turkish potentate, with all commands given in sign language (*Epicoene*, 2.1.31–5). Such visions of perfection represent one of Jonson's most effective dramatic means for presenting the fruits, both wholesome and poisonous, of the human imagination and the human will.

The visionary propensities of the tragic hero, although not so obviously displayed as those of a Mammon or a Morose, contribute to his tragic standing and his tragic fall. The conflict in each of Shakespeare's mature tragedies, as in Jonson's comedies, may be described as a collision between the world as it is and the world as the protagonist imagines it. Bernard McElroy, writing of the four great tragedies, argues that they all 'embody at least one essential experience in common, the collapse of the subjective world of the tragic hero. . . . the world picture of each of the title characters is undermined at a fundamental level; his most basic assumptions about who he is and what reality is are rendered untenable.'[10] Since the action of

---

8 On this point see Alvin B. Kernan's introduction to his edition of *The Alchemist* (New Haven, 1974), p. 8.
9 Jackson, *Vision and Judgment*, p. 114.
10 *Shakespeare's Mature Tragedies* (Princeton, 1973), p. 3. McElroy confines his study to the four major tragedies because the particular qualities of mind he develops seem truly appropriate only to these four figures and because the later plays, such as *Antony and Cleopatra* and *Coriolanus*, do not concentrate upon the 'collapse' of the subjective world. I believe it is fair to say, however, that Shakespeare does reveal in each figure commitment to a subjective reality. See the quotation from *Coriolanus*, below.

the tragedies depicts the collapse of the unrealistic vision, or the hero's awakening to the limits of mortality, the ideal conception is not always given the elaborate expression that it is in Jonson. Sometimes the initial attachment to an absolute world must be inferred from its opposite, as in the second scene of *Hamlet*, where the Prince's reflections upon the lost realm of benevolence and order symbolized by his father proceed from his expressed contempt for the mutability and corruption of the present. Such a commitment to a noble domain is always present, however, a concomitant of the hero's exceptional imagination and strength of will, and it is both the source of his greatness and the cause of his ruin.

The relation of the Shakespearian hero's vision to the specious Jonsonian paradise is most evident when the protagonist, usually as the pressures of the fallen world become most intense and its limits most restrictive and intolerable, offers a pure expression of the visionary impulse. Coriolanus so indulges himself when he stands before the populace and finds himself unable to satisfy the demands of custom:

Better it is to die, better to starve,
Than crave the hire which first we do deserve.
Why in this wolvish toge should I stand here,
To beg of Hob and Dick that does appear
Their needless vouches? Custom calls me to't.
What custom wills, in all things should we do't,
The dust on antique time would lie unswept
And mountainous error be too highly heaped
For truth t' o'erpeer. Rather than fool it so,
Let the high office and the honor go
To one that would do thus.
                              (*Coriolanus*, 2.3.108–18)

The hero has devoted himself to his imaginative understanding of a just society, a world in which merit is absolute, not subject to the constraints of ceremony or form. And yet the crucial ambiguities of the play depend upon the conflict of opposites that the speech contains.

Alfred Harbage puts the matter this way

when he summarizes the characteristics of Shakespeare's heroes as a group: 'If we ask what qualities his tragic protagonists come nearest to sharing in common, we must say their *unworldliness*, their incapacity for compromise.'[11] The hero makes his entrance committed to his own inadequate but ideal conception of experience, bearing a firm conviction that the world functions as he understands it. To describe this ideal as simply as possible, we may say that he believes in a perfect correspondence between the way things are and the way they appear to him. This heroic conception is normally marked by its radical simplicity. In the opening scene of *King Lear*, for instance, the ceremony throws into relief Lear's childlike faith in his own interpretation of his kingship, his family, and himself. The King is ague-proof, the ultimate arbiter of value, a believer in the identity of words and meanings. Like Lear, all the tragic heroes are distinguished by their extraordinary *naïveté*; perhaps Shakespeare even implies that they exist in a state of innocence. According to Arthur Sewell, 'There is a sense, indeed, in which Othello is at first imagined as without original sin.'[12] That Othello has often been considered a simpleton is partly a function of his devotion to an elementary and clearly-defined sense of honour, honesty, loyalty, and conjugal love. His famous credo, 'To be once in doubt / Is to be once resolved', testifies to his uncomplicated ethical system, a mode of behaviour appropriate to his naive understanding of human intercourse. The other heroes' ideal visions are easily discerned: Macbeth acts upon a faith in his own strength and privilege; Timon is committed to the benevolence of humanity; Antony believes 'There's not a minute of our lives should stretch / Without some pleasure now' (1.1.46–7).

---

11 Foreword to the section on the tragedies in *The Complete Pelican Shakespeare*, p. 821.
12 *Character and Society in Shakespeare* (Oxford, 1951), p. 94.

This commitment to a noble ideal ought not to be oversimplified, however. Shakespeare takes pains, even as he suggests the appeals of the vision, to show that the visionary is hubristic, self-absorbed, and blind to the potential dangers of his ideal view. His devotion to a heroic conception of the world is predicated upon his location at the centre of that world – all the heroes are solipsists. When the ideal is challenged, which is the main business of the play, the hero's own identity is threatened, and he responds with a violence that reveals the dark underside of heroic commitment. McElroy describes the reactions of Hamlet, Othello, Lear, and Macbeth in just these terms: 'They demand that the world conform to what they desire it to be, and, when it refuses, they attack furiously, procuring their own destruction.'[13] The volley of curses with which Lear meets Cordelia's opposed view of her filial responsibility, a reaction which almost invariably troubles students, represents the efforts of the self to preserve its identity. In every play Shakespeare insists that the audience recognize the ambiguous combination of beauty and danger. The honourable murderer is as much a murderer as he is honourable.

These Shakespearian visions lead back to Jonson, whose comic protagonists also maintain unrealistic conceptions of themselves and their relation to other men. The connection should be clear between Shakespearian idealism and the heavenly visions of such buffoons as Morose and Mammon, whose naïveté and fertile imaginations reach heroic proportions; but perhaps it is less easy to identify the resemblance between the tragic heroes and the Jonsonian rogues, whose cunning and manipulative skill would seem to link them with such scheming villains as Edmund and Iago. (In fact, this is also a tenable connection, as I shall argue shortly.) Whereas the Shakespearian hero pursues his ideal in innocence of the fallen world, the Jonsonian shark is alert to its corruption and seeks to profit thereby. And yet such schemers as Mosca and Subtle and Face,

for all their clear-sighted understanding of man's penchant for folly, imagine themselves to be exempt from the general weakness. Plague or no plague, the alchemist and his assistants have created their own private world in which the dross of society may be converted into gold. Truewit thinks of himself as a man immune to the stupidities of such gulls as Daw and LaFoole, and yet the play's final revelation leaves him as incredulous as the rest. Volpone illustrates better than any other Jonsonian figure this mixture of insight and blindness, of earthy wisdom and high-flown imagination. The temptation to regard him as a tragic figure, an impulse to which some critics have yielded, implies yet another crucial link with the tragic protagonists. He shares with them, as with Face, an immensity of will that makes him unable to compromise. His arrogant view of himself as the champion trickster requires that he reveal himself to the court in order to outfox Mosca. Like Coriolanus, he will sustain the ideal regardless of the cost.

'You are too absolute', says Volumnia to her son, and her phrase elucidates the dilemma faced by both the tragic and comic extremists. A supremely powerful will is coupled with the wealthy imagination, yet the world inevitably resists transformation or control. Shakespeare emphasizes the tragic failure and waste that attend the hero's devotion to his cause: each of the protagonists is betrayed by the strength of his will. Even when it becomes clear that the ideal conception cannot be sustained, the hero insists upon fulfilling its conditions. Othello in his suicide judges himself by the same standards he has applied to others, Antony must fight Caesar in the most heroic and challenging manner ('by sea! by sea!'), and Macbeth 'bearlike . . . must fight the course'. Even though such rigidity is self-destructive, it ennobles the hero in the same way that his vision magnifies him. Both the will and the object of that will provoke an ambivalent response and contribute

---

13 *Shakespeare's Mature Tragedies*, p. 28.

to Shakespeare's exploration of the tragic paradox.

The comic version of heroic intractability
appears in Jonson's depiction of the rampant
human will, especially where his emphasis falls
upon the relentless pursuit of absurd desire.
The great fools exhibit the most obviously rigid
attachment to their hopes, as when Mammon
finds ways to accommodate each of Surly's
objections to the alchemical operation.
Morose's first appearance shows the extremity
of his attempts to secure his silent realm: the
servant who has 'fastened on a thicke-quilt, or
flock-bed, on the out-side of the dore' and oiled
the locks and hinges must announce that he has
done so only with nods of the head, shrugs, and
bows, as Morose reminds him before every
response. Others reveal the same kind of
monumental stubbornness. Ananias, the
younger and more zealous of the Puritans who
deal with Subtle, is so full of his new religious
fervour that he attempts to dictate even the
terms of his conversation with the alchemist:
'Christ-tide, I pray you.' This portrait constitutes a sketch for that most extreme of Jonson's
Puritan fanatics, Zeal-of-the-Land Busy, who
cannot restrain himself from 'prophesying'
against the corruption of Smithfield. Busy's
hypocrisy complicates the issue a bit, for when
he cannot prevent the Littlewits from sampling
the delights of the Fair, he manages to endorse
the venture and even to justify his own participation: he resolves 'by the publicke eating of
Swines flesh, to professe our hate, and loathing
of *Judaisme*, whereof the brethren stand taxed.
I will therefore eate, yea, I will eate exceedingly'
(*Bartholomew Fair*, 1.6.95–7). Yet even with
the obvious inconsistency, Busy illustrates
the absurdity of extremism, his rigid devotion
asserting itself regardless of the position
adopted.

It may seem inappropriate to charge with
intransigence those great Jonsonian intriguers
who thrive by means of their protean talents.
Adaptability, here a wicked *sprezzatura*, is the
main subject of Mosca's boast in his famous

encomium to the genuine Parasite, who can

> be here,
> And there, and here, and yonder, all at once;
> Present to any humour, all occasion;
> And change a visor, swifter, then a thought!
> (*Volpone*, 3.1.26–9)

Yet it is ironically true that flexibility is the one
point on which the schemer is dogmatic. Volpone's firm insistence upon the supremacy of
his wit, the example already cited, is characteristic of all the Jonsonian intriguers. Their
capacity for being all things to all men is central
to their arrogant view of themselves and their
world, and it is the one value they will not alter
or compromise. The quarrel in the first scene of
*The Alchemist*, with each contestant claiming
that his role is more important, is a dispute
over precedence; and even though both agree
to disagree, neither changes his position
because it is not in his nature to do so. Dol
accuses them of being madmen, and their rigid
views clash again at every lull in the action.

Busy becomes a comic madman in the last act
of *Bartholomew Fair*, disputing with a puppet
whether dramatic representation should be
considered profane. Similarly, Morose is said
to have 'run out o' dores in's night-caps, to
talke with a *Casuist* about his divorce' (*Epicoene*, 4.5.3–4). If such fits do not constitute
madness in the strict sense, they do at least
represent the disorientation that occurs when
the dreamer is suddenly awakened and his
vision shattered. Much of the 'humorous'
behaviour in the earlier plays is sufficiently
aberrant to be called madness; the danger of
the *idée fixe* was one of Jonson's earliest
concerns.[14] And when the fixed idea is as grand
as those cherished by the mature Jonsonian
fools, the destruction of it creates a comic ex-
plosion. Mammon 'will goe mount a turnep-
cart, and preach / The end o' the world, within

---

14 G. R. Hibbard, 'Ben Jonson and Human Nature', in *A
Celebration of Ben Jonson*, ed. William Blissett, Julian
Patrick, and R. W. Van Fossen (Toronto, 1973), p. 76.

these two months' (*The Alchemist*, 5.5.81–2). The rigid mind snaps under the pressure of failure or denial and spins into confusion, to the delight of the audience and often of the stage spectators.

In tragedy such dislocation produces a horrific insanity. The boldness and beauty of the hero's dreams invite assault from the malign forces of the tragic universe, an attack which his mortality cannot withstand: the result is the ravings of Lear, 'the lunatic king', in act 4, or Hamlet's brutal treatment of Ophelia in the nunnery scene. Even when the hero is not literally demented but merely out of control, like Othello in the latter half of the play or Antony in his assault upon Cleopatra and Thidias, the wild actions and the fragmented language create a similar impression. As events combine to challenge his conception of the world and his relation to it, the hero clings all the more tenaciously to his vision, and the ensuing tension creates an outburst corresponding to the moment of comic dementia.

The imaginary worlds to which these characters madly cling are of a piece. They are realms of infinite possibility. Particular details vary, of course, according to the nature and taste of the dreamer, from Volpone's quest for exotic physical sensations to Lear's hope 'to take upon's the mystery of things', but each vision implies an easy leap beyond the limits of the fallen world. It is in many respects a version of the golden world realized at the end of Shakespeare's romantic comedies, but without the questions or tinges of darkness. Since certain of the tragedies have been shown to portray the stage of experience inevitably succeeding the comic happy ending,[15] we may think of the tragic hero – Othello comes to mind – as attempting to maintain single-handedly that state of bliss and harmony. The limitations of mortality will be forgotten, quotidian cares banished, the grandest desires for self and state easily gratified. So the imaginist sees things.

So Shakespeare would like things to be. He encourages his audience to assent to the beauty of the vision, first by supporting the natural dramatic alliance between dreamer and spectator and second by contrasting the appeals of the imagined world with the brutality and malevolence of the tragic environment. The audience's sympathy with the tragic hero is connected with its willingness to endorse the attractions inherent in the heroic vision of world, misguided though it is. It is tempting to contemplate the kind of world Othello believes in, where 'Certain, men should be what they seem', and this desire for consistency is an appealing feature of most of these heroes' visions. I would contend that Shakespeare even invites limited approval for Coriolanus's dedication to an ethic of merit, although he ironically subverts that commitment in his depiction of Marcius's arrogance and inhumanity. An audience is probably less inclined to sanction Macbeth's mistaken conception of the world, for the idealistic hero rapidly becomes a criminal and most of the play exhibits the consequences of his villainy. It is possible, quite early in the play, to sense the seductive power of Macbeth's dreams: if only this were a world where power could be achieved and retained by an 'easy' act, where 'it were done when 'tis done', where a little water could clear one of the deed. But in this context *Macbeth* differs from the other tragedies because the emphasis is unusual: Shakespeare dwells here upon the hideous personal and political effects of the imaginist's subjective view.

*Antony and Cleopatra* illustrates more persuasively than any other play the lure of the hero's vision. Since Alexandria is an actual location, not just an imagined state of being, the audience must participate in that glittering, sensual world. Shakespeare's success in representing the glories of this realm is demonstrated by the terms of the critical conflict surrounding the play: is it 'a tragedy of lyrical inspiration, justifying love by presenting it as triumphant over death, or is it rather a

---

15 See Susan Snyder, *The Comic Matrix of Shakespeare's Tragedies* (Princeton, 1979), pp. 56–90.

remorseless exposure of human frailties, a presentation of spiritual possibilities dissipated through a senseless surrender to passion?'[16] Although the sensual temptations give to Egypt a particular identity and flavour, it nevertheless can stand for the idealized world to which the Shakespearian hero commits himself, and it serves as a guide for our response to that world.

Even Jonson, unlikely as it might seem, betrays some sympathy for his dreamers' fancies. Although the moralist and the moderate in him regularly subvert these imaginative flights with irony and finally condemn the solipsist and voluptuary, the great passages given over to the realms of gold are too prominent, frequent, and impressive to be scorned and dismissed. We may, while admitting the risks of such a position and the need for interpretative restraint, suggest that the pleasures of the imagined world are sometimes even celebrated. Jonson's fascination with extremism and excessiveness, what one writer calls his 'fascinated respect for the eccentric and absurd',[17] is a primary determinant of his comic method in all the plays, and his success in articulating the desires and aspirations of his most imaginative figures may also be a measure of his own response to such wishes. In other words, it seems clear that these dreamers have captured the imagination of their creator.[18] The poet, after all, is responsible for having imagined and described these visions of power and pleasure. What is more, the audience also responds to these temptations. Just as Jonson's management of the intrigue in the major comedies is calculated to inculpate the audience by involving them in a network of morally dubious plots, so his exhibition of physical delights leads them to share the yearnings of libertines and fools. Like Shakespeare, Jonson seeks to win his audience over to an appreciation of the character's ideal; the difference is that in the comedies we are seduced by the satisfactions of luxury or absolute sway.

Jonson and Shakespeare construct these visions only to destroy them. The dramatic action, both comic and tragic, is concerned chiefly with the disillusionment of the idealist. And just as we notice resemblances among the dreamers and their dreams, so may we identify similarities among the agents of destruction. In Shakespeare these are the villains – Iago, Edmund, Claudius, perhaps Octavius; in Jonson they are the intriguers who originate the 'plots' – Volpone and Mosca, Subtle and Face, Truewit and Dauphine, Quarlous and Winwife. The comparison here is admittedly not exact: Shakespeare clearly separates his dreamers and villains; but Jonson, while he does create merely foolish dreamers such as Morose and Mammon, makes his protagonists both visionaries and realists. They resemble the villains, however, in that most of the action depends upon their ability to identify, exploit, and shatter the unrealistic hopes of others.

These agents of disappointment are, above all, rationalists, clear-sighted individualists who understand and seek to profit from foolish imaginings. The connection between villainy and chicanery appears most clearly in Iago's manipulation of Roderigo and the relation of this practice to his deception of Othello. Even in the tragedies with less obvious comic connections, *Hamlet* or *King Lear*, it is not difficult to see that Claudius's use of Laertes or

---

16  D. A. Traversi, *An Approach to Shakespeare*, 2 vols. (rev. edn, London, 1968; New York, 1969), vol. 2, p. 212.

17  R. V. Holdsworth, review of Parfitt's *Ben Jonson, Review of English Studies*, 30 (1979), 208.

18  Alvin B. Kernan contends that 'the brilliance of phrase and urgency of rhythms in such speeches as Volpone's praise of his gold and his temptation of Celia guarantee that Jonson himself responded powerfully to this [Renaissance] optimism'. Introduction to *Volpone* (New Haven, 1962), p. 25. See also Robert Ornstein, 'Shakespearian and Jonsonian Comedy', *Shakespeare Survey 22* (Cambridge, 1969), pp. 43–6: 'in deliberately rejecting the earlier romantic mode of comedy, Jonson, I suspect, denied something of his own genius. . . . Contemptuous as he was of romantic fabling, Jonson had, moreover, an instinct for romantic variety and multiplicity which, though severely disciplined in *Volpone* and *The Alchemist*, burst forth in the noisy carnivals of *Epicoene* and *Bartholomew Fair*' (p. 43).

Edmund's deception of Gloucester depends upon techniques essential to the comic schemes in *Volpone, Epicoene*, and *The Alchemist*. Hamlet, as Claudius tells Laertes, will not suspect their confederacy because he is 'Most generous, and free from all contriving'; Iago identifies Othello's 'free and open nature'; Edmund relies for the success of his plans upon 'A credulous father, and a brother noble / Whose nature is so far from doing harm / That he suspects none'; and Enobarbus points out that Caesar is too canny to accept Antony's naive proposal of single combat. The schemers are quick to discern the idealism that insulates the victims from awareness of the malignant forces around them, a credulity related to the elevated, visionary tendencies common to the heroes. In Jonson, although the fool's *naïveté* is a function not of his goodness but of his misplaced self-esteem, it nonetheless serves as the handle by which the schemer twists his victim. In both cases the scheme depends upon the victim's unworldliness. As Subtle says of Mammon, 'If his dream last, he'll turn the age to gold.'

The two dramatists insist upon different responses to the practical-minded manipulators, just as they demand different judgements on the idealists. The fundamental distinction is between villainy and roguery, according to the conventions and limitations of the two modes. The pragmatists in Shakespeare's tragedies are among his most reprehensible characters. Even though his treatment of the heroic vision is mixed, Shakespeare's presentation of the villainy which subverts that vision suggests one of the plays' ethical themes, the perils of aggressive individualism.[19] Such criminality is in fact an interesting variation on the single-minded nobility of such characters as Hamlet and Coriolanus, who cling stubbornly or heroically to an untenable moral, ethical, or political position. Jonson too attacks selfish desire, evident in the hopes of the *captatori* or the indiscriminate wishes of a Bartholomew Cokes, but best displayed in the scheming of

his intriguers. The compacts formed to take advantage of others inevitably break apart from the pressures of competition: the selfish impulses that brought them into being necessarily destroy them. But these comically-conceived manipulators are no villains, and we find ourselves in league with them. Our relationship with these types is thus determined chiefly by the mode: in the comedies we join with the realists, while in the tragedies our lot is with the dreamers. Such alignments correspond to the attitudes the two playwrights encourage toward the characters' visions: generally speaking, Shakespeare invites us to admire and sympathize, Jonson to enjoy and to judge.

Although the comic and tragic action is given over to the contest between visionary and realist, the conclusion is clear from the start. The visionary is easily defeated, not so much by the power of his enemy as by his own inherent weakness, his incapacity for adapting to the demands of this world. The tragic hero is responsible for his own fall, just as the comic butt must take the blame for his humiliation. Their antagonists merely assist in the process of debasement. Furthermore, the pragmatist cannot be said to win, for in helping to bring down the visionary he usually confounds himself as well. Just as the shape of the struggle is identical in each case, so the end of the action is inevitably the same. Whether considered tragically or comically, the result is always failure.

> The greatest comedy seems inevitably to deal with the disillusion of mankind, . . . the failure of men to realize their most passionate desires. . . . Cannot we see from the very periods in which it arises in its greatest forms with what aspect of humanity it needs must deal? It comes when the positive attitude has failed, when doubt is creeping in to undermine values, and men are turning for comfort to the very ruggedness of life and laughing in the face of it all.[20]

---

19 L. C. Knights, 'Shakespeare's Tragedies: with Some Reflections on the Nature of Tradition', *Further Explorations* (Palo Alto and London, 1965), pp. 21–2.
20 Bonamy Dobrée, *Restoration Comedy: 1660–1720* (Oxford, 1924), p. 15.

Although Bonamy Dobrée does not here mention Jonson, the summary identifies the tone and the ideological underpinnings of the comic masterpieces from *Volpone* forward. Moreover, the emphasis upon 'the disillusion of mankind' reveals the pertinence of these remarks to great tragedy, particularly to the major works of Shakespeare, and to the spirit of the age that produced all these plays. The first decade of the seventeenth century, it may be fairly said, introduced an age of doubt. Modern efforts to identify the nature, specify the origin, and estimate the prevalence of the 'new philosophy' have rightly altered the convenient notion that the thinkers and writers of the Renaissance exchanged theistic optimism for doubt and pessimism as they changed their calendars, but it is generally agreed that the philosophical tone of the reign of James differs from that of the age of Elizabeth. The enthusiasm and hope of the 1590s, owing to changes in the political, social, economic, religious, and scientific spheres, began to dissipate and to give way to fear and dubiety. It is well known that Shakespeare's own canon offers a record of this growing scepticism: the darkening vision evident from *Twelfth Night* through *Timon* and *Macbeth*, once associated with the playwright's personal disappointment or unhappiness or crisis, is now seen usually as a reflection of the changing philosophical temper of the age. What is not so well established is that a corresponding pattern of disillusionment appears in Jonson's drama of the same period. *Every Man in His Humour* (1598), with its comparatively gentle ironies, playful tone, and festive conclusion, is followed shortly by the comical satires which, while more acerbic and critical, still imply some faith in human improvement and the power of art to influence behaviour. *Sejanus* (1603) reveals for the first time the negative conception of experience that informs the comic masterpieces. Both dramatists, in other words, exhibit an increasingly disillusioned view of man's nature, and such a view is fully formed by

the time they create their most meaningful works.

All these plays convey to the spectator a profound sense of pessimism about the possibility of human happiness, goodness, or achievement. Forgetting for the moment the generic distinctions, we find that the actions depicted arise from similar motives and take a similar shape: attempts to take unfair advantage, betrayal of one's fellows, efforts to satisfy the self at the expense of others, the desire to dictate or dominate behaviour, the destruction or infection of good by evil, engagements in losing battles. If the degree of villainy is more extreme in the tragedies, it is balanced by the ubiquity of folly and evil in the comedies. The relation of such pessimism to larger systems of religious or natural philosophy is unclear for either playwright, and those attempts to connect Shakespeare or Jonson with specific traditions of belief have been unsuccessful.[21] What matters, it would seem, are the metaphysical issues that arise from the authors' repeated dependence upon the same kinds of actions: the collapse of order, the lure and power of evil, the failure of hope, and the inescapability of human weakness and pride. Their pessimism becomes most apparent when we consider that all these comedies and tragedies are insistently anti-romantic.

Jonson throughout most of his career was notoriously distrustful, even contemptuous, of romantic stagecraft, a bias which produced some of his most famous attacks on Shakespeare. Thus, the assaults on romantic illusion that occur repeatedly in his mature plays are familiar and consistent with his method and dogma. Of such episodes, the introduction of Dapper to the Queen of Faery is perhaps the

---

21 Roland M. Frye discusses the abuses that have attended efforts to Christianize and de-Christianize Shakespeare, for example. See *Shakespeare and Christian Doctrine* (Princeton, 1963). An unconvincing attempt to read Jonson in Christian terms is found in Robert E. Knoll's *Ben Jonson's Plays: An Introduction* (Lincoln, Nebraska, 1964).

most obvious; its simplicity makes it one of the most illuminating. The young lawyer, who hopes only for a key to victory in the gaming houses, is a pedestrian version of the grand imaginists in Jonson and Shakespeare. The scheme to dupe him is carefully adjusted to his romantic turn of mind. Dapper is willing to believe Face's assurances that 'a rare starre / Raign'd at your birth'; that 'There must a world of ceremonies passe, / You must be bath'd and fumigated'; and that finally he will be presented to Her Grace. His suitability as a candidate for such romantic folderol reveals itself in the preparatory ritual, when the servants of the 'Queen' demand all his worldly goods: 'I ha' nothing but a halfe-crowne / Of gold, about my wrist, that my love gave me; / And a leaden heart I wore, sin' she forsooke me' (*The Alchemist*, 3.5.43–5). This credulous optimism leads to humiliating consequences: left alone and gagged in the privy, nearly overcome by the stench, and finally granted an interview with a punk whose 'departing part' he is invited to kiss, Dapper rushes from the house illusions intact. So absurd and negligible is he that the audience does not even need to witness his inevitable come-uppance. In all the comedies Jonson repeats this pattern, exploding dreams of success, wealth, and distinction, and laying traps for those whose inflated self-conceptions give them unrealistic expectations.

What all this has to do with romance is that Jonson's visionaries share a romantic view of the world. Richard Harter Fogle offers a deliberately simplified and therefore useful definition of the romantic attitude: 'to be romantic is to expect a great deal from life; to believe in ideals, like true love; to be regardless of limits; not to count costs until we have paid the price, at which we may then be everlastingly outraged'.[22] In discussing the visionary tendencies of the Shakespearian and Jonsonian characters, I have postponed identifying the distinctively romantic features of their visions, but the suitability of the adjective should be

clear. Jonson's fools, with varying degrees of awareness, accept the conventions of romance literature and interpret the actual world accordingly. Theirs is a universe in which 'out of the first fire of meeting eyes, (they say) love is stricken' (Morose); in which sons or other troublesome relations may be disinherited or debased at will (Corbaccio and Morose); in which fortunes may be won with magic formulae (Mammon); in which one need 'trust no learning but inspiration' (Busy); in which a fairy spirit selects and blesses her favourite (Dapper). Adam Overdo thinks of himself as carrying on the tradition of the disguised ruler, Justice at work in a world where vice and folly may be corrected by a cloak-and-dagger game. But the characters' romantic inclinations are not always so concrete: even more interesting and pertinent is the air of romantic optimism common to all. At the centre of this world view, securely protected by pride, is the self. Sharks and dupes alike display a vigorous individualism accompanied by disregard for social circumstance or legal restraint. Hope is unbridled in such a realm of luck, where miracles may occur at any time. This is a progressive attitude toward human experience, and it is foreign to Jonson's classical, conservative temper.

In plays such as *A Midsummer Night's Dream, As You Like It*, and *Twelfth Night*, Shakespeare employed, adapted, and expanded the traditional material of romance literature, and in so doing he sanctioned the positive, romantic view of mankind that such conventions promote. This is not to say that these plays do not raise serious questions about the validity and reliability of such a vision; indeed, the balance between doubt and acceptance contributes to the impression of truth that distinguishes these works from lesser efforts. Nevertheless, the romantic comedies offer hope and reassurance, and they do so with familiar

---

22 'Romanticism Reconsidered', *The Sewanee Review*, 82 (1974), 383.

materials: escapes from the sea, a devoted friend who rescues his 'fellow' from a duel, benevolent spirits who favourably alter the course of love, charmed forests where mistakes are forgiven, enemies or perfidious relations who repent, and a controlling Providence whose interventions are always benevolent and timely. Shakespeare's fondness for such romantic devices has proved to be one of the major lines of distinction between him and his major contemporary. In the mature tragedies, however, Shakespeare puts these conventions to new use, inverting or employing them ironically so as to examine critically and sceptically the attitudes he has formerly endorsed.

The major tragedies are so virulently anti-romantic because Shakespeare deliberately evokes and then destroys romantic expectations. One of his most valuable instruments for subverting such hopes is his ironic reference to the conventions of romance literature, the machinery of his own comedies, a method he employs most liberally and impressively in *King Lear*. As Leo Salingar has recently demonstrated in an important essay, 'Romance in *King Lear*', Shakespeare almost invariably altered his sources so as to clarify the connections with romance and thus to emphasize the bleak failure of romantic possibilities. The faithful servant, son, and daughter, the debased ruler, the joyful reunion of parent and child, the disguises – all these are relics of the romance tradition, and their appearance in this savage world underscores their failure: 'a repeated consequence of Shakespeare's innovations in the plot is to set up a dialectic between expectations belonging to romance and those attached to tragedy, between inalienable hopes and the sternest moral realism'.[23] In the tragedies, the enchanted forest is transformed into the heath or a dark island; benevolent sprites become deaf and pitiless gods; swordfights inevitably reach their bloody conclusions; and joyful meetings, if they occur at all, are cut short by imminent disaster. Even when Shakespeare does not present

characters or settings or actions associated particularly with romance, he still insists upon the contrast between vain hope and bitter truth, placing the visionary hero in the centre of the dialectic. Most of the great protagonists may be thought of as romantic figures – solipsists, individualists, men willing to set themselves against the furies of the world and sustained by a mysterious faith in their power to survive, even to triumph. For all the tragic grandeur they are able to suggest, their self-inflicted misery is both humiliating and frightening. Shakespeare organizes the action of these plays to reveal the dangers of the hero's vision, to adumbrate the pain and suffering it creates, to strip ragged these romantic pretensions, naked as at their birth. Although a recent critic may be liable to charges of exaggeration, there is truth in his contention that Shakespeare's tragedies are 'the greatest anti-romantic structures ever created'.[24]

When romantic illusions are punctured, the worlds that remain are similarly stale, flat, and unprofitable. Always in the background are the inescapable consequences of the Fall. The settings chosen, regardless of the action, suggest pollution, limitation, and danger: a savage heath (*King Lear*), a decaying imperial city (*Volpone*), a barbarous island (*Othello*), a neighbourhood afflicted by the plague (*The Alchemist*). In *Antony and Cleopatra*, as Howard Felperin indicates, Rome is such a world: 'When Samuel Johnson praised Shakespeare for representing "the real state of sublunary nature", he might have had the Rome of this play in mind, for Rome corresponds to the world as Bacon and Jonson conceive of it in everyday consciousness: a hard, unyielding, brazen reality.'[25] It is such a world that fosters and dooms the effort at imaginative escape. The visionaries cannot accept the im-

---

23 *English*, 27 (1978), 20.
24 Howard Felperin, *Shakespearean Romance* (Princeton, 1972), p. 62.
25 *Ibid.*, pp. 135–6.

plications of man's fallen condition. Their resistance, the refusal to accommodate themselves to the limitations of mortality, sentences these imaginists to a re-creation of the Fall. The struggle is intensified by the other major group – the serpents in these dramas – who not only perceive the conditions of the corrupt world but embrace and seek to profit from evil. Their trickery or villainy is equivalent to the idealists' wish for imaginative transcendence; it is an alternative response, another kind of effort to liberate the self from the constraints of the earth. For both authors the outcome of the struggle is never in doubt, for the world will tolerate neither exploitation nor escape. But their attitudes toward their characters' falls determine the kind of plays they make from the same conflict.

A blunt statement of the distinction is this: Jonson regards the destruction of illusions with scornful amusement, while Shakespeare laments the waste of imaginative gifts. The difference here is related to the point of view each playwright establishes, the bond he seeks to form between stage and audience. Shakespeare's creation of a bond between audience and visionary leads the spectators to assent to the attractions of the vision, to sympathize with the destruction of such an individual. In Jonson, on the other hand, the structure of the play and the nature of the characters require that the viewers cast their lot with the witty destroyer and delight in the puncture of grandiose dreams. Both dramatists emphasize the impossibility of realizing the illusions sustained by their characters: the dénouements leave no doubt on this point. But their own responses to their characters' imaginative myopia are very different. Jonson demands sharp critical judgement. He underscores the absurdity of the dreamer's vision, exposes it as immoral, anti-social, and a perversion of creative energy. Shakespeare is more tolerant of the vision itself: without ignoring its moral, ethical, or political perils, he nevertheless reveals and seems even to relish its promised

beauties. Here the two artists offer complementary views of the same landscape. And yet the two attitudes are closer than might be expected, for each is complicated and balanced by intimations of an opposing view.

It is on this issue that the traditional characterization of Jonson as the stern and dogmatic moralist needs to be amended. Aldous Huxley perceived the complexity of the playwright's mature vision when he proposed that Jonson 'might have been a great romantic, one of the sublime inebriates'.[26] What Huxley notices is the sound of the opposing voice, heard most plainly in the comic masterpieces, chanting the beauties and pleasures of romantic desire. That Jonson grants a hearing to this voice is one of the artistic decisions that distinguish these great works from the journeyman efforts, the comical satires. There the satiric targets – social, political, and aesthetic vices and their dramatic embodiments – are so large and easy to demolish that there is little sense of challenge or conflict. In these mature masterpieces, however, the targets not only spring up again but also fire back at the marksman. The claims of Jonson's visionaries are universal and compelling, and the playwright allows the audience to feel them and to consider, if only briefly, their legitimacy.[27] The greatness of the mature comedies owes much to this tension, the careful balance between Jonson's firm opposition to romantic speculation and his willingness to admit the attractiveness of such visions.

Shakespeare is pre-eminent among playwrights when it comes to matters of revaluation and qualification and balance; the fashionable word for this practice, supplied by Norman Rabkin, is 'complementarity'.[28] And

---

26 'Ben Jonson', *London Mercury*, 1 (1919), 187.
27 This ambivalent view of the imagination and the force of illusion is consistent with Jonson's mixed attitude toward the theatre itself. See Jonas A. Barish, 'Jonson and the Loathéd Stage', in *A Celebration of Ben Jonson*, p. 52.
28 *Shakespeare and the Common Understanding* (New York, 1967), pp. 22 ff.

it is true that the tragic power of plays such as *Othello* and *King Lear* is released by the collision of two truths: that the ideal world is supremely beautiful and valuable, and that the ideal world is impossible to realize. Shakespeare's depiction of his characters' notions of perfection differs from Jonson's, of course, in that the visionary speculations of the tragic heroes are given greater and more straightforward consideration. We are conscious of the unreality, to be sure, for the context guarantees it: Edmund is on the stage as Lear imaginatively constructs his walled paradise. But Shakespeare does insist upon the desirability of the vision, actively encouraging his audience to wish for Hamlet's world of truth, for a state where Coriolanus need not demean himself, for the prison in which Lear and Cordelia can 'laugh and sing and tell old tales'. Within the passages devoted to such ideals there is far less irony and exaggeration than in the equivalent Jonsonian fantasias. In short, it is hardly surprising that Shakespeare's treatment of his heroes' ideal visions is mixed. What is shocking, however, is the brutality with which Shakespeare demolishes the illusions he has invited us to contemplate. The juxtaposition of the beautiful dream with its immediate destruction is a fearsome spectacle which, because this is tragedy, is unmatched by anything in Jonson. But this ruthless disillusionment is the Shakespearian version of the terrible ironies attendant upon the Jonsonian visions: both methods serve to distance the romantic view, to expose its quixotic nature, and to generate a grave pessimism about human possibility.

Such pessimism goes virtually unrelieved until the later works of Shakespeare and Jonson. Still concerned with the conflict between romantic vision and human imperfection, both adopt new and similar perspectives. Perhaps it is ironic that the two artists, having dwelt in their great middle plays upon the vanities and evils of imagination, should ultimately take a visionary turn themselves. Shakespeare's romances and Jonson's masques assert that the main defence against the fact of mortality is to be found in the realm of the imagination, the province of art. Such an answer is implicit in almost all the earlier plays, especially Jonson's comedies, where the rogues employ artistic means for improper ends. But in the later works both dramatists explore the positive and consolatory uses of the imaginative faculty. Like Lear and Sir Epicure, Shakespeare and Jonson seek liberation from the penalties of a corrupt universe by constructing an imaginary realm of beauty, harmony, and unity. The fools' paradises are ephemeral; the artists' illusions are attainable and permanent, unlikely to vanish *in fume*.

Human aspiration, like most human activity, may be noble or it may be ludicrous, depending upon the viewer's standpoint. The categories of comedy and tragedy are useful guides to point of view, for they help the playwright to evaluate as well as to organize the action. Although Shakespeare's interpretation of man's visionary impulses is essentially tragic and Jonson's comic, each dramatist qualifies and complicates his presentation so thoroughly that he stretches the conventional limits of the genres, revealing the fundamental relation between ridiculous and heroic forms of human activity. Bernard Shaw perceived the complexity of the issue when he called *Coriolanus* Shakespeare's greatest comedy.[29] The resemblance between the richly suggestive visions of the two playwrights ought to indicate that firm generic distinctions can be a hindrance as well as an aid to interpretation. Stephen Orgel has recently challenged the rigid modern division between the two modes, arguing that this separation was not maintained so faithfully in the Renaissance, that the great tragedies were always followed by merry songs and bits of foolery, and that the age accepted the Socratic view that the arts of

---

29 *The Collected Works of Bernard Shaw*, vol. 10 (New York, 1930), p. xxxiii.

comedy and tragedy are identical.[30] Removal of this generic barrier reveals important similarities of purpose and achievement in the work of these playwrights and leads into territory that ought to be explored more extensively.

The common ground occupied by Shakespeare and Jonson, the area I have been attempting to survey, is identified in Salingar's phrase 'the sternest moral realism', a description which brings to mind Joseph Conrad's dictum that the purpose of great art is 'to make you see'. Jonson and Shakespeare seek to promote moral realism in much the same way, by dramatizing the experience of characters who lack or disregard it. And what is more important is that the visions that proceed from their rigorous scrutiny are similarly sceptical and negative. The characters' visions give promise of great possibility, universal order, limitless pleasure, correspondence between word and deed, unblemished love, transcendence, the conquest of nature. The creators' visions emphasize failure. To observe this stress is not to indulge in the easy nihilism that has afflicted a number of modern interpretations and damaged too many recent stage productions. As I have tried to establish, the balances achieved by both Shakespeare and Jonson forbid such a label. These plays do exhibit actions that suggest vitality, creative talent, the awareness of error, and great heroism. But they also stimulate a sense of limitation, foster a climate of doubt, and illustrate what man is and what he can never be. And the paradox of their authors' achievement is that the creation of plays like *Hamlet* and *The Alchemist* adds new dimensions to our understanding of what man is.

---

30 'Shakespeare and the Kinds of Drama', *Critical Inquiry*, 6 (1979), 118.

# SHAKESPEARE IN PERFORMANCE, 1980

## ROGER WARREN

This article covers the Shakespeare productions which had opened at Stratford-upon-Avon and at Stratford, Ontario by August 1980, four each, and the National Theatre's production of *Othello*.[1]

## I

The Stratford-upon-Avon season began with Terry Hands's production of *As You Like It*. An obvious companion-piece to his 1979 *Twelfth Night*, it was primarily about love, and only very secondarily about anything else: the centre of the play was marvellous, the frame questionable. As with *Twelfth Night*, a wintry, black-and-white first half gave place to a variegated, dappled world of warm browns and greens in the second. The white fur surfaces of Farrah's set, suggesting luxury at court and snow in the country, were replaced by moss-covered trees and (again as in *Twelfth Night*) a profusion of daffodils and other spring flowers. Everyone at court wore uniform black and silver, even Rosalind and Celia, whose severe black velvet dresses were edged with more white fur.

Both Duke Frederick and Oliver were neurotic to the point of melodrama; the other Duke was a sententious windbag who seemed to have gained nothing from his experience, as Jaques emphasized in his accusing 'your *abandon'd* cave'; Adam was a garrulous yokel ('providently caters for the spar*rer*'), falling over a farcically oversize broadsword: it was hard to grasp exactly what point was being made when

Orlando presented *this* Adam to Jaques after 'sans everything' (an illustration? a contradiction?).

The main approach seemed to be that formality and artifice of any kind were to be rejected in favour of spontaneity and naturalness: Rosalind and Celia settled down informally on the floor to discuss Nature's work and Fortune's, competed for Orlando's attention, vigorously hissed Charles the Wrestler and even lent a hand in his overthrow; Joe Melia's easy, unforced Touchstone set one kind of natural behaviour against another in his encounter with Tom Wilkinson's very persuasive Corin, a sturdy countryman with a real point of view, who presided over the final fertility rites as a rural Hymen; and Derek Godfrey's superb Jaques was vigorous and energetic in his enthusiasm for the Fool's patter ('And then from who-er to who-er we rot and rot'), and his relish for the language of the Seven Ages speech had a vitality and authority which seemed, as the lights faded on his lonely seated figure for the interval, to give his viewpoint central importance.

But in fact Mr Hands was having none of that. Even before the interval Rosalind, arriving disconsolately among the swirling mists of Arden, had seemed as exhausted by sheer erotic frustration as by her journey, and had established an immediate rapport ('Alas, *poor*

---

1 The review of the Ontario season was made possible by a grant from the Research Board, University of Leicester.

shepherd!' typically tender) with Silvius, whose frustration was even expressed in his physical stance, arms twisted round a shepherd's crook slung across his shoulder-blades. It was, indeed, a striking aspect of this production, as of Mr Hands's *Twelfth Night*, that the lovers' ardours, ecstasies, sorrows, frustrations were expressed in vigorous physical movement. The famous shifting quality of the central scenes, moving between laughter and tears, was not merely a verbal process but a physical one, even to the point of varying the lighting to reflect gaiety or sadness. Crucial to this approach was the superbly sustained partnership of Susan Fleetwood and Sinead Cusack as Rosalind and Celia; together with John Bowe's warm, sympathetic Orlando, they got right to the heart of the play.

Miss Cusack's Celia, by turns mocking, sympathetic, concerned, amazed, was both foil and accomplice to Miss Fleetwood, who poured out her high spirits almost to the point of physical exhaustion. After 'Love is merely a madness', for instance, both collapsed on the floor in gales of laughter; but in seconds Rosalind had modulated to a rapt, still 'Yet I profess curing it by counsel'; she held the mood as she described her love-cure, dissolved into mockery again at 'sound sheep's heart' and then reverted to a still, infinitely tender delivery of the line 'I would cure you, if you would but call me *Rosalind*', contrasting with Orlando's brash gaiety and Celia's alarm and concern.

Similar varied details packed the second encounter: Orlando's head was in Rosalind's lap at 'men have died from time to time, and worms have eaten them, but not for love' (lighting appropriately dimmed); Rosalind's hand hovered in pent-up desire above Orlando's head at 'By this hand, it will not kill a fly' – whereupon she *did* kill a fly against Orlando's chest, thus shattering the sweet–sad moment and effecting the transition to 'now I will be your Rosalind in a more coming-on disposition'. The atmosphere of the mock marriage became so charged at Rosalind's 'I do take thee, Orlando' that they both had to break away for a moment, as the mood of the text changes – always a sign of an *As You Like It* that is working well. 'Say "a day" without the "ever"' was strident rather than wry, anticipating the 'giddiness' of her desires later in the speech; Orlando's clumping attempt to match her wit ('Wit, whither wilt?') did not pass unmocked by this Rosalind; she used the full range of her voice for 'how many fathom deep'; and 'I cannot be out of the sight of Orlando' verged on desperation.

These scenes were as fascinating and enjoyable as I have ever known them; but in others Mr Hands characteristically pushed his approach too far. It was quite in character for this Celia to sympathize with Silvius's near-breakdown at Phebe's letter to Rosalind, but both reactions were excessive in the wrong way, and when she and Oliver expressed their love at first sight by using Oliver's factual narration about the lioness as a means of gaining her interest, they distracted attention completely from the narrative itself. The lovers' formal litany ('And so am I for Phebe', etc.) became the verbal release of pent-up frustration which – just – managed to stave off mocking laughter. The weirdest moment came when Jaques enveloped Rosalind in his cloak as if in huge sinister wings for their casual conversation about travel (pronounced 'travail') and appeared to attempt to seduce her, with much stress on 'experience' – but Rosalind? or Ganymede? And why? To demonstrate the dangers of her disguise, the other side of the natural, liberated coin, 'licence of free foot'? But such affectations were decisively outweighed by the achievements; it was an exhilarating start to the season.

Ron Daniels was clearly aiming at a 1980 image for *Romeo and Juliet*. Ralph Koltai provided two tattered, plaster-exposed walls (as if ready for the decorator) which could swivel to re-define the acting area but which always presented a remorselessly blank view, a faceless precinct for urban violence, where rival gangs lounged, hands in pockets; for if Nadine Baylis's costumes hinted at the doublets of Renaissance bravos, their leather and boots carried a much stronger suggestion of modern muggers, wielding clubs and belts: Mercutio and Tybalt fought with their sword-sticks as blunt weapons before actually drawing the blades.

Mr Daniels also interpreted the play's verbal elaboration in these terms: the word-play between Benvolio, Mercutio and Romeo in act 2, scene 4 upon 'pink', 'courtesy' and 'goose' was played as street-corner-gang in-joking, with no attempt to get laughs off the faded quibbles themselves; Mercutio's very young page was given Benvolio's Q1 question 'Queen Mab, what's she?', to which Mercutio improvised an increasingly imaginative explanation, illustrated in mime by the others; above all, Anton Lesser's Romeo was an embodiment of his society in his black leather gear, working out, indeed hammering out, his conceited definitions of 'brawling love'. 'What is it else?' was followed by a pause, as if to say 'let's think – ah yes, a *madness*', barked out desperately, an internal version of the violence around him. But more straightforward lines were equally broken up into mannerism: 'Sin? From my lips? Oh! Trespass sweetly urged' won a laugh; 'yonder blessed moon' in the balcony scene was a grotesque parody, all flailing arms; and moments like ''Tis TAW-CHER, and not mercy' in the Friar's cell became merely another form of rant – the oldest sins the newest kind of way.

The Friar's rebuke 'such die miserable' seemed very pertinent, whether by directorial intention or simply because Edwin Richfield's Friar was an oasis of calm authority amid destructive violence; but should the Friar's view dominate so much? The approach seemed to trivialize the play, reducing the importance of Mercutio, well though Jonathan Hyde played the part along the chosen lines; on the other hand, with no more scenes of urban violence after Mercutio's death, Mr Daniels could no longer use his main line of interpretation, and

had nothing to replace it with apart from a formal laying-out of Juliet to the sung accompaniment of Nashe's 'Adieu, farewell earth's bliss', which only served to prolong a second half which dragged more than ever.

And that modern urban world which gave a context to Anton Lesser's Romeo had no place for great houses and so tended to deprive Juliet of *her* context. Also, Judy Buxton had a very different, un-mannered way with verbal elaboration: her performance was clear and direct, and if it did not seem much more than that, it was partly because she was so isolated from everyone but the Nurse. Brenda Bruce played the Nurse with easy mastery, capturing all her garrulity with a welcome lightness of touch which had no need of eldritch cackling. Vigorously middle-aged rather than addled, warmly affectionate, she was by far the most attractive character on stage, so that her worldly-wise advice to marry 'with the County' came as an especially severe blow to a Juliet already so isolated.

Most of John Barton's first production of *Hamlet* took place on a small wooden forestage, surrounded by low benches; behind it were set the major props (halberds, rapiers, stoups of wine, the Players' property basket and thunder-sheet) needed to tell the story – or, more precisely, to *enact* the story. There was much stress on this being a *performance* of the events, an action 'that a man might *play*': at the start, Francisco appeared upstage, getting ready for his entry rather than on patrol, lit by a naked light bulb suspended over the up-stage area; the performance proper began with a sudden change from rehearsal lighting to stage lighting at Barnardo's 'Who's there?'. That naked bulb lit up again at the arrival of the Players, for the play scene, and at the end, when Hamlet finally performs his part and kills the King. But there was no attempt to establish Elsinore as a busy administrative and political centre, or indeed as a court of any kind, which was surprising and disappointing in a Barton production.

So Tony Church could obviously not present Polonius here as the crafty political operator he had played so brilliantly in Peter Hall's very political 1965–6 RSC version; but he substituted an equally brilliant study of an even more complex figure: ripely genial, superbly pacing and timing his lines for maximum humorous effect without loss of shrewdness, and able to modulate from sternness with Ophelia to genuine affection for her, comforting her after Hamlet's brutality in act 3, scene 1, and furious with Hamlet for his treatment of her in the play scene. Another aspect of this rounded Polonius was a genuine enthusiasm for the Players, arriving ebulliently in jester's cap and bells to announce them. 'This is too long' and a murmured, absorbed ' "mobled queen" is good', catching Hamlet's own tone, were evaluative comment, not philistinism, and Hamlet bantered good-naturedly with him.

The Players themselves were sober, unextravagant professionals: Aeneas' tale to Dido was at first quiet and measured; as it grew more intense, the other Players added external 'effects', rattling the thunder-sheet and building to a climax by wailing Hecuba's 'instant burst of clamour', cut off as the First Player ended the speech but held the mood, until, at Polonius's comment, he smiled and switched off the performance, to Polonius's laughing admiration. The whole scene was extremely effective and interesting; avoiding the extremes of ranting and naturalism, these Players were dignified and accomplished, yet also making unconcealed use of artifice.

Hamlet became increasingly involved in their performance. Struck by his resemblance to Pyrrhus, 'a neutral to his will and matter', he audibly anticipated the First Player's 'Did nothing'; the programme quoted Anne Barton's comment: 'The momentary indecision of Pyrrhus, . . . *in itself neither bad nor good*, presents Hamlet with an image of his own, mysterious inactivity.'[2] This exactly reflected the open, 'neutral' aspect of Mr Barton's approach to the character, clinched later in Hamlet's in-creasingly passionate admission 'I do not know / Why *yet I live to say* "THIS THING'S TO DO"', ever more exasperated with his own inaction. During the play scene, when the forestage itself became the Players' stage with the court seated on the benches around it, Hamlet's increasingly abusive interruptions, abetted by the Player Queen's accusing glances at the references to second husbands, initially disturbed and infuriated Gertrude more than Claudius; Hamlet's frenzied rattling of the thunder-sheet at 'the croaking raven doth bellow for revenge' screwed up the tension and provoked Claudius into breaking up the play contemptuously, his chest even resting against Hamlet's property sword.

The 'neutral' approach and the avoidance of conjuring up any 'world' other than that of the stage itself also characterized the treatment of the Ghost, a corporeal figure in very solid-looking armour who astonishingly *sat down*, and laid his helmet and truncheon beside him, to deliver part of his narration in a quietly conversational manner. This had a nice sequel in the closet scene when the Ghost again sat down, in his nightgown, a quietly domestic figure with his son and ex-wife: and this enabled Mr Barton to make a startlingly original point. Gertrude, having clearly realized the truth in her thunderstruck 'As kill a king!', actually heard the Ghost; she hardly dared look, until Hamlet turned her face towards him, and she collapsed in terror. This certainly disposed of the inconsistency of her inability to see a ghost visible to everyone else; and its apparent contradiction of the text was resolved by her trying not to admit her guilty realization of the truth, so that Hamlet's

Lay not that flattering unction to your soul,
That not your trespass but my madness speaks

seemed a factual comment and a logical rebuke.

Hamlet seemed badly shaken, mentally ex-

---

2 Introduction to the New Penguin *Hamlet*, ed. T. J. B. Spencer (Harmondsworth, 1980), p. 30 (italics mine).

hausted, after both Ghost scenes; 'I essentially am not in madness, / But mad in craft' was almost a question; and it seemed a pity that the violent hysteria of 'it hath made me MAD', as he struck Ophelia, should arise from the hoary old routine of having Hamlet suspect that he is being spied on, rather than from a morbid aspect of his own personality. But this was probably part of Mr Barton's declared aim of restoring a more poetic, romantic, princely Hamlet, for which Michael Pennington was ideal: handsome, attractive, friendly, with a natural, easy delivery and confident authority on stage.

But crucial scenes have to be tailored to fit this view. When Hamlet spared the praying Claudius, he did so merely because the action needed to be 'scann'd'; there was no sense of Hamlet arrogating to himself Claudius's damnation, not just his death. And in the graveyard, Hamlet's obsessive tracing of the noble dust of Alexander till 'a find it stopping a bung-hole had to be softened with soothingly elegiac recorder music played by the Second Gravedigger at complete variance with the words. Both the old king and Claudius were presented wholly from Hamlet's point of view, the first quiet and fatherly, the second a mere satyr, a ranting, melodramatic, red-coated hussar who reduced his prayer, from which vital phrases were cut, to a series of sophistries.

Such cuts, like others[3] which reduced the potential impact of performances like Tom Wilkinson's gentle, thoughtful, almost withdrawn Horatio, ultimately hampered Mr Pennington's own performance by depriving him of a detailed court world around him. In the middle acts, especially, the production lost some of the impact of acts 1, 2 and 5, where Mr Barton's absorbing interpretation, warts and all, renewed one's interest in the inexhaustible text.

To fit *Timon of Athens* into the cramped conditions of The Other Place, Ron Daniels used a kind of Japanese (possibly Noh-influenced) stylization: Timon and the sena-

tors wore kimonos; Alcibiades and his army were Samurai; the feasters squatted on cushions, picking decorously with chopsticks at diminutive dishes of what looked like prawn cocktail. There was no riotous excess in this hushed, smiling ceremony, nor a corrupt society later: the thumb-nail satirical sketches of the three false friends were played very soberly, without a hint of caricature. Timon himself was neither opulent benefactor nor foolish prodigal, but a sweet-natured, smilingly courteous host. In so low-key a world, after so cool a feast, the effect of the banquet of stones (in *tiny* 'covered dishes') was very restrained.

The stage floor was made of planks, with five of them up-ended at the back; in the second half, much of the floor was removed for Timon's pit, and nets suspended from the uprights to suggest breakwaters on the 'very hem o' th' sea'. But here Mr Daniels's production seemed to lose its line: stylization gave way to a kind of realism with a very intrusive sound-track of waves and howling beasts (but sounding like cows), and a violent thunderstorm which completely distracted from the bandit scene. Richard Pasco's Timon was at his best in the quiet, ironic passages, especially with the Poet and Painter, arms round them and piercing eyes fixed upon them as he drew them out: 'Y' have heard that I have gold; / I am sure you have. Speak truth; y'are honest men' had a witty alertness which strongly recalled Hamlet drawing out Rosencrantz and Guildenstern. Like his sweet-natured courtesy

---

3 In the first scene, these included: 'That are so fortified against our story' (32); 'Together with that fair and warlike form / In which the majesty of buried Denmark / Did sometimes march' (47–9); most of Marcellus's speech about the brazen cannon and impress of ship-wrights (73–8); 'The source of this our watch, and the chief head / Of this post-haste and romage in the land' (106–7); much of Horatio's account of the portents in Rome (117–25); 'For it is, as the air, invulnerable, / And our vain blows malicious mockery' (145–6); 'No fairy takes, nor witch hath power to charm' (163). Such omissions seem to me to weaken the distinctive *idiom* of the play.

at the start, this suggested a Timon more at home with 'the middle of humanity' than with 'the extremity of both ends'. Since he had not seemed one 'Who had the world as my confectionary', the extended curses of the second half seemed unrelated to the first half, especially since the production failed to maintain its chosen style and so could offer no support to its Timon in sustaining those curses, as John Schlesinger's had done so successfully in the main theatre in 1965. There, with room to manoeuvre, vivid detail and a strong company set a lavishly excessive Athens against a wilderness of concentrated desolation, within which Paul Scofield could range from large-scale prodigal to misanthrope, and could sustain those curses by emphasizing their formal structure ('If thou wert the lion . . . if thou wert the lamb . . . the fox . . . the wolf . . . the unicorn . . .') with his hypnotic, incantatory delivery, whereas sensitivity and fluency alone were not enough to carry Mr Pasco through.

## II

Mr Scofield himself, meanwhile, was playing Othello at the National Theatre. John Bury set a central, formal gateway with an upper level into a bare wall the width of the Olivier stage. Venice was suggested by projecting the windows of the Doge's palace and reflections of rippling water on to the wall; the Sagittary was defined simply by two rows of senatorial chairs facing each other; the move to Cyprus was achieved with minimum fuss by projecting clouds on to the wall, using the upper level as a look-out tower, and rearranging the furniture to form a guardroom where the visitors were received and offered drinks. Effected with Mr Bury's usual smooth mastery, scenes were quickly established with appropriate, detailed business which in no way inhibited actors from standing bang centre-stage and delivering passages like the expository Iago/Roderigo exchanges straight out into the house. For the temptation scene, which began the second half, a lightweight canopy was lowered and lit from above, shielding the characters from the Cyprus sun.

The boldly simple, functional design matched Peter Hall's direct, often quite literal, interpretation: as so often, he seemed concerned to explore and communicate the precise meaning of each scene. Paul Scofield's Othello was visually ideal: the handsome, craggy features, greying hair, bloodshot eyes, that characteristically upright military bearing and graceful movement, all stressed the ageing, alien professional soldier. This impression was reinforced by his initial costume, a mercenary soldier out of Dürer, contrasted with the sober Jacobean style of the Venetians, which Othello himself adopted in Cyprus until he changed into a red dressing-gown-cum-judge's-robe for the 'judicial' murder. He delivered much of the part evenly, perhaps somewhat monotonously, in his lowest register, obviously seeking to establish the difference between Othello's origins and those of the Venetians.

The Venetians themselves were strongly played. Felicity Kendal was a direct, girlishly unaffected Desdemona, very much attuned to Scofield's simple professional soldier. Mark Dignam's decades of invaluable experience in playing major supporting roles in Shakespeare gave his Duke real distinction: genial, humane, trying to arbitrate between Brabantio and Othello by taking up 'this mangled matter at the best'. Basil Henson's stern Brabantio responded to the Duke's consolatory couplets with a sharply ironical delivery of his own, mocking such consolation as empty cliché, however well meant: here, the implications of the constantly fluctuating language, as blank verse contrasts with rhyming couplets which in turn give way to business-like prose and revert to blank verse in Othello's elaborate replies, were all unerringly brought out by director and actors.

So, to an even greater extent, were those of the temptation scene. At the start, Othello was genially reasonable, his questions guileless, genuine inquiries. 'What dost thou mean?' was the straightforward question of a man

IA *As You Like It*, Royal Shakespeare Theatre, 1980.
Sinead Cusack as Celia and Susan Fleetwood as Rosalind

B *As You Like It*, Royal Shakespeare Theatre, 1980. The lovers' litany.
John Bowe (Orlando), Susan Fleetwood (Rosalind), Allan Hendrick (Silvius),
Julia Tobin (Phebe)

IIA *Romeo and Juliet*, Royal Shakespeare Theatre, 1980.
Judy Buxton as Juliet and Brenda Bruce as the Nurse

B *Romeo and Juliet*, Royal Shakespeare Theatre, 1980.
Mercutio (Jonathan Hyde) and Tybalt (Chris Hunter) fight with sword-sticks

IIIA *Hamlet*, Royal Shakespeare Theatre, 1980.
Polonius (Tony Church) announces the players

B *Hamlet*, Royal Shakespeare Theatre, 1980. The
Queen (Barbara Leigh-Hunt) sees the Ghost (Raymond
Westwell). Left, Michael Pennington as Hamlet

IVA *Timon of Athens*, The Other Place, Stratford, 1980. The first banquet, with James Hazeldine as Alcibiades and Richard Pasco as Timon at the central table

B *Timon of Athens*, The Other Place, Stratford, 1980.
Richard Pasco as Timon

VA *Othello*, National Theatre, 1980.
Felicity Kendal as Desdemona and Paul Scofield as Othello

B *Othello*, National Theatre, 1980. Paul Scofield as Othello

VIA *Titus Andronicus*, Stratford, Ontario, 1980.
William Hutt as Titus

B *Titus Andronicus*, Stratford, Ontario, 1980.
Rodger Barton (Chiron), Stephen Russell (Demetrius), Errol Slue (Aaron)

VIIA *Twelfth Night*, Stratford, Ontario, 1980.
William Hutt (Feste), Brian Bedford (Malvolio), Pat Galloway (Olivia)

B *Twelfth Night*, Stratford, Ontario, 1980.
Patricia Conolly (Viola), Jim McQueen (Orsino), William Hutt (Feste)

VIIIA *Much Ado About Nothing*, Stratford, Ontario, 1980.
Maggie Smith as Beatrice

B *Much Ado About Nothing*, Stratford, Ontario, 1980.
Stephen Russell (Claudio), Jim McQueen (Don Pedro), Brian Bedford (Benedick)

completely at a loss to understand what Iago was talking about, and when Iago warned him to beware of jealousy, his reaction was equally bewildered ('why is this?'); so his clear-cut approach to issues ('Away at once with love or jealousy') seemed more characteristic and more ominous than ever. When Iago makes his crucial suggestion that he knows Venetian infidelity as Othello doesn't, Michael Bryant was so plausible that Othello's 'Dost thou say so?' and 'And so she did' seemed the obvious responses to apparently incontrovertible truths. When the seeds of doubt are sown with this conviction, the damage is immediately done: there was a hint of the instability of the fit scene in 'not m-m-much mov'd' and in 'my relief / Must be to l-l-loathe her', and a sudden outburst on the word 'haggard', which returned with full primitive power at Othello's re-entry. So sensitive and responsive were actors and director to every detail of the scene that all questions about plausibility seemed irrelevant: it seemed quite natural that this Othello should span the whole gamut from faith to collapse in one tremendous long scene.

This was the high point of the production; thereafter, its very directness incurred some penalties. The huge, open stage was fine for the build-up to the fit as Othello circled Iago, the still point at the centre, and for the striking of Desdemona; but it robbed several episodes, especially the 'brothel' scene, of the murky, claustrophobic intimacy which they must have if we are to be drawn fully into the agony and humiliation of Othello's collapse. Nor did Mr Scofield's outbursts become as volcanic as might have been expected: he made surprisingly little use either of his lithe panther-like movements (so effective in his Volpone) or of his range of vocal mannerisms, to the point where the animal howls seemed oddly insulated from the performance as a whole, unlike, for instance, his amazing delivery of Lear's four-fold 'Howl', which had been an expression of unbearable intensity, a climax to which everything in that performance had logically built.

Here, however, there seemed to be something curiously uncertain, even evasive, at the heart of the performance: both 'once put out thy light' and 'I look down towards his feet – but that's a fable' were delivered with his back to the audience, and it was very hard to see what could be gained from denying Othello direct communication with the audience at such vital moments. It seemed at odds, too, with the directness of so much of the production, especially the quiet earnestness of Felicity Kendal's 'No, by my life and soul' and 'I never did / Offend you in my life; never lov'd Cassio', as if she was at last being given the chance to clear things up, and Mr Scofield's own return to his earlier patiently reasonable manner as he questioned Cassio about the handkerchief. The production's probing clarity had the great advantage that Othello's 'not easily jealous, but, being wrought, / Perplexed in the extreme' seemed a literal description of the process we had been shown in the temptation scene, but the disadvantage that it didn't seem able to illuminate the murky emotional complexity of the scenes that follow.

### III

At Stratford, Ontario, Brian Bedford made the maximum use of the huge thrust stage and upper level of the Festival Theatre for *Titus Andronicus* without using any additional set. The measured, formal disputes of the opening scene, with Marcus 'aloft', and the elaborately gilded procession in which Titus brought his prisoners and his dead sons back in glory to Rome, immediately established a convincing world of barbaric ritual where the violence and killing seemed explicable, almost inevitable, as Titus killed his son for dishonouring him in public, or Demetrius eyed Lavinia with fierce desire, or, later, Aaron killed the Nurse out of necessity rather than gratuitous blood-letting.

Dappled lighting was all that was needed to transform the permanent stage to the forest, where the central pillar served easily for the tree where Aaron hid the gold, and the central trap for the pit into which Titus's sons fell – not at all awkwardly, on a darkened stage; for the forest lighting varied as the characters' descriptions of the forest vary, from the 'chequer'd shadow' of Tamora's first speech to the sinister gloom of the 'barren detested vale' as she later calls it when her mood changes from lust to savagery. The dappled forest lighting and birdsong were unexpectedly used again later, to reinforce Lavinia's use of Ovid's account of the rape of Philomel to reveal her own – a subtle detail which indicated Mr Bedford's precise grasp of the tone and style of the play.

'The woods are ruthless, dreadful', fit setting, in their darkened state, for Errol Slue's superb Aaron, whose rich emphatic delivery gave lines like 'Blood and revenge are hammering in my head' full impact, and for Stephen Russell's lithe Demetrius, crouching warily, resting on his heels, hands balanced on his knees, as if watching for his prey, and exactly communicating brutish satisfied lust after savaging Lavinia. These two performances strongly supported J. C. Maxwell's view that their scenes stand out in their 'power to convey a real impression of dramatic interchange',[4] especially when Aaron defended his black baby with bravura and ribald humour, easily holding and dominating the centre of the stage: this Aaron was always placed in emphatically strong positions, on the upper level for his first Marlovian speech ('I will be bright and shine in pearl and gold'), and strapped to a ladder suspended from the upper level from which he could deliver his self-congratulatory account of his villainy in act 5, scene 1 straight out into the house with unimpeded impact.

William Hutt's Titus was a smilingly confident general, an innocent in politics, turned to crazed revenge. The climax of his performance was the speech leading to his cutting the throats of Demetrius and Chiron, in which he turned his rather mannered habit of breaking up verse lines into abrupt chunks to positive advantage: he built up the whole speech bit by bit, faster and faster, to suggest a mind half-crazed but also ruthlessly logical as it worked out the cannibal banquet, culminating in a tremendous

> For worse than Philomel you us'd my daughter,
> And worse than Progne I will be reveng'd,

the last word extended into a terrifying howl, the climax both of Titus's mad revenge and of the play's use of the Philomel story as a running motif.

It is instructive here to compare this *Titus* with Trevor Nunn's at Stratford-upon-Avon in 1972. Mr Nunn, assuming that a modern audience wouldn't understand the Philomel references, cut them all; Mr Bedford, who can scarcely have had higher expectations of his Ontario audience's familiarity with the classics, nonetheless retained them, obviously realizing that they are a crucial strand in the writing, and that such passages of verbal elaboration are essential to the play's theatrical impact: hence, in large part, the success of his Aaron scenes and the failure of Mr Nunn's, where an atmosphere of *dolce vita* decadence was not enough. On the other hand, Mr Nunn's Titus, Colin Blakely, vividly made us share the experience of a man of oak enduring a series of agonizing blows, as William Hutt did not. Indeed, Mr Hutt's mannerism of whipping out a knife to kill or maim with lightning suddenness meant that he had severed his own hand in act 3, scene 1, almost before we knew it had happened, a far cry from the 'enormous physical agony' that Olivier apparently communicated at this point.[5]

The final ritual slaughter was superbly controlled by Mr Bedford's unerring sense of rhythm; but he then cut everything from the death of Saturninus, so that the play did not end with Marcus's attempts to 'knit' Rome's 'broken limbs again into one body', but with Aaron spotlit on the upper stage as an amplified

---

4 *Titus Andronicus* new Arden Shakespeare (1953, repr. 1968), p. xxxvii.

5 See Richard David, *Shakespeare Survey 10* (Cambridge, 1957), p. 127.

voice spoke a passage from the Sibylline oracle prophesying that 'inexorable wrath shall fall on Rome'. This falsification of the ending was the more surprising since it didn't fit in with the way in which the production as a whole, most successfully, took the play at face value; for the other major cuts (the whole of Marcus's notorious, emblematic description of the ravaged Lavinia, or the squabbling over 'whose hand shall go' in act 3, scene 1) seemed to be made out of nervousness rather than the desire to alter. The final impression was of an uncomplicated but very powerful revenge play.

*Henry V* was somewhat similarly treated by Peter Moss as an uncomplicated but certainly not uninteresting chronicle play. Douglas Rain's Chorus walked quietly on to the empty stage and spoke confidentially, persuasively, evoking the night before Agincourt with especial mastery. Apart from a few props (ships' rigging, banners) the actors themselves 'dressed' the stage, the three darkly-clad conspirators ominously appearing on the forestage steps as the Chorus referred to them, and the stage suddenly filling for the embarkation at Southampton.

Within the simple, fluid staging, Jack Wetherall gave an interestingly rounded performance as a very young but serious, thoughtful Henry, bringing out especially clearly the way in which the King makes the most of any situation with which he is presented. Kneeling at a prayer-desk, he listened attentively to the Archbishop's advice; although this was obviously given out of ecclesiastical self-interest (to the marked distrust of the court), that didn't necessarily invalidate his claim; so when the ambassadors presented the tennis balls, Henry *used* the insult to build up an impassioned claim to the French crown which had already been decided on before the insult was delivered. So with the conspirators: having lured them into advising against mercy for another offender, he could then stress that their 'own counsel' had suppressed 'the mercy that was quick in us but late', whipping

himself up to passionate indignation against the ingratitude of Scroop (a technique which recalled William Hutt's Titus building up his plan of revenge). In each case, the effect was an interesting blend of expediency and personal involvement.

There was similar involvement in his soliloquy 'Upon the King', developing into heartfelt envy of the peasant's security as opposed to the King's responsibility; and this in turn developed into an almost desperate *bargain* with God for victory in return for obsequies to 'Richard's soul'. This desperation returned at the command to kill the prisoners; then, typically, he worked himself up to the threat to 'cut the throats of those we have' in apparent response to the killing of the boys, having *already* given the command. He was close to breaking-point as he asked Montjoy 'Com'st thou again for ransom?', and almost collapsed at the news of victory; but he was able to switch to boyishly impish plotting, Hal-like, with Williams and Fluellen – and back again, to a seriousness with Williams prepared for by his passionate envy of the peasant's lot in the earlier soliloquy. It was of a piece with this interpretation that 'O God, thy arm was here' should seem perfectly sincere: the fact that he made the most of every situation, including bargaining with God for aid, did not necessarily make him a hypocrite; and the way that he involved himself personally in those situations made 'Davy Gam, Esquire' intensely moving. The splendid courtship of Katherine was a fitting climax to the interpretation: it was typical of this Henry that, while making it clear that she is his main political demand of her father (the repeated 'it shall please him, Kate' very steely), he should use the Hal-style device of getting to *know* her first, with much humour.

The substantially Canadian company gave strong performances throughout, especially the very nicely timed and paced French scene before Agincourt, and the still account of Falstaff's death, with a desolating sense of loss from Bardolph; it was the more frustrating that, though sitting well forward in the centre, I could not see Henry's face as he ordered Bardolph's execution: he was completely hidden from me by a soldier placed on the steps at the very front of the stage. This raises important points about the use of this aggressively open stage. Unless actors stand in the position of advantage dead-centre (Aaron defending his baby, Henry brooding 'Upon the King'), they are in real danger of losing the attention of the third or so of the audience from whom they are turned away. A glaring example was the night before Agincourt: Williams and the others sat by a brazier on the front steps off-centre in an attempt to suggest something intimate on that vast stage; so the absolutely crucial debate between Henry and Williams about a king's responsibilities lost most of its impact by being huddled into a disadvantageous position where a large proportion of the audience couldn't concentrate on it. This is not a stage which encourages conversation, or even much communication, between actors; and here the theatre's Artistic Director, Robin Phillips, has developed his personal inclination towards elaborate interpretation and large-scale visual effects in response to the nature of his stage. Sometimes the results are marvellous, as in the dazzling evocation of Elizabeth I's court in the 1977 *Midsummer Night's Dream*, which I described in *Shakespeare Survey 31*; but at other times they are distracting, as in the use of a large company of walk-on actors merely to 'dress' the stage, even in intimate scenes where they are plainly not required and are therefore an intrusion.

The elaboration of Mr Phillips's *Much Ado About Nothing* and *Twelfth Night* contrasted with the direct simplicity of *Titus* and *Henry V*; in both comedies, he used rich costumes, set and furniture, and 'mood' music often during, as well as between, scenes to create a very specific atmosphere. It was a pleasant change to see a *Much Ado* for once *not* set in the nineteenth century but in a Cavalier world of warm, mellow 'Old Master' brown velvets,

bucket-top boots and Henrietta Maria hairstyles, with the first dissembly of the Watch gathered round a table after Rembrandt's *Night Watch*, and with more than a hint of Cromwell in Dogberry's broad hat and burly appearance. Mr Phillips's approach can be summarized by the two 'stage pictures' that closed each act: in the first, Beatrice made a long, love-sick exit accompanied by slowly dimming lights and mood music; at the end, the company took hands for a dance and then 'froze' as the lights dimmed to a spot on Beatrice and Benedick embracing.

This certainly left no doubt where the emphasis was laid, on two star performances by Maggie Smith and Brian Bedford which certainly did not miss a trick from start to finish. Miss Smith was as enchanting as ever, though her vocal mannerisms are becoming very pronounced, especially a habit of pausing at eccentric points in a sentence and then running the rest of it into the next ('Can this [*pause*] be-true-stand-I-condemn'd', for instance); like Mr Hutt's 'short-winded' breaking up of verse into fragments, this seems an unhealthy example to the less assured or less experienced members of the company; but certainly the elaborate technique of this Beatrice and Benedick was entirely in keeping with the deliberate pace of Mr Phillips's production.

Mr Bedford's meticulous timing of his extended prose speeches, delaying laugh lines by strategic pauses, yielded more laughter than any other Benedick I recall, particularly in the scenes with Claudio and Don Pedro, a trio of laughing cavaliers whose gaiety established a real sense of camaraderie. The easy friendship between this Benedick and Claudio helped Stephen Russell to establish a more convincing and sympathetic Claudio than usual; in the church scene he began to question Hero almost gently, as if regretting his decision to shame her, before becoming violent. Mr Bedford's new, sobered response to his friends' behaviour was impressive here, and even more so in his quiet challenge to Claudio, 'You are a villain';

and Jim McQueen treated Don Pedro's very tricky, ill-timed speech about how Beatrice praised Benedick's wit as an embarrassed attempt to restore their earlier friendly relaxation, rather than as the piece of heartless indifference to the news of Hero's apparent death which it seems in the text.

Here, as in the earlier scenes for these three, Mr Phillips's slow pace enabled these experienced players to make difficult passages convincing and to make sure-fire passages, like the gulling of Benedick, better than ever. But in contrast, with less experienced players, the gulling of Beatrice went for nothing, and the audience lost interest; they also seemed quite unable to cope with the play's shifts between humour and sombreness: because Mr Phillips had released such tremendous gaiety early on, they subsequently sniggered remorselessly at everything, even Maggie Smith's 'there is no love in you', delivered with a quiet earnestness that was exactly right. And though the massed attendants ought to have given the church scene its sense of sinister occasion, it seemed to lose its way, to lack a focal point, and the rhythm of the production faltered in the second half generally.

So it did in the second half of *Twelfth Night*, which took place in an eighteenth-century world of 'sentimental comedy', with drawing-room chairs for Olivia's house and a large iron-work structure at the back, topped by foliage, part garden for the box-tree, part prison for Malvolio, part funeral monument – to underline the sadness of the play? Mr Phillips clearly wanted to emphasize its bitter-sweet complexity, at the risk of some confusion.

Jim McQueen's Orsino, for instance, seemed an odd mixture of vigorous confidence and fashionable doting, genial towards a court who appeared, again oddly, both to flatter and overtly to mock him. Perhaps the idea was that Patricia Conolly's fresh, direct Viola was the only person in his court who could really communicate with him; it was as if she brought out the best in him, made him generous, especially

in one notable episode: William Hutt's elderly Feste, less a clown than a relaxed, studious 'corrupter of words' with his lorgnette and satchel of books, sang 'Come away death' beautifully; this Feste really did 'take pleasure in singing', and instead of rewarding him with money, Orsino presented him with the song-book: '*Truly*, sir?' asked Mr Hutt in delight. Later, Mr McQueen made no attempt to soften the male chauvinism of 'There is no woman's sides / Can bide the beating of so strong a passion / As love doth give my heart', delivered slowly and emphatically; Miss Conolly very deliberately corrected his view with her allegory of her sister. In this scene, Mr Phillips certainly reached the complex heart of the play; and his steady, thoughtful approach to the text also helped Miss Conolly as she almost improvised her way into the 'willow cabin' speech. But Pat Galloway was a very mature Olivia in what we are told was the style of the old 'stock' companies. For all her authority, her declaration of love ('Cesario, by the roses of the spring') lost all its fresh lyricism in rant and physical groping, to the derision of the audience – an extremely serious miscalculation.

There was, in fact, a curious stylistic contradiction at the centre of the production: for while Brian Bedford's Malvolio began as a sober steward signing bills, his (very funny) letter scene seemed too long drawn out and too obviously played to the audience; and while Barry MacGregor's quietly Scottish Sir Toby was nicely unexaggerated, Sir Andrew was exaggeration run riot, a grotesque frog-faced mannequin without a trace of humanity. Moreover the finale, like the church scene in *Much Ado*, seemed to lose its way: Orsino, bantering rather than threatening, did not build on what he and Viola had achieved earlier; Olivia's 'Most wonderful' and Sebastian's 'So comes it, lady, you have been mistook' were played for crude guffaws at complete odds with the treatment of the Viola/Sebastian reunion which, supported by atmospheric music, was clearly meant to be a charged, held moment, but wasn't. Mr Hutt got the scene back on the rails with Feste's edged jibe at Malvolio 'Why, "Some are born great"', and the rain spattering down after his final song was a very characteristic Phillips touch.

That seemed to reinforce Mr Phillips's concern with the play's bitter-sweet complexity; too often, however, we were more aware of elaborate contrivance instead, especially when he 'dressed' the stage with wholly unnecessary (and extremely irritating) hordes of courtiers, bewigged servants, ladies' maids in mob-caps, and so on. Even so, these four productions were continuously stimulating, demonstrating the various approaches possible to a stage which offers opportunities and pitfalls in almost equal measure.

# THE YEAR'S CONTRIBUTIONS TO SHAKESPEARIAN STUDY

## 1 CRITICAL STUDIES

*reviewed by* HARRIETT HAWKINS

### PART I
### BOOKS AND COUNTERBOOKS

'A book which does not contain its counterbook is considered incomplete', wrote Borges, describing the books of 'Tlön' which invariably include 'the rigorous pro and con of a doctrine'.[1] This also seems a strikingly accurate account of Shakespeare's plays and poems. Possibly because his strongest case in favour of something is, characteristically, countered by the best possible arguments against it – and vice versa – Shakespeare often seems to confront us with the very books and counterbooks of life itself. This, of course, has provided critics with countless subjects for fruitful speculation. But it poses grave difficulties for those who attempt to interpret his works in terms of a single doctrine or one-sided theory. And there is always the danger of mistaking a counter-argument for the main one. Several recently published books, as well as certain articles which will be considered later on, may serve to illustrate these points.

Kenneth Muir's new books on the sonnets and the comedies reflect his continuing concern with the differences between Shakespeare's accomplishments within a single genre:

In the Sonnets the Poet's attitude both to W. H. and to the Dark Lady – and even to his own feelings – is wildly inconsistent . . . W. H. is sometimes de-picted as a man whose character is as praiseworthy as his beauty, sometimes as a rake, sometimes as selfish and cold-hearted, if slow to temptation. . . . The Poet himself vows eternal fidelity to W. H., but on occasion partially admits he has neglected him for newer friends . . . Some critics would have preferred a tidier story . . . But, it may be argued, it is the very untidiness which helps to give the illusion of truth to life.[2]

Discussing *Shakespeare's Comic Sequence*,[3] Muir reminds us that, while 'it is true that every one of his comedies could be recognized as his, and could not possibly be mistaken for one of Dekker's, or Jonson's or Middleton's', no single formula can be found to apply to Shakespeare's various experiments in the comic mode: 'To adapt what I once said about his tragedies, "there is no such thing as Shakespearian Comedy; there are only Shakespearian comedies"' (pp.1–2). Although the fashion, nowadays, is to insist that even the gayest comedies are ultimately disturbing because they acknowledge that, in the natural course of human events, not every

---

1 Jorge Luis Borges, 'Tlön, Uqbar, Orbis Tertius', in *Labyrinths*, ed. Donald A. Yates and James E. Irby (Penguin Books, Harmondsworth, 1974), p. 37.
2 *Shakespeare's Sonnets* (George Allen & Unwin, London, 1979), p. 122.
3 *Shakespeare's Comic Sequence* (Liverpool University Press, 1979).

Jack gets his Jill, and all does not always end well for everyone, Muir argues that we need not be unduly upset by the fates of certain comic losers like 'the forsaken William, or Sir Andrew, a sadder, poorer, and not much wiser man' (p. 52). In Muir's discussions of them, the major key still dominates in Shakespeare's merriest plays.

By contrast, in his Marxist study of the comedies,[4] Elliot Krieger relentlessly decomicalizes and flattens out the different plays discussed. Here is his ideological steamroller in operation:

[As You Like It] articulates an ideological process, whereby the ruling class uses Nature, or its own translation and redefinition of *nature*, to justify its freedom from labour and the subordination of, or struggle against, other social classes. (p.96)
[In *Twelfth Night*] the ruling class ideology that 'all is fortune', that fortune creates and determines nature, is meant to keep people, especially servants, blind to the opposite proposition: that people create nature . . . as they bring about changes in the social order. (p. 130)
[In *The Merchant of Venice*] the emphasis on harmony, especially through its association with heavenly hierarchies . . . protects the social position of the ruling class. (p. 10)

Readers familiar with the criticism of the nineteen-fifties and sixties will remember having read eerily similar conclusions about Shakespeare's plays in countless books and articles that then *lauded* them for affirming the hierarchical values of the time. And the new 'dialectical' packaging given them by Krieger does not make the same old conclusions concerning these plays sound any less reductive and irrelevant than they did fifteen years ago. For no matter whether it is posed by reactionaries or by revolutionaries, the true answer to the question, 'Do Shakespeare's plays and characters uphold hierarchical values?' obviously has to be 'Some do; some don't.' Krieger himself simply ignores any comedies, characters, lines or situations that do not conform to his thesis. There is no notice of the

sometimes hilarious, sometimes profound processes of inversion and levelling that go on in several plays that are discussed, no reference to Shakespeare's celebration of 'bourgeois' virtue in *The Merry Wives of Windsor*, no mention of his sending up – and putting down – of aristocratic pretensions and characters in *Love's Labour's Lost* and *All's Well That Ends Well*. Krieger's book therefore seems (on the one hand) incomplete, and (on the other hand) twice again too long.

In his Christian interpretation of the comedies,[5] R. Chris Hassel, Jr, tries to keep his priorities clear: 'The Christian doctrine, the Pauline and Erasmian allusions, elucidate the comic action – not the other way around' (p. 17). Yet he still treats the comedies as sugary sermons on set texts, i.e., '''Love'' vs. ''Charity'': Folly in *Love's Labour's Lost*', '''Man is a Giddy Thing'': Repentance and Faith in *Much Ado About Nothing*', 'Faith in *A Midsummer Night's Dream*', '''Man's Estate'': The Festival of Folly in *Twelfth Night*', and '''I Stand for Sacrifice'': Frustrated Communion in *The Merchant of Venice*'. It is undeniably true that Shakespeare, St Paul and Erasmus agree that nobody's perfect, and to recognize one's own frailty and folly is a form of wisdom. But their agreement concerning such issues does not explain the differences between the various needs satisfied by, and diverse insights to be derived from receiving the sacrament in church, reverently reading the Bible, relishing the ironies in *The Praise of Folly*, and watching *Twelfth Night*. Neither does Hassel's book, which is concerned only with correspondences between them: 'Comic festivity . . . achieves its fullest potential in *Twelfth Night*, by becoming associated with both the sacrament and the festival of Christian humility and Christian love' (p. 175). Biblical references to olive trees (and branches) are alleged to associate Olivia

---

4 *A Marxist Study of Shakespeare's Comedies* (Macmillan Press, London and Basingstoke, 1979).
5 *Faith and Folly in Shakespeare's Romantic Comedies* (University of Georgia Press, Athens, 1980).

with peace, fertility, fidelity, 'the body of Christian believers' and 'the Christian tradition of edifying humiliation'. Her name thus predicts Olivia's 'successful humbling' and makes her 'intended monasticism even more richly ironic' (p. 158). Sebastian's baffled delight at her favour ('Or I am mad, or else this is a dream') is associated with a 'blessed humility' which is 'too closely analogous to the madness of religious ecstasy described by Erasmus' to be 'dismissed as completely coincidental' (p. 168). Alas, Hassel does not say whether Sebastian's name predicts a future martyrdom that makes his eagerness to marry Olivia even more richly ironic – doesn't the feast of St Sebastian follow Twelfth Night too closely for this association to be dismissed as purely coincidental? One also wonders whether Antipholus of Syracuse, who expresses identical sentiments in a similar situation ('Am I . . . sleeping or waking? Mad or well advis'd?') is, likewise, associated with religious ecstasy. He could be, since he is visiting the very Ephesus to which St Paul directed an Epistle. But, then, given this mode of reasoning, that banquet in *Titus Andronicus* wherein flesh and blood are actually *consumed* might be said to realize the fullest potential of tragedy by becoming associated with the Eucharist itself. Readers of all such interpretations had better heed J. C. Maxwell's warning, and adopt a sceptical attitude towards conclusions based on correspondences alleged to result from 'more than mere' coincidence.

Focusing on the question of authority in *Measure for Measure*, D. C. Biswas's account of 'The Administration of Justice in Elizabethan England'[6] cites actual statutes and case-histories that reveal the cruelty, tyranny, and sheer arbitrariness then sanctioned by the laws on the books. One may not always agree with Biswas's interpretations, but his quotations so illuminate the human realities behind Shakespeare's references to the 'law's delay', to 'beggars in the stocks', to trumped-up charges against men and women of the highest rank, to having to plead one's case without being

allowed to summon witnesses, that it becomes impossible to account for them in purely ideological or literary terms. Biswas's book also includes specially useful discussions of 'Witches in Shakespeare' and '*Troilus and Cressida* and the Renaissance Concept of Value'. It seems to me that in *Troilus and Cressida*, as elsewhere, Shakespeare's answer to the question, 'Does the worth of a thing ultimately depend on the way it is valued by others?' is 'No' – at least so far as human beings are concerned. Some individuals (like Cordelia) may prove to be worth more, others (like Cressida) worth less than the value we once placed on them. Still, as Biswas argues, there is also truth in the argument that value, insofar as the *valuer* is concerned, does dwell in particular will. And he is surely right to conclude that the counter-arguments concerning this issue are as powerfully presented in *Troilus and Cressida* as they are ever likely to be.

In *Shakespeare's Tragic Practice*,[7] Bertrand Evans is unconcerned with any counter-arguments whatsoever. This book seems based on the assumption that no one, before or since Evans published his earlier book on Shakespeare's comedies, has ever heard of dramatic irony, or written about Shakespeare's ironies in particular. Sometimes he writes straightforwardly (as if no one else had) about the levels of knowledge and awareness shared by, or restricted to, Shakespeare's characters and his audience. At crucial points, however, his refusal to admit the extant evidence against his own conclusions results in disaster. Completely ignoring the critical and theatrical testimony of centuries – along with the emotional impact of the dramatic poetry and the genuinely tragic ironies here involved – Evans announces that Antony never loved Cleopatra, that his passion for her was feigned in order to cover up his real reason for staying out of

---

6 *Shakespeare in His Own Time* (Macmillan, India, 1979).

7 Clarendon Press, Oxford, 1979.

Rome (his terror of Caesar), and that he intended to betray her 'in the worst way possible' through that final, misdirected warning, 'None about Caesar trust but Proculeius' (pp. 241–69). One waits in vain for the answer to the obvious technical query: in the absence of any soliloquies or series of asides so stating, how is the actor portraying Antony supposed to inform everyone in the audience that he is only faking it, and, *simultaneously*, convince everybody on the stage that his passion is real? Moreover, if Evans is right, then we have to blame Shakespeare for a virtually total failure of communication – for having so long, so grievously, and (worse still) so unwittingly misled the rest of us concerning the emotional and sexual affinity between Antony and Cleopatra. And this seems a terribly sad thing to do to him, 'considering' – in the immortal words of Robert Benchley – 'the hard work that Shakespeare must have put in on his wording' when he was writing this particular play.

It is, therefore, a relief to open a rich collection of essays on *Shakespeare's Styles*[8] and find an explicit discussion, by G. R. Hibbard, of 'That "happy valiancy of style" which Coleridge singled out as the most striking and characteristic quality' of *Antony and Cleopatra*. This volume also contains articles on 'Rhetoric and Insincerity', by L. C. Knights; 'Style in the *Henry VI* plays', by Wolfgang Clemen; 'Poem and Context in *Love's Labour's Lost*', by G. K. Hunter; 'The Declaration of Love', by Philip Edwards; 'Juliet's Nurse: The Uses of Inconsequentiality', by Stanley Wells; 'Language and Speaker in *Macbeth*', by Nicholas Brooke; 'Poetic Language and Dramatic Significance', by R. A. Foakes; 'The Language of Recognition', by Inga-Stina Ewbank; 'Language and Speaker in Shakespeare's Last Plays', by Anne Barton; 'Shakespeare's Bombast', by E. A. J. Honigmann; 'The Defence of Paradox', by Geoffrey Bullough; 'Some Off-stage Conversations', by A. C. Sprague; 'Shakespeare's Recollections of Marlowe', by M. C. Bradbrook; 'Caliban as a Red Man', by

G. Wilson Knight; and 'Shakespeare's Dark Lady: A Question of Identity', by Samuel Schoenbaum. Here, chosen pretty much at random, are samples of the problems posed and subjects pursued:

The 'I' of a character in a play . . . is open all the time to the question Why: Why is it that he is saying this? What does his language tell us about the kind of man he is or will become? (Hunter, p. 29)

Given almost any protestation of love by a 'good' character in Shakespeare one could transfer it without indecorum to a hypocrite. Only the situation teaches us how it should be read. (Edwards, p. 46)

As the Nurse talks, her memories not only throw our minds back to the infancy of this girl, they also recall a prediction made at that time of how Juliet would react when she . . . came 'to age'. The child who is talked about as an innocent infant is now before us, the subject of marriage plans. (Wells, pp. 61–2)

Editors of *The Tempest* have often wished to transfer Miranda's verbal assault upon Caliban in Act 1 ('Abhorred slave, / Which any print of goodness wilt not take') to Prospero. . . . Even so, Miranda says to Caliban . . . what the situation, as opposed to maidenly decorum and the pliability of her own nature, would seem to demand. (Barton, p. 137)

Sometimes again, the spoken words following the imagined ones are of extraordinary naturalness, 'sounding from the page' and characterising the speaker. '*Shylock*. Three thousand ducats – well. . . .' The beginning of the negotiation is left for us to re-create. Its sinister progress is dramatised later in the scene. But Shylock already lives for us in those first words of his and in the pauses which accompany them. (Sprague, p. 185)

Such essays seem designed to stimulate further speculation about the problems concerned. For instance, R. A. Foakes argues that his 'balanced phrases, "With mirth in funeral, and with dirge in marriage" . . . may suggest a prepared speech, even a certain pomposity, but the speech could be regarded as a brilliant tactic by Claudius (or Shakespeare) to *conceal* rather

---

8 *Shakespeare's Styles: Essays in Honour of Kenneth Muir*, ed. Philip Edwards, Inga-Stina Ewbank and G. K. Hunter (Cambridge University Press, 1980).

than distil his personality' (pp. 84–5). This seems to make specially good sense given the methods of exposition in the opening scenes of *Hamlet*. His speech is just fishy enough to arouse suspicion, but for Claudius (or Shakespeare) to manifest his villainy more overtly here would diminish the impact of the Ghost's subsequent revelations to Hamlet – and to us. Thus these essays serve to set the reader thinking.

Individual chapters in Alvin B. Kernan's *The Playwright as Magician* are devoted to 'Shakespeare's *Sonnets* and the Failure of Patronage', 'Actors and Audiences in *The Taming of the Shrew, Love's Labour's Lost, A Midsummer Night's Dream*, and *1 Henry IV*', 'Politics and Theater in *Hamlet*', 'The Morality Play in *King Lear*', 'The Public Playhouse and the Ideal Theater of *The Tempest*'.[9] To some of the fundamental problems posed in his works, Shakespeare offers no final solution: in *A Midsummer Night's Dream*

Shakespeare claims for the dramatic poet all the powers which the Renaissance conferred on art, but his image of the theater still acknowledges the crudity and accidents of stage presentation, the clumsiness of actors, the incomprehension of audiences, and the danger that plays may be mere fantasy without much relation to reality. (p. 79)

Although he discusses some familiar subjects, Kernan's book serves as a useful reminder that what counts are the ways in which Shakespeare's greatest works defy all attempts to 'sum up life too neatly, round it off too perfectly' (p. 128).

In his book on *Measure for Measure: The Law and the Convent*, Darryl J. Gless discusses 'the full implications of the biblical measure-for-measure text; the complex interrelationships among Renaissance conceptions of civil law, theological law, charity, and providence; the ethical import of Protestant salvific doctrine; and the currency, complexity and potential literary uses of antimonastic satire'.[10] According to Gless, a consideration of these

issues provides solutions to the following questions:

To what extent can characters in the play be considered 'allegorical'? Does Isabella's defense of her chastity mark her as an aspiring saint or as an unfeeling prude? Why are the Duke's attitudes . . . consistently inconsistent? Why does the subplot focus repeatedly on Lucio's comic slanders of the Duke? How are we to assess the often-remarked discordance between the play's early scenes and its conclusion? How does the Duke's famous death speech function? And why does Isabella agree to marry? (p. x)

It seems to me that the human and dramatic problems posed by this play are immeasurably more interesting than the solutions propounded by modern critics like Gless. But, then, anyone who writes about *Measure for Measure* is going to run into resistance from readers who admire the play for diametrically opposite reasons, or who interpret it in opposite ways.

Rolf Soellner and Jeanne Addison Roberts have published studies of *Timon of Athens* and *The Merry Wives of Windsor* that are intended to remedy the comparative neglect of their subjects. Yet an obvious reason why their books seem so interesting is that one has not read innumerable other discussions of the plays concerned. In *Shakespeare's Pessimistic Tragedy*,[11] Soellner provides a detailed discussion of *Timon's* dramatic and cultural context which points to the peculiar problems posed by its structure and characterization. Individual chapters are concerned with Renaissance pessimism, the boundaries of tragedy, the 'Turn of Fortune's Wheel', 'The Rise of Alcibiades', 'Apemantus and the Others', the 'Ills of Society' and the 'Uses of Nature and Art'. Soellner's attack on the faithful Flavius seemed most odd – he is 'interested in gold' (p. 17). But who would want a steward that wasn't?

---

9  Yale University Press, New Haven and London, 1979.
10 Princeton University Press, 1979, p. ix.
11 *Timon of Athens: Shakespeare's Pessimistic Tragedy*, with a stage history by Gary Jay Williams (Ohio State University Press, Columbus, 1979).

In *Shakespeare's English Comedy*, Jeanne Addison Roberts discusses the text, criticism, sources, stage history and characterization of *The Merry Wives*.[12] Her brief account of Verdi's *Falstaff* (p. 118) is suggestive – does the music supply the dimension of poetic power that, in comparison with his greatest works, Shakespeare's language here lacks? In an effort to demonstrate that this is not mere farce, Roberts occasionally seems transported by the mode for criticism that tends, rather like the melancholy Jaques, to moralize the spectacle, augmenting it with tears:

*The Merry Wives* is not a lighthearted midsummer romp, or a springtime celebration, but rather a record of the transition from fall to winter – an effort to put the house in order, to become reconciled to the passing of fertility from the old to the young. Just beyond the frivolity of the play's pranks and the 'innocent' revenge of its night-wandering spirits lie the gravity and earnestness of a sober New Year. Allhallow Eve must give way to the Feast of All Saints. (p. 83)

*Query*: Would the management at the Globe have advertised this particular play in such gloomy terms? A modern producer might do so precisely because modern critics have already imposed the kind of interpretation appropriate to the end of *Love's Labour's Lost* on so many other comedies that these sombre criteria of analysis have come to seem criteria of *comic* merit. Yet it is so obviously true that youth's a stuff will not endure, that winter winds will blow, etc., that one wonders why we need always make Star Chamber matters of it when discussing Shakespeare's comedies. Sometimes, surely, 'gravity and earnestness' must give way to present mirth and present laughter.

Couldn't it be that the serious undertones in certain comedies serve to reinforce – by taking into account what most threatens them – their glowing affirmations and celebrations of life in a holiday humour? Conversely, as Susan Snyder has observed in her superb discussion

of *The Comic Matrix of Shakespeare's Tragedies*,[13]

comedy can become the ground from which, or against which, tragedy develops. By evoking the world where lovers always win, death always loses, and nothing is irrevocable, a dramatist can set up the false expectations of a comic resolution so as to reinforce by sharp contrast the movement into tragic inevitability. . . . Finally, comedy can become part of the tragedy itself, providing in its long-range, leveling, anti-individual perspective the most radical challenge to heroic distinction. (p. 5)

Charles Frey's involvement with *The Winter's Tales: Shakespeare's Vast Romance*[14] began about twenty-five years ago – just before the deluge of commentary on the romances – and in spite of all his citations, he concludes that this is a 'still much-too-neglected masterpiece'. His discussions of 'Critical Views and Reviews', of *Pandosto*, and 'The Play in Time' are knowledgeable and seem deeply felt. Yet it's been a long time since this beautiful play was the subject of 'casual and uninformed' dismissals (p. 170), and there's no need for anyone, nowadays, to exhort us to 're-examine our more skeptical and no doubt more prevalent assumptions' about it. For that matter, the sceptical reader is unlikely to be persuaded by Frey's references to 'temporal-affective' responses, 'post-play rumination' and 'pre-play preparation' which make the experience of watching or reading *The Winter's Tale* sound rather like having, or performing, an operation:

Given the play's resistance to conceptual analysis, a sound interpretive strategy . . . would be to provide not post-play rumination but a collection of mat-

12 *Shakespeare's English Comedy: The Merry Wives of Windsor in Context* (University of Nebraska Press, Lincoln and London, 1979).

13 *The Comic Matrix of Shakespeare's Tragedies: Romeo and Juliet, Hamlet, Othello, and King Lear* (Princeton University Press, 1979).

14 *Shakespeare's Vast Romance: A Study of The Winter's Tale* (University of Missouri Press, Columbia and London, 1980).

erials most useful to pre-play preparation . . . My triangulation of chapters that follow attempts to provide . . . a recurrent focus upon the developing, cumulative, drama of the play in performance or reading and upon the uses of a temporal-affective criticism responsive to that drama. (p. 3)

In a news release issued on the Bard's birthday (1980), A. L. Rowse decreed that there is nothing more to be learned from purely critical discussions of Shakespeare.[15] But do not fear. Having arrived at similar conclusions concerning *Julius Caesar and its Source*, David C. Green proposes the following solution: although 'critical study of the play alone runs us aground', we can 'free ourselves by dredging deeper – by studying the sources with that same zeal with which we apply ourselves to the play' (p. 123).[16] Speaking of sheer zeal, the time has come for the publishers of Green's monograph, Professor Erwin A. Stürzl and Dr James Hogg, of Salzburg Studies in English Literature, to justify their practice of photo-reproducing, binding up in paper covers, and selling (at book prices) what appear to be unedited facsimiles of any doctoral theses that happen to come their way. Is 'Publication for Publication's Sake' their motto? If so, why shouldn't all Ph.D. theses be reproduced in this fashion? John Dean's thesis, *Restless Wanderers: Shakespeare and the Pattern of Romance*[17] is certainly as good as most – it clearly demonstrates the author's understanding of various classical, medieval and Renaissance traditions at work in the last plays, and two sections have previously been published elsewhere. Indeed, the same ground has, by now, been covered so many times that one wonders what was gained by reproducing the thesis in Salzburg.

It is, surely, obligatory for those who publish critical studies of Shakespeare to let their readers know what (if anything) of importance is being said and *why* it is important that it should be said – *or said again*. It is hard to see, harder still to say, just what Larry S. Champion is trying to tell us about *Perspective in Shakespeare's English Histories*.[18] He simply

informs his readers that he does not aim to do what there's no earthly reason for him – or anyone else – to do: the 'aim here . . . is to insist neither on a crude simplicity in his earliest pieces nor on some narrowly focused progression of excellence' (pp. 10–11). One also wonders what sort of audience Champion is addressing. Readers who are unfamiliar with these texts are unlikely to consult this specialized study of them, while those who are acquainted with the plays are not going to find their learning much advanced by a series of announcements like these:

*Richard II* like its predecessor is fundamentally a history play, as that term was so ambiguously used in Shakespeare's day. (p. 69)
[In *3 Henry VI* sympathies shift back and forth] from pro-Lancastrian (I, i), to pro-Yorkist (I, iii–II, ii), to pro-Lancastrian (II, vi–III, i), to pro-Edwardian (III, ii–IV, iv), to pro-Lancastrian (v, v–v, vi), to pro-Edwardian (v, vii). (p. 48)
[In *1 Henry IV*] Shakespeare simultaneously develops three individually significant plot strands: Henry IV's apprehensions concerning both his kingship and his relations with his son, the activities of the rebellious feudal lords which center on the impetuous Hotspur, and Hal's escapades at Eastcheap

---

15 Rowse certainly has a point. Things *are* in a sorry state when the man proclaimed to be the greatest of all Elizabethan scholars writes about Shakespeare in clichés worthy of Dick Minim – see Rowse's discussion of 'Shakespeare's Universal Appeal' in *Deutsche Shakespeare-Gesellschaft West, Jahrbuch* (1980), pp. 59–72: 'Drama is a basic human activity, and Shakespeare is the world's greatest dramatist.' His work, which 'holds the mirror up to nature' is like life in its 'infinite variety'. 'The intensity of Shakespeare's imagination is a prime source of his power over us.' Another 'chief source of fascination is the endless variety of his characters', a 'vast gallery exhibiting every rank and class and age'. Moreover, 'Shakespeare was the greatest master of the English language and for ever its poet.' (Obvious comment: 'There needs no ghost, my lord, come from the grave to tell us this.')

16 *Jacobean Drama Studies*, 86 (Institut für Anglistik und Amerikanistik, Salzburg, 1979).

17 *Elizabethan and Renaissance Studies*, 86 (Institut für Anglistik und Amerikanistik, Salzburg, 1979).

18 University of Georgia Press, Athens, 1980.

involving the world of Falstaff and his debauched associates. (p. 111)

[In *Richard III*] Shakespeare has consciously shaped his material to create a villain-hero of consuming interest. (p. 69)

The question raised by Champion's book which is of most consuming interest to this reader is the one so frequently asked by that same villain–hero himself: 'How, now . . . what's the news?'

Engrossed in writing about his subject, any critic is likely to assume that his readers 'will not know what all but he do know', and no lover was ever more blind to the faults of his mistress than a scholar infatuated by his own hypothesis. Much criticism, in any age, is, therefore, both good and original – but what is good is not original, and what is original is not good. The subject of Marlies K. Danziger's too brief little edition, *Samuel Johnson on Literature*,[19] and J. P. Hardy's *Samuel Johnson: A Critical Study*,[20] provides the best possible corrective to certain critical assumptions precisely because Johnson takes the reader's side. Although the response of 'the audience' or 'the reader' to works of art is the subject of great concern to modern criticism, the authors of that criticism itself sometimes lose sight of the nature of their own audience, mistakenly assuming that it consists of enthusiasts who are incapable of boredom, and willing to credit everything printed about Shakespeare. But the best spokesman for our real audience is, of course, Dr Johnson, who damned scholarship that 'explains what no reader has found difficult, and, I think, explains it wrong', and who observed that 'the power of tedium propagates itself'. Like Johnson, our real readers are bound to be bored to distraction at hearing the same theories parroted over and over again, and justifiably infuriated by insults to their common sense and intelligence. These readers deliver the final verdict on the books and articles that they commit, in perpetuity, to the shelves.

J. P. Hardy thus summarizes Dr Johnson's view, which 'requires the critic . . . to articu-late his response in a way that is faithful to the work in all its compelling detail' (p. 177). At best, scholarly notes are 'necessary evils': 'Let him . . . who desires to feel the highest pleasure that the drama can give, read [Shakespeare's plays] from the first scene to the last, with utter negligence of all his commentators.' This, surely, is truth beyond all controversy. But where does it leave us? Many people today wonder what is left to be learned about Shakespeare's works. Happily, however, one need only re-read Johnson's *Preface*, to be reminded, in words which sound like the trumpet calls in *Fidelio*, that there is no limit to what we may learn *from* them. How many lifetimes would it take to discover, for ourselves, anything like as much about the 'real state of sublunary nature' as may be learned from those scenes through which 'a hermit may estimate the transactions of the world and a confessor predict the progress of the passions'?

### Reprints, Retrospects

Several works of proven value have recently been reprinted. Among them are John Wain's (deservedly) popular introduction to the plays, *The Living World of Shakespeare: A Playgoer's Guide*,[21] and Kenneth Muir's justifiably famous discussion of *Shakespeare's Tragic Sequence*.[22] The reprint of *An Approach to Hamlet*, by L. C. Knights, has been enriched by a selection of his major articles.[23] Reading through these essays, from 'How Many Children had Lady Macbeth?' to 'Shakespeare and History' is to survey the major concerns of Shakespeare criticism from 1933 to the day before yesterday. It is, moreover, a pleasure to disagree with Knights. For instance, he has most forcefully argued that we know *only* as much about Shakespeare's characters as the

---

19 Frederick Ungar, New York, 1979.

20 Routledge and Kegan Paul, 1979.

21 Reissued with a new introduction (Macmillan, 1978).

22 Liverpool University Press, 1979.

23 *'Hamlet' and Other Shakespearean Essays* (Cambridge University Press, 1979).

plays require us to know (pp. 213–14). Yet what, in *Hamlet*, so urgently requires us to know that Claudius once served against the French, or that Polonius played Julius Caesar? Such seemingly irrelevant details surely serve to give these characters past histories all their own. Knights emphatically disagrees with Morgann's observation that Shakespeare often makes characters 'act and speak from those parts of the composition which are *inferred* only, and not distinctly shown', and so convey a 'relish of the whole' (p. 281). Still, in Shakespeare's most extensive account of the art of characterization, he himself appears to have anticipated Morgann:

> For much imaginary work was there;
> Conceit deceitful, so compact, so kind,
> That for Achilles' image stood his spear,
> Gripp'd in an armed hand; himself, behind,
> Was left unseen, save to the eye of mind,
> A hand, a foot, a face, a leg, a head,
> Stood for the whole to be imagined.

To a degree, anyway, we cannot but see some of Shakespeare's characters in terms of what is inferred only: 'Even as subtle Sinon' there was painted, 'So sober-sad, so weary, and so mild / As if with grief or travail he had fainted'.

## PART II. ARTICLES

Specific ways in which Shakespeare appeals to the 'mind's eye' are the subject of Kathleen M. Lea's excellent essay on 'Shakespeare's Inner Stage'.[24] There are events and scenes which 'we suppose belong to the play until we have seen it staged, and . . . realize that what we seem to have seen has come to us by hearing only'. There are vivid images of times past and to come, of characters who never appear on stage ('no one was ever cast for Queen Mab'), and of abstractions like Time, the fashionable host, seeing off his parting guest. 'Who', asks Lea, 'is more horrifying to the imagination: Macbeth trembling, withered Murder and his sentinel wolf, or Tarquin striding to ravish?' (p. 134).

When Marvin Rosenberg put the text of *King Lear* through a computer, he noticed that the word 'if' showed up over a hundred times. His discussion of 'Shakespeare's Tragic World of "If"'[25] illuminates the conditional dimensions of the tragedies by citing crucial occurrences from Horatio's multiple 'ifs' – the first of 111 instances in *Hamlet* – to 'If it be now, 'tis not to come.' Othello's 'ifs' at first reflect his self-confidence, and, with ironic foreshadowing, express his love ('If after every tempest come such calms'). Subsequently, of course, they breed with Iago's, and finally serve to communicate his tragic recognition to us: 'If heaven would make me such another world'. Macbeth and Lady Macbeth gamble on success in the 'if-world' of the witches until Macbeth realizes the extent of their equivocations: 'If thy speech be sooth / I care not if thou dost for me as much.' In *Lear*, many of the play's hundred-plus 'ifs' come from the King himself, culminating in the most tragic of all uses of the conditional: 'If it be so, / It is a chance which doth redeem all sorrows / That ever I have felt.'

Shakespeare's great 'ifs' force critics to use the word themselves. Discussing the ending of *King Lear*,[26] Joseph H. Summers quotes Bradley: 'If to the reader . . . that scene brings one unbroken pain, it is not so with Lear himself' (p. 77). Summers then argues that, 'If at the end we respond to Lear's death as heroic rather than merely pathetic' it is because 'his final powerful fluctuating responses cast doubt on the "realities" which we often assume as "objective" or "self-evident".' Moreover, even 'if one insists' that Lear's insight is sheer delusion, 'one may still consider it a consummation devoutly to be wished'. Yet this holds true only if, as Summers argues, what

---

24 In *English Renaissance Studies Presented to Dame Helen Gardner* (Clarendon Press, Oxford, 1980) (hereafter cited as *English Renaissance Studies*), pp. 132–40.

25 *Deutsche Shakespeare-Gesellschaft West, Jahrbuch* (1980), pp. 109–17.

26 Joseph H. Summers, '"Look There, Look There!" The Ending of *King Lear*', *English Renaissance Studies*, pp. 74–93.

King Lear finally sees is 'reality and truth that triumph over death and fate and time' (pp. 89, 92). Discussing 'The Case of Hamlet's Conscience',[27] Catherine Belsey quotes Maynard Mack: 'The world of *Hamlet* "reverberates with question".' Thus it leaves us wondering 'what ought Hamlet to have done? What else could he have done?' 'If revenge is evil, so are Claudius's crimes' and it is hard to believe that an audience – 'however influenced by the morality tradition' – would admire a Hamlet 'who simply washed his hands of the whole matter'.

In an article appropriately entitled '"Very Like a Whale": The Problem of Knowledge in *Hamlet*', Don Parry Norford provides a classic example of the 'Fluellenist' ('There is salmons in both') approach to Shakespeare's characters:

Hamlet, in fact, resembles Iago: both distrust appearances, try to unmask others. Hamlet has that within that passes show, and Iago does not wear his heart on his sleeve. . . . Both desire revenge and go about it by playing with appearances . . . Iago hates *the Moor*; and Hamlet, holding up the two pictures . . . asks: 'Could you on this fair mountain leave to feed, / And batten on *This moor*?' (my italics)[28]

I hope they had lascivious Moors in Denmark: 'Away!' cried Gertrude – anticipating Shelley – 'The Moor is dark beneath the moon.' Who wouldn't relish the romantic possibilities inherent in Norford's confusion between topography and race? But, alas, the word refers to entirely different things in Shakespeare's texts. Anyway, as Richard Levin has demonstrated in a series of devastating attacks on this particular methodology, the approach which deems such comparisons more significant than the blindingly obvious differences between Shakespeare's characters has nothing going for it but applicability. Given five minutes or so, any of us could come up with a series of correspondences comparable to Norford's, i.e. Juliet resembles Tamora, Queen of the Goths: Tamora has a secret affair with Aaron, and Juliet is secretly married to Romeo. Tamora's

lover is himself black, and Juliet's lover compares her to a 'bright jewel in an Ethiope's ear', etc., etc. ['A man might write such stuff forever, if he would *abandon* his mind to it' – Dr Johnson.]

In 'Kingship of the Silent Knight: A Study of Shakespeare's Bolingbroke'[29], B. J. Baines concludes that Bolingbroke represents Shakespeare's ideal king, since he realizes that 'the duty of kingship is to mirror as nearly as possible divine virtue' and 'also understands that this duty must be fulfilled within the limitations of the fallen world'. Baines's whitewashing of Bolingbroke's rise and reign in effect deprives one of Shakespeare's toughest customers of all his individuality in favour of platitudes that could be applied, with equal validity, to any half-way competent prince in Christendom. A more complex account of Bolingbroke is provided in Robert J. Fehrenbach's account of 'The Characterization of the King in *1 Henry IV*':[30] Shakespeare appropriately denies us intimacy with this troubled ruler 'who in his dual struggle against past sins and present threats must always be a masker'. And see also Gordon Ross Smith's critical discussion of Bolingbroke in 'A Rabble of Princes: Considerations Touching Shakespeare's Political Orthodoxy in the Second Tetralogy':[31] the most obvious thing about his troubled reign is that 'he does not and cannot establish order'. Discussing the political and religious ferment which had 'generated books on all sides of every question', Smith concludes that 'no extraliterary way exists to approach Shakespeare's intentions' and 'our only recourse is examination of what is said and goes on in the plays'.

In an interesting discussion of 'Substitutions in Shakespeare's Problem Comedies',[32] Nancy

---

27 *Studies in Philology*, 76 (1979), 127–48.
28 *ELH*, 46 (1979), 559–76 – the quotation is from p. 569.
29 *English Studies*, 61 (1980), 24–36.
30 *Shakespeare Quarterly*, 30 (1979), 42–50.
31 *Journal of the History of Ideas*, 41 (1980), 29–48.
32 *English Literary Renaissance*, 9 (1979), 281–301.

S. Leonard concludes that they 'compel interpretation without confirming it'. The Duke's behaviour as Friar Lodowick 'is surely charming enough in his half-studied, half-improvised plans for reunion and ransom'. 'Yet shiftingly he does appear in dark corners', falsely preparing Claudio for death, and falsely reporting that death to Isabella. Discussing *The Taming of the Shrew* in the same journal,[33] Marianne L. Novy considers the 'ambiguous coalescence between Petruchio the dominant husband and Petruchio the game-player, between a farce assuming patriarchy and a comedy about playing at patriarchy'. Discussing 'Shakespeare's hypocrites',[34] Brian Vickers sensibly argues that it is an 'odd misuse of modern theater aesthetics' for some of our contemporaries to believe that asides and soliloquies are 'distancing' devices. In fact they bring us closer to the various characters, so that we share their hopes and fears.

In a sensitive essay on *The Winter's Tale*, 'Shakespeare's Humanist Enterprise',[35] Louis L. Martz discusses the play's movement from its original associations with classical tragedy, through the 'cyclical, pagan world of great creating nature', to an ending wherein 'in humanist terms, faith, nourished by art and grace', witness the triumphant restoration of Hermione. 'Yet Mamillius and Antigonus are dead, and Hermione's wrinkles remain, the finest touch of Shakespeare's realism.' Discussing 'Double Exposure' in Shakespeare's Sonnets,[36] Jane Roessner concludes that, beginning with Sonnet 100, the speaker turns 'from using poetry to hide or deny or dissuade his friend's untruthfulness to the complex trick of appearing to praise him while in fact exposing just how and why those praises are written'. In an article on '"Solitariness": Shakespeare and Plutarch',[37] Janette Dillon concludes that 'Solitude, whether physical, spiritual, or both, is the common factor in the lives of Plutarch's Antony, Coriolanus, and Timon.' Thus, 'As Shakespeare adapts history to drama, solitude becomes the essential structural element on which their tragedies are made to hinge.' As Dillon acknowledges, it is difficult to see how the solitude of these characters is more essential to their tragedies than the isolation of Macbeth is to his.

In his essay on 'The "Compulsive Course" of *Othello*',[38] G. A. Wilkes concludes that, although on one level 'the possibility nags us' that the misunderstandings might easily be cleared up, 'at another level the play keeps indicating that it cannot be turned from its course'. Discussing 'Shakespeare and Italy',[39] Mario Praz attributes Shakespeare's remarkably accurate references to Italy to the influence of Florio, and to frequent occasions to talk to Italian merchants. Praz goes on to discuss Italian translations of his works which (like certain critical and directorial interpretations of them) are of such wretched quality that one could repeat about Shakespeare 'what was said once about the Church of Rome, that he must really rest on divine foundations if he has been able to outlive the corruption of the interpreters'.

## PART III. PERIODICALS[40]

### Hamlet Studies

The question, 'How many critical studies of Shakespeare do we wish to see published?' should not be divorced from the question, 'How many should we be required to read?' *Hamlet Studies*, 'the first journal devoted exclusively to a single literary work', contains some good essays and reviews. But it sets a

33 'Patriarchy and Play in *The Taming of the Shrew*', *English Literary Renaissance*, 9 (1979), 264–80.
34 *Dædalus*, 108 (1979), 45–83.
35 *English Renaissance Studies*, pp. 114–31.
36 *ELH*, 46 (1979), 357–78.
37 *Journal of English and Germanic Philology*, 78 (1979), 325–44.
38 *Sydney Studies in English*, 5 (1979–80), 31–7.
39 *Sydney Studies in English*, 3 (1977–8), 3–18.
40 Relevant issues of *Studies in English Literature* were at the library bindery at the time this was written, and will be reviewed in next year's survey.

precedent that makes the mind reel. If similar journals were devoted to nine other plays, the result would be one hundred essays *in addition to* the ones that annually roll off our assembly lines. And one longs to know how many people make the Canute-like effort required to keep up with the current volume of commentary.

The first issue of this journal includes Alvin B. Kernan's essay on 'Politics and Theater in *Hamlet*' (also published in *The Playwright as Magician*), as well as an interesting essay on '*Hamlet*: The Transitional Play Between Shakespeare's Two Major Dramatic Methods' by Gordon Ross Smith (pp. 13–21): in *Hamlet* and henceforth, 'the verse as well as the plot is suffused with a degree of feeling that appears to be the dramatist's'. Smith's view, by the way, is confirmed elsewhere by J. M. Newton: 'It had to be Hamlet' who gives us all those 'highly intelligent reflections of Shakespeare's about tragic drama.'[41] Discussing 'Yeats and the Hamlet Mask' (pp. 45–53), R. W. Desai argues that 'The merger of the soldier and the sage that Yeats speaks about is exemplified in Hamlet's death.' I could not follow certain arguments in Robert F. Fleissner's article on 'Subjectivity as an Occupational Hazard of "Hamlet Ghost" Critics' (pp. 23–33) – and not just because he did not mention my own (absolutely definitive) discussion of the Ghost. For instance, in the course of making a distinction between literature and life, Fleissner asserts that, 'Although Christians are supposed to believe that, so far as they know, there is no one in hell, that all may be saved, Marlowe commits Faustus to hell' and thus his tragedy is 'more medieval than Renaissance'. But *when* – in literature or in life – do these generalizations apply? Were Christians supposed to believe that there was 'no one in hell' in Marlowe's time? In Bunyan's? In the eighteenth century? [*Dr Adams.* What do you mean by damned? *Johnson* (*passionately and loudly*). Sent to Hell, Sir, and punished everlastingly.] And what about the fire-and-brimstone sermon that terrified young Stephen Dedalus? Fleiss-

ner is, however, absolutely right in arguing that interpretations of the Ghost by critics who claim superior objectivity (like Eleanor Prosser), are no less subjective than others. But the real issue, to my mind, anyway, is not the subjectivity or objectivity of the individual critic, but the validity of the interpretation posited: Paulina and Leontes held equally subjective theories concerning Hermione, but one was true and one was false.

### Shakespeare Survey

In a retrospective article on 'The Middle Comedies' (*Shakespeare Survey* 32, pp. 1–13), M. M. Mahood reviews 'A Generation of Criticism' in which descriptions of these plays as 'happy', 'gay', 'golden', 'festive', and 'joyous' have given way to accounts of the 'hard', 'abrasive', and 'aggressive' qualities of *Much Ado About Nothing* and *As You Like It*, 'while unnumbered critics stress the underlying sadness of *Twelfth Night*'. Thus the critical pendulum swings, and swings again: 'Not all readers', Mahood correctly observes, will agree with Gareth Lloyd Evans's argument that 'Beatrice, after telling us she was born under a dancing star, leaves the stage in tears.'

A number of subsequent articles in this volume are devoted to other problems of continuing interest. As Russell Jackson reminds us, the depiction of Rosalind, Beatrice and Viola as 'Perfect Types of Womanhood' in Victorian criticism and performance had serious limitations (pp. 15–26). Still, Dorian Gray raises a fascinating question in his description of Sybil Vane's appearance as Imogen, Juliet and Rosalind (quoted in full, pp. 25–6): 'I have watched her wandering through the forest of Arden, disguised as a pretty boy in hose and doublet and dainty cap. . . . Ordinary women never appeal to one's imagination. . . . Why didn't you tell me that the only thing worth loving is an actress?'

---

41 '*Hamlet* and Shakespeare's Disposition for Comedy', *The Cambridge Quarterly*, 9 (1979), pp. 39–55.

Perhaps significantly, the same conclusion was recently arrived at by a man who told me that he had fallen forever in love with Vanessa Redgrave, as Rosalind. Whatever 'it' is, several of Shakespeare's heroines have that certain something which appeals to the imagination of generations with very different ideals of perfect womanhood, and which carries over to the actresses who play them.

In an interesting account of 'The Stage Representation of the "Kill Claudio" Sequence in *Much Ado About Nothing*' (pp. 27–36), J. F. Cox illuminates 'both the variety of legitimate interpretations' and the extent to which this episode has been falsified in the theatre. In her discussion of *Love in a Forest*, Charles Johnson's adaptation of *As You Like It* (pp. 37–48), Edith Holding concludes that 'The variety of intellectual and emotional life which Shakespeare offers' is often more than a given adapter – or director, or critic – may want. The result is an 'enormous reduction of Shakespeare's breadth of vision'. Speaking of which, Elliot Krieger's conclusions about 'Social Relations and the Social Order in *Much Ado About Nothing*' (pp. 49–61) seemed just as reductive as the ones in his book: 'the emptiness of the aristocratic personality in *Much Ado* is a function of the lack of opposition that the aristocracy faces as a class, the absence of difficulty in delineation of social boundaries' (p. 61).

Discussing 'Sexual Disguise in *As You Like It* and *Twelfth Night*' (pp. 63–72), Nancy K. Hayles argues that in the early plays Shakespeare uses disguise to explore the implications of sexual role-playing, while in his later works he uses it as a means 'to investigate, and eventually resolve, the disparity between appearance and essence'. In a characteristically learned and elegant essay on 'Twelfth Night and the Myth of Echo and Narcissus' (pp. 73–8), D. J. Palmer illuminates Ovidian allusions and overtones that occur throughout the play: in its opening lines, in its treatments of unrequited love and self-love, and in its reflected

images. Roger Warren seemed to me to get everything right in his essay, ' "Smiling at Grief": Some Techniques of Comedy in *Twelfth Night* and *Così Fan Tutte*' (pp. 79–84). Like Mozart's 'tender benediction on human nature', Shakespeare's is open-eyed, aware, inclusive, and thus 'half gay, half sad, like the smile on the face of a departing friend'. Feste's last song 'provides a perspective on the happiness achieved by the lovers, on their "golden time", without invalidating the golden time itself'.

In 'My Lady's a *Catayan*, We are Politicians, *Maluolios* a Peg-a-Ramsie' (pp. 85–104), Gustav Ungerer clarifies a number of enigmatic passages in *Twelfth Night*. Discussing 'The Antecedents of Clarence's Dream' (pp. 145–50), Harold Brooks surveys classical and medieval precedents for that great dream-vision of Hell. In 'The Importance of Being Marcade' (pp. 105–14). J. M. Nosworthy discusses the *coup de théâtre* through which Shakespeare transforms a good comedy into a masterpiece. Some of the associations in 'A Hebrew Source for *The Merchant of Venice*', by S. J. Schönfeld (pp. 115–28), seemed far-fetched, to say the least. He supports the theory that there is a Jewish source for this play by arguing that, since 'The Hebrew name, Daniel, can be translated "a God-like judge" ', it looks as if Shylock 'must have been thinking in Hebrew' in uttering his cry: 'A Daniel come to judgement!' The word for lead in Hebrew is transcribed ØPRT, while Portia's name in Hebrew is transcribed PRT, and so we have 'the Hebrew Portia, PRT, actually "locked in" ØPRT, which could not fail to vastly amuse Hebrew listeners'. Hebrew puns on ḤOZEH (bond) and ḤAZEH (breast) explain why Portia insists that the pound of flesh must be 'cut off nearest the merchant's heart'.

One hopes that Karl P. Wentersdorf has finally put an end to the scholarly controversy concerning 'what kind of pre-contract had Angelo?'. Discussing 'The Marriage Contracts in *Measure for Measure*' (pp. 129–44) Wentersdorf poses the problems arising from the facts that (a) although the pre-contract between Claudio and Julietta, and the pre-contract between Angelo and Mariana are described in markedly similar terms, (b) the Duke reprimands Julietta for her 'sin' in having had sexual intercourse with a man to whom she had been contracted, but had not yet married in church, and then (c) positively states that there will be 'no sin' involved when Mariana goes and does likewise. According to Wentersdorf, the historical evidence 'makes it clear that, for traditionalists, the enjoyment of sexual intercourse between validly contracted parties did not raise any question of morality'. On the other hand, 'for those influenced by the teaching of Calvinistic reformers', consummation of the contract before the public wedding was gravely sinful. Therefore, even as the various characters veer between these diametrically opposed views, the play mirrors contradictory attitudes held in Shakespeare's time. I never have believed that the moral and legal conundrums built into the action of *Measure for Measure* could be solved on the basis of technical distinctions between the two pre-contracts, and it is good to have Wentersdorf's evidence that the great questions concerning sex, marriage and society, were as wide open to discussion then as they are right now. For other views of the pre-contracts, see Margaret Loftus Ranald, '"As Marriage Binds, and Blood Breaks": English Marriage and Shakespeare', *Shakespeare Quarterly*, 30, pp. 68–81, and Darryl J. Gless's book (cited above), pp. 200–1.

Another controversial question, 'Did the King see the dumb-show?', is the subject of M. R. Woodhead's essay on 'Deep Plots and Indiscretions in "The Murder of Gonzago"' (pp. 151–61): 'Claudius is upset not by the play but by the direct accusation which Hamlet blurts out.' In an interesting discussion of 'Proverbs and Logic in *Hamlet*' (pp. 163–76), Joan Larsen Klein points out that Shakespeare often uses proverbs so that his audience can anticipate

discoveries or events: 'When Hamlet tells himself, before he sees the ghost, that "Foul deeds will rise, / Though all the earth o'erwhelm them, to men's eyes", Shakespeare plays upon the expectations of an audience conditioned to hear that it is murder that will out.' Discussing '*The Tempest*: Language and Society' (pp. 177–87), Stanton B. Garner, Jr, overstates the case that 'The question of language lies at the thematic center of *The Tempest*' (what about Art, Nature, Magic, etc.?). According to Garner, this play instructs us that 'language can be redeemed by an awareness of its inadequacies and that, in its purest moments, founded on soul-spoken simplicity and feeling, it can genuinely bind and communicate'. But why should Shakespeare have written a whole play to make a point quite effectively communicated by Sir Philip Sidney in just fourteen lines, and, for that matter, already made any number of times in his own earlier works?

### Shakespeare Studies

*Shakespeare Studies*, 12, begins with A. Robin Bowers's discussion of '"Hard Armours" and "Delicate Amours" in Shakespeare's *Venus and Adonis*' (pp. 1–23). Bowers is certainly right in observing that 'one of the greatest difficulties' for present critics is the problem of 'how to accommodate the comic and the serious' in Shakespeare's work without over-stressing one or the other. The problems posed in *Venus and Adonis* are never-ending: 'The poem is circular . . . with the two sides of the rolling coin showing the two basic images of worldly love – one seductively pleasant, the other inevitably harsh.' In disagreement with M. C. Bradbrook, Bowers stresses its sobering commentary. But Bradbrook's counterview has obvious validity. What *does* one remember most about this poem? Its warning about the awful consequences of lust? Or its beauty?

Discussing 'The Witty Idealization of the French Court in *Love's Labour's Lost*' (pp. 25–33), Albert H. Tricomi concludes that 'At no other period could Elizabethans have . . .

known more about the Bourbon king and the toughened generals.' Yet Shakespeare portrays them as uniformly graceful, young, attractive, and available for marriage. Why? 'The relationship between the present world and that of Nérac is the relationship between an immediately recognizable world of process, and a world seemingly out of time, for in the dream of this wittily romantic comedy . . . time holds no power to decay.' Tricomi's interpretation, however, seems refuted by the ending.

Discussing 'Helen Faucit's Rosalind' (pp. 65–94), Carol J. Carlisle defends the romantic interpretation that finally prevailed against the saucy, robust interpretations by Mrs Jordan and Mrs Nisbett, who 'seem to have played the boldness of the swagger and the impudence of the wit for all they were worth'. Helen Faucit's emphasis was on the basic femininity of the character, and her Rosalind was characterized by the good taste and elegance suitable to a Duke's daughter. Again considering Shakespeare's heroines who are alternatively – or simultaneously – capable of being played as gentle and impudent, passionate and sensible, merry and pensive, one wonders what roles for women created since then seem so authentically attractive, yet so adaptable to varying tastes. Why, then, are some of his comic heroes so unappealing?

In what seems a desperate defence of Bertram (pp. 95–111), John Edward Price argues that *All's Well that Ends Well* is an answer to 'perfunctory and self-serving moralism' wherein Shakespeare favours the 'independent actions of Helena and Bertram' against the useless platitudes and 'nearly suffocating restraints of the Countess and the King'. For instance, the Countess's advice, 'Love all, trust a few, / Do wrong to none' is 'blandly conventional', the kind of advice 'young people will react against'. One wonders how – by loving none, trusting few, and doing harm to all? Price's arguments will not convince those of us who find his elders far kinder and less snobbish than Bertram, who might best be defended as

Shakespeare's definitive portrayal of a stinker.

In an interesting essay unfortunately entitled 'Hermeneutical Circularity and Christian Interpretations of *King Lear*' (pp. 113–25), René E. Fortin argues that 'the great diversity' of possible interpretations is 'our best defence against critical dogmatism'. The 'open form of tragedy, its respect for the limits of human experience, allows readers to draw different conclusions: enough is given to allow interpreters to "see feelingly", to infer an interpretation based upon their own personal experience of the play; but enough is withheld to compel respect for the tragic mystery'. Fortin's conclusions seemed eminently fair to other critics, and true to the text.

In an article on 'Obstetrics and Gynecology in *Macbeth*' (pp. 127–41), Alice Fox discusses the play's manifold references to sterility, fertility, pregnancy, miscarriage, and abortive births. This vocabulary underscores those references to their spiritual pain and loss, and to the utter barrenness of their lives, which enable us to accept a murderer and murderess as tragic figures. In a rich discussion of *Coriolanus* (pp. 143–58), Christopher Givan argues that the hero's 'sense of identity' constantly wavers between words and deeds, and 'ultimately between destroying others or destroying himself'. Like Macbeth, Coriolanus is trapped in patterns of repetition, and, like Antony, he is confronted with mutually contradictory alternatives. His last lines sum up the fatal way that he can assert his identity only by declaring himself the victor of Corioli in the very citadel of the Volsces.

Discussing '*Timon of Athens* and the Morality Tradition' (pp. 159–77), Lewis Walker considers Timon's relationship to 'the generic Mankind figure' who is seduced by worldly riches and pleasures. The arguments in this essay will be utterly predictable to those who have read the same conclusions about countless other Elizabethan plays. The banquet is 'a direct descendant of the worldly feasts of Herod and Mankind', and 'in the morality tradition', eating and drinking are 'sure signs of sensuality'. Yet the banquet 'also resembles the Last Supper, with its images of eating the body and blood of a sacrificial victim', although 'Timon is not Christlike in every respect.' But, then, again, I kept thinking, neither were Chiron and Demetrius. Needless to say, Lewis ignores any classical sources for *Timon of Athens* which might account for certain situations and themes quite independently of the morality play tradition discussed here. For an argument against the morality play as a major influence on *Timon of Athens* see Rolf Soellner's book, pp. 17–18, 70.

In his essay on ' "Perishing Root and Increasing Vine" in *Cymbeline*' (pp. 179–93), J. S. Lawry argues that the competing literary and dramatic genres in the play – romance, history, tragedy, satire and pastoral – are 'not so much reconciled' as 'mutually transformed'. Discussing 'Witchcraft in *The Winter's Tale*' (pp. 195–213), D'Orsay W. Pearson cites images of the 'urban witch' as 'Bawd, midwife and agent of evil forces' all of which Leontes projects upon Paulina ('mankind witch', 'intelligencing bawd', 'gross hag') and which are echoed, even as they are transformed, when she oversees the statue scene. Numerous precedents for 'The Magic Banquet in *The Tempest*' are discussed by Jacqueline E. M. Latham (pp. 215–27), and Edward I. Berry (pp. 229–46) defends *Henry VIII* as a 'history play that redefines truth', a *'de casibus* play that moves beyond tragedy'. Although it is a bit too moralistic for my taste, his account of Queen Katherine is specially interesting. As Claire Bloom demonstrated in the BBC production, this ranks among the major parts for women in Elizabethan drama.

## Shakespeare Quarterly

Critical studies in volume 30 (1979) that have not been previously cited include Russ McDonald's discussion of 'Othello, Thorello, and the Problem of the Foolish Hero' (pp. 51–67): 'Othello's misdirection of his imaginative and

histrionic gifts produces the same sense of loss that we feel when Macbeth unleashes the ambition that made him a great warrior.' Discussing 'Shakespeare's Industrious Scenes' (pp. 138–50), Bernard Beckerman forcefully concludes that 'Shakespeare's practice in general is to provide a vigorous reaction to a strong assertion as a foundation for a scene.' For instance, 'He juxtaposes characters of contradictory temperament or conflicting desire. He then has them argue, give orders to inferiors, persuade one another . . . address offstage figures, abstract ideas, natural objects and bodily parts.' On stage, lines like 'Blow, winds, and crack your cheeks', or 'Bow, stubborn knees' help to establish 'a projected opposition against which the player strikes'.

In a most welcome essay on 'Shakespeare – and the Others' (pp. 324–42) – too few critical discussions of Shakespeare, nowadays, acknowledge the existence of any other playwrights – Maurice Charney observes that, although Shakespeare managed to lead his contemporaries in most respects, he did not follow them in others. 'Certain kinds of plays and certain kinds of characters and situations were foreign to his temperament.' He did not choose to portray the drama of London life, or to deal with characters of a 'high, hard, and even cynical sexual sophistication'. Reading Jean Howard's discussion of 'Shakespearean Counterpoint: Stage Technique and the Interaction Between Play and Audience' (pp. 343–57), I wondered why she felt obliged to use such ponderous prose in order to make points familiar to anyone who has read Maynard Mack's famous essay on 'Engagement and Detachment':

Each instance of dramatic counterpoint sets in opposition two lines of stage speech which are separate and yet are concurrently presented so that the audience must tolerate a division of its attention. This division is always purposeful. It is, in part, a means of controlling the audience's perspective upon stage events and thus for controlling its responses to those events – inviting, at times, identification with one stage party; forcing, at other times, ironic detachment; mandating, at still other times, an active quest for a point of view more comprehensive than the limited or partial perspectives articulated on the stage. (p. 357)

In his discussion of 'Shakespeare's Aural Art: The Metaphor of the Ear in *Othello*' (pp. 358–66), John N. Wall concludes that 'in Shakespeare's theatre' the ear is the 'agent of delusion, creating in various characters visions of the truth which do not accord with the reality known to the audience'. *Query*: In what theatre *aren't* characters 'aurally' deceived? Shakespeare was surely not the first or last playwright to observe that people often believe lies, misinterpret what they hear, etc. 'As I have noted earlier', Wall observes – in case the rest of us haven't – 'the main action of *Othello* is the destruction of a marriage.' Discussing 'Portia, the Law, and the Tripartite Structure of *The Merchant of Venice*' (pp. 367–85), Alice N. Benston reminds us that Portia dominates the three major actions: the casket scene, Shylock's trial, and the ring episode.

## CONCLUSIONS

Although a different reviewer would have chosen different works to blame or praise, anyone attempting to survey recent critical studies of Shakespeare is bound to notice common problems.

1. Given the richness of the plays and poems, it is easy to find in them confirmations that would seem to verify nearly every theory posited – that is, if one ignores all evidence that might refute it, as well as any alternative explanations for the same features of the works discussed.

2. A theory which is not refutable by anything that might occur in the complete works of Shakespeare *cannot* serve to explain specific events that do occur in individual works. Thus, the universal applicability of a theory is not its greatest virtue, but, arguably, a vice resulting in dogmatic, one-sided and boring books and articles that slavishly apply the reigning theory to whatever works it has not previously been applied. It might be more fruitful to consider ways in which a theory which does illuminate certain works does *not* apply to others. Thus, our various 'approaches' might serve as incentives to independent thought rather than substitutes for it.

3. Authors (and their editors) should be on guard against the process of selective citation, whereby previous discussions which (a) have made the same points, or (b) have criticized the theories propounded, are simply ignored. The question 'How much homework should be required?' needs serious consideration at all levels of the profession.

4. Questions concerning our readership also need fresh discussion. It may be true that more of us (I preach as yet another castaway) are publishing critical discussions of Shakespeare than reading them. Of the books and articles produced annually, how many are read by anyone *but* reviewers, or other authors in search of subjects for their own publications, which, in turn, will be read by. . . . Does the fact that more and more is published each year mean that more and more – or less and less – is read?

## 2 SHAKESPEARE'S LIFE, TIMES AND STAGE

*reviewed by* GĀMINI SALGĀDO

By far the most exciting book I have read in the last twelve months within the general category of 'Life, Times and Stage' is Philip Edwards's masterly study of Elizabethan and Irish drama in relation to emergent nationalism.[1] Most of

the material which the author considers, whether plays or masques on the one hand or

---

1 *Threshold of a Nation: A Study in English and Irish Drama* (Cambridge University Press, 1979).

historical information on the other, is thoroughly familiar, which makes his achievement in juxtaposing them to make them yield new insights into both drama and history all the more striking. Among the many fine things in the book is an excellent account of court masque with a keen-edged discussion of flattery and the moral problems raised by it for Jonson as masque-maker, as well as the connection between the 'flattering' and the 'non-flattering' works. This occurs within a wider-ranging inquiry into the way in which Jonson 'theorized on, dramatized and lived out his view of the relationship between prince and poet' which illustrates very well Professor Edwards's gift for setting familiar material in a new and revealing light. Similarly stimulating is the comment that in *The Tempest* Shakespeare finds room for both epic and burlesque views of colonization, or that in the Histories national pride is transformed from belief into longing, or the inquiry prompted by the question: why, around 1630, should two of England's leading dramatists (Massinger and Ford) choose to write a play sympathetic to a defeated pretender to the throne? Inevitably, in a book which takes so much for its province, there are minor disagreements and disappointments. The view of *Henry V* as an empire-building epic pure and simple strikes me as unacceptably 'straight' and should be set against Ralph Berry's discussion of the play in *The Shakespearean Metaphor*. Irish drama gets only fifty-odd pages in a book five times that length, though there is an incisive treatment of the role of Shakespeare's Histories in developing national awareness outside England in the late eighteenth and early nineteenth centuries. I am puzzled by the remark that there is no evidence as to exactly why the Elizabethan dramatists came to write for the public stage. I suppose it depends on what one means by 'evidence' and 'exactly' (and even 'why?'!), but the decline of patronage, the over-production of graduates in relation to available employment in court or church and the magnetic attraction of London seem to be some among many other factors. But Professor Edwards knows all this better than I do, so he is clearly looking for some other kind of evidence (autobiographical? legal?) and a different degree of exactitude. Why? Finally I would question the propriety of bracketing Yeats and Shakespeare as both 'bourgeois with a nostalgia for feudalism'. To my mind Shakespeare was too hard-nosed to be nostalgic about anything. But in spite of these and a few other points of difference, and in part because of them, *Threshold of a Nation* remains for me the prize catch in last year's netful.

It will come as no surprise to anyone reasonably familiar with Chambers and Bentley that there was 'a tradition of plays and masques which are relevant to the feast-day of their performance'. R. Chris Hassel undertakes to demonstrate in detail the nature of this relevance[2] by examining the correlations between some Elizabethan and Jacobean plays and masques known to have been performed during certain Christian festival days in terms of particular 'thematic, imagistic and narrative facets' which they allegedly share. The value for literary studies of such an enterprise must depend almost entirely on the light it sheds on the works themselves. By this standard Professor Hassel's book is far from having the indispensable status which the publishers claim for it, for two main reasons. In the first place, the author's insistence on discussing every extant work which may be supposed to relate to some liturgical occasion in a volume of less than 200 pages of text makes it almost inevitable that the level of engagement is fairly shallow. Shakespeare, Jonson and Beaumont and Fletcher account for fifty-six of the ninety-six works discussed. There are a mere three pages on *Lear*, two apiece on *The Tempest* and *The Winter's Tale* and five on *The Comedy of*

---

2 *Renaissance Drama and the English Church Year* (University of Nebraska Press, Lincoln and London, 1979).

*Errors* and *Othello*. *Twelfth Night* is the subject of the most extended discussion, yet even here the insights offered do not go very far beyond comments such as 'Looking at Feste through the perspective of Epiphany will also suggest how closely the liturgical festival of humiliation and enlightenment might be related to the interest of all Shakespearean comedy in the benevolent edification of its most prideful characters', which is true as far as it goes, except that humiliation and enlightenment are comic themes whose provenance extends in time far beyond Christian liturgical patterns; unless a closer connection between the play and the related liturgical occasion than is here offered can be established (and the suggested application to *all* Shakespearian comedy merely dilutes the force of the specific correspondence urged), the latter seems little more than an interesting irrelevance. The question of relevance leads to my other objection. The author's categories of 'genetic' and 'affective' correlation are sound enough, one describing a work 'clearly named for a festival or written for festival performance', the other a work whose 'significance might have been affected for the court audience by its liturgical occasion'. The trouble arises with the degrees of 'slight, moderate and extensive' correlation which Professor Hassel also employs, but with a generous inclusiveness which does little to give his comments depth or pertinence. In general the masques gain more from his approach than the plays and the lesser plays more than the greater ones. My understanding of the way in which assumptions about divine authority behind political order and the centrality of man in the cosmos are 'explicitly and strenuously questioned in *Lear*' is not notably strengthened or sharpened by quotation from the Lessons for Candlemas. The chosen method of interpretation – a summary of the chief characteristics of each festival followed by an account of how its theme, etc., is reflected in the work discussed – also tends to flatten out the individuality of the latter. But the book contains much useful in-

formation about the Christian year and there is something to be said for an i-dotting demonstration of what one would have expected to be the case anyway.

The prestigious shadow of the Globe has for a long time tended to obscure earlier Elizabethan theatres and reshape them in its own image; so much so that some theatre historians and many literary historians still talk with unwarranted confidence about *the* Elizabethan playhouse. In different ways most of the contributions to *The First Public Playhouse*[3] (based on papers presented to a seminar at the second World Shakespeare Congress held in Washington in 1976) are designed as counterweights to this essentialism, emphasizing the variety of theatrical and architectural forms which the first public theatres could draw on. Of the six papers collected here, three are directly and one largely concerned with the playhouse from which the volume takes its title. Glynne Wickham attempts some further tentative demolition to go the way of the inner stage. He questions the existence of the 'heavens', their furniture and all that upheld them in the earliest public theatres. He points out that there is no evidence that they existed before the building of the Rose (1591), and that one factor which may have induced Henslowe to add them was that Greene's spectaculars called for them. Within the limits imposed by negative evidence the argument is persuasive though not conclusive; the heavens may not have fallen but they are certainly beginning to look pretty insubstantial. Herbert Berry lists for the first time in one place all documentary evidence relating to the Theatre in Shoreditch and in a second contribution considers in detail aspects of its design and possible use. The relation of the Theatre's design to available traditions of theatre construction and to later playhouses is the subject of Richard Hosley's

---

3 *The First Public Playhouse: The Theatre in Shoreditch 1576–1598*, ed. Herbert Berry (McGill – Queen's University Press, Montreal, 1979).

contribution. The design may not have been based on Burbage's experience of playing in innyards, halls and baiting rings (another contributor is sceptical whether plays were ever performed in the last of these). A building specially erected for entertainment, the Calais banqueting hall put up on Henry VIII's orders in 1520 to welcome Charles V, may, according to Hosley, have been the immediate precedent. William Ingram speculates on the financial arrangements entered into in 1585 between James Burbage and Henry Lanman, holder of the nearby Curtain. On his own admission Ingram's essay is largely conjectural but, on the evidence he offers, his conclusion that Burbage senior virtually owned both the Theatre and the Curtain for several years from 1585 is attractive and plausible. Oscar Brownstein questions the view that baiting rings ever provided an arena for players or that any theatre building (apart from the purpose-built Hope) was ever designed as a multi-use auditorium. The thrust of his argument is largely optical–architectural but the question he uses as a title is as stimulating as it is obvious, though no one has ever asked it before to my knowledge, namely: if baiting rings had been so frequently used for playing, 'Why didn't Burbage lease the Beargarden?'

The contributions in *The First Public Playhouse* will certainly provoke rethinking of received ideas about playhouse structure. A modest and small-scale digest of received opinion comes from the Bear Gardens Museum and Arts Centre on the Bankside.[4] It offers, in just over fifty pages of illustrated text, a necessarily brief but quite detailed and accurate view of what is known about Elizabethan, Jacobean and Caroline playhouses and their immediate forerunners. The whole range of playing sites from innyards to court theatres is glanced at, and there is a short but up-to-date bibliography (which does not, however, list *The First Public Playhouse*). The illustrations are well chosen and not all of them are by any means deadeningly familiar. My only slight misgiving is

whether the editor and contributors (Robert Cannon, Rosemary Linnell, Anthony Hozier, Diana Devlin and Jenny Naish) have not tried to do too much in too short a space. Will even the informed reader find the charts of the principal acting companies, for instance, clear and helpful? I didn't.

The first two volumes of *Records of Early English Drama*[5] are devoted to the dramatic and ceremonial activities associated with the civic and guild authorities of York. Volume I is largely taken up with the records themselves, which run from 1220 to 1642 and consist of a variety of items including minutes of council meetings, letters, wills and legal contracts. The introduction, while eschewing any attempt to interpret the documents or assess their significance, sets them in their historical context, dating them and giving their provenance in as much detail as possible. Volume II contains various related appendices, as well as translations, notes and glossaries. While there is little or nothing of *direct* Shakespearian interest here (till the last third of the sixteenth century the records are mainly concerned with the York Corpus Christi performances), there are fascinating details regarding dramatic activity and its relations to civic affairs in the largest fortified northern city. These include an eyewitness account of James I's visit to York in 1603 – 'about the bearing of the sword there was some small contention, the Lorde President taking it for his place, the Lorde Mayor of the Citie esteeming it to be his'. When complete the series will contain all surviving records relating to drama, minstrelsy and civic ceremonial in Great Britain.

*Shakespeare's World: Renaissance Intellectual Contexts*[6] is introduced by the compiler as 'uniquely, a *non*-literary bibliography for

---

4 *The London Theatre Guide 1576–1642*, ed. Christopher Edwards (Burlington Press, Cambridge, 1979).

5 Ed. Alexandra F. Johnston and Margaret Rogerson (Manchester University Press, 1979).

6 By W. R. Elton assisted by Giselle Schlesinger (Garland Publishing Inc., New York and London, 1979).

Shakespeareans – as well as a selective compilation for Renaissance students generally'. The extent of the selection is indicated by the fact that out of over 40,000 possible items covering the period 1966–71, less than a tenth are included. The days when one could hope to read all the secondary material even within a subsection of a subsection in one's field have of course long passed (were they ever really here?) and we are rapidly approaching the time when we shall be unable to keep track even of bibliographies, though rescue by computer is promised us. But it will always be useful to be reminded of the many contexts of Shakespearian drama suggested by the various divisions of this volume – Economic–Social, Educational, Iconographic, Legal and so on. The bibliography also cites reviews and is briefly and briskly annotated. Scholars will doubtless find the two concluding sections – a 128-page dictionary of 'Topoi, Themes, Emblems etc.' and a guide to 'Research Tools' especially useful in conserving midnight oil and many other forms of energy.

Michèle Willems's *La Genèse du Mythe Shakespearien*[7] is wider ranging than Babcock's pioneering study in that it takes in both critical and popular opinion as factors in the making of the Shakespeare myth. She sees the latter, unsurprisingly, as the product of a collision between a critique dominated by rationalist criteria and the Shakespearian *oeuvre* which cannot be adequately accounted for by such criteria. The author painstakingly plots the various stages in the evolution of the image of the Bard as a quasi-divine creator whose characters inhabit an autonomous world, noting that adaptations were often determined by considerations of public favour rather than by neoclassical rules of propriety. Perhaps she underestimates the extent to which a Shakespeare myth already existed before the Restoration. Dr Willems makes the slightly paradoxical but valid point that it was precisely the *simplification* of Shakespeare by the adapters – turning characters into heroes or villains *tout simple*,

plot into intrigue and metaphor into explicit utterance – that helped to create the myth of Shakespeare as divine creator, and documents the way in which the Romantic Shakespeare of the facile pen and the never-failing untutored inspiration is already present in Addison and others. In the early part of the study I felt there is insufficient distinction made between private and public theatres in the matter of audience participation and that altogether too much religious orthodoxy is postulated for the pre-Civil War period. Dr Willems also has a tendency not only to say the same thing three times but to use the same quotation to illustrate it. But most of what she says is true and worth saying (once) and for Wodehouse addicts, of whom this reviewer is one, the longueurs of the book are relieved by a couple of shrewd pages on the Shakespearian dealings of Jeeves and Bertie.

Margot Heinemann's study[8] should convince anyone who still needs convincing that the terms Puritan and Puritanism should be handled with extreme caution in connection with sixteenth- and seventeenth-century social and cultural history. They are especially lethal if one attempts to use them to understand attitudes to the stage in this period. The focus of this study is the dramatic career of Thomas Middleton, with particular emphasis on the political satire and the late great tragedies. The author demonstrates, by close attention to historical evidence and the plays themselves, that a rigid antithesis between a pro-theatre court and an anti-theatre city faction is simply untenable. Her view that Middleton was able to write great tragedy at a time when conditions for serious drama were bad and getting worse because he was in sympathy with the increasingly vocal opposition to the court and its doings has a good deal to recommend it. She also shows how anti-court sentiment persisted in plays right up to the Civil War in spite of

---

7 Presses Universitaires de France, Paris, 1979.
8 *Puritanism and Theatre: Thomas Middleton and Opposition Drama under the Early Stuarts* (Cambridge University Press, 1980).

censorship and finds a link between early Stuart theatre and the popular radical pamphleteering of the 1640s. Her view of some of the plays, particularly *A Fair Quarrel*, is oversimple (she attributes an authority to the Captain's scruples which the play does not support), and she occasionally gets a date wrong (the accepted date for *A Chaste Maid* is 1613, not 1611). There is also something odd, to say the least, in attributing *The Peacemaker* to Lancelot Andrewes in a footnote (p. 115) when (a) there is no evidence whatever that Andrewes had any hand in it and (b) the footnote quotes the very article by Rhodes Dunlap which draws attention to an actual payment to Middleton for the tract.[9] Nevertheless *Puritanism and Theatre* is a bracing example of a cross-disciplinary study which does not trivialize the works it looks at in the interests of propounding a thesis.

*Night's Black Agents*[10] is a sketchy and often tired-sounding survey of elements of witchcraft and magic in a few seventeenth-century plays. There is nothing here as far as the background is concerned which one cannot find in R. H. West's *The Invisible World* and K. M. Briggs's *Pale Hecate's Team* and the insights offered into the plays are neither frequent nor profound. The speculations on staging and the accounts of the subsequent stage history of plays are probably the best parts of the book, though the intrinsic interest of the material is almost enough to hold the reader's attention. I cannot help feeling that the author has missed an opportunity to use the vast body of seventeenth-century material on witchcraft to illuminate a few carefully chosen plays instead of filling out his study with easily available general information on masque and other irrelevances.

I conclude this section with a brief glance at two voluminous studies of individual plays. John Ripley looks minutely at 375 years of *Julius Caesar* on the stage[11] in almost as many pages. Inevitably most of the evidence comes from the nineteenth century and Kemble and

his imitators hold the stage until the 1930s, till the entire *beau idéal* tradition is exploded by Orson Welles's Mercury Theatre production which fathered the over-simplification of Fascist Caesar versus muddled-liberal Brutus which has been around almost ever since. Professor Ripley divides his study into four principal sections, text, staging, type of theatre and audience taste, though the last does not count for much in his study. His critical comments are often either distressingly banal or unsupported where one would like support, but his afterword, consisting of tentative notes for future producers, is both sensible and timely. This is the definitive study of the play's stage history – I hope.

*Shakespeare's Typological Satire*[12] delivers considerably less than or rather something different from what its title promises. It is a study of a related group of plays rather than a single play. The subtitle 'A Study of the Falstaff–Oldcastle Problem' represents much more accurately the scope of the book. Alice-Lyle Scoufos pursues the connection between Shakespeare's Falstaff and the Brookes of Cobham with a meticulous tenacity which inspires awe even where it does not compel belief. A goodly load of old Cobhams make their conspiratorial and sometimes confusing way through the book, because it is the author's view that in all the Henry plays, as well as in *The Merry Wives of Windsor*, Shakespeare is poking fun at a variety of Cobhams past and present. 'Typological satire' is her term for this conflation of past and present, predominantly in the Falstaff figure. The argument depends not so much on any newly discovered evidence (though there are one or two items of new information) as on the presentation of what is

---

9 I owe this point to my friend Brian Parker.
10 By Anthony Harris (Manchester University Press, 1980).
11 *Julius Caesar on Stage in England and America, 1599–1973* (Cambridge University Press, 1980).
12 By Alice-Lyle Scoufos (Ohio University Press, Athens, 1979).

already known and, in the words of one of the chapter titles, 'An Accretion of Minuscule Clues'. It is impossible even to summarize all these here and each reader will judge for himself what weight to give to the clues individually and collectively. For my own part, while I believe there is nothing inherently implausible in the idea that the Falstaff figure satirizes Cobhams past and present, especially in the two *Henry IV* plays, I find the evidence for the satire on Elizabethan Cobhams meagre and unpersuasive. Sir John Brooke (Cobham) may have behaved like Falstaff in regard to paying his soldiers in the Low Countries but so did many others, as the very letter from Thomas Randolph quoted by Dr Scoufos notes. Similarly, the author describes in great detail the involvement of one of the Cobhams with diplomatic waylayings on Gad's Hill but is compelled to concede that there is no clear evidence linking any of them with Shakespeare's play, and is obliged to lay her argument to rest in the ample and treacherous bosom of 'the larger idea of the Gad's Hill robbery' being *'apparently* based upon the historical episodes at Gad's Hill' (my italics). The other question raised by her study, namely what difference it would make to our appreciation of the plays if we made the generous assumption that the author's case has been substantiated, I thankfully evade, noting only that a critical standpoint which sees *The Merry Wives of Windsor* as 'a complex and highly symbolic recapitulation, of [Shakespeare's] satire of the Cobhams' is, to say the least, in danger of being unduly reductive.

Among longer articles that have come my way are two apiece on *Cymbeline* and *Timon* (and two other Roman plays), one each on *Richard III, As You Like It, Hamlet* and *The Tempest* and one on *The Phoenix and the Turtle*. I shall glance briefly at each in that order. In *Le Secret de 'Cymbeline'*[13] James Dauphiné offers to relate romance to astrological lore, an enterprise not self-evidently absurd. There are some

mildly relevant comments on the significance of Imogen's cinque-spotted mole and I could go along with the identification of Belarius with Bel-Aries = *bélier* (Ram), and even Arviragus with Greek αἰγό-κερως (Capricorn) though a reference to 'rain and wind beat dark December' is hardly strong enough to establish a connection between Arviragus and Capricorn (the December birth-sign). There is an intolerable deal of starry speculation to a meagre ha'p'orth of critical insight. I am unimpressed by the application to Shakespeare of a statement about James I made by the astrologer Lilly thirty years after the dramatist's death, and wonder why, if *Cymbeline* is so riddled with astrological allusions as the author makes out, that compulsive astrologer Simon Forman makes no mention of the fact in his comments on the play. But the article will undoubtedly make a strong appeal to those who find impressive arguments such as the one that because the Queen confesses that her daughter was 'as a scorpion to her sight' she (the Queen) was a Scorpio or that Cloten is a Pisces because Guiderius says he will 'tell the fishes' Cloten is the Queen's son.

More rewarding is David Bergeron's reading of *Cymbeline* as 'Shakespeare's Last Roman Play' where the discussion of sources and in particular the notion that the Augustan family may lie behind the play as a kind of paradigm is put to good critical use.[14]

Janette Dillon provides an interesting background to Timon, Antony and Coriolanus by setting them against the contemporary controversy about solitude ('solitariness') versus society. She charts the varieties of isolation, from spiritual desolation and loss of others' respect (Antony) through 'a stillborn aspiration to self-sufficiency' (Coriolanus) to physical exile (Timon and Coriolanus). Her discussion of Timon is perfunctory and the notion of Antony's isolation as that of 'the actor, who is

---

13 *Études Anglaises*, 2, April–June 1979.
14 *Shakespeare Quarterly*, 31 (1980), 31–41.

never physically alone, but also never spiritually engaged' strains my sense of the character to the limit (if Antony is as lacking in an inward sense as Miss Dillon alleges, it is difficult to see how we can sense his spiritual isolation), but on the whole I found my understanding of the plays enriched by seeing them against this setting.[15]

Challenging the usual view that the Athenian background of *Timon* is either anachronistic or irrelevant or both, Robert S. Miola points out that the Elizabethan idea, inculcated in school-books and the like, of Athens as a democracy and hence a seed-bed of licence, disorder and sensuality is central to the play. His view of Timon's banquet as merely self-indulgent excess is itself excessive and should be modified by Miss Dillon's comments on the Shakespearian feast as an image of social intercourse.[16]

A suggestion in Geoffrey Bullough's *Narrative and Dramatic Sources of Shakespeare* (duly acknowledged) is convincingly developed by Harold Brooks to show Shakespeare's indebtedness to Seneca's *Troades* for the chorus of women in *Richard III* and to *Hercules Furens* (and to a lesser extent to the *Hippolytus*) for the courtship scene between Richard and Anne.[17] This is a sequel to Professor Brooks's discussion of the possible sources for Clarence's dream in Golding's Ovid, *The Mirror for Magistrates* and the Cave of Mammon and the sea episodes in the first three books of *The Faerie Queene*.[18]

An instructively detailed comparison between Rosalind and her counterpart in Lodge's romance enables Edward I. Berry to trace the process of self-discovery in, and hence the relative complexity of Shakespeare's heroine.[19]

In 'Hamlet, Nationhood and Identity'[20] Ralph Berry achieves the difficult task of saying something at once new, true, and exciting about the play. I do not know whether Berry has read Philip Edwards's book, but his discussion of the relationship between drama and the developing awareness of national iden-

tities is a richly various extension of Edwards's theme – 'for Hamlet the drama of his consciousness unfolds through areas of national definition. The geography of Europe becomes, in the end, countries of the mind.'

John Bender's 'The Day of *The Tempest*'[21] considers the play in relation to the date of its first recorded court performance – All Saints' Day, 1611 – citing certain passages selected for the Anglican celebration of the feast which promise that the righteous dead 'will miraculously confront those who despised them and shall be instruments of judgement'. This is much the same territory as that explored in R. Chris Hassel's study, though Hassel stresses texts about the virtues of forgiveness rather than miraculous confrontation. As with the book, I learned much about Hallowmas but little that helped me to respond more fully to the play.

The parallels cited by Alur Janakiram between 'The Phoenix and the Turtle' and the first of Leone Ebreo's *Dialoghi d'Amore*[22] in regard to the paradoxical union of oneness and the love–reason relationship are certainly there, but his discussion of the poem is remote and reductive because the strange framework of mock solemnity is not taken into account at all.

Short notes can receive only the shortest of notices. In the issue of *Notes and Queries* devoted to Shakespearian topics, Jane Belfield draws attention to an entry in the Court Min-

---

15 '"Solitariness": Shakespeare and Plutarch', *Journal of English and Germanic Philology*, 83 (1979), 325–44.
16 'Timon in Shakespeare's Athens', *Shakespeare Quarterly*, 31 (1980), 21–30.
17 '*Richard III*: Unhistorical Amplifications: The Women's Scenes and Seneca', *Modern Language Review*, 75 (1980), 721–37.
18 *Shakespeare Survey* 32 (Cambridge University Press 1979), pp. 145–50.
19 'Rosalynde and Rosalind', *Shakespeare Quarterly*, 31 (1980), 42–52.
20 *University of Toronto Quarterly*, 49 (1980), 282–303.
21 *ELH*, 47 (1980), 235–58.
22 *English Studies* (Lisse), 61 (1980), 224–35.

ute Book of the Goldsmiths' Company of 27 January 1603/04 recording that Robert Armin was made a freeman of the Company, and to another one dated 15 July 1608 which notes that Armin took as an apprentice one James Jones, possibly an actor rather than a trainee goldsmith.[23] A source in Whitney's *Choice of Emblems* for Shakespeare's 'dyer's hand' (and Donne's 'huge hill, cragged and steep') is suggested by Bernard Richards.[24] R. A. L. Burnet identifies further echoes from the Geneva Bible in Shakespeare (and Milton) and wonders whether Macbeth's 'I have lived long enough' is a reminiscence of a passage in Antony Gilby's 1551 commentary on Micah.[25] Nine verbal parallels, some of them plausible, between *Romeo and Juliet* and Nashe's *Have with You to Saffron Walden* are noted by J. J. M. Tobin.[26] James Neil argues with due solemnity that *A Midsummer Night's Dream* contains astronomical references which make it clear that a specific date – 1 May 1595 or 11 June 1594 – or possibly both, are being referred to. The assumption that because there were two full moons in their prime on these days Shakespeare designed the play to refer to them needs more arguing, to say the least.[27] David Scott Kasten and Nancy J. Vickers suggestively link Jaques's lover's ballad to his mistress's eyebrow to the tradition of the *blason anatomique* exemplified by a poem of Maurice Scève's.[28] The all-too-flourishing art of labouring the obvious is well demonstrated by Dale G. Priest in 'Rosalind's Child's Father'.[29] Robert T. Levine argues that in Ophelia's question 'Could beauty, my lord, have better commerce than with honesty?' the central terms should be transposed. I am not convinced that the confusion is not Ophelia's rather than Compositor Y's.[30]

*Hamlet* elicits two other notes, one an emendation to Polonius's advice to Ophelia on how to treat Hamlet's 'tenders of affection', by Richard Jacobs,[31] the other by Robert Bozanich, offering an elucidation of Hamlet's verse to Ophelia based on at least two senses of 'doubt'

(suspect to be the case or not to be the case);[32] I doubt he may be right. Naseeb Shaheen demonstrates that a source for Iago's 'trifles light as air' in the scripture Paraphrases, suggested by Thomas Carter, could not have been a source as it did not appear there till 1781. Perhaps it is as well that no one but Carter seems to have noticed the coincidence of phrase.[33] Elsewhere, Professor Shaheen shows that Shakespeare was more likely to have written 'base Judean' rather than 'base Indian' because one of his sources, Geoffrey Fenton, twice compared the villain to Judas in retelling Bandello's version of the Othello story in *Certaine Tragical Discourses*.[34] Addressing himself to a well-known crux in the same play, Michael Srigley makes out a good case for glossing 'defunct' as achieved or consummated and makes more sense of the whole speech than most commentators.[35] Though Horst Oppel concludes his note on 'Edgar's Refrain "Hey No Nonny" (*Lear* III. iv. 97)' by reminding us that 'there is no need to overstrain the relation between Coverdale and Shakespeare' the re-

---

23 'Robert Armin, Citizen and Goldsmith of London', *Notes and Queries*, n.s. 27 (1980), 158–9.

24 'Whitney's Influence on Shakespeare's Sonnets 111 and 112 and Donne's Third Satire', *ibid.*, pp. 160–1.

25 'Some Echoes of the Geneva Bible in Shakespeare and Milton', *ibid.*, pp. 179–81.

26 'Nashe and *Romeo and Juliet*', *ibid.*, pp. 161–2.

27 'A Calendar, A Calendar! Look in the Almanac', *ibid.*, pp. 162–4.

28 'Shakespeare, Scève and "A Woeful Ballad"', *ibid.*, pp. 165–6.

29 *Ibid.*, p. 166.

30 'Honesty and Beauty: An Emendation for *Hamlet* III, i, 109–110', *ibid.*, pp. 166–9.

31 'Sex and Money: A Note on *Hamlet* I, iii, 108–10', *Shakespeare Quarterly*, 31 (1980), 88–90.

32 'The Eye of the Beholder: Hamlet to Ophelia II, ii, 109–122', *ibid.*, pp. 90–3.

33 '"Trifles light as air": A Note on *Othello* III.iii.313' *Notes and Queries*, n.s. 27 (1980), 169–70.

34 'Like the Base Judean', *Shakespeare Quarterly*, 31 (1980), 93–5.

35 'A Note on *Othello* I.iii.288–293', *Studia Neophilologica*, 52 (1980), 61–7.

minder comes, in my view, after the fact.[36] David Everett Blythe helpfully points out, what most editors appear to have missed, that 'soiled' as applied to a horse in Lear's great speech has the specific sense of an animal fed in order to increase its sexual potency (Posthumus's 'full-acorn'd boar' is adduced as an analogous example).[37] A distant echo of some lines in a late twelfth-century Latin poem by Joseph of Exeter is heard by Peter Dronke in Enobarbus's famous description of Cleopatra's barge.[38] Three of the five women mentioned by Stephano in his drunken song are plausibly identified with actual seventeenth-century 'roaring girls' by Patricia Gartenberg, who goes on to suggest, much less plausibly, that a fourth, Kate for whom 'none of us car'd', was the heroine of the *Shrew*.[39] Donald S. Lawless indulges in some singularly pointless speculation about 'Shakespeare's Death, Funeral and Burial'.[40] Richard A. Levin's suggested analogy between Davenant's claim that he was Shakespeare's bastard son and the behaviour of the Bastard in *King John*[41] may have a point, but it eludes me.

## SHAKESPEARE ON THE STAGE

We draw our readers' attention to two ambitious works of reference relating to Shakespeare on the stage. *Theatre at Stratford-upon-Avon* (2 vols., Westport, Conn., and London, 1980), compiled by Michael Mullin, Karen Morris Muriello, and others (including a computer), is described as 'a catalogue-index to productions of the Shakespeare Memorial/Royal Shakespeare Theatre, 1879–1978'. It is essentially a computerized guide to the Theatre's archives, now housed in the Shakespeare Centre at Stratford-upon-Avon and available on microfilm at the University of Illinois. The first of these volumes offers a catalogue of productions, listed alphabetically with full information about directors, designers, actors, etc. The second reshuffles the basic material, indexing playwrights, theatre personnel (directors, designers, actors), and re-

viewers, and offering also a chronological calendar of productions. Michael Mullin contributes an introductory survey of the Theatre's history and the material included in its archives. The scope of these volumes is limited, inevitably, by the selectivity imposed on the Theatre archives: the reviews, for example, do not extend to *Shakespeare Survey* or *Shakespeare Quarterly*. The volumes will be of great value, but users should be aware that the archives, though rich, are not comprehensive.

*Shakespeare as Spoken* (12 vols., Ann Arbor and London, 1977–80) represents William Halstead's own collation of about 2,500 printed acting editions and 'all promptbooks in English through 1975 of professional productions held in public collections'. The basic list of acting texts was supplied by Jaggard's *Shakespeare Bibliography* (1911), of promptbooks by Charles Shattuck's *The Shakespeare Promptbooks* (1965). Each of the twelve volumes, published 'on demand', prints on verso pages a blown-up reproduction of the Globe text of three or four plays, faced by line-by-line collations of cuts and indications that a line has been revised or an addition made – though such alterations are not given verbatim. There are additional items, such as a General Bibliography (in the first volume), a bibliography for each play which includes summaries of alterations in each acting version, and reproductions of Garrick's adapted endings to *Romeo and Juliet* and *Hamlet*. The editorial material is described as an 'unedited facsimile of the author's typescript', and there are evident errors. But this is a heroic enterprise carried through with extraordinary energy and devotion. The

---

36 *Notes and Queries*, n.s. 27 (1980), 170–2.
37 'Lear's Soiled Horse', *Shakespeare Quarterly*, 31 (1980), 86–8.
38 'Shakespeare and Joseph of Exeter', *Notes and Queries*, n.s. 27 (1980), 172–4.
39 'Shakespeare's Roaring Girls', *ibid.*, pp. 174–5.
40 *Ibid.*, pp. 176–7.
41 *Ibid.*, pp. 177–9.

terrain is now mapped out, and others can refine upon it in matters of detail. Perhaps this is a step towards the replacement of G. C. D.

Odell's *Shakespeare – from Betterton to Irving* which is so greatly to be desired.

S.W.W.

## 3 TEXTUAL STUDIES

*reviewed by* GEORGE WALTON WILLIAMS

The Arden Shakespeare has graced the year with the publication of two volumes, *A Midsummer Night's Dream* and *Romeo and Juliet*, so happily paired that we are tempted to suppose that the General Editors, joined now by Brian Morris, planned it that way from the beginning. It is not so, of course, for Brian Gibbons, the successor to the late John Crow in the editorship of *Romeo and Juliet*, began his work 'from scratch in 1973'; and Harold F. Brooks confesses in his preface that '*A Midsummer Night's Dream* has had a pre-eminent place' in his affections since the afternoon in 1914 when he attended Granville-Barker's golden production. It is not too much to say that Brooks's edition, bearing yet the marks of that inspiration, began at that matinée.

The conjunction of the two volumes sharpens our perspective on the relationships between the two plays. The most interesting of these to this reviewer is the question of dating. Brooks assembles all possible material on the date of *A Midsummer Night's Dream* from literary, topical, occasional, and stylistic considerations (twenty-three pages) and concludes that it 'was composed in the winter of 1595–6, for the Carey wedding' on 19 February 1596 (p. lvii) and that it probably followed *Romeo and Juliet* (p. xliii). In recognition of Brooks's extensive treatment, Gibbons gives less space to this topic in his edition; he accepts, in general, Brooks's dating, but he seems reluctant to follow Brooks in giving *Romeo and Juliet* the precedence: 'only if we suppose that the artisans' difficulties with [bringing a wall on to the stage] . . . allude to the scene in *Romeo and Juliet* where Romeo says he has leapt Capulet's orchard wall, can we argue that *Romeo and*

*Juliet* was performed earlier than *A Midsummer Night's Dream*' (p. 30).

If there was an actual property wall in *Romeo and Juliet*, it must have been either (a) so routine and efficient a mechanism that a parody of it later would have been meaningless or (b) so clumsy a contraption as to invite not only parody later but also merriment at the moment. It is unlikely that Shakespeare would have allowed a device (b) that would evoke the wrong kind of response at the start of the tenderest scene in the play.[1] But if there was no actual property wall on stage in *Romeo*, then a reference to it in *A Midsummer Night's Dream* is scarcely admissible, and we must conclude that the artisans' difficulties with the wall are of a piece with their difficulties with moonshine. The question of the precedence of *Romeo* depends not on the bringing in of a physical wall (3.1.58) in *A Midsummer Night's Dream* but on the removal of a psychological one (5.1.204, 342) and the consequent reconciliation of the parents of Pyramus and Thisbe, a matter that Shakespeare twice mentions. The presence of the parents – who are not in Plutarch – and their reconciliation are elements meaningless in terms of the themes of *A Midsummer Night's Dream*, which has no hostility between any feuding parents, and meaningful only in reference to some situation

---

1 It should be observed that the dialogue requires no wall. Benvolio tells us that Romeo has 'leapt this orchard wall', and we may well believe that the wall is as imaginary as are the light wings of love with which Romeo o'erperched it. Insistence on a physical wall derives from the tradition of nineteenth-century staging or from the movies. Gibbons is entirely correct in rejecting a physical wall (p. 123).

which does and which must therefore already have been in existence in the mind of the poet if not of the audience, i.e. *Romeo and Juliet*. On this reconciliation Gibbons writes movingly, seeing it as an anticipation of the late romances. But Brooks warns that the priority 'cannot be firmly determined' (p. xliii).

In the matter of sources, both editions are unusually rich. Brooks gives us thirty pages of discussion and twenty-four pages of quotation; Gibbons gives us ten pages of discussion and forty pages of quotation. In Brooks, we have a display of source material of unexpected breadth: quotations from Chaucer, North, Golding, Seneca (*Oedipus, Medea, Hippolytus*), *Huon of Bourdeux*, and Reginald Scot, with surprising emphasis on the classical background of, for example, Oberon's description of the pageant, which derives from Seneca and Ovid, as well as from Marlowe, Chaucer, and Elyot's *Governour*, to say nothing of its presumed source in an actual event.[2] Gibbons's special contribution lies in his analysis of the poetic tone and style of the play which he finds, source-like, in the sonnet sequences, particularly in Sidney's *Astrophil and Stella*.

The two editions tend to be cautious in matters of text, each providing one new emendation only. At *A Midsummer Night's Dream*, 5.1.205, Brooks emends Quarto 'Moon used' (F 'morall downe') to 'mure rased'; he argues cogently for these words which do certainly provide a plausible and attractive reading though one not easy for an actor to say. Gibbons, at *Romeo and Juliet* 3.5.181, emends Quarto 'liand' (F 'allied') to 'lign'd', Harold Jenkins's refinement of Crow's 'lien'd', i.e. with good family lines. Though this is the easiest explanation of the Quarto error, 'ligne' is not a standard spelling of Shakespeare's. In matters of stage direction, Gibbons is quite correct in regarding 'Away Tybalt' (3.1.87) as a speech (following T. J. B. Spencer and others), and in adjusting Rowe's error in the location of the first kiss of Romeo and Juliet so that it shall terminate the sonnet (lines 91–104) and not

pointlessly follow the first line of the following quatrain. (There is no occasion to suppose that these four lines (lines 105–8) begin 'a fresh sonnet' (p. 119); they form a quatrain and that is enough.) This quatrain also should be terminated with a kiss, not interrupted by one as here, so that the Nurse may burst in upon a kiss, not a conversation. Gibbons rightly observes (at 2.2.149) that the Nurse's repeated intrusions form a 'miniature conceit for the tragic action as a whole'; this is just such an intrusion. At 3.3.108, Gibbons declines to introduce the Q1 direction the 'Nurse snatches the dagger away' on the grounds that 'There is nothing in the dialogue (or the characterization of the Nurse generally) to prepare for or to support this intervention by the Nurse; indeed this piece of business looks like a gratuitous and distracting bid' by the actor to call attention to his part (p. 180). This is a just observation.[3] Gibbons recognizes the proper staging of act 3, scene 5, and of act 4, scenes 3 to 5, and he notes Shakespeare's ingenuity in arranging for Mercutio to die off stage so that Tybalt's corpse — one corpse only — lies on the stage conspicuous for sixty-six lines; 'the action of bearing [Tybalt] off gives visual emphasis to the turn-

---

2 Brooks's discussion of dating includes the topicalities suggested by this description (2.1.148–68). On page xxxix, Brooks dates the Kenilworth spectacle at 1571, the Elvetham one at 1591; on page lxviii he dates Kenilworth at 1591 and Elvetham at 1595. The dates are, respectively, 1575 and 1591. The difficulties that some critics sense as to the impropriety in Shakespeare's evoking in Elizabeth's mind past *amours* are surely unfounded. The juice of the little Western flower produces error and confusion; Dian's bud, i.e., Elizabeth's flower, has force and blessed power to correct all such error. The associations with chastity and blessedness confirm the Elizabethan compliment of 1.1.74–5.

3 But its justness depends in part on the tone of the production. In the 1980 production at Stratford-upon-Avon, the Friar rushed forward to prevent Romeo from stabbing himself. As the Friar, struggling with Romeo, had no hand free, the Nurse removed the dagger from Romeo's hand. She did not 'snatch the dagger away', for that would indeed have been uncharacteristic violence; but her action seemed appropriate in context.

ing point of the action: the dark second half of the play begins' (p. 168). Gibbons appropriately assigns the 'grey-ey'd morn' passage to Romeo (following Hosley and Spencer).[4]

In a footnote, Brooks offers an observation salutary to directors of *A Midsummer Night's Dream*. In defiance of the eroticism of most modern productions, Brooks remarks that 'carnal bestiality [between Titania and Bottom] is surely impossible: jealous Oberon would not have cast his spell to cuckold himself' (p. cxv).

The new editions of Shakespeare from the Oxford and Cambridge University Presses have progressed so far as to issue instructions to their several editors. These are of general interest as well. For the Oxford Shakespeare, Stanley Wells, the General Editor, has prepared in typescript for private circulation his 'Editorial Procedures'. Here he explains the double nature of the edition; there will be a single-volume edition (the *Complete Oxford Shakespeare*), and a multi-volume edition (Oxford English Texts). Samuel Schoenbaum is co-editor for the former and American Advisory Editor for the latter. Gary Taylor is Associate Editor; special advisers are G. R. Proudfoot for text and F. W. Sternfeld for music. The texts of the plays in the two formats will be the work of different editors and will, therefore, be different. For the New Cambridge series, Philip Brockbank has done the same (in printed form and generally available) in company with his Associate General Editors Brian Gibbons, Bernard Harris, and Robin Hood. In his 'Editorial Guide' we are told that the new edition in order to be attentive 'to the realisation of the plays on the stage' has secured Maurice Daniels of the Royal Shakespeare Company as Theatre Adviser. Plays more than usually complex will have supplementary volumes in a series, New Cambridge Shakespeare Studies and Supplementary Texts, a revival of the old Shakespeare Problems Series.

Both of the multi-volume editions will follow, in general, the Arden format of the page,

but the Cambridge will record the collations in an appendix. Both editions will follow the Pelican edition in placing act and scene numbers in the margin and will eschew conspicuous location indicators.[5] Both editions will be modern-spelling, but the Oxford will evidently be more extreme than the Cambridge, going even so far as to adopt 'jail' for 'gaol'.

As its ripe first-fruits, the new Oxford Shakespeare edition has produced a volume entitled *Modernizing Shakespeare's Spelling, with Three Studies in the Text of 'Henry V'*. The *Three Studies* are discussed later in this review, but here we notice the lead essay by Stanley Wells. Confronted with the problems of modernizing for the new edition, Wells remarks that, though many critics worry about spelling, few have discussed it in print. His essay explores the problems and suggests ways in which they may be faced (p. 4). Wells confirms the position of his predecessor, Alice Walker, admitting that he sees no virtue 'in conscious conservation of archaic and obsolete spellings' (p. 4). He considers variants that are semantically indifferent and those that are semantically significant and concludes that in cases of ambiguity or where 'additional resonances' are important, the editor should modernize and annotate. Though such a policy may lead to many annotations, it has certainly the virtue of clarity. Wells also considers contractions, elisions, metrical markings, and punctuation. His conclusion is that the 'mod-

---

4 In his extensive review of this edition, 'The Bettering of Burby', Stanley Wells properly notes that the fact that Q1 gives the speech to the Friar is 'very strong evidence indeed that this was Shakespeare's own final decision' (*Times Literary Supplement*, 20 June 1980, p. 710). It is very strong evidence that the Friar spoke the lines on stage, but it is not quite so strong evidence that arrangement was Shakespeare's final decision. It is possible to argue rather that the location in Q1 derives from errors of the reporter (so Richard Hosley) or of the theater scribe (so the present reviewer).

5 Wells's review (cited in n. 4 above) seems to indicate that the Oxford edition will provide more stage directions than have been customary in recent texts.

ernizing process could, and should, be taken further than has been customary' (p. 34), and he cites preliminary studies in *As You Like It* which suggest that modernization, 'responsibly undertaken', will indicate clearly that Shakespeare located the scene specifically in France. Modernization becomes in such an instance 'a means of exploring Shakespeare's text that can make a real contribution to scholarship' (p. 34).

Unafraid to admit that he is one of those critics who 'quite enjoy counting things' (p. [vii]) MacD. P. Jackson has contributed an important volume to the bibliography of studies of authorship, *Studies in Attribution: Middleton and Shakespeare.*[6] Following the examples of Cyrus Hoy and other scholars (and working independently of D. J. Lake), Jackson has here applied evidence from linguistic preferences, oaths and exclamations, and function words to provide almost incontrovertible data for the establishment of the Middleton canon. Of interest to readers of this review are his assignment on the basis of such evidence of two plays of the Shakespeare Apocrypha – *The Puritan* and *A Yorkshire Tragedy* – to Middleton and his argument that in *Timon of Athens* Middleton was a collaborator. Such claims have been advanced before by other scholars – Archer, Oliphant, William Wells – but Jackson's analyses are compelling; and, since his data of various kinds tend to support and confirm one another, it will be difficult to set his findings aside. In *Timon,*

the linguistic pattern of I.ii, III, and one or two other patches . . . is as like Middleton's as it is unlike Shakespeare's. Middleton strongly prefers *has* and *does* to [Shakespeare's preferences,] *hath* and *doth*, and he uses *h'as, h'ad, 'tas, ha', 'em, I'm, e'en, ne'er, on't,* and other *'t* contractions [in his undoubted works] at roughly the rate at which they are used in the anomalous scenes. . . . [There is] nothing un-Middletonian about the linguistic pattern of I.ii and III of *Timon.* (p.58)

Furthermore, preliminary studies of the frequency of thirteen function words (*a/an, and,*

*but, by, for, from, in, it, of, that, the, to, with*) demonstrate that the patterns in the two shares of the play are clearly 'Middletonian' and 'Shakespearian' and fit exactly into the patterns of those dramatists in their undoubted plays of the same period (pp. 89–90). Similarly, an examination of 'rare words' in the play reveals that, though Middleton's share bears no relationship to the use of such words in Shakespeare's chronology, Shakespeare's share fits precisely where we would expect it to on the basis of customary tests (pp. 155–6). Finally, the forms of *Oh* and *O* exclamations and the variant spellings of proper names both confirm the presence of another author in the play.

Jackson also provides, incidental to his analysis of 'rare words' and chronology in *Timon*, arguments for two strata of work in *Titus, Henry VIII,* and *Pericles,* noting that the strata may be explained in terms either of authorship or of chronology.

Questions of authorship are further treated in those perennials, *Pericles* and *Sir Thomas More.* Two monographs review the 'case' of *Pericles.*[7] The later of the two (1980), a general survey by James O. Wood, maintains Wood's steady thesis that the play is an early work of Shakespeare, acts 3 to 5 having been revised late in his career. He dismisses the arguments supporting Wilkins as a contributor to the play as 'not supported by any substantial evidence' (p. 48) – disregarding the article by Willem Schrickx published in these pages in 1976 – and he counters the argument for John Day as author by supposing that Day was in fact borrowing from Shakespeare's play which he had seen in manuscript (unlikely) or on the stage (no performances recorded). Wood dates the

---

6 *Studies in Attribution: Middleton and Shakespeare,* Jacobean Drama Studies, 79 (Institut für Anglistik und Amerikanistik, Salzburg, 1979).
7 'The Case of Shakespeare's *Pericles*', San José Studies, 6 (1980), 38–58; 'Shakespeares "Pericles" Gedanken zu einem umstrittenen Drama', in *Jahrbuch der Wittheit zu Bremen,* 23 (1979), 113–33.

first writing of the play to the early 1590s and the revision to 1605–6. (The dates that Jackson gives in the book reviewed above are 1597–8 and 1604–5 for the two strata.) This reviewer is not yet convinced that Wood's thesis is to be accepted, but he finds Kenneth Muir's tolerance of it a mark in its favour. In the earlier monograph on the topic (1979), a comparable general statement about the nature of the play, Johannes Schütze defers in matters of authorship to Wood: 'Die Aufsätze von Wood verdienen unsere volle Auferksamkeit' (p. 128). The problem of *Sir Thomas More* is also with us again. Thomas Merriam has announced in the public press that, by using a computer program that distinguishes unconscious word habits appearing consistently in a writer's work, he can demonstrate that *More* is entirely Shakespeare's.[8] His data derive from 'the frequency of common combinations of words and the position in sentences of commoner words such as 'and', 'the', or 'but'; he has then compared his findings in *More* with comparable tests in *Titus Andronicus*, *Julius Caesar*, and *Pericles*. Evidence drawn from such a trio might well be expected to support any hypothesis.

Two articles address the problems in editing texts presumed to be from foul papers and, concentrating on various kinds of errors in the printed versions, argue that we may see in them 'Shakespeare at Work'. Stanley Wells deals with *Much Ado About Nothing*; Fredson Bowers, with *All's Well That Ends Well*.[9] From the presence in entry directions of characters who never speak (and the reverse), both critics see evidence of Shakespeare changing his mind as he worked his way through the play; of such famous ghosts, Wells discusses 'Innogen' and Bowers 'Violenta'. Both critics also consider the problems of variant prefixes for the same character. Wells returns to the question of Margaret's partner in the dance (act 2, scene 1), and Bowers attacks the 'complex and textually important problem of the two French Lords' (p. 68). Bowers brings to bear on his text a careful analysis of the stints of the compositors as they bear on the variant prefixes. Wells offers a salutary conclusion: in texts based on foul papers, an editor 'is dealing with a work of art which, however fine in some respects, has not been polished in all its details . . . it should be possible to reveal more of the possibilities inherent in the text than are suggested by editors who take the attitude that there must be a final solution to every problem' (p. 16).

In a long and important article Fredson Bowers addresses a particularly annoying problem in editing Shakespeare's verse – or, perhaps more exactly, in printing it on the page: the problem of the short line.[10] Bowers notices the various kinds of short line in Shakespeare's plays – internal line, pentameter divided between two speakers, concluding line of a speech, line without metrical relationship to the dialogue (which may be verse or prose), beginning line of a speech – but the last category is the one of greatest concern in the article, and Bowers returns to it constantly. By a rough count, Bowers finds in fifteen plays approximately 354 short concluding lines that are not linked and approximately 117 short beginning lines that are not linked – a ratio of three to one; this ratio Bowers describes as 'general prevalence' as opposed to 'relative rarity' (pp. 78–9). He then deduces from the evidence of three late plays only that 'the statistics are five or more to one that when linking part lines are present Shakespeare will end a speech with a short line than that he will begin a speech with less than a full pentameter' (p. 80).

'The general pattern . . . indicates that un-

---

8 *The Times*, 2 July 1980, p. 2.

9 Stanley Wells, 'Editorial Treatment of Foul-Paper Texts: *Much Ado About Nothing* as Test Case', *Review of English Studies*, 31 (1980), 1–16; Fredson Bowers, 'Shakespeare at Work: The Foul Papers of *All's Well That Ends Well*', in *English Renaissance Studies Presented to Dame Helen Gardner*, ed. John Carey (Oxford, 1980), pp. 56–73.

10 'Establishing Shakespeare's Text: Notes on Short Lines and the Problem of Verse Division', *Studies in Bibliography*, 33 (1980), 74–130.

linked final short lines are common whereas unlinked short beginning lines are rare' (p. 81). Therefore, in editing Shakespeare's verse, 'the odds strongly favor the principle that in ordinary circumstances [wherever linking is possible, the linking should be made with the] short line beginning a speech . . . [rather than with] the short line ending . . . a speech' (p. 81). Bowers finds that Steevens, the Globe, and most subsequent editors have tended to link in the opposite direction. He argues against this tendency, though he admits that there are occasions when the short beginning line is 'inserted for special purposes and therefore acceptable: when it is associated with 'change of address, stage-business, or strong syntactical shifts' (p. 105). There is no fault to find with such a general principle, but when we discover that the 'principle' of page 81 becomes by page 105 'the really significant rule' we have reason to fear that the case may be being overstated. Editors will differ on the strengths of strong syntactical shifts and on the varying significances of changes of address and of the nature of stage directions. So that in *Antony and Cleopatra* (TLN 34–7) where 'the Globe faultily arranges' (p. 106) thus:

| | |
|---|---|
| Perform't, or else we damn thee.' | 34 |
| *Ant.* How, my love! | 35 |
| *Cleo.* Perchance! nay, and most like. | 36 |
| You must not stay here longer; your dismission, | 37 |

Bowers arranges:

How, my Love?

Perchance? Nay, and most like:

The Globe gives us a regular line of ten syllables; Bowers, a bumpy one of nine. Bowers violates his own finding that 'the beginning line of a linked speech will more often be three than two feet' (p. 105). The Globe arrangement of the full line includes a taunt and response between the lovers that are more intimately connected than are Bowers's. To this reviewer, it seems that the syntactical shift between lines 36 and 37 (marked in the Folio by a colon)

is sufficiently strong to justify the short beginning line. Bowers would brush aside these arguments as 'weak reeds [that] must bend before the superior force of the evidence against ordinary beginning short lines of speeches' (p. 106).

Similarly, in *Julius Caesar* (TLN 2367–70), the Globe arranges thus:

| | | |
|---|---|---|
| And leave them honeyless. | | 2367 |
| *Ant.* | Not stingless too. | 2368 |
| *Bru.* | O, yes, and soundless too: | 2369 |
| For you have stol'n their buzzing, | | |
| Antony | | 2370 |

Bowers would read as the full line 'Not stingless too. O, yes, and soundless too', though he admits that the interchange between Cassius and Antony is 'more direct' (p. 105) within the single line of the Globe than is that between Antony and Brutus in his arrangement. Yet 'here there is insufficient reason to break the really significant rule that run-on lines without . . . strong syntactical shifts should not begin a speech as an unlinked unit' (p. 105). Such an assertion is based on a subjective response; to this reviewer at least, it seems that line 2369 is not a run-on line and that there is a sufficiently strong syntactical shift between lines 2369 and 2370 (marked in the Folio by a colon) to justify the short beginning line and so retain the more direct interchange. Bowers concedes that the matter is 'debatable'.

It is evident that some clear guidelines will be useful in the treatment of these 'amphibious' part lines (as Abbott called them).[11] Bowers's study, a strong leading statement of the problem, is certainly correct in its general conclusions. What is yet needed, however, rather than a rough survey of the canon, is an exact analysis of each play. Bowers recognizes

---

11 The new Oxford edition proposes to print the three lines of such an amphibious crux flush left, numbering them as separate units. This is to follow typographically the consequences of Abbott's suggestion (§ 513). As one of his examples, Abbott cites the lines from *Antony and Cleopatra* quoted above.

that Shakespeare's techniques changed over the years; a ratio drawn from the entire canon or from three late plays will prove an inadequate guide for editing any single play. Bowers calls attention to the problem and provides many valuable examples of it with penetrating analysis for each; he also discusses the problem of part lines as they bear on tetrameter and hexameter lines. The paper is a seminal one and will provoke much profitable discussion.

The year has produced some interesting work on compositors and printing practices. T. H. Howard-Hill refines and enlarges Hinman's analysis of Compositor E.[12] He demonstrates that, contrary to Hinman's belief, Compositor E did set from manuscript copy: he did so in *Titus Andronicus* (on dd4) where he revealed that he was not competent to handle manuscript copy quickly enough and he was therefore given only printed copy until he became more fluent in setting, i.e. in quires ss and following: *King Lear, Othello, Antony and Cleopatra* and *Cymbeline.* Howard-Hill, using the reattribution of twenty-eight and a half pages that he has presented earlier, observes also that E's spelling preferences changed in the course of his experience in the Folio work. He argues vigorously for compositor identification based on typographical evidence (spacing of internal commas in short lines, lines containing contractions but not driven out, turn-overs, stage directions set in, marginal divergence of entries, catchwords, and dashes – evidence of varying degrees of usefulness) rather than on orthographical preferences – evidence subject to influence of copy and to changing tastes. We see from this article 'more clearly than before the closeness of E's working relationship with compositor B, and, throughout the Tragedies, we can observe E's gradual acquisition of typographical expertise. The consolidation of his spellings warns that his relationship with copy in general may have changed significantly between the first and the last plays on which he worked' (p. 178).

Paul Werstine continues his study of the

printing of *Love's Labour's Lost* with a list of press variants in the 1598 Quarto.[13] Of nineteen formes, seven exist in corrected states; seventeen variants occur. This is a tiny body of evidence on which to support an hypothesis of the quality of the proofreading, and the fact that the proofreader left unchanged the faulty translation of Caesar's boast – 'came, See, and overcame' – on a page where he changed other forms is not a powerful argument. All that can be said is that this negative evidence does not conflict with positive evidence found elsewhere in the text. For his thesis that the faulty Latin of the Braggart and the Pedant are literary and not compositorial, Werstine finds support in the same evidence that proofreading left unchanged the faults in the Quarto. He is right to establish again the reliability of the compositors, but he should not assume too much comfort for the accuracy of individual readings. Werstine elsewhere reports also on his examination of Folio proofreading.[14] In the Church copy of the Folio at the Huntington, he has discovered evidence that one forme (qq1v: 6) was corrected not three, as Hinman thought, but four times. He concludes that Jaggard's workmen were anxious 'to produce a typographically attractive book'.

In a brief note, MacD. P. Jackson comments on a typographical curiosity, first noted by Robert F. Welsh in a study of Edward Allde's printing of plays by Marlowe: the use of the

---

12 'New Light on Compositor E of the Shakespeare First Folio', *The Library*, 2 (1980), 156–78. A specific product of this general inquiry was a paper that Howard-Hill presented to the seminar on *King Lear*, mentioned below, in which he demonstrated on the basis of Compositor E's known fidelity to copy that the Folio text of *Lear* must have been printed from manuscript and not from Quarto copy.

13 'Variants in the First Quarto of *Love's Labor's Lost*', *Shakespeare Studies*, 12 (1979), 35–47. In 'Correspondence' to the *Papers of the Bibliographical Society of America*, 73 (1979), 493–4, Werstine points to some errors in the article by George R. Price on the printing of the play (*ibid.*, 72 (1978), 403–34).

14 'An Unrecorded State in the Shakespeare First Folio', *ibid.*, 74 (1980), 133–4.

triple ligature 'ſſı' and its alternates, 'sſı' and 'ſsi'.[15] Distinctions among these three may prove of value in determining compositors or printing shops. The need for scrutiny of ligature sorts is demonstrated in a note on *Coriolanus*. Theobald emended the Folio 'unroost' (*Coriolanus*, 1.1. 216) to 'unroof'd' (all editors follow), but now W. Riehle reads in the Hinman facsimile 'unrooft' after all.[16] Such a discovery presumes that the letters 'f' and 't' (like 'ſ' and 't') form a ligature. In fact, they do not, as a glance at the kerned 'f' in 'after' at 1.3.61, 63, 70 will show. Theobald's emendation is necessary; Riehle's 'crossbar' is a smudge.

At the 1980 meeting of the Shakespeare Association of America, G. B. Evans chaired a seminar on 'The Textual Problem in *King Lear*', the chief interest of which centred on the theory that the Quarto and Folio represent two distinct versions. Michael Warren renewed his arguments for the independence of the two texts, and he was ably supported by Randall McLeod and Steven Urkowitz; in an important paper Gary Taylor demonstrated that the two texts 'present coherent but distinct accounts' of the military actions of acts 4 and 5. Specifically, the Folio systematically deletes all references to the French origin of Cordelia's army which becomes, thereby, 'not an invasion but a rebellion'. Stanley Wells admitted at the seminar that he had reluctantly come to the conclusion that 'the differences between the two are organic'; the present reviewer shares that opinion – and that reluctance.

In the volume from the Oxford Shakespeare Studies already cited, Gary Taylor offers three lively articles on the text of *Henry V*, focusing on the bad Quarto:[17] the first tries 'to refute the theory . . . that the Folio was printed from an annotated copy . . . of the Quarto. . . . The second . . . attempts to prove that the Quarto is based upon a deliberate adaptation and abridgement . . . designed for performance . . . by a cast of eleven. . . . The third essay investigates how far the Quarto can be trusted in . . . verbal detail' (pp. 40–1). Taylor's first

essay by close attention to compositorial practices in the Folio effectively knocks on the head Cairncross's improbable thesis that annotated exemplars of Q2 and Q3 served as copy for the Folio. His second is a most ingenious analysis of the Quarto text from the point of view of doubling. He concludes that the abbreviated version could have been and was played by eleven actors and that in fact such doubling accounts for 'virtually every major anomaly in the Quarto's distribution of scenes and characters' (p. 72). This is an impressive correlation of data. His third essay takes the position that where the Quarto diverges from the Folio it is not necessarily corrupt, that it may be in fact 'an accurate text of a different version' (p. 125), that 'version' being the abbreviated version that he has postulated. Taylor identifies the reporters as Gower and Exeter and considers a number of interpolations in Q, 'theatrical additions which post-date the foul papers behind F' (p. 149), spoken in performance (with Shakespeare's approval – or acquiescence). Taylor concludes that the Quarto represents 'not an . . . abridged copy of a report of a full performance . . . but a straightforward (if corrupt) report of an abridged performance' (p. 98). That abridgement, though it reflects 'merely the mechanical consequence of a limited cast' (p. 110), generally aims throughout at simplifying both 'the portrayal of Henry and the moral issue' (p. 157).

J. J. M. Tobin, noticing eleven unusual words or phrases in the Quartos of *Romeo and Juliet* that appear also in Nashe's *Have with you to Saffron Walden*, concludes that this particular vocabulary in the play derives from Nashe.[18] As several of these phrases are com-

---

15 '"A Curious Typesetting Characteristic" in Some Elizabethan Quartos', *The Library*, 2 (1980), 70–2.

16 '*Coriolanus*, I.i.217 unroof'd', *Notes and Queries*, 27 (1980), 174.

17 *Modernizing Shakespeare's Spelling, with Three Studies in the Text of 'Henry V'* (Oxford, 1979).

18 'Nashe and *Romeo and Juliet*', *Notes and Queries*, n.s. 27 (1980), 161–2.

monplace, the relationship between the two works is perhaps not so firm as is here proposed. Two of the list are moreover, as Tobin recognizes, words over which editors have disagreed: 'fantasticoes' (2.4.29) and 'pallet' (5.3.107). 'Fantasticoes' (Steevens recorded the parallel in Nashe) appears in the reported bad Quarto, whence it used to be admitted to the received text until Crow explained why the authoritative good Quarto 'phantacies' should be preferred. Subsequent editors read 'phantasimes', a word used twice elsewhere in the canon ('fantasticoes' is not used elsewhere). 'Pallet' is one emendation for the good Quarto 'pallat'; 'palace' is the other. Because the Quarto 'pallat' can probably be explained more easily as a misreading of a presumed manuscript 'pallac' than of 'pallet', the emendation 'palace' (from 'pallac') is probably to be preferred; the choice remains, however, one on which editors may reasonably disagree. Those who on literary grounds choose 'pallet' may find some support in the fact that Nashe also uses it (Shakespeare uses it twice elsewhere); those who choose 'palace' will not be affected. (The new Arden reads, correctly, 'phantasimes' and 'palace'.)

Comments and emendations for the text of *Hamlet* lead the editorial field in number and in interest, and it is no surprise to find an old favourite at the head of the list.'"Sullied" is the Word' Lin Tung-chi announces, and he maintains that position with force and clarity.[19] Demonstrating first that 'solid' is not the word that Shakespeare would have used to describe flesh (which in Christian terms is always seen as frail), Lin Tung-chi then explains on the basis of parallel readings in *Hamlet* and elsewhere in the canon that 'sullied' is such a word and that in both physical and moral senses it is particularly appropriate in the larger dramatic context. Furthermore, the term applies also to the political and social situations. 'The sense of tainted blood and tainted honour . . . [gives] the image the immediate concreteness and cogency it carries.' But the term gains 'in preg-

nancy and scope' when we realize that it qualifies also 'the foul body of the infected world' (p. 10). This is a significant contribution – perhaps the final one? – to the controversy.

Robert T. Levine suggests that in the conversation between Hamlet and Ophelia on honesty and beauty (3.1.103–15), the two words should be reversed in Ophelia's reply.[20] He bases his argument on the lack of coherence in the dialogue: Hamlet questions whether honesty should admit discourse with beauty, and Ophelia replies that beauty should admit discourse with honesty. There is indeed a *lapsus* in the progression of the argument, but Ophelia does not consider so curiously as does Levine; she is satisfied that the virtues should admit discourse with one another. Levine attributes the error to compositorial forgetfulness in dealing with the sequence of the two terms (the pair of words occurs six times). Though this argument might be appropriate in another situation, it seems inadequate here, for the three independent witnesses concur in the sequence of the words in Ophelia's reply. In Q2 and F, the dialogue begins and ends with speeches by Hamlet in which the sequence is 'honesty/beauty' (or 'fairness'); in the middle section of the dialogue, the speakers use the sequence 'beauty/honesty'. Levine's rearrangement requires that Hamlet initiate the change; the received text, requiring that Ophelia initiate the change, offers a situation probably more interesting dramatically and rhetorically than does Levine's.

For Polonius's deprecatory comment on his own punning with 'tender' (*Hamlet* 1.3.108–9) – 'not to crack the wind of the poor phrase, / Running it thus' – Richard Jacobs recommends accepting two emendations – 'not to crack the ring of the poor phrase, / Wronging it thus' – the first from Inez Scott, the second from

---

19 '"Sullied" is the Word: A Note in Hamlet Criticism', *Waikuoyu* (Foreign Languages) (Shanghai, 1980), no. 1, pp. 1–11.
20 'Honesty and Beauty: An Emendation for *Hamlet*, III.i.109–10', *Notes and Queries*, n.s. 27 (1980), 166–9.

Pope.[21] Recognizing the paleographical problems behind these emendations, he points to the sexual and monetary connotations that they carry: 'tenor and vehicle, warning and image, are made one. Polonius' "art," here, is literally his "matter" ' (p. 89). Carter Revard supports 'oft adulter' for the 'of a doubt' in *Hamlet* (Q2) (1.4.37), a reading proposed by Tannenbaum (1933) and adopted by Brooke (revised Yale Shakespeare, 1942).[22] If the manuscript spelled the word 'adoult', the misreading was easy: 'l' was misprinted as 'b', and the terminal scribal flourish (=*er*) was omitted (Kellner, §§ 60, 184). The reading 'adulter' is certainly appropriate to the context of the play at large which constantly considers the corrupting or debasing of things once noble.

Stanley Wells discusses the problem of assignment of two speeches in *Much Ado About Nothing* to Conrade (3.3.156, 159), and he notes that the Quarto prefixes '*Conr.*' are press corrections for '*Con.*'.[23] He considers the possibility that the Constable (i.e. Dogberry) should be the speaker, but he concludes that the received text is probably the reading still to be preferred. Naseeb Shaheen re-examines the problem of Indian/Judean at *Othello*, 5.2.350.[24] He argues that for the death of Desdemona, Shakespeare finds his source not in Cinthio but in Geoffrey Fenton's version of the fable where Judas Iscariot is twice mentioned. Judas's kiss of betrayal seems to Shaheen to underlie Othello's farewell kiss to Desdemona (5.2.361–2). Correspondents to the *Times Literary Supplement* have discussed two troublesome readings in *Henry V*. At 3.2.111, T. W. Craik senses a disconnectedness in Jamy's phrase 'ay, or goe to death'; he most ingeniously conjectures 'I owe god a death'.[25] Priscilla Bawcutt argues for retaining in the same speech the Folio reading at 3.2.114, 'I wad full fain heard some question', as a form 'common in colloquial Scottish syntax'. Harold Jenkins approves the retention also, finding parallels in *Coriolanus* and *Hamlet*.[26]

Charlotte F. Otten supports the common gloss for Ophelia's 'long purples' (*Hamlet*, 4.7.170), recently challenged, by demonstrating on the basis of the medico-botanical environment that the *Orchis Serapias* or the *Satyrion Royall* are the members of the orchid family that the court of Denmark would have associated with Ophelia's garlands:[27] the roots resemble the genitals; the flowers 'suggest shamelessly immoderate copulation' (p. 400); the grosser names of the plant are legion, the classical names connote the licentious worship of Serapis and the traditional lechery of the satyr (cp. 1.2.140). These garlands are a sad anticipation of Laertes's prayer for violets (5.1.233–4) and Ophelia's virgin crants (line 226). Donald K. Anderson, Jr, explains the 'three-nook'd world' in *Antony and Cleopatra* (4.6.6) by noting the obsolete meaning of 'nook', a sector of a circle, and by recognizing that the medieval T-in-O map was a circle cut into three nooks.[28] This is certainly a happy solution to a very puzzling phrase. Thomas L. Berger and the present reviewer contribute some occasional notes on the text and staging of *2 Henry IV*.[29]

T. H. Howard-Hill has compiled a supplement of ninety-five new items to his *Shakespearian Bibliography and Textual Criticism* (1969); it is included in *British Bibliography and Textual Criticism, A Bibliography* (Oxford, 1979). Papers by Philip R. Rider, Paul

---

21 'Sex and Money : A Note on *Hamlet* I.iii.108–9', *Shakespeare Quarterly*, 31 (1980), 88–90.
22 '*Hamlet* I.iv.36–38: *of a doubt* and *OED adulter v.*', *English Language Notes*, 17 (1979), 106–8.
23 'A Crux in *Much Ado About Nothing* III.iii.152–63', *Shakespeare Quarterly*, 31 (1980), 85–6.
24 '"Like the Base Judean"', *ibid.*, pp. 93–5.
25 *Times Literary Supplement*, 29 February 1980, p. 236; 21 March, p. 324; 13 June, p. 672.
26 *Ibid.*, 21 March, p. 324; 11 April, p. 415.
27 'Ophelia's "Long Purples" or "Dead Men's Fingers"', *Shakespeare Quarterly*, 30 (1979), 397–402.
28 'A New Gloss for the "three-nook'd world" of *Antony and Cleopatra*', *English Language Notes*, 17 (1979), 103–6.
29 'Notes on Shakespeare's *2 Henry IV*', *Analytical and Enumerative Bibliography*, 3 (1979), 240–53.

Werstine, William P. Williams, and O. M. Brack, Jr, originally delivered as a seminar on 'Research Opportunities in the Early English Book Trade' at the Modern Language Association meeting in 1978, call attention to the directions for further research in printing and publishing.[30] William P. Williams cites, for example, the need of a bibliography of all studies of compositors, 'organized by printing shop' (p. 185). Editors of Shakespeare's works will heartily support that suggestion.

---

30 'Research Opportunities in the Seventeenth-Century Book Trade', *ibid.*, pp. 165–200.

# INDEX